"GO YE THEREFORE AND TEACH ALL NATIONS"

THE STORY OF THE BIBLE

**RETOLD FROM GENESIS TO REVELATION
IN THE LIGHT OF PRESENT KNOWLEDGE
FOR BOTH THE YOUNG AND THE MATURE**

WALTER RUSSELL BOWIE

ABINGDON PRESS
NEW YORK ● NASHVILLE

1106
Copy 2

THE STORY OF THE BIBLE

Copyright 1934 by Walter Russell Bowie

Ω

SET UP, PRINTED, AND BOUND BY THE
PARTHENON PRESS, AT NASHVILLE,
TENNESSEE, UNITED STATES OF AMERICA

To
BERTHA MAUD GARVIN
EDWARD FELIX KLOMAN
MYRA STETSON BAKER
COMRADES IN HAPPY ENDEAVOR
WITHOUT WHOSE COÖPERATION
MUCH WHICH HAS BEEN COMPLETED
MIGHT NEVER HAVE BEEN BEGUN

CONTENTS

CONTENTS

CONTENTS

CONTENTS

CONTENTS

CONTENTS

ILLUSTRATIONS

PREFACE

T IS an oddity of books that the preface, which is printed first, is usually written last. The author sets down at the front of his book his apologia or explanation of what he has tried to do in the pages which are to follow. So it is in this case. With the manuscript of THE STORY OF THE BIBLE finished, I must try to tell those who may begin to read it what I have wanted to do.

Some two years ago the Editor of The Abingdon Press came to me and asked that I should undertake this work. "But why another story of the Bible?" I said. "There are several of them which have been in print these many years." "Yes," answered the Editor, "but we want one from another point of view. The increasing study of the Bible and the researches of scholarship have set the Bible in a new light. We want a story of the Bible written from the perspective of the best we know to-day about its various books and their relationships, and yet a story which will keep the religious reverence which the Bible has always inspired."

Obviously, this was not a simple thing to do. Was it possible, on the one hand, to tell the story of the Bible so that people of this generation, acquainted to some extent at least with modern science, history, and biblical criticism, would find here a narrative which should not evade difficulties of reinterpretation and should square with their standards of honesty and truth? Was it possible, on the other hand, to make the story of the Bible, retold in this fashion, seem not less but rather the more inspiring to those older people who have always loved it? Certainly, no one would imagine that he could carry through

11

this double undertaking to complete success. I am under no illusions concerning the imperfections of this book. But, at any rate, I can make clear what has been its purpose, and say that I have followed that purpose as well as I knew how.

More than once the question has been asked, "Is this story of the Bible being written for grown people or for children?" I have always answered with another question, "Which is the Bible written for, for grown people or for children?" The answer, of course, is that it is meant for both. And that is true of this book also. There are some explanatory passages which could not be expressed without the use of some words which children will not readily understand; but, similarly, there is much which children will not understand in the Bible itself. What I have tried to do is to tell the Bible story in such a way that mature and intelligent people will feel its fascination, and yet at the same time reproduce its incomparable pictures of human life in language simple enough for every child to follow and to grasp.

It will be observed that not everything which is included in the Bible is included in this book. There are some incidents, and much more teaching, which are not even mentioned. This, of course, was inevitable, and for two reasons. In the first place, to reproduce everything in the Bible, including, for example, all the long messages of the prophets, would have made the book too long; and even if this had not been true, the necessity for selection and discrimination would still have remained. The Bible itself is always there for those who wish to go to it and to get its message in completeness. This book is not a paraphrase of the Bible, but it is the story of the Bible. That is to say, it is an effort to present in its high vividness the mighty pageant of the life which moves through the Bible from its earliest to its latest days, the pageant of the soul of man in its ascending quest for God. In order that the figures in this pageant might stand out vividly, and that they might move with that same dramatic interest which really belongs to them, it was necessary that minor incidents should be subordinated to major ones; and that of what these men of the Bible said, there should be given no more than would best serve to make clear what they did and what they were.

In quoting from the Bible I have not followed any one version. Sometimes I have used the Authorized and sometimes the English Revised translation. Now and then I have incorporated—and I pay my thanks to him—some of the graphic phrases from the translation of Dr. James Moffatt. Often I have not attempted to reproduce the language of the Bible with literal exactness, but have sought to use such expressions as would mirror the meaning and color of the story most clearly in terms of our understanding to-day. Of how delicate and difficult a thing this is to do, I have been particularly aware when I came to deal, not with the Old Testament, but with the New. The words of Jesus in the phraseology of the Gospels are so full of sacred associations that one hesitates to vary from the tradition in the least. Moreover, there is the added complication of the differences between the several Gospels, and the question as to which account of an incident or report of teaching should be preferred. Often for the sake of the whole story, and in order not to clog it with comparative references, I have chosen that one portrayal of the figure of Christ which seems to me most convincing, and have dared to trust that it may seem so to others too. Whether or not this result has been in the main achieved will be the test of the success or failure of this book. For the one thing which makes a story of the Bible true is that the long procession of its human figures should seem to culminate in "the measure of the stature of the fulness of Christ."

WALTER RUSSELL BOWIE.

INTRODUCTION

SOME GENERAL CONSIDERATIONS ABOUT THE BIBLE; HOW IT GREW,
AND HOW IT MAY BEST BE UNDERSTOOD TO-DAY.

HERE ARE two ways of beginning a story of
the Bible. One way is to launch at once, with
no preliminaries, upon the retelling of that
story itself as the long record from Genesis to
Revelation presents it. But another way is
to take account first of certain questions which
trouble people about this book. They have heard and read of a
conflict between the Bible and modern knowledge. The Bible,
as it is read in churches and Sunday schools, seems to say one
thing; and science and history, as these are taught in day-schools
and colleges, seem to say another. To read the Bible happily,
we must get rid of this confusion.

That is the reason, then, for this introductory chapter. It
is meant to help us see the whole Bible, in its whole perspective,
before we begin to turn its pages. Even if we have to take a
little time for that, it will be worth while.

The Bible is one of the oldest books in the world, and it is
also one of the newest. It is old; for the latest parts of it were
written eighteen hundred years ago, and much of it hundreds of
years before that. But it is new; because it is read with new
interest continually by living men, and in its old pages new
needs are freshly met.

More people have read the Bible than have read any other
book since time began. It was written in Hebrew and in Greek;
but it has been translated in whole or in part into more than
nine hundred languages and dialects, and made understandable
to people and tribes from the Arctic Circle to the Equator, and
from the ancient civilizations of India and China to the rudest
inhabitants of the islands of the seven seas. If, when a new book

is published, two or three thousand copies of it are sold, the publishers think it has done well; but every year there are published in the world, of the whole Bible or of parts of it, about twenty-seven million copies.

Why is this?

It is because the Bible deals with the great questions which men are forever asking:

Where did we come from, and whither are we going?

What does life mean, and what should we do with it?

What is wrong, and what is right?

And who is God, and where shall we find him?

Other great books of the world have set out to answer these same questions. The sacred books of India, for example; the ancient writings of Egypt; the philosophies of Greece—all these and others, have pondered the mysteries of man and of what lies beyond him and above him. But the singular power of the Bible is found in the fact that it has brought an answer which comes closer home than any other answer seems to come. It helps us to understand life because it tells so much of life itself. It does not deal with abstractions. It tells of real people, good people and bad people, people half good and half bad, people high and low and middling, and it tells of them just as they were. Thus and so they thought and did; thus they saw clearly and walked straight, or thus they blundered and went wrong; in such and such a fashion they followed their own ignorant or evil devices, and in such another and better way they caught the beauty of the meaning of God and followed that. Little by little God is revealed to us by these figures of the Bible in whom he is reflected. And at last, out of all the lesser crowd, one great Person rises, splendid with God's shining—like some snow-clad mountain which, above the valleys still in shadow, stands crowned with the beauty of the risen sun. That one is Jesus. He is the climax of the Bible story. He is the final meaning which shows the partial meaning in all the rest. Looking at him and experiencing his spirit, men in every time have said, "This is what God must be like."

Some elements in our understanding of the Bible do not change. Men who are in earnest have always realized that the one thing which matters in reading the Bible is to find God and to be found of him. And whether they were scholars, or only ordinary unlettered folk, they have learned that in their reading of the Bible God did find them. "I know this book is the word of God," said an old Mohave Indian chief, "because it pulls my heart."

Now, all the while, through the long centuries since the Bible as we now have it came into being, people who took the whole Bible into their hands and honored it because it was to them the Word of God, have actually been loving some parts of it more than others. If not in what they said, then more importantly in what they did, they have showed that here rather than there, and in this book of the Bible rather than that, they felt that they were hearing the voice of God himself. They might have been taught some particular theory of the Bible's inspiration; but their hearts had a surer instinct which made them rank the different books of the Bible according to the measure of inspiration which these different books actually put into them. They knew that their own living was more apt to be inspired by the parables of Luke than by the laws of Leviticus. They knew that they got more light and leading from the Gospel of John than they did from the book of Judges. They knew that there seemed to be more of God in the Psalms than in the Song of Solomon. They had no concern for "biblical criticism," but meanwhile some whisper of the Holy Spirit in their hearts went on being their own sufficient critic; and they read the parts of the Bible which most seemed to do them good.

So, as we have already said, some elements of our understanding of the Bible do not change—and never will. Men will continue to turn to the Bible, as they always have, because they hope to find God there; and they will go to those parts of it where they hope to find God closest. But one element of our thinking about the Bible *has* changed, and it is this: we have commenced to recognize explicitly what we used implicitly to feel. We have begun to say to ourselves: "Of course it *is* true

that the different parts of the Bible have different values for
people who are in earnest about religion. Why is that? And
what more does it suggest to us about the Bible than we understood before?"

When we set about answering those questions, we discover
that the Bible opens before us into a rich variety. This Book is
not merely a book. It is a library. It happens to be bound in
one cover, and is printed, generally, in close type on paper so
thin that we hardly appreciate how many pages it contains. It
might well be many volumes; for it comes from many centuries
and brings us the records which were written in very various
times. All through it there runs one golden thread—the thread
of a great desire after God; but that thread is woven into many
different patterns upon the background of such knowledge as
men had. Being men, their knowledge was conditioned by the
age in which they lived and by the facts surrounding them. The
oldest parts of the Bible were originally not writings at all. They
came into existence long before anyone had dreamed of such
things as libraries; before the people on most of the earth knew
how to write, or had any alphabet to use in writing. In those
far-off days of the Bible's beginnings there were songs of poets
who were stirred by the mystery and wonder of the world, and
whose spirits had that strange inner illumination which poets
often have. There were stories told about the campfires of the
early people who pitched their tents here and there and whose
history began through tenacious memories and through tales
handed down from father to son. Later on the art of writing
developed among the great peoples who inhabited the Tigris
and Euphrates valleys, and was acquired also by the Jews; and
they too began to set down in their Hebrew language the
gradual writings which grew into the Old Testament. That age
of writing commenced, so far as we can tell, about 950 B. C., but
the substance of the Bible did not begin only then. Long before
that—how long nobody knows—its earliest messages had been
echoed down from generation to generation. Then these
immemorial traditions were gathered by the scribes and set
down upon their papyrus rolls; and the process was fully

launched which was to lead through the long history of accumulating manuscripts, sifted by experience, to the finished Bible
as we have it now.   The first compilers of the Jewish Scriptures
were not governed by any nervous fear lest they should include
material that was not perfect.   They gathered together everything they could discover which seemed to them to express what
their fathers had believed about God, and about this world they
lived in, and about the meaning of life.   They included poems
about the creation, and immemorial stories about Adam and
Eve, and about the Garden of Eden, and the serpent which
could talk; they even put into the opening chapters of the book
of Genesis two separate stories of the creation and left them
there side by side for all who chose to read.   They included a
narrative of the Flood, much like the narrative which was current in the literature of Babylon, except that it is more beautiful, and is marked—as it is the characteristic of the Old
Testament repeatedly to be—by a clearer insight into the character of God.   They included ancient sagas of battle and
adventure, and traditions which had gathered round the names
of far-off heroes; together with lovely stories of human love and
friendship which rank with the great literature of all time.   They
recited their nation's history as the report of this had come down
to them, glamorous with mighty miracles which they exulted to
believe in—miracles such as those of Moses in the deliverance
from Egypt, or of Joshua commanding the sun and moon to
stand still.   They were not bothered, as our modern historians
are, by considerations of documentary evidence; it was enough
that they could say, "We have heard with our ears, and our
fathers have declared unto us, the noble works that thou didst in
their days, and in the old time before them." They codified the
nation's laws: not only the moral law which had to do with the
supreme relationship of men to God and to their fellow men,
but also all the lesser laws that had to do with buying and
selling, and sanitation, and everyday community behavior.
They put into immortal words their own and their fathers' confession of the Everlasting God, and along with that they put
down also the minutiæ of how they built the tabernacle, and

what they built it of, and of how they killed the animals for the sacrifices which formed men's idea of appropriate worship in that day. They were hospitable to everything which revealed the life and spirit of their people, since to them every detail of that story had importance because of the covenant which they believed their people had with God.

Reading to-day that library which they were forming—those sacred Scriptures which have become our Old Testament—we see that they were right. It *was* important that they should preserve everything that had to do with the history and the tradition of this nation which so proudly, yet so reverently, thought of itself as "the people of God." But it is equally important that we to-day should understand intelligently what they did. We can see their work now in the perspective of that riper knowledge, gathered from many aspects of God's growing revelation, which throws its light back along the years. We can avoid the mistakes of previous generations of devoted but uninformed readers of the Bible who loved the Word of God with all their hearts, but had not learned the happy freedom of loving it also with all their minds. We can discriminate, because that is always the way of truth. We can see that the Bible has gathered into its spacious richness poetry which it is bunglesome to treat as if it were prose, and the intuitions of seers which it is impossible to twist into exact science. The geologists can tell us more accurately how this earth was formed than the book of Genesis can; and the anthropologists can deliver us from the mistaken literalism with which we used to read the story of Adam. The Holy Scripture in which the truth of God has revealed itself can be written as majestically and read as reverently in the everlasting record of the rocks, and in the actual remains which men have left behind them, as in the sacred rolls.

Does it discredit the Bible then, that some of its pictures which our fathers used to think of as exact descriptions must be supplemented and corrected by the discoveries of later times? Does this rob the Bible of its unique honor? Clearly it does not.

For the Bible (in its Old-Testament beginnings particularly) is like the maps which were drawn by the first intrepid explorers who set out from Europe to discover the New World which no living man then had seen save with the eye of faith. Out into the unknown seas they sailed, out upon the heroic venture which their high courage made them dare; and at the end of their voyaging they found their belief was vindicated. Another great continent of reality was proven to exist, and they had blazed the way to find it and to add it to men's life forever. But what of the maps they drew? Did they conceive exactly the facts they had discovered? Look at those old maps and see. The outlines of the new-found continent seem to our later knowledge so inadequate and so quaintly crude that we smile to look at them. And those same maps were embellished also with vivid pictures of other things which the explorers believed in as implicitly as they believed in the lands they found—sea monsters and dragons and naïvely imagined miraculous portents of all kinds. The coastlines were and are far different from what the great discoverers thought; the weird and wonderful creatures which they saw on their horizons were not there; but nevertheless the innumerable perfect maps which have been made in our later days, all put together, do not equal in immortal value the maps of the pioneers. For they first of all proved that there was something to look for which could be found. They first exhibited the reality which they could leave all succeeding generations to define.

And so it is with the Bible. Even in its most primitive books it is the record of those great spirits of our race who have been discoverers of God. Not all the pictures they drew are accurate. Not all the poetry of their superb imagination can be pressed into literal form. Even the ships of the ideas they sailed in can be followed by larger thoughts that steer on straighter ways. But nevertheless theirs is the immortal honor of the pioneers. They have showed the way to God, and have encouraged all who will to follow on that rewarding way.

It does not matter, therefore, that later criticism amends the story of the Bible here and there. Science and history and archæology, inspired by that love of truth which is the gift of God, will do that. Moreover—and more important—the Bible itself has been doing that all the while. Its later and maturer books have been correcting its earlier and more primitive ones. The old-time readers of the Bible might not have admitted this in theory, but they recognized and reflected it in fact. The differences in the Bible are like a change of climate; and in the spiritual climate of the prophets, and in the diviner air of Christ, many of the ideas which were native to the earlier days gave way to new and higher things. The early forms of Jewish worship, with their animal sacrifices and other customs parallel to those of other tribes round about, change to the magnificent understanding of the prophets which finds voice in words like those of Micah: "He hath showed thee, O man, what is good; and what doth the Lord require of thee, but to do justly, and to love mercy, and to walk humbly with thy God?" The ideas of the patriarchs, who approved of polygamy and slavery, give place to those more sensitive ideals which governed the little Christian communities to whom Saint Paul wrote. The conception of a tribal God of the armies of Israel, in whose name Samuel believed himself commissioned to order the slaughter of the Amalekites, grows into the revelation through Jesus of the God whose law is love. The Bible shows life in process, reaching on from that which was partial to that which should be complete.

With freedom of mind, therefore, and with enrichment of spirit, we can follow the story of the Bible. That story is like a road that leads uphill. It starts in the shadowy places where the dawn is just beginning to break, in the misty glades of men's earliest thinking where all sorts of wonderings are abroad. It goes forward across the plains where men with the divine spark in their souls are working out their first crude relationships with one another. It passes by altars where a worship still imperfect is yet made beautiful by the adoration of worshipers whose eyes are lifted to the highest that they knew. It climbs the great slopes of expanding vision along which the prophets point the way. On and up it goes, until it reaches the mountain peak of the mind and heart of Jesus, beneath which the long gradations of the journey fall into their perspective and before which a new world lies.

THE OLD TESTAMENT

CHAPTER I

FROM THE beginning of time men have wondered about the things which no man knew. That is the difference between a man and an animal. The animal roams the woods, or grazes in the meadow, and as long as there is food to eat, and springs and rivers to drink from, and a place to sleep, never concerns himself about any further questioning. But men are not made that way. They cannot be content dumbly to take things as they are. They must forever be asking how this world came to be as it is. Who made the mountains and the rivers and the sea? How did the stars get into the night sky? Back of everything we see there must have been a beginning; and what was that beginning like?

Among the people of Israel men were thinking about these things, just as they were in other lands. And various traditions grew. As we start to read the book of Genesis, which is the book of Beginnings, we need to remember that. This book is put together from many pieces. Most of the various narratives which are woven into it had been written probably before the middle of the eighth century B. C.; and fragments, such as battle-songs and other scraps of poetry, may well be older than a thousand years B. C. The unknown scribe who put the book of Genesis into final form used thus what others had written long before, and arranged these writings within his own framework. He did not even rewrite these earlier materials, for that was not the way of the compilers of Hebrew history; he put the different materials bodily into his story, like cloth of different colors sewn side by side into his final pattern. The separating lines can still be traced. The first chapter and the first four verses of the second chapter of Genesis, for example, are quite unlike the rest of the second chapter. Here are two accounts of the creation, not one. And the one which is put second is the older one. Down the stream of time it had come, this ancient story, to the hands of the Hebrew historian who was to complete the book of Genesis. So old it was that it bears the marks of the earliest folklore; God is pictured as like a human figure who walked in a garden, and a serpent can stand up and converse like a man. Nobody to-day thinks that God, and the beginning of the world, were like that; and nobody needs to think so. But we can be glad, none the less, that the compiler of the book of Genesis put into the book this naïve old tale which dates back to the far-off years when the world was young—and that he put in also the following stories of Cain and Abel, and of the days when "there were giants in the earth," and of the Flood, and of Noah and his ark. The historian saved all these because they belonged to the traditions of his people; and as the foreword to them all, he put another and maturer account of the creation which is like a chord of mighty music, striking the essential keynote for everything that follows. "In the beginning"—so the Bible opens. "In the beginning"—what? This thing and that thing and the other, said some of the myths of the various peoples. In the beginning, the body of the monster Tiamat who was slain by the god Marduk, said the Babylonians; in the beginning, a cosmic egg made from the mud of the Nile, said men in Egypt; in the beginning, the dissevered limbs of a giant, said one of the hymns of the Rigveda. But the book of Genesis says, "In the beginning—God!"

That is what matters. It makes a difference to believe that not accident, and not blind working of blind matter, and not indifferent fate, but the living God, is before all things, and through all life, forever. That is the faith the Bible proclaims; but it is upon the whole story of its pages, and not upon the old quaint pictures which the first men drew, that this faith is based.

So much, then, for prelude to the first book of the Bible. Let us listen to it not with anxious uneasiness lest it fail to conform to our later science and our developed history. Of course it will not conform; and that is the spontaneous beauty of it. For much of it is poetry—the poetry which grew like a flower from the virginal religious imagination of men's souls.

How did the world begin? And where did people come from? And who made them live? And why must they die? These questions are as old as the minds of men, and in the second chapter of the book of Genesis is the oldest answer which the Bible contains. Thus it is written, as long before it had been told and sung:—

In the day when God made the earth and the heaven, no grass or flowers had yet sprung up, for the whole earth was like the sands of the desert where no rain falls. Then God caused a mist to rise which softened all the ground. And God took the moist dust and molded it into the figure of a man, and breathed into his nostrils the breath of life, and man became a living soul.

And God planted a garden in the east country, in Eden; and there he put the man which he had formed. He made all manner of pleasant trees to grow in it, and a river watered the garden. And God told the man to take care of the garden, and to eat whatever he wanted of the fruit of the trees—except of one tree. For in the middle of the garden was the tree-of-the-knowledge-of-good-and-evil; and the man was to have nothing to do with that. "If you eat of that," said God, "you shall die."

But the man was lonely in the garden. "It is not good that he should be alone," said God; "I will make a companion for him." So God made all beasts of the field, and he made all sorts of birds; and they came, playing about the man's feet and hovering around his shoulders. And God said, "What will you call them? for you may give them names." So the man gave names to all the animals and birds; but he was lonely still.

Then God put the man into a deep sleep; and while he slept, God took one of his ribs and closed up the flesh where it had been; and out of the rib he made a woman. And he brought her to the man. And when the man waked and saw her, he loved her and was glad. He called her name Eve; and his name was Adam. So they walked in the garden together, and they had no trouble and no care.

Meanwhile, in the midst of the garden was the one tree of which God had said that the fruit must not be eaten. Adam told Eve what God had said; but the more they thought of the tree, the more they wondered what it would be like to eat the fruit, and the more they wished they could.

Now, the craftiest of all the living things which God had made was the serpent; and one day as Eve was walking in the garden, there the serpent was. "What is this I hear?" said the serpent. "God has said that you shall not eat the fruit of any of the trees of the garden?"

"No," said Eve. "We may eat of the trees of the garden as much as we will, that is, all except of one tree, the tree in the middle of the garden. Of that God has said that we must not eat of it nor even touch it; for if we do, we shall die."

"Die?" said the serpent. "If you eat the fruit of that tree, your eyes will be opened to things good and evil, and you will be like God, and know what he knows."

So Eve looked again at the fruit on the tree, and she saw that it was good to eat, and a delight to the eyes; and she heard the serpent say that if she ate it, it would make her wise; so she took it, and ate some, and she told Adam to eat the rest.

Then the eyes of them both were opened; they knew that they were naked, and they went and sewed fig-leaves together and made themselves clothes, because they were ashamed.

Then evening came; and they heard a voice. It was God's voice; for God was walking in the garden in the cool of the day. They went deeper among the trees and tried to hide.

"Adam," said the voice of God, "where art thou?"

Slowly Adam came out from his hiding. "I heard thy voice in the garden," he said, "and I was afraid, because I was naked; and I hid myself."

Then God said: "Who told thee thou wast naked? Hast thou eaten of the tree whereof I commanded that thou shouldst not eat?"

"The woman whom thou gavest to be with me, she gave me of the tree, and I did eat," said Adam.

But Eve said the serpent tempted her, and that the serpent was to blame.

So one tried to accuse another; but God saw that all of them together had disobeyed his voice, and all of them must suffer for their wrong.

This was the punishment of the serpent: He should never again walk and talk, as he had done when the world was new. He should crawl in the dirt, and strike at men with his fangs, and men should crush his head with their heels.

And this was the penalty upon the woman: Because she had tempted her husband, henceforth she should be made subject to him; and when children came to her, they should come with pain.

And as for man, this should be his doom: He should not any longer live in a garden where all good things grew. He should have to dig in the ground, with labor and sweat, and struggle with weeds and brambles; and die at the end of his toil, and go back to the dust from which he came.

So God drove Adam out of the Garden of Eden, to till the ground out of which he was taken; and at the gate of the garden God placed an angel with a flaming sword to block the path that led to the tree of life.

Thus the oldest story of the creation ran; and people listening to it in the far-off times looked at one another and seemed to hear their questions answered. So this was the way evil began, and this is why all human beings hate crawling snakes and kill them when they can; and this is why women suffer, and this is why men must work, and be weary, and lie down at last in the dust.

But the writer who drew together the many traditions which have entered into the book of Genesis and who made the book finally a whole, saw that this story belonged to the days when the minds of men were very simple; and he took another story of the creation, which had in it no talking serpent nor childlike picture of God walking among the trees, and this other and majestic story he put first.

As we listen, this is the picture which appears:

In the beginning, God created the heavens and the earth. The earth was without form, and void; and darkness was upon the face of the deep. But the spirit of God moved upon the waters, and God said, "Let there be light." Then through the darkness light began to dawn, and God saw that the light was good, and he said, "I shall call it day." So the light was divided from the darkness, and the first day had come to be.

But still the earth was wrapped in mist and cloud, until God said, "There must be a sky to separate the waters of the rain from the waters that roll upon the earth." So God made the blue dome of the heavens to be the home of the clouds. And that was his work on the second day.

Still upon the earth the seas washed everywhere. But on the third day God said, "Let the waters be gathered together, and let the dry land appear." Then the mountains lifted their mighty flanks above the ocean, and the rivers poured down toward the valleys, and the lakes shone in the hollows of the hills, and the yellow sands of the shore were spread as the threshold of the sea. But the earth was barren as a rock. And God said, "There must be grass to make it green, and plants that bear seed, and trees that give fruit." So God made the grass and the growing plants and trees; and the earth was beautiful with blossoming, and sweet with the scent of forests and of meadows where the flowers grew.

Also, the times and seasons must be divided; so God made the stars to march across the heavens and to shine upon the earth. And he made two great lights, the greater one to shine throughout the day, and this he called the sun; and the gentler one to shine with the stars at night, and that he called the moon. So the fourth day came to its end.

Meanwhile in the waters there was no moving thing, nor in the sky anything that had breath. Therefore God made the fishes to swim in the sea, and the birds with wings to fly in the air; and that was the fifth day.

Still on the earth there was silence, except as the songs of birds drifted down from the treetops; for there were no animals anywhere. Then God said, "Let the earth bring forth living creatures after their kind, cattle, and creeping things, and beasts of the earth after their kind." And it did. Everywhere the animals appeared. The little furry creatures ran in the forests, cattle stood in the meadows, deer came down to drink at the rivers, and on the plains the lions roamed and great elephants went on their way.

But still the work of God was not complete. "I will make man," he said, "after my own image, and I will make him master over everything else which has been created: over the fish in the sea, and the birds of the air, and the cattle, and the animals of every kind." So God made man, and he made woman, and he blessed them, and he said, "Be fruitful, and multiply, and replenish the earth; for I have given the whole world, and all growing things and all living things upon it, to you."

Then God saw that everything he had made was very good. The heavens and the earth were finished, and he rested from his work. That was the seventh day; so he blessed the seventh day, and made it holy, because it was on this day that he rested from all that he had created and made.

But the oldest traditions did not deal only with the creation. In the same fashion as in the story of the Garden of Eden, and of Adam and Eve, and the serpent, they go on to tell of what happened after that. The Hebrew people were asking not only how the world began, but how the different races and tribes began. And, particularly, how was it that *they* began? They knew that they were different from other peoples, and they believed that God had destined them for a great purpose in the world. How had this happened? they asked; and they loved to listen to the legends which gave an answer.

Thus these ran:

After Adam and Eve had been driven from the garden, Eve bore a son; and she called his name Cain. Afterward she had another son; and him she named Abel. When they grew up,

Abel was a shepherd; but Cain cultivated the ground, and raised grain. One day Cain brought some of his crop and offered it as a sacrifice to God; and Abel brought young lambs and goats from his flocks, and offered them. They put their offerings on the altars which they had built of stones and lit the fires which were to consume them; but as Cain watched Abel's sacrifice burning, and looked at his own, he thought that God was accepting Abel's sacrifice and despising his. So he was very angry, and his face grew hard.

Then his conscience began to speak. There was a voice from which he could not seem to get away, and it was saying: "What is the reason for your being angry, and why is your face so sullen? If you do right, all will be well; but if not, beware—for evil is crouching like a wolf at the door to seize you. Master it quickly."

But Cain did not want to master the jealous hate he felt for Abel. He told Abel how he thought God favored him; and as he told it he felt more humiliated and bitter than before. So as the two of them were in the field together, Cain sprang at Abel and struck him dead.

Then came the voice of God: "Cain, where is Abel your brother?"

"How should I know?" he answered. "Am I my brother's keeper?"

But God said to him, "The voice of your brother's blood cries out to me from the ground."

Then upon Cain fell the judgment. Henceforth upon the ground where he should walk there should be a curse. No longer should it yield as it used to do; and Cain should be driven to wander here and there, a fugitive upon the earth.

Then Cain was terrified. "My punishment," he said, "is greater than I can bear! I am driven from my own land, and I shall be hid from the face of God. I shall be a fugitive upon the earth, and any man that finds me will try to kill me."

But God said it should not be so. No man should slay Cain. There should be a mark upon him, and as a branded man he should wander up and down the earth.

CHAPTER II

SO ABEL was dead, and nobody was left on earth except Adam and Eve and the wicked Cain. At least, there was nobody else on earth so far as the book of Genesis explains how anyone had got there. If we had any doubt that the early part of the Bible is made up of fragmentary stories, the doubt would disappear when we see the gaps which the stories do not cover. For the next thing we know, Cain goes off into the land of Nod and marries a wife. Who was the wife, and where did she come from? Nobody knows, and the book of Genesis does not bother to explain. Anyhow, according to the old tradition, Cain was married, and he had children, and his children had children, and they were mostly rather troublesome and unpleasant people, as might have been expected from a family who had Cain for their father and grandfather.

Fortunately for the people of Israel and for their pride in the story of their ancestry, Adam and Eve had another son. They called his name Seth. Seth also had a son, and the various generations of his family went on till they came to Noah, of whom more is to be told presently. Meanwhile it is to be noticed that in this line of the descendants of Seth there came Methuselah. Methuselah's name has emerged from the old traditions because he was reputed to have lived to be so old. According to the legends which had been handed down, for a man to be three score years and ten was nothing. In those days people lived for centuries instead of decades, and Methuselah lived longest of all. He lived nine hundred and sixty-nine years, and the odd part of it is that by counting up other figures about the age of Noah and Noah's father it appears that Methuselah died in the year when the whole world and everybody in it except Noah and his wife and children were drowned in the great Flood. It looks as though the old tellers of the story assumed that Methuselah might never have died at all unless the Flood had drowned him. Anyway, he did establish the record of living longer than anybody else ever did, or is likely to. But, unfortunately, that is the only thing he did do. "All the days of Methuselah were nine hundred and sixty-nine years," says the book of Genesis, "and he died." With the exception of the fact that he had a son, that is the only fact which they could find about him to record. His life had length, and that was all it did have. He was the father and the forerunner of many other people since his time—people who exist and keep on existing for long years, but have never successfully shown any reason why it did any good to anybody that they should exist at all.

But we must come back to Noah. By the time of Noah, with the bad start that the world had got when Adam and Eve listened to the serpent in the Garden of Eden, and when Cain made things worse by killing his brother Abel, people had grown so wicked that it looked as though the patience of God himself must be exhausted. All through the Eastern lands there was the tradition of a vast Flood which had taken place once in that great plain through which the Tigris and Euphrates rivers run. And the people of Israel had a tradition about this Flood which has come down to us in the brave old story of Noah.

The earth was corrupt before God, and the earth was filled with violence. The people in it who were fit to be saved could be counted on the fingers of two hands. "God saw that the wickedness of man was great in the earth, and that every imagination of the thoughts of his heart was only evil continually. And it repented God that he had made man on the earth, and it grieved him at his heart." The only thing left to do seemed to be to wash the earth clean with the Flood and to start the human race again with Noah.

So God told Noah that this was what he meant to do, and presently it would begin to rain, such a rain as the world had never seen since the beginning; and the plains would be covered, and the valleys flooded with water, and the hills and mountains drowned before the waters should get through rising; and every living thing on the earth would be destroyed except those which Noah was going to be instructed how to save.

"Build an ark," said God to Noah; "build it out of gopher wood, and make its seams tight with pitch. Make room in it for people, and for all kinds of birds and beasts. When the time comes, you will go into it, and your wife, and your children and their wives, and you will take into it a pair of every kind of animal and bird and creeping thing which exists in the world; so that after the Flood they will be left to start life anew."

So Noah and his sons began to build the ark. It was a huge flat-bottomed boat, with windows and doors and first, second, and third stories. It needed to be big, and it needed to have various stories, considering what was going to be in it.

It does not take much imagination to know that the building of this ark must have caused comment. The neighbors looked at Noah in astonishment. Had Noah and his sons gone crazy to be building a huge boat in a dry meadow? Whoever heard of building a boat where there was no water to float it in? And what was this boat for, anyhow? But Noah kept on working. As for the water, he said, it would be provided, and it would be provided so plentifully that his gibing neighbors would not be laughing when that day came.

Presently the day did come. It began to rain, and it rained harder, and it kept on raining. Day by day the flood of waters poured out of the sky as if the earth had been turned upside down and the ocean had been put on top and was coming down again. Forty days and forty nights it rained, while Noah and his family had gone into the ark, and into the ark they had collected also the male and female of every kind of living thing which came walking and running and creeping and flying from the face of the earth. Everywhere the Flood swirled and deepened. The ark was lifted up and floated above the meadows.

The whole wicked population of the earth and all the rest of the living things clambered up on high places and hills, but that did not give them safety. Presently the waters had covered the hills too, and except for Noah and his family and all his birds and beasts, nothing of all the first creation was left alive, and the ark floated on a great sea of unbroken water as desolate as the empty chaos had been before the world was made.

For a hundred and fifty days the waters covered the earth, and then a wind began to blow, and the rain stopped, and the sun came out, and little by little the waters began to recede. At last, when more than five months had gone by, there was a jolt and a grating sound, and Noah discovered that his ark had touched the solid earth. He had gone aground on the top of Mount Ararat, which now for the first time was thrust up again above the waters of the flood.

Then Noah opened a window in the ark; and he went into the place in the ark where all the birds were, and took a dove and held the dove outside the window and let it fly away. But presently the dove was back again, for there was no dry place on the whole earth where it could alight. So Noah knew that, though the waters were going down, they were still too deep for the earth to be uncovered.

He waited a week. Then he sent the dove out again. This time, in the evening, back again the dove came flying, and in her mouth was a leaf plucked from an olive tree. From this Noah knew that the waters were abated, and he waited another week, and he sent the dove out again. This time the dove did not come back; so Noah knew that the Flood was vanishing, because the dove had found a place to nest.

Then Noah opened up the ark, after he had been in it with his wife and Shem and Ham and Japheth, his sons, and their families, and all the animals, for nearly a year. Out they all came, the people and the animals, glad enough to be back on the solid earth again. So Noah built an altar and did what men in those old simple days thought was pleasing to God. He killed some of the animals as a sacrifice and burned their flesh upon the altar, so that the smoke of the sacrifice went up toward the sky; and in his heart he felt very content because it seemed to him that God was promising that never again would he send a flood upon the earth to destroy its life. And this was the message which he believed that he heard from God: "While the earth remaineth, seedtime and harvest, and cold and heat, and summer and winter, and day and night shall not cease." Moreover, on that day when the rain had stopped and the sun had come out, there was a rainbow in the sky, which seemed to Noah the most beautiful and blessed thing he ever had seen; and always afterward the rainbow had become to him a sign of the covenant of God that the Flood was finished and no such flood as that would come again.

After the story of the Flood and of the ark and of the deliverance of Noah and his family, there follows in the book of Genesis a story about Noah himself which is not such pleasant reading. When he had got back to the earth again and the good, warm sunlight, Noah planted himself a vineyard; and the unhappy truth is, that after his vineyard had commenced to produce grapes and he made his grapes into wine, he drank more wine than he should have, and the next thing anyone knew, Noah was drunk. The writer of the book of Genesis does not say any harsh words about Noah. Perhaps he felt that a man who had been shut up in the ark for nearly a year, with lions and tigers and hippopotamuses and elephants and hyenas to feed and look after, must not be judged too harshly. But in any case this frank and unvarnished picture of Noah, in his badness as well as in his goodness, is a witness to a very significant fact about the Old Testament which needs to be borne in mind. These men of the early days were no completed saints. They must not be judged by the standards of our own times. They lived a long time ago when the world had moral standards which were very primitive. We shall see presently that the worst men did hideous things, and even the best men did things which would shock our times. They took several wives instead of being true to one. They held slaves, and sometimes were cruel to their slaves. They were pitiless in war. Yet these same men were very religious. When we think of them we must avoid two mistakes. We must not think their religion was hypocritical because they did not live in all respects up to what we think to-day must be expected of good men. Neither, on the other hand, must we suppose, as people sometimes used to do when they read their Bibles, that because these men who worshiped God did thus and so, therefore we must believe that what they did really represented the will of God. The truth is that in that primitive time even the best men were only beginning to understand the spirit of God, like children who still have a vast deal to learn. Their greatness was that they did turn their faces toward God, and they did understand a great deal more about his will than the other average people of their day. They did not have all the enlightened ideals which we have now; but they had ideals far above the ordinary level of their age, and that is what made the best of them leaders in the religious progress of the race.

There was another reason, however, beside the impulse of frankness which made the compiler of the book of Genesis put in the story of Noah's drunkenness. It was important in his eyes to separate the people of Israel from the rest of the people of the world, and especially to explain satisfactorily how those people whom the Jews despised and hated got to be as unregenerate as the Jews were convinced they were. So the story tells how two of Noah's sons were very considerate with his weakness and the third son, Ham, was quite indecent. Then there follows a list of the descendants of Ham, and in these are included all the Canaanites and the Assyrians and Babylonians and other people whom the Jews by this means consigned to the infamy where they thought they belonged.

One other ancient legend is incorporated in the book of Genesis before we come to the appearance of Abraham, and with him the tradition of the choice of Israel itself as God's peculiar people. How did it happen that there are so many languages on the earth? How did it happen that, if all people sprang from Adam and were alike in the beginning, they should be so unlike in their ways of thought and of speech now? The answer is given in the account of the building of the tower of Babel. Once upon a time, when the whole earth was of one language and of one speech, people thought that they would make a great tower which should reach up to heaven. So they set to work in a wide plain to make bricks and to pile them higher and higher toward the sky. But God saw their arrogance, and to put an end to what they were trying to do, he confounded their language; so that one part of the people could not understand what the other part were saying. The clamor and confusion that followed broke up the effort to build the tower, which ever since has been referred to as the Tower of Babel; and it broke up the unity of the people too. So that was the way, according to the story, in which the various nations began.

CHAPTER III

WHICH HAS TO DO WITH ABRAHAM, AND WITH LOT, AND WITH THE
WICKED CITY OF SODOM AND THE FIRE THAT FELL UPON IT; AND
WHICH GOES ON TO TELL OF ISHMAEL, AND OF HOW ABRAHAM WAS
READY TO SACRIFICE ISAAC, HIS SON.

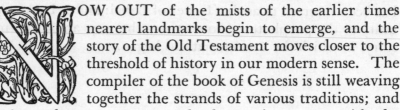

OW OUT of the mists of the earlier times
nearer landmarks begin to emerge, and the
story of the Old Testament moves closer to the
threshold of history in our modern sense. The
compiler of the book of Genesis is still weaving
together the strands of various traditions; and
sometimes these are not completely consistent one with the
other, and sometimes they duplicate incidents of the story.
Much of his material is legendary, and angels and other bright
forms of religious poetry move in and out of his narrative. But
on this borderland between the oldest creation stories and the
later and surer history to which the Old Testament advances,
there appear the great figures to whom the people of Israel always
looked back as having been the founders of their nation.

The first of these was Abraham. One tradition said that
he came from Ur of the Chaldees, another that he came from
Haran, which was in Babylonia. In either case he was one of
those men who now and then arise, men not content with the
ordinary facts of the life surrounding them, men morally and
spiritually taller than the crowd, who have that strange, haunt-
ing desire for the ideal beyond the horizons of the actual which
is the creative spark in this our human life. In the Epistle to
the Hebrews it is said of Abraham that "he looked for a city
which hath foundations, whose builder and maker is God."
In the poetry of those words, more than in any mere prose, is
expressed the thought of what Abraham has always represented
in the belief of the Hebrew people. He appears first in that

great region of the valleys of central Asia which has been the cradle of so many mighty movements of the human race. There in those countries beneath the wide sky men watched the white moon at night; and moon worship was the religion which was most popular. But Abraham was not satisfied. He was not satisfied either with his neighbors or with his neighbors' religion.

From out of the East, then, Abram (for that was his name until later) started with his wife Sarai and his nephew Lot, and all their possessions and their sheep and camels. Over the plains and past the hills they came, until they entered the little strip of country lying between the Mediterranean Sea and the Jordan valley, which we know as Palestine but which then was called the land of Canaan. Being nomads, they did not settle in any one place. With the herds and flocks which they had, it was necessary that they should be continually moving. The sheep ate up the grass in one valley and had to be moved to another. So Abram and Lot pitched their tents here and there in Canaan, especially wherever they could find a well of water. The names of some of the places where they stayed have come down to us, and some of them linger in the geography of Palestine to this day. One of them was Sichem on the plain of Moreh; another was Mamre; and another was Bethel. There Abram built his altars of stone and worshiped God.

During this time Abram and his nephew Lot had continued tranquilly together; but after a while it began to look as though they had too many animals to manage in one group. Lot's herdmen and Abram's herdmen got to quarreling with one another as to whose sheep should have which pasture, until at length Abram suggested to Lot that he should choose one part of the country and take that for his own, and Abram would take the rest.

Now Lot thought that this was a very favorable opportunity. Abram was generous and had given him the first choice, and he would be clever and take advantage of it. So he looked to the east, where all the land seemed pleasant and well watered, and he said that he would go in that direction. It looked like a shrewd act, but it was not as shrewd as Lot thought, for in that valley to the east lay Sodom and Gomorrah, the wickedest cities in the world. Lot thought that he was overreaching Abram, but the fact was that he was overreaching himself.

Off he went, however, toward the valley lands along the Jordan River, and they seemed to him the garden of the Lord. But people were living there, as we have already suggested, who had little concern for the Lord or the Lord's ways. In Sodom and Gomorrah men seemed to think of nothing except gratifying their own hot, wild passions, and there were no places for anyone with a decent inheritance to move into. But Lot established himself in Sodom; and whether or not he liked the place, it appeared that his wife and daughters did.

After Lot had gone to live in Sodom and Abram was still living in the open spaces, as he had lived before, Abram was sitting one noonday in the door of his tent, which he had pitched in the plain of Mamre. He looked up and saw three men standing out in the glare of the sun. Abram was a kind man, and hospitable, and he immediately left his tent and ran out to meet the strangers. He brought them in under the shade of a tree by which his tent was pitched. He had his servants wash the dust from their feet, and he asked Sarai to knead some fine meal quickly and to make cakes upon the hearth. He had one of her servants kill a calf, and he took the meat, together with butter and milk, and set these before the strangers.

After they had eaten, these men rose up, and they looked toward Sodom. They had heard about Sodom, and they thought they would go and see for themselves what sort of a place it was. Then suddenly Abram's compassionate heart was frightened. He began to think that these men were messengers from God, and he knew that if God ever dealt with Sodom as it deserved, it would go hard with Sodom. So Abram began to pray:

"Wilt thou destroy this whole city, the righteous with the wicked?" he said. "Perhaps there may be fifty good people in the city. Wilt thou also destroy, and not spare the place for the fifty good men who are there? Be it far from thee to do after this manner, to slay the righteous with the wicked! Shall not the Judge of all the earth do right?"

So the Lord said to Abram that if there were fifty righteous in Sodom, he would spare the whole town for their sakes. But Abram kept on. "Behold now," he said, "I have taken upon me to speak unto the Lord, which am but dust and ashes. Perhaps there shall lack five of the fifty righteous: wilt thou destroy all the city for lack of five?"

And the Lord said that if there were even forty-five, he would not destroy Sodom.

But Abram was still troubled, and he kept on. What if there were forty good people?

Yes, the Lord would spare Sodom if there were forty good people in it.

But if there were thirty? Yes, the Lord would spare it even for thirty.

If there were twenty? Yes, for twenty.

And then Abram said, "O let not the Lord be angry, and I will speak yet but this once: Perhaps ten shall be found there." And the Lord said, "I will not destroy it for ten's sake."

But it turned out that there were not even ten righteous people in all Sodom.

One evening to the gate of Sodom came two angels, though nobody knew that they were angels because they looked like other men. Lot sat in the gate of Sodom, and seeing them he rose up to meet them. He asked them into his house, and bade them stay all night. They said no; they would stay in the street; they wanted to walk about and see what Sodom was like. But he urged them greatly, so that finally they did come into his house, and he baked bread for them, and they sat down to a feast which he prepared.

But presently a crowd of the men of Sodom gathered outside Lot's house. They had heard that two strangers were there with Lot, and they wanted to get hold of them. Lot went out of the door and shut it after him, and tried to persuade them to go away; but their reply was to jeer at Lot. "This fellow came into our town to sojourn here," they said, "and now he sets himself up to be a judge. We will deal worse with you," they said to Lot, "than with the men inside;" and they pressed about Lot and tried to break down the door.

Then the two messengers from God whom Lot had sheltered opened the door, pulled Lot in, and shut it again; and they struck the men outside with blindness, so that they groped about and could not find the door. Then they said to Lot: "Are there any others here besides you? Whatever others there are, your sons and your daughters and your sons-in-law, whatever else you have in this city, bring them out of this place, for Sodom is going to be destroyed."

Then Lot went and told his sons-in-law, "We must go out of Sodom." But they were no better than the rest of the people in the town, and they laughed at him.

When the morning came, the two angels told Lot that there was no more time to lose. "Arise," they said, "take your wife and your two daughters and come, for if you do not, you will be consumed along with the rest of Sodom." Then while Lot hesitated, they laid hold of his hand and of his wife's hand and of the hands of his daughters, and they hurried away from the place. "Escape for your life," they said. "Do not look behind, and do not stop in the plain. Get up into the mountain."

But Lot thought that he never could reach the mountain, and he begged that he might be allowed to enter into the little town of Zoar, which lay not far from Sodom. So he did go to Zoar and was sheltered there.

Then the end came for Sodom and for Gomorrah also. The region north of the Dead Sea, where those cities stood, is a region in which there are swamps where oil and pitch bubble out of the ground. A bolt of lightning set fire to this oil and pitch, and a great wind blew it upon the cities, till they were turned into flaming furnaces, and most of the people in them were destroyed.

Lot was thankful to be out of Sodom, but his wife did not want to leave it. When the others were running, she was looking behind. The flames overtook her, and the furious wind, laden with the sands of the desert and the dried salt from the shores of the Dead Sea, blew about her and covered her; and so the saying arose that Lot's wife became a pillar of salt.

Abram meanwhile had gone on his peaceful way, and one day there came to him a vision from God, and the voice of the Lord said to him: "I am the Almighty God; walk before me, and be thou perfect. And I will make my covenant between me and thee, and will multiply thee exceedingly." The voice said that Abram should be the father of many nations and the ancestor of kings, and that the land in which he was wandering should be the land of his children and his children's children, and that God would be their God forever.

Moreover, Abram's name was to be changed to Abraham, and his wife's name was to be changed to Sarah; and, notwithstanding that Abraham and Sarah both were growing old, they should have a son.

In due time the promise was fulfilled. Sarah's son was born, and he was named Isaac.

But Abraham had already had another son, whose mother was Hagar, Sarah's maid. This fact was a blemish on the record of Abraham which the Old Testament chronicler does not attempt to conceal. It seems strange to us in our later time to read, not in this instance only, but in others, of how it is written almost casually concerning heroes of the world's religious history that they had more than one wife, or women of their household whom they openly treated as their wives. But in that primitive society marriage to one person only had not yet risen as an ideal. Abraham and others who came after him must be measured, not by our standards, but by the standards of his age; and his greatness lay in the fact that, if he did not transcend the average moral consciousness in everything, he did transcend it in very much.

The name of Hagar's son was Ishmael. Not unnaturally, Sarah was jealous of him, and one day after Isaac was born, she looked at Hagar and Ishmael and her dislike flared. She did not want anyone to be the rival of Isaac; so she said to Abraham,

"Cast out this bondwoman and her son: for the son of this bondwoman shall not be heir with my son Isaac."

Abraham was much distressed; but he did not know what else to do except to let Sarah have her way. So he rose up early next morning, took bread and a bottle of water and gave these to Hagar, and he told her to take Ishmael and to go away. Then Hagar, leading the little boy, turned away from Abraham's tents, and set her face toward the wilderness. They walked and walked until they could walk no more. The water in the bottle was exhausted, and the empty wilderness was round them everywhere. She laid the tired child on the ground in the shade of one of the desert shrubs, and went and sat down a good way off, for she said, "Let me not see the death of the child." But as she sat there weeping she seemed to hear a voice like the voice of an angel of God, and the voice told her not to fear, for Ishmael should not die. Instead, he should live and be the ancestor of a great nation. Then she lifted up her eyes and looked about, and there in the sands not far off was a little pool of water, and she ran and filled the bottle with the water and gave it to Ishmael to drink. So Ishmael lived and grew up, and he became an archer, and the people of Israel thought of him afterward as being the father of the Arabs and other tribesmen of the desert.

Meanwhile Isaac was growing up also, and Abraham loved him better than anything else in the world. Then one day Abraham had an awful thought. He wanted to love God with his whole heart. Perhaps he ought to give Isaac to God. Other tribes and peoples in that world he lived in believed in human sacrifice. If they could do that much for their gods, ought he not to do it for his God? Isaac was the best he had, and perhaps the best he had was what God wanted. When he began to think thus, Abraham determined that there was only one thing which he could do. There seemed to be a voice speaking in his soul which he could not silence; and it kept saying to him that he had to go away into the mountains and take Isaac with him and offer Isaac there as a sacrifice to God. "Thy son Isaac," it was saying, "thine only son Isaac, whom thou lovest."

So Abraham rose up early one morning, though his heart was like lead within him, saddled his ass, and took two of his young men with him, and Isaac his son. He cut wood for the sacrifice, and started off into the lonely hills. It took him three days to get to a place which was far enough away.

Then Abraham told the two young men to stay where they were. "The lad and I," he said, "will go farther on and worship." He did not tell them what he was going to do. Neither did Isaac know. He took the wood for the fire with him, and he took a torch in his hand, and also a knife. Then Isaac said, "Father," and Abraham said, "Yes, my son;" and Isaac said: "I see the fire and the wood. But where is the lamb for the burnt-offering?" He did not know that he was to be the lamb.

Abraham answered: "My son, God will provide himself a lamb for a burnt-offering." So they went both of them together.

Presently they came to a solitary place, and Abraham built an altar out of stones. He laid the wood on the altar. Then he bound Isaac's hands and feet, and laid him on the altar upon the wood. And he took the knife in his hand, and was about to kill his son for the glory of God.

Then in an instant the truth flashed upon him. It came to him with a sudden brightness, like an angel out of heaven. Another voice, mightier than the first voice, was speaking, "Lay not thine hand upon the lad, neither do thou anything unto him." Moreover, there beside the altar Abraham caught sight of a ram held in the tangled thicket by his horns, a ram which could be sacrificed in place of Isaac. So he lifted Isaac up in his arms, and offered that other sacrifice in Isaac's place. And the two of them who had come up the hill together, went down together again; and a great wonder was upon Abraham, and his heart which had been heavy was at peace.

Always afterward that story represented in the mind of the people of Israel two things. In the first place, it recalled the devotion of the man who was willing to give up the one whom he loved the dearest when he thought it was the will of God. Because of such devotion they believed that Abraham was worthy of the promise which was written as having come to him from God: "I will multiply thy children and thy children's children as the stars of the heaven, and as the sand which is upon the seashore; and thy descendants shall possess the gate of their enemies, and in them shall all the nations of the earth be blessed."

And the second significance of this story of Abraham who started to sacrifice Isaac and then had his hand withheld is that it stands as the explanation why the people of Israel, though they lived in a world where human sacrifice still continued, never permitted that terrible thing to be a part of their religion. Abraham was the representative of the moral discovery that the true God does not ask that life and love shall be destroyed. The love he seeks is not something different from but something to be found through our human loves. That great illumination which had come to Abraham made it plain for religion ever afterward that real worship is to "offer and present our selves, our souls and bodies, to be a reasonable, holy, and living sacrifice" unto Him whose will is more abundant life.

CHAPTER IV

THE STORY OF THE JOURNEY OF ELIEZER INTO THE EAST TO FIND A
BRIDE FOR ISAAC, AND OF HOW HE FOUND REBEKAH AT THE WELL;
AND THE STORY OF HOW JACOB STOLE THE BIRTHRIGHT OF HIS
BROTHER ESAU.

IT WAS a glad day for Abraham when he came
back from the hills with Isaac alive. But not
long afterward sorrow came to him. Sarah,
his wife, died. Then Abraham realized afresh
the loneliness which comes sometimes to a man
who has gone out of his own country into a
new land. The burial places of his fathers were far away, and
he had no place in which to lay the body of Sarah; so he went to
some of the Hittites who lived in that country of Canaan and
begged them to let him have a burying place. A man named
Ephron was kind to Abraham and said he would give him a
cave in a field which he had. But Abraham would not take it
so. He would buy it, he said, for Sarah's tomb. So he bought
from Ephron a field which was in Machpelah, near Mamre,
and the cave which was in the field and the trees around it; and
there at last in the cave of Machpelah he laid the body of
Sarah to rest.

And now Abraham was growing old, and he was lonely.
Moreover, he realized that Isaac had now grown up, and he
wanted to see Isaac married. According to the custom of the
East, parents had a great deal more to do with choosing husbands or wives for their children than the children themselves
did. So Abraham began to wonder who should be the bride for
Isaac. He wanted Isaac to live in this new country to which
he had come, but he did not want to see Isaac marry one of the
girls of these people around him who were not of his own blood.
His heart turned back to his own early associations. "Back

there in the old country and among our own kinsfolk," he thought, "may be a wife for Isaac."

So Abraham called his most trusted servant to him and he told him what he had planned. He wanted him to go as his representative back to the East from which so long ago Abraham himself, as a young man, had come; and by the blessing of God he was to find there a bride for Isaac.

So Abraham's servant, whose name was Eliezer, took ten camels out of the herds of Abraham, which had now grown numerous and rich. He loaded the camels with provisions for the journey and with presents. Then he turned the head of his caravan eastward toward the desert country and the great valleys of Mesopotamia beyond. After long traveling, he arrived one evening outside the town where dwelt Nahor, the brother of Abraham.

He halted his camels at the village well to which the women were accustomed to come to draw water, and at the trough alongside, from which the flocks and herds also were brought to drink. Now he had come to the country of Abraham's own people, and this was the place, therefore, where he might hope to find the sort of wife he had been sent to win for Isaac.

But when the women and girls came out from the village how should he know which should be the one for him to seek? Thus he wondered as he waited with his camels where they rested by the well.

Then a clear thought came to him. He could not tell these girls one from another by their looks, he could not tell what they really were by their clothes or by their ornaments, but there was a way by which he could tell something more important than appearances. So he made this prayer: "O Lord God of my master Abraham, I pray thee, send me good speed this day, and show kindness unto my master Abraham. Behold, I stand here by the well of water; and the daughters of the men of the city come out to draw water: And let it come to pass, that the damsel to whom I shall say, Let down thy pitcher, I pray thee, that I may drink; and she shall say, Drink, and I will give thy camels drink also: let the same be she that thou hast appointed for thy servant Isaac; and thereby shall I know that thou hast showed kindness unto my master."

Before he had finished speaking, out from the village came a girl whose name was Rebekah, carrying an earthen jar upon her shoulder. She was young and very fair to look at. She went down the stone steps that led from the level of the plain to the pool of water in the well, filled a jar and came up the steps again. Eliezer came toward her, and asked her if she would let him drink a little water from her pitcher. Quickly she took it from her shoulder, held it out toward him in her hands so that he might drink, and when he had finished, she said, "I will draw water for the camels also." So up and down the steps to the well she went in her quick, graceful way, filled the jar again and again and emptied it into the trough for the camels, until all the great thirsty beasts had drunk their fill. And Eliezer, Abraham's servant, wondering at her, held his peace, considering whether it might be true that God was bringing his journey to a prosperous end.

When the camels had finished drinking, he took a golden earring and two heavy bracelets and gave them to her. He asked her whose daughter she was, and would there be room, perhaps, for him to lodge at her father's house? Then she told him she was Rebekah, and Abraham's servant recognized at once that she was a great-niece of Abraham, a granddaughter of his brother Nahor; and she said there was straw and provender enough at her father's house to take care of the camels, and room for him to lodge. And when she had said all that, and he listened to the welcome in her voice, Abraham's servant bowed his head and blessed God.

Then Rebekah ran home and told her family what had happened at the well. Out then came her brother, whose name was Laban; and he gave a hospitable welcome to Eliezer and told him that he had the place ready for him to lodge, and room for the camels. So Laban ungirded the camels and took their packs off and gave them provender, and, according to the custom of the East, brought water to wash the feet of Eliezer and of the camel drivers of his caravan. Also he wanted Abraham's servant to sit down at once and have something to eat. But he said no, that he would not eat until he had told his errand.

Then he told about Abraham, how God had blessed him and given him flocks and herds and silver and gold and men servants and maid servants and camels and asses. Being devoted to Abraham and proud of the family, he probably made the whole story sufficiently glowing; and then he told about Isaac and about Abraham's desire that Isaac should not marry one of the Canaanitish girls but find a wife in the land from which his ancestors had come. Also he told of the prayer he had made by the well as to the sign for the kind of girl he should choose, and how Rebekah had come and how she had answered him when he asked her for a drink, and how she had drawn water for all the camels—how, in short, she was exactly the one person he was looking for; and would they let her go back with him to Abraham in order that she might be Isaac's wife?

Laban, Rebekah's brother, and Bethuel, her father, conferred together. They said to Eliezer: "This thing proceeds from God. We cannot answer you either well or ill. It is not for us to object." Rebekah would go with him according to the message which he had brought.

Then Eliezer was full of joy, and he took out from the packs which he had brought on the camels jewels of silver and jewels of gold, and raiment, and gave them to Rebekah; and he gave handsome gifts also to her brother and to her mother; and that evening they had a feast together.

In the morning Eliezer said that he wanted to start home. "Send me away," he said, "to my master." But Rebekah's brother and mother were reluctant to have her go so soon. Let her stay a few days—at least ten. After that she should go. But Eliezer was urgent that he ought to get back at once. So they said they would call Rebekah and let her answer. They called her and said, "Will you go with this man?" And she said, "I will go." So the camels were saddled again, and Rebekah and her nurse told her family good-by, and they started away westward by the same way upon which Abraham had gone upon his adventure long years before.

Over the many miles the caravan rocked upon its way, and at last it was drawing near to Abraham's country. It was the end of the day, and Isaac went out into the field at eventide to meditate. Perhaps he was thinking of his father's servant who had gone on that exciting journey, and was wondering what was happening to him. He lifted his eyes and there were the camels coming. At the same moment Rebekah caught sight of the figure of Isaac. "What man is this that walks in the field to meet us?" inquired she of Eliezer. And when he told her that it was Isaac, she alighted quickly from her camel and drew the veil which she wore as a maiden across her face. Then Eliezer told Isaac all the story of his journey, and of how he had brought Rebekah back. When Isaac saw her, he loved her, and Rebekah became his wife.

About this time Abraham married again, and his second wife's name was Keturah. He had a number of sons, but none of them did he love so well as Isaac, and toward the end of his life he gave Isaac all his possessions. Then Abraham died, and Ishmael, his eldest son, who had gone away years before with his mother Hagar, came home for the funeral, and Isaac and Ishmael buried the body of their father in the cave of Machpelah, which Abraham had bought from the Hittites and in which Sarah had been laid before.

So Isaac and Rebekah were left alone, and they had no children. They prayed to God that children might come. At length their prayer was answered, and Rebekah had twin boys. She and Isaac named the first of them Esau, and the second one Jacob.

The years went by, and they were almost grown up. Although they were twins, they were not alike at all, but most remarkably different. Esau had red hair and a ruddy face—the sort of person who seemed to be all strength and burliness. Strong as a bear he was, and he had hair on his hands and his arms, so that if you put your hands upon him, his skin seemed as rough as a bear's. All his life he had been an out-of-doors boy. He spent his days hunting. He knew the ways of the animals, and he could go out and kill and skin a deer when he wanted food, and make its meat into the kind of dishes which he loved and which his father Isaac loved also. Perhaps Isaac leaned toward Esau all the more because Esau could do what he had never done. Isaac himself had been a quiet sort of person, and he was proud of this big, strong son who could roam the fields and bring a deer home over his shoulder.

But Rebekah preferred Jacob. Jacob stayed at home, and very probably helped his mother. He was not always tramping about in the hills and woods and coming in with the smell of wild things on him. He was not so strong as Esau, but he did more thinking. He had a quick mind which worked very nimbly, even if sometimes along rather curious paths, and Rebekah was so partial to him that, for Jacob's sake, she could bring herself presently to practice upon Isaac, her husband, an act of deceit which she would never have thought of for her own sake.

It came about in this way:

One evening Esau, his father's favorite, came back to the tents from having been out as usual on a hunt. Either this day he had not killed anything or he was too tired to cook it. At any rate, he was hungry and wanted something to eat, and wanted it quickly. Jacob had been making himself some broth out of reddish brown beans called lentils. Esau smelled it as soon as he came in, and he wanted some. "Feed me," he said to Jacob, "for I am faint."

Then Jacob had a crafty thought. Esau was the elder of the two, therefore he possessed the birthright. That meant, according to the custom of the tribes in that day, that he would inherit twice as much of his father's property as anyone else. Moreover, he would be the head of the family. Jacob had always envied Esau for that, and now he saw his chance. "Will you sell me your birthright, then?" he asked.

"What do I care about a birthright," thought Esau, "when I am about to starve to death?" Esau was not given to much reflection. He had strong appetites and hot impulses. If he wanted something, he wanted it then and there. "What profit shall this birthright be to me?" he said. Jacob could have the birthright if he wanted it. What Esau wanted was some of that good hot broth of beans which was cooking on the fire.

Jacob asked Esau to swear that if he gave him the beans, Esau would give him the birthright. Esau gave his oath; and he sat down and ate the broth and some bread which Jacob gave him, and rose up when he had finished and went on his way. So Esau despised his birthright.

At first Esau did not seem to give much thought to what he had lost, but something was to happen which should bring it sharply to his mind. As Isaac grew older, his sight began to fail. He could not even recognize his own sons except by listening to the difference in their voices, or by putting his hands upon them. He thought that the time was drawing near when he might die; and because he loved Esau he wanted to give him his particular blessing. He called him to him. "My son," he said; and Esau, drawing near his blind father, said, "Behold, here am I."

Isaac said: "I am old. I do not know when the day of my death may be. Take your weapons, your quiver of arrows and your bow, and go out into the fields and shoot a deer, so that we may have some venison. Make me some savory meat, such as I love, and bring it to me, and my soul will bless you before I die."

Now, Rebekah overheard what Isaac said to Esau, and Esau had no sooner disappeared into the fields to look for a deer than Rebekah called Jacob. "Listen," she said, "I heard your father speaking to your brother Esau, asking Esau to bring him some venison, that he might eat it and bless Esau before the Lord. Now, do as I tell you, according to what I am going to say. Go out to the flock and fetch me two of the best kids out of the goats, and I will make them into a savory dish such as your father loves, and you can take it in to him, and he will give his blessing, not to Esau, but to you." But Jacob replied, "My brother Esau is a hairy man, and I am a smooth man. Suppose my father should feel me, and I should appear to him as a deceiver, and I should bring a curse upon myself and not a blessing." Then his mother answered: "I will take care of the curse; only do what I have said, and go and fetch me the kids."

So Jacob went and brought the kids, and his mother very soon made them into a savory dish, seasoned the way in which she knew Isaac took delight. Moreover, she got some of Esau's clothes and put them on Jacob, and she put the skins of the kids which had just been killed upon the backs of his hands and upon his neck. Then she told him to take the meat and bread and carry them in to Isaac.

So Jacob went in to where Isaac was and spoke to him to make him know he was coming near. "My father," he said, and Isaac said, "Here am I. Who art thou? My son?"

Jacob said, "I am Esau, your firstborn; and I have done as you bade me. Rise now, I pray you, and eat of my venison, that your soul may bless me."

Isaac was surprised that Esau could come back so soon. "How is it that you found it so quickly, my son?" he said. And Jacob, brazening out the first lie with a worse one, said, "Because the Lord your God brought it to me."

The old man began to feel that something was strange about this. "Come near, I pray you," he said, "that I may feel you, my son, whether you are my very son Esau or not." And as Jacob came close to him, Isaac stretched out his hands, as a blind man does, and passed them over Jacob's head and neck as Jacob bowed before him. Then he told Jacob to hold out his hands. "The voice is Jacob's voice," he said to himself, "but the hands are the hands of Esau." He was troubled. "Are you my very son Esau?" he insisted, and Jacob said, "I am."

"Then bring the venison to me," he said, "and I will eat it, and my soul will bless you." So Jacob brought it and put it into his hands, and Isaac ate, and he drank some wine which Jacob also brought. "Come near now, and kiss me, my son," said Isaac. When Jacob came near and kissed him, Isaac smelled the smell of Esau's clothes which Jacob had on, and then he thought that certainly he could not be wrong. This certainly must be Esau, the son he loved. "The smell of my son is as the smell of a field which the Lord hath blessed," the old man said.

"Therefore may God give you of the dew of heaven, and the fatness of the earth, and plenty of corn and wine. May people serve you, and nations bow down to you. You shall be lord over your brethren, and your mother's sons shall bow down to you. A curse be upon every one that curses you, and a blessing on every one that blesses you."

Scarcely had Isaac finished pouring out this blessing, as he thought, upon Esau, but actually upon Jacob, and scarcely had Jacob gone out of his father's presence, when in from his hunting came Esau. He had killed his deer. He had made it into the savory meat which Isaac had asked for, and his big, cheerful voice was saying, "Let my father arise, and eat of his son's venison, that your soul may bless me."

Then, startled, Isaac said, "Who are you?"

"I am your son," he said, "your firstborn Esau."

Then Isaac trembled exceedingly. "Who?" he said. "Then where is he that took venison, and brought it to me, and I have eaten of it before you came, and I have blessed him? And it is he that shall be blessed."

When Esau heard that, he gave a great and bitter cry. "Bless me," he said, "O my father, bless even me also."

But Isaac said, "Your brother came with craftiness, and has taken away your blessing."

"Rightly is he named Jacob!" said Esau (for "Jacob," by a play of words in the Hebrew, meant "a supplanter"), "for he has supplanted me these two times: he took away my birthright, and now he has taken away my blessing. But," he said to his father, "have you not reserved a blessing for me?"

What could Isaac answer? Already he had solemnly given Jacob the blessing that was meant for the firstborn. "I have made him your lord, and all his brethren I have given him for servants," he said. "With corn and wine have I sustained him; what now can I do for you, my son?"

But Esau said: "Have you only one blessing, my father? Bless me, even me also, O my father, bless me." And Esau, the strong man, wept.

Then Isaac gave him such blessing as he could, the blessing of the man who should not inherit the leadership of the family, but at least could have the wild, fierce freedom of the out-of-doors. "Behold," he said, "thy dwelling shall be the fatness of the earth, and of the dew of heaven from above. You shall live by your sword, and shall serve your brother; but it shall come to pass that when you have the power, you shall break his yoke from off your neck."

CHAPTER V

THE FLIGHT OF JACOB, AND HIS LOVE FOR RACHEL, AND HIS DEALINGS
WITH LABAN; AND HIS COMING HOME AGAIN, AND HIS WRESTLING
WITH AN ANGEL BY THE BROOK.

SO ESAU was stripped of the firstborn's blessing, and it was not surprising that he hated Jacob. He would not do anything to Jacob while his father lived; but he said to himself, "The days of mourning for my father are not far off; when they come, I will kill Jacob."

The report of what Esau had said was brought to Rebekah, and she immediately sent for Jacob and told him how she had heard that Esau was restraining himself only because he was planning to kill Jacob by and by. She advised him to flee into Haran, from which she herself had come, and where her brother Laban was still living. She told Isaac also that Jacob ought to go away, although she gave him a different reason. Esau had already married two of the young women of the Hittites, which had displeased both Isaac and Rebekah exceedingly, and she said to Isaac that if Jacob stayed at home he might presently do the same thing; and if Jacob married a girl of that kind, "What good," said Rebekah, "shall my life be to me?" Isaac listened to her, and agreed, and he sent for Jacob and advised him to go into the east country and find himself a wife.

Then Jacob started away from Beer-sheba, where his father's tents were pitched, and he went eastward toward Haran. When night fell, he was in a desolate and lonely place where rocks were strewn among the fields. The only pillow he could make for himself was a heap of small stones, and he lay down with his head upon these to sleep. That night he had a dream, and he seemed to see a ladder set upon the earth, the top of which reached to heaven, and angels of God were passing up and down the ladder. Above the ladder stood the Lord God himself, and Jacob dreamed that God told him that he would bless him as he had blessed Abraham and Isaac before him, that he would be with him in all places where he should go, and bring him home in safety again.

When Jacob waked, he was greatly awed. "Surely the Lord is in this place and I did not know it," he said. "How dreadful this place is! This is none other than the house of God, and this is the gate of heaven." So he set up a stone to be a sign, and he poured oil upon the top of it by way of showing that it was sacred, and he called the name of the place Bethel. Then he made a vow which was a curious combination of what little religion Jacob at that time possessed and his shrewd instinct of bargaining, of which he possessed a great deal. He said that if God would bless him and protect him on his journey, and give him food to eat and clothes to wear, and bring him back to his home in peace, then he would certainly worship God, and of what God should give him, he would give a tenth of it back again to God.

So Jacob continued on his journey, the journey which was to result in large consequences for future times. He did not seem to be very promising material for God to make anything out of; but at least he was a person who did not live for his stomach, as Esau was disposed to do. He could see beyond the impulse of the actual moment. He could think and wonder, and he was to have a long, hard chance to learn.

Still traveling eastward, he arrived at last within the borders of the land from which his mother had come with Eliezer long before. One day as he looked ahead, he saw that he was approaching a well, and in the field around the well three flocks of sheep were lying. A large stone was over the mouth of the well, and the flocks were waiting until the stone should be rolled aside and they could drink.

Jacob went up and spoke to some of the shepherds and asked them where they lived and what this region was. They told him that it was Haran. He asked them if they knew Laban, and they said they did. He asked them if Laban was well, and they said he was. "Look yonder," they said, "there is Rachel, his daughter, coming with the sheep." When Jacob saw Rachel and realized that this was his cousin, a daughter of his mother's brother, he went up and kissed her and shed tears for joy at seeing someone who reminded him of home. He rolled the stone from the mouth of the well and drew water for the sheep of Rachel's flock.

Then Rachel ran and told her father who had come, and Laban hurried out to meet Jacob, and embraced him, and brought him to his house. "You are my bone and my flesh," said Laban; and he invited Jacob to come and stay there for a visit.

Meanwhile Jacob began to help with the flocks and be useful generally. After a time Laban said to Jacob: "Even if you are my nephew, that is no reason why you should serve me for nothing. Tell me what your wages shall be."

Now, Laban had two daughters; the name of the elder one was Leah, and the younger one was Rachel. It seemed to Jacob that Rachel was much more beautiful and well-favored than Leah. He loved Rachel, and he said to Laban that if he would give him Rachel for his wife, he would serve him seven years.

Laban replied that, if Rachel were to marry, he would rather have her marry Jacob than someone else, so he agreed to Jacob's words and told him to stay there and begin his seven years of service. Therefore Jacob served for seven years, and he loved Rachel so much that even that long time seemed but a few days.

But Laban was hiding a crafty purpose in his mind. He did not like the idea of Rachel being married before her elder sister. Consequently, at the end of the seven years, instead of giving Rachel to Jacob as his bride, he gave him Leah instead.

Jacob, of course, felt very bitter about this; but Laban insisted that "it must not be so done in our country, to give the younger before the firstborn." However, he said that if Jacob would serve him seven more years, he would give him Rachel also for his wife. And since in that time people had never questioned the idea of having more wives than one, Jacob consented.

He took Rachel also for his wife, and began to serve the seven more years which Laban said he owed for her.

As the years went on, a large family began to grow up. Altogether Jacob had eleven sons and one daughter, but only one of these was the child of Rachel. His name was Joseph, and Jacob loved him better than all the rest.

At length the time came when Jacob began to think that he would go back to his home country; but Laban did not want him to go. Things had resulted very prosperously for him during these years while Jacob had been helping to look after his affairs. "Tarry longer," Laban urged, "for I have learned by experience that the Lord has blessed me for your sake." Let Jacob name his wages, and he would pay them.

But Jacob said: "You shall not give me anything. There is one thing which, if you will do, I will again feed and keep your flock." Then Jacob went on to explain what he meant. He would take out of the flocks and herds all the speckled and spotted cattle and goats and all the brown sheep. These should be his portion, and all the rest should belong to Laban.

No sooner had Laban agreed to that than he began to think of a method by which he could get the better of Jacob. He separated all the speckled and spotted cattle and sheep and goats from the rest, and had his sons drive them off into another region, three days' journey distant. Then he left Jacob with the remainder of the flock, which did not seem likely to breed any speckled or spotted calves or goats or lambs which could belong to Jacob.

But when Laban or any other man tried to match wits with Jacob, he was launched on a risky enterprise. Jacob saw what Laban had done, and he set to work to accomplish his own purpose. Before he had finished, he had contrived it so that practically all the good, strong sheep and goats and cattle had been bred brown or speckled, and so they belonged to him. He was growing rich. He had not only large flocks and herds, but maid servants and men servants and asses and camels.

By that time Laban's sons were beginning to grow disgruntled and envious. "Jacob has taken away all our father's

NOAH BUILDING HIS ALTAR

JACOB AND ESAU

property," they said, "and of that which used to be our father's
has he gotten all this glory." Moreover, Jacob noticed that
Laban's countenance had changed, and that he did not look at
him with the same expression as before. Therefore, he made
up his mind that he would leave Laban's country and go back
home.

He called Rachel and Leah out into the fields with him,
where they could talk in private. "You know," he said, "that
with all my power I have served your father. And your father
has deceived me, and changed my wages ten times: but God did
not suffer him to hurt me." Also he told how Laban had tried
to get all the flocks for himself, but how he, Jacob, had out-
witted Laban. Rachel and Leah agreed with him. They did
not like their father's ways, and they were ready to leave with
Jacob.

So one day, when Laban had gone out to shear his sheep,
Jacob gathered up all his possessions and all his people and
crossed over the river and set his face westward toward Mount
Gilead. Some time elapsed before Laban knew that he had
gone, and then he and his men pursued Jacob, and after seven
days overtook him. He complained loudly because Jacob had
gone off in such a secret fashion, and had not even let him kiss
his daughters and his grandchildren good-by. Moreover, he
accused Jacob of having stolen his gods. The little images he
had kept as his household deities had disappeared when Jacob
left. As a matter of fact, Rachel had taken them, though Jacob
did not know it; but she had concealed them in her tent so
well that Laban, though he searched everywhere, could not find
them.

Then Jacob was very angry, and gave Laban a piece of his
mind. He wanted to know what Laban meant by following
after him and searching his tents and claiming that he had stolen
his gods. He launched into an eloquent summary of all the
work he had done for Laban, and of the ways in which Laban
had tried to cheat him and defraud him. "Unless the God of
my fathers, of Abraham and of Isaac, had been with me, surely
you would have sent me away empty. God saw my affliction

and the work of my hands, and rebuked you yesternight," he said.

So Laban was silenced, and there was nothing left to do but to agree peaceably with Jacob. They put up a sacred pillar and named it Mizpah, and they said, "The Lord watch between me and thee when we are absent one from another."

Then early the next morning Laban kissed his daughters and their children good-by and returned to Haran.

A long time had gone by now since Jacob had started away, a fugitive, from home. He had learned a great deal, and he was a better man than when he had set out; but the memory of the old wrong he had done to Esau was still vivid, and he began to be afraid as he drew near to Esau's country. One night he had another dream, and he saw a vision of a host of the angels of God, and that encouraged him. He sent a messenger to Esau, and he told the messenger to say: "Thy servant Jacob saith thus, I have sojourned with Laban, and stayed there until now: and I have oxen, and asses, flocks, and menservants, and women-servants: and I have sent to tell my lord, that I may find grace in thy sight." When the messengers came back, they told Jacob that Esau was coming to meet him with four hundred men.

Then Jacob was more afraid and distressed than ever. But his mind still worked quickly. He determined to send retinues of presents out ahead to meet Esau, first one group and then another. He told his shepherds and herdsmen to keep a space between the different droves, so that Esau, as he came to meet him, would encounter one flock of sheep and learn that it was a present for him, and presently encounter a drove of camels and learn that this was another present, and so on through the long procession. By this means he thought that Esau would be in a favorable humor by the time he came where Jacob and his family were.

Meanwhile that night Jacob had a strange experience. He walked out into the darkness and the solitude, and suddenly he seemed to find himself caught in the grip of a terrible foe. All night long they wrestled, and Jacob's thigh was thrown out of joint: but even thus Jacob would not let go. That, perhaps, was the one great trait in him which, in spite of his bad beginning, made him in the end a bigger man than his brother Esau. No matter what the difficulty was with which he grappled, he never would let go. As the day began to break, his antagonist tried to shake himself loose; but Jacob said, "I will not let you go unless you bless me."

"What is your name?" he inquired, and Jacob told him. Then said this unknown figure, "Your name shall no longer be called Jacob, but Israel: for as a prince you have power with God and with men, and have prevailed."

Though Jacob tried to learn the name of the other, he would not tell. Ever afterward Jacob believed that in the experience of that night he had been wrestling with an angel of God himself. He named the place Peniel, and he said, "I have seen God face to face, and my life is preserved."

The next morning, as the light came over the plains, Jacob looked, and, behold, Esau was coming with his four hundred men. Jacob divided his family and put the servants in front, and Leah and her children next, but in the last, and what he thought might be the safest place, he put Rachel and Joseph. Then he went past them and bowed himself seven times to the ground before Esau.

But Esau, if he was hot-tempered and impulsive, was also big-hearted and forgiving. To Jacob's relief and amazement, he fell on his neck and kissed him, and they wept together. He came and greeted all Jacob's family, and he asked Jacob what he meant by all those droves of cattle and camels which he had been meeting; and Jacob said, "These are to find grace in the sight of my lord." But Esau said, "I have enough, my brother; keep what you have for yourself." Nevertheless, Jacob pressed him to take a present, until at last Esau consented. He wanted Jacob to come back with him to where he was living; but Jacob thought to himself that it was wiser not to do that. So Esau went back to his own dwellings, and Jacob went on in another direction and pitched his tents and folded his cattle outside the town of Shalem. Soon after that he went to Bethel, where he had had the dream of the ladder reaching up to heaven, and he set up an altar there.

Thus he had returned in peace to the land from which he had set out so doubtfully years before. But his happiness was to be shadowed by a great sorrow. Near Bethel Rachel gave birth to another son, who was to be named Benjamin. But when he was born, Rachel died. Isaac, his father, who had lived much longer than either he or anyone else had expected, died also. But it was Rachel whom Jacob had loved best of all people, and now that she was dead her two sons, Joseph and Benjamin, were dearer to him than ever before.

CHAPTER VI

FTER THE death of Rachel, Jacob settled in
the land of Canaan with all his sons and his
shepherds and his other servants, and there he
pastured his flocks. The little boy Joseph
grew up until he was a lad of seventeen. He
was not like his older half-brothers. They were
mostly rough, matter-of-fact men, busy about the ordinary
affairs of their day and not bothering much about anything
beyond. But Joseph had the eyes of one who saw things which
were far away. As he grew up, Jacob, his father, loved him
more and more. Perhaps Joseph reminded Jacob of old lovely
forgotten things in his own youth, such as his vision of the
ladder of God at Bethel.

The other sons were not long in seeing that their father
loved Joseph more than he loved them. He gave Joseph a coat
dyed with many colors, so that no one could ever fail to see it.
It was another sign, so they thought, that their father preferred
Joseph to all the rest.

Moreover, Joseph began to have dreams which he recounted
to his brothers, and these dreams angered them all the more
because it seemed that Joseph was always dreaming of how he
would be greater than they. He said one morning that he had
dreamed the night before that he and his brothers were all
together in the field binding sheaves, and his sheaf stood straight
up from the ground and their sheaves bowed down and made
obeisance to his sheaf.

"Indeed?" said his brothers. "So you are to reign over us,
and you are to have dominion over us!" And they hated him
yet the more for his dreams and his words.

67

But that was not all. Another morning Joseph said he had had another dream; and this, according to his brothers' ideas, was worse than the other. He said that the sun and the moon and eleven stars in the sky bowed down to him. He told that to his brothers and also to his father, but that was too much even for Jacob.

"Shall I and your mother and your brothers indeed all come to bow down ourselves to the earth before you?" he asked. And he rebuked Joseph. Nevertheless, even though he rebuked him, Jacob kept wondering about this thing. He could not conceal from himself his belief that Joseph, in some strange way, was destined for great things.

Meanwhile, however, his brothers had no such idea. It is not hard to understand their feeling. Joseph seemed to them an impudent upstart. All these dreams of his seemed to be a reflection upon them. It was true also that they did have some grounds for grievance. Joseph had the assurance of youth. He was so possessed with the strange budding life which he felt within himself and so carried away by his own imaginings, that he did not stop to realize how these grated upon his brothers. He was struggling free, like a bird in its first flight, and was not conscious whom he was striking with his wings.

One day Joseph's brothers were feeding the flocks in the plains of Shechem, and Jacob said to Joseph that he wanted to send him on an errand to see how everything was faring with them. "Go," he said, "see whether it be well with your brothers and with the flocks, and bring me word again." So Joseph went out of the valley of Hebron and came to Shechem. He met a man as he was going on his way. The man asked him what he was looking for. Joseph said he was looking for his brothers and their flocks, and the man told him they had left Shechem and moved on to Dothan. So Joseph went farther; and there in Dothan, a considerable distance away from home, he found them.

As soon as he came to the edge of the fields his brothers saw him. His coat of many colors could be recognized a long way off. They put their heads together and began to talk.

"Look who is here," they said contemptuously. "Behold, this dreamer comes! Come, let us kill him and throw him into some pit, and we will say a wild beast devoured him. Then we shall see what will become of his dreams."

But Reuben, who was the eldest of all the brothers, was a kinder man than some of the rest. And he said, "No, let us not kill him. Shed no blood. Cast him into a pit here in the wilderness if you want to do that, but do not lay any violent hands on him." What he purposed was to deliver Joseph, when he had the chance, out of the hands of the rest of the brothers and to bring him back to his father.

The others yielded to Reuben to this extent. When Joseph came up to them, they did not kill him, but they tore that hated many-colored coat off him and threw him into a pit. The pit was without water and empty, so he was not hurt. Then the brothers sat down to eat some bread, and as they happened to look toward the horizon they saw a caravan of Ishmaelites coming from the direction of Gilead with their camels, carrying spicery and balm and myrrh on their way down into Egypt. Then Judah, who agreed perhaps with his brother Reuben, said, "What profit is it if we slay our brother and conceal his blood? Come, let us sell him to the Ishmaelites. Let us not do violence to him; for, after all, he is our brother and our flesh."

So the others agreed, since this method would be profitable, and they pulled Joseph up out of the pit and sold him to the Ishmaelite traders for twenty pieces of silver; and they carried Joseph with them on the long trail toward Egypt.

Now, Reuben had been away somewhere at the moment when the caravan came by, and when he came back he was dismayed to find the pit empty. He rent his clothes and came to his brothers and said, "The child is gone; and I, whither shall I go?" Apparently they did not tell him what they had done; but they contrived a story to tell to their father Jacob. They killed a young goat and took Joseph's coat and dipped it in the goat's blood, and then they took this coat all stained with blood to Jacob, and they said: "We found this. You can tell whether this is your son's coat or not." Of course Jacob knew it, and he cried out: "It is my son's coat! A wild beast has devoured him. Joseph is rent in pieces." Then Jacob put on sackcloth and mourned for Joseph many days, and no one could comfort him. He said, "I will go down into my grave mourning for my son."

Meanwhile Joseph had been carried into Egypt, and there the Ishmaelites sold him as a slave to a man named Potiphar, who was an officer of the Pharaoh, king of Egypt, and captain of the guard. Thus it appeared that Joseph's dreams had come to their end. He had thought the whole world was before him, and now here he was in Egypt, alone and friendless and a slave. It had been easy to dream when he was a favorite son in his father's household; but what would happen now when every fact seemed to make a mockery of the old, bright belief that his life would lead to something great?

Even the fact that he was a slave was not to end his troubles. For a while it seemed only a beginning for worse things following.

It was true that Potiphar liked Joseph and made him the steward of his house. But Potiphar's wife liked Joseph altogether too much. She saw that he was young and handsome, and she wanted him for herself. Potiphar by this time had given Joseph much responsibility and freedom in his house, and confidently left Joseph in charge when he himself was away. One day when Potiphar was absent, his wife made love to Joseph, and tried to persuade him to come and make love to her.

But Joseph answered: "My master does not know what is with me in the house. He has committed all that he has to my hand. How, then, can I do this great wickedness, and sin against God?"

Still day by day Potiphar's wife pursued Joseph with her advances, and day by day he would not listen. But once when he came into the house where she was alone, all the other servants being absent, she caught at his robe; and when he tore himself away, a piece of his robe was left in her hand. Then, in a passion, she shrieked and called the other servants. When they came running, she showed them the piece of Joseph's robe which she had in her hand, and she accused him of having tried to do violence to her, and of having been frightened away. When Potiphar came back, she made the same accusation to him. Potiphar was enraged. He turned Joseph out of his house, and had him put in prison.

If Joseph had kept any remnants of his dreams in Potiphar's house, it would have seemed that they must be dead now that he found himself shut up in an Egyptian jail. But again there was something in his spirit which could not be overcome by circumstance.

Before long Joseph had led the keeper of the prison to like him so well that this man made Joseph a sort of deputy. He put him in charge of the other prisoners, and treated him generally with respect. Moreover, the other prisoners began to turn to Joseph and to tell him what they were thinking and of how—like prisoners in every other time before or since—they were hoping to get out. One night two of them had dreams which they recounted to Joseph. Both of them had been servants of Pharaoh, one of them his butler, and the other his baker. The butler dreamed a dream of how he had seen grapes grow on a three-branched vine, and of how he had pressed wine from the grapes and filled Pharaoh's cup with the wine, and had given it into the king's hand. The baker told of how he had been carrying three baskets of bread and cakes for Pharaoh, and birds had flown down and eaten them. Joseph said he believed the dreams meant that in three days the butler would be restored to his old place of serving Pharaoh, and that within the same time Pharaoh would take the baker and hang him, and that the birds would eat his flesh. Unfortunately for the poor baker, that was exactly the way in which events turned out. Pharaoh did restore the butler to favor, and the baker he did have hanged. But for all the good it did Joseph, the butler might have been hanged too. Being out of prison, he promptly forgot everybody in it, including Joseph. He went on his way of restored fortune; as for Joseph, he could stay where he was.

There in jail Joseph did stay for two more years. Then Pharaoh himself had a dream. In fact, he had two dreams, and they were so vivid and so much alike that they disturbed him greatly. In one dream he saw seven fat cattle feeding in a meadow; and as he looked, he saw seven other cattle come up out of the river, scrawny and ugly, and these lean, ill-favored cattle ate up the fat ones. In the next dream Pharaoh saw seven ears of corn blossom on one stalk. They were round and full. Then after them there grew out seven thin ears, looking as though they had been blasted by an east wind, and these seven shrunken ears devoured the seven good ones.

Pharaoh could not rest until he had found out what these dreams meant. He sent for all the magicians he knew, who were numerous. He sent for the soothsayers, and all the learned men generally. He told them his dreams, but no one could explain them. Then the chief butler, now that it was useful to remember Joseph, remembered all about him. He came and told Pharaoh what had happened to him in connection with his own dream, and that perhaps this same Joseph could interpret the dream of Pharaoh. So Pharaoh had Joseph summoned, and Joseph, having made himself as presentable as he could, was brought into Pharaoh's presence. The king told Joseph that he had had two dreams. "I have heard it said of you," he continued, "that you can understand a dream and interpret it."

Joseph answered very simply: "It is not in me: God shall give Pharaoh an answer of peace."

Then Pharaoh told Joseph his dreams about the seven fat and seven lean cattle and about the seven good ears and the seven blasted ears of corn. "I told all this to the magicians," he said, "but there was not one of them who could declare it unto me."

The two dreams, said Joseph, were one. God had showed Pharaoh what he was about to do. The seven fat cattle and the seven good ears of corn meant the same thing. They stood for seven years of abundant harvests. The seven lean cattle and the seven blasted ears of corn also meant one thing. They meant seven years of famine. There should be a time of plenty in Egypt, and after that should come such a time of scarcity and hunger that all the good years should be forgotten as though they had never been.   Moreover, he said, the fact that the dream was doubled was in order that it might more surely be believed.

Pharaoh was impressed.   In view of these things, what was to be done?

Then Joseph gave the answer.   Pharaoh, he said, ought immediately to find some able person who could be given authority in the whole kingdom of Egypt, to make provision ahead against the famine which was coming.   He should be Pharaoh's food administrator, and during the period of plenty he should gather the surplus crops and store them in preparation for the time of need.

Pharaoh saw at once the wisdom of this.   He wondered whom he should appoint to this position.   And then he knew. Where could there be a more fit man than Joseph himself? When Pharaoh decided, he decided thoroughly.   All the people, he said, should henceforth be ruled according to Joseph's word. "Only in the throne," he declared, "will I be greater than you." He took a ring from his hand and put it on Joseph's hand.   He hung a gold chain about his neck, and gave him royal vestures of fine linen.   He had his second-best chariot brought out for Joseph to ride in; and from that time on, wherever Joseph went, people bowed down before him as they did before the king himself.

In the next seven years the land of Egypt brought forth huge crops, and Joseph had great quantities of food gathered up in the royal storehouses.   In those same happy years Joseph was married; and he had two sons, one of them named Manasseh, and the other named Ephraim.

But the seven years went by, and then began seven very different ones.   There came a famine in Egypt grievous beyond all ordinary famines.   The whole people of Egypt began to be hungry.   "Give us bread," the crowds said to Pharaoh, and Pharaoh answered, "Go to Joseph; what he says to you, do."

Then Joseph opened the storehouses into which he had gathered the grain of the abundant years; but the famine grew worse and worse.

CHAPTER VII

WHEREIN THE BROTHERS WHO HAD SOLD JOSEPH INTO SLAVERY COME DOWN INTO EGYPT, AND FIND THEIR BROTHER ON A THRONE; AND WHEREIN IS SHOWN THE LOVE THAT JOSEPH HAD FOR HIS BROTHER BENJAMIN AND FOR HIS FATHER JACOB.

EANWHILE THE famine had spread to near-by countries also. It was in Canaan as well as in Egypt, and here there was no food stored up. The rumor spread across the desert and up into the plains and hills of Canaan that the Egyptian storehouses still had grain, and Jacob, Joseph's father, heard it. It had been some twelve or thirteen years since Joseph had disappeared, and Jacob had long since lost any hope which he had at first that Joseph could be alive. But the ten elder half-brothers were living, and so was Benjamin, Joseph's brother, the son of Rachel, and the youngest of all Jacob's children.

One day Jacob said to Reuben and Simeon and Judah and the others: "I have heard that there is corn in Egypt; go down there and buy food for us before we shall all die." So the ten brothers mounted their camels and started toward the Nile; but Jacob kept Benjamin at home, "lest," he said, "by any chance mischief befall him." He was still remembering Joseph; and Joseph and Benjamin together, the two sons of Rachel, were always the ones whom he had loved best.

Presently the other brothers arrived in Egypt by the same caravan route along which, years before, Joseph had been carried by the Ishmaelite traders to whom they had sold him. They knew nothing of what had happened to him since, and little did they imagine the way in which now they were about to meet him. Out in their own plains they were bold enough, but in Egypt they felt lost and strange. They were mere rude tribesmen, looked at indifferently by the people of the cities which had grown up beside the Nile. No wonder they were ill at ease when they came into the courts of Pharaoh, and no wonder that the last thing they were likely to do was to recognize the man there on the seat of power as their own brother.

But Joseph recognized them. He had gone a long way— from the bottom of the pit in the plains of Dothan to a throne in Egypt. In the lines of his face and in his Egyptian garb he was very different from the earlier Joseph; but these brothers were not much different from what they had been before. He did not let them see that he knew them. Instead, he assumed a roughness of speech and attitude to hide his real emotion. "Where did you come from?" he demanded.

"From the land of Canaan," they said, "to buy food."

"You are spies!" he said. "You have come here to see the nakedness of this land."

But they protested, "Thy servants are twelve brethren, sons of one man in the land of Canaan; and the youngest is this day with our father, and one is dead."

So the youngest was with their father! That meant that Jacob was alive, and Benjamin alive also. Joseph determined that he should see this his own brother, who, when he last laid eyes upon him, was only a little boy.

"I said," he went on, "that you are spies. Now, this is the way you shall be proved. By the life of Pharaoh, you shall not go forth unless your youngest brother come hither. Send one of you and let him fetch your brother, and you shall be kept in prison, that your words may be put to the test whether there be any truth in you. If not, by the life of Pharaoh, surely you are spies!" So he had them seized, and they were held under guard three days.

On the third day, Joseph had them brought before him, and he said: "If you are honest men, let one of you be kept as an hostage. The rest of you can go and carry corn for the famine of your households. But bring your youngest brother to me; so shall your words be verified, and you shall not die."

Then they commenced to talk together. They were frightened, and old, guilty memories began to stir their consciences. They were thinking of what they had done to Joseph.

"We are certainly guilty concerning our brother," they said, "because we saw his anguish of soul, when he besought us, and we would not listen; that is the reason why this distress has come upon us."

And Reuben said: "I told you not to sin against the child; and you would not hear. Now you see that his blood must be avenged."

Meanwhile they had no idea that this Egyptian before whom they were whispering understood their language, for he had taken care to speak to them through an interpreter. And still less did they have any dimmest notion that the man whom they thought was an Egyptian was really Joseph.

But Joseph, as he listened, was overcome with his emotions, and he turned away from them, so that they should not see his tears. Then he came back and took up the conversation with them again. He picked out Simeon as an hostage and had him bound before their eyes. After that he said no more to them; but he ordered his servants to fill all their sacks with grain, to put every man's money which he had paid for the grain back into the sack, and to give them provisions for the journey. So they laded their pack-mules with the grain and set out homeward.

After they were well on their way, one of them opened his sack, and there he discovered his money. He showed it to his brothers, and they were all afraid. They thought this was some sort of magic, and they had a feeling that trouble might come out of it before they were through. As soon as they reached home they told the whole story to Jacob: how they had arrived in Egypt; how the man in command there had treated them roughly and accused them of being spies; how they had denied it and told him of their father and Benjamin; how he had given them food; how he had taken Simeon as an hostage, and sent them back with the demand that they bring Benjamin down to Egypt; and, lastly, how their own money had somehow got back into the mouth of their sacks.

Jacob's heart sank. "You have bereaved me of my children," he cried. "Joseph is gone, and Simeon is gone, and now you talk of taking Benjamin away. Everything is against me!"

Then Reuben said to his father that he would be responsible for bringing Benjamin back to Jacob. "Slay my two sons," he said, "if I do not bring him back to you. Give him into my keeping, and I will see that he comes home safe."

But Jacob said: "My son shall not go down with you. His brother is dead, and he is left alone: if mischief should befall him in these ways of yours, then you will bring my gray hairs down with sorrow to the grave."

But the famine in Canaan grew no better, but worse instead, and the time came when all the corn which the brothers had brought from Egypt was eaten up, and Jacob had to appeal to them again: "Go again and buy us a little food."

But Judah answered: "The man in Egypt solemnly protested that we should not see his face unless Benjamin should be with us. If you will send him, we will go down and buy food. But if you will not send him, we will not go. I tell you again the man said that we should not see his face unless our brother came with us."

"Why did you do me such evil as to tell the man that you had another brother?" asked Jacob.

Then the whole group joined in to explain how the Egyptian had pressed his questions about them, and about their kindred, and had demanded to know whether their father was alive, and whether they had another brother. They had to answer him. "How could we know," they said, "that he would say 'Bring your brother down'?"

Then Judah said to his father, as Reuben had said before, that he would be surety for Benjamin, and that he would take the blame forever afterward if Benjamin did not come home safe. "Unless we had lingered," he said, "by this time we could have gone there and returned a second time."

So Jacob yielded, and he said: "If it must be so, then do this: take the best fruits in the land, and carry the man a present, some balm and honey, spices and myrrh, nuts, and almonds. And take double money with you, and also the money that you found in the mouth of your sacks. Carry that again in your hands. Perhaps it was an oversight. Also take your brother and go. May God Almighty give you mercy before the man in Egypt, that he may send away your other brother, and Benjamin. If I be bereaved of my children, I am bereaved!"

So the nine brothers took the present and took double money and Benjamin, and down into Egypt again they went and appeared before Joseph. When Joseph saw Benjamin, he said to his steward, "Bring these men home and have a feast made ready, for these men shall dine with me at noon."

So the steward did as Joseph bade, and he conducted his brothers into Joseph's house.

When they saw where they were being led, they were more alarmed than ever. They said one to another: "This is because of the money that was returned in our sacks. We shall be accused. They will set upon us and make slaves of us all, and take the pack-mules we have brought down." They surrounded Joseph's steward before they went through the door. They told him how they had found the money in their sacks, and that they did not know how it got there, and that they had brought it back, and here it was.

If he had answered them with threats, they would not have been surprised, but what he said to them was, "Peace be to you, fear not; your God and the God of your father gave you treasure in your sack; I had your money." And he brought Simeon out to them. Moreover, in Joseph's house he had water brought to wash their feet, as with distinguished guests; and he had provender given to their beasts.

Presently Joseph came home, and his brothers came up to him with the present of money and other things which they had brought from Canaan, and they bowed down to the earth before him. He asked them of their welfare: "Is your father well, the old man of whom ye spake? Is he yet alive?"

"Thy servant, our father, is in good health," they answered. Then Joseph lifted his eyes and saw his brother Benjamin, his mother's son. "Is this your younger brother," he said, "of whom you spoke to me?" And without waiting for their answer, he said to Benjamin, "God be gracious to you!" Then Joseph was so moved that he could not control himself, so much did his heart yearn toward Benjamin. He went out to his own room and wept there. Then he washed his face and came out again; and, holding his feelings in check, he said, "Set on bread." So they all had dinner together, but Joseph saw to it that Benjamin was served more lavishly than any of the rest.

Still he did not tell them who he was.

That evening he told his steward to fill the sacks of all these men with food, as much as they could carry, and again to put every man's money into his sack's mouth. Furthermore he told him to hide his own silver cup in the grain of Benjamin's sack. The steward did what Joseph told him, and as soon as it was light next morning the whole group started away.

When they were scarcely out of the city, Joseph said to his steward, "Follow after those men, and when you overtake them, say to them, 'Why have you rewarded good for evil?' " Then he was to seize Benjamin's sack and find in it Joseph's cup.

After them the steward hurried, and when he overtook them he spoke to them as Joseph had instructed. They all protested earnestly. Why should he speak to them in this way? God forbid that they should do any such thing as he had accused them of! The money which had been in their sacks' mouths before, had they not brought it back again out of the land of Canaan? How could it be supposed that they would steal silver or gold out of Joseph's house? If any one of them had done such a thing, they said, let him die; and, as for the rest of them, they would be bondsmen in Egypt.

"Very well," said the steward, "let it be according to your own words. At least, he who is found with the cup shall go back to be a servant; the others shall be blameless."

Quickly, then, every man took down his sack, laid it on the ground and opened it. The steward searched. One sack after another he examined, but the cup was not in any of them,

At last, he came to Benjamin's sack, and there in Benjamin's sack was Joseph's cup.

Then they all rent their clothes in dismay, loaded their asses again, and all of them went back into the city.

When they reached Joseph's house, Joseph was there, and they fell before him on the ground. "What is this that you have done?" said Joseph. "Did you forget that such a man as I am can divine things?"

Judah answered for the others. "What shall we say unto my lord? What shall we speak? Or how shall we clear ourselves? God has found out our iniquity. We are your servants, both we and also him with whom the cup is found."

"No," said Joseph. "God forbid. Only the man in whose hands the cup was found shall be my servant; as for the rest of you, go back in peace to your father."

Then Judah came near and begged to speak to him. He told him the whole story as it had happened from the first. "Oh, my lord," he said, "I beg you to let me speak a word into your ears. Do not let your anger burn against your servant, for you are even as Pharaoh. My lord, you asked us, 'Have you a father or brother?' and we said, 'We have a father, an old man, and a child of his old age, a little one; his brother is dead; and he alone is left of his mother, and his father loves him.' And you said, 'Bring him down to me, that I may set my eyes upon him.' And we said to my lord, 'The lad cannot leave his father: for if he should leave his father, his father would die.' But you said, 'Unless your youngest brother come with you, you shall see my face no more.'

"Then we went to your servant my father, and we told him my lord's words; and our father said, 'Go again, and buy us a little food.' We told him that we could not go down unless our youngest brother went with us. Only then would we go down. We told him again that we could not see your face unless our youngest brother were with us. Then my father said to us, 'You know that my wife bore me two sons. One of them went out from me, and all that I could know was that he must have been torn to pieces. I have not seen him again: and if you take this one also from me, and mischief befall him, you will bring down my gray hairs with sorrow to the grave.'

"So, then, when I come to my father, and the lad is not with us, because his life is bound up in the lad's life, when he sees that the lad is not with us, he will die, and your servants will have brought their father down sorrowing to his grave. I was surety for this lad to my father. I told him, 'If I do not bring him back to you, then I shall bear the blame forever.' Now, therefore, I beg you, let me stay instead of the lad a bondsman to my lord, and let him go up with his brothers. For how can I go up to my father if the lad is not to be with me? How can I look upon the evil that should come to my father then?"

When Judah had finished, Joseph could refrain no more. "Let every man go out from me," he cried to his servants and to all the other Egyptians in the hall. When no one was left except Joseph himself and his brothers, Joseph broke down and wept aloud, so that the Egyptians heard him beyond the door. But his brothers were amazed. What did it mean that this lord of Egypt was moved this way?

Then Joseph made himself known. "I am Joseph," he said.

They looked at him terrified. "I am Joseph," he repeated. "Is my father alive?" His brothers could not answer him, for they were speechless in his presence.

"Come near me, I pray you," Joseph said, and hesitantly they drew near. "I am Joseph," he said again, "your brother, whom you sold into Egypt. Do not be grieved nor angry with yourselves because you sent me hither: God sent me before you to preserve life. For these two years the famine has been in the land, and there are yet five years in which there shall be neither earing nor harvest. God sent me before you to preserve you a posterity in the earth, and to save your lives by a great deliverance. So now it was not you that sent me hither, but God; and God has made me a helper to Pharaoh, and lord of all his houses, and ruler through all this land of Egypt.

"Go quickly up to my father and say to him, 'This is the message of your son Joseph: God has made me lord of Egypt. Come down to me, come and do not tarry.' Tell him too that he shall dwell in the land of Goshen, and he shall be near me, he and his children, and all his children's children, and his flocks and herds. I will nourish him there through the five years of famine which are to come, lest he and all his household come to poverty."

Still his brethren stood like men dazed, scarcely yet taking in that his words were real.

"Look," said Joseph, "your own eyes can see for yourselves, and my brother Benjamin can see, that this is my mouth that speaks to you. Go tell my father of all my glory in Egypt, and of all that you have seen. Hasten and bring my father here!"

Then Joseph fell upon Benjamin's neck and wept for joy, and Benjamin wept on his neck. He kissed all his brothers, and after that they talked with him.

No wonder the excitement ran all through Pharaoh's house. Joseph's brothers had come, men told one another. It pleased Pharaoh well, and his servants also. The king said to Joseph: "Tell your brothers to lade their beasts and go back to the land of Canaan. Let them get your father and his household and come to me, and I will give them the good of the land of Egypt, and they shall eat of the fat of the land. Tell them that this is my commandment: that they are to take wagons out of the land of Egypt for their little children and their wives, and they are to bring your father, and come. Never mind about packing up any possessions. The good of all the land of Egypt shall be theirs."

So the brothers did as they were bidden. Joseph gave them wagons according to Pharaoh's command, and provision for the journey. New clothes he also gave them, but to Benjamin he gave three hundred pieces of silver and five new robes to wear. He sent also asses laden with grain and bread and meat for his father, and he told his brothers not to lose time by the way.

So up out of Egypt again the brothers went, and came into Canaan to their father Jacob. "Joseph," they said to him, "is still alive! Joseph is alive, and he is governor over all the land of Egypt."

At those words the old man's heart almost ceased beating.

He heard what they said, but he could not believe that it was true. "children. Joseph brought the two boys near before his"

But they told him it was true. They told him all Joseph's words—everything he had said to them. And then when he saw the wagons which Joseph had sent to carry him, his spirit revived. "It is enough," he cried; "Joseph my son still lives, and I shall see him before I die!"

So down toward Egypt Jacob started on his way, past Beer-sheba, where he had a vision, and seemed to hear a promise from God which comforted him greatly, and on then over the desert, he and his entire family—some seventy souls in all. As they drew near the borders of Egypt a chariot came rolling up to meet them, and in that chariot was Joseph. For the first time since he had gone as a boy with that message to the plains of Dothan, Jacob looked again on his son's face. "Now," he said, "I am ready to die, since I have seen your face and know that you are still alive!"

They all went together, therefore, into the realms of Pharaoh, and Pharaoh, as he had promised, gave them land in the rich region of Goshen. The famine was still continuing, and the chronicle in the book of Genesis goes on to recount how Joseph administered food from his storehouses, and what he required of the people of Egypt whom he fed; but this has nothing directly to do with the story of his father and his brothers. They lived peaceably in Goshen until Jacob grew to be a very old man. And one day he sent for Joseph, and Joseph came to see his father and brought with him his two sons, Ephraim and Manasseh. Jacob's mind went back, as an old man's will, to the years long ago, and he began to talk of the happy things and the sad things which had happened to him since he was young. He told Joseph how his mother Rachel had died in the land of Canaan, when they had only a little way to go to come to Ephrah, and of how he had buried her near Bethlehem. Then as with his failing sight he saw Joseph's two boys, he said, "Who are these?" And Joseph told him that they were his two sons. "Bring them near," said Jacob, "and I will bless them. I had not thought to see thy face," he said to Joseph, "and now God has showed me also thy children." Joseph brought the two boys near before his father, Manasseh before Jacob's right hand, and Ephraim before his left. Then Jacob blessed Joseph and the two boys, and he said, as he blessed the lads, "Let my name be named on them, and the name of my fathers Abraham and Isaac; and let them grow into a multitude in the midst of the earth."

But as Jacob blessed the boys, Joseph saw that he had crossed his hands, so that his right hand was stretched out to be laid on the head of Ephraim, who was the younger of the two, and his left hand laid on the head of the firstborn, who was Manasseh. Joseph was displeased, and he said to his father, "Not so, my father: this is the firstborn"—and he showed him Manasseh; "put your right hand upon his head." But Jacob shook his head. "I know it, my son, I know it," he said: "he also shall become a people, and he also shall be great; but truly his younger brother shall be greater than he, and he shall become a multitude of nations." And Jacob, who had himself been a younger son, blessed the younger son first.

After that he called together all his own sons, the half-brothers of Joseph, and Joseph's own brother Benjamin. He gave each one of them his own blessing, and said that each one of them should be the head of a family which would grow into one of the tribes of Israel.

Then he died, but not before he had charged them not to bury him in Egypt. He wanted his body to be laid in the old tomb in the field of Machpelah, which his grandfather Abraham had bought, and where Abraham and Sarah and his own father and mother, Isaac and Rebekah, had been buried. With a great retinue, therefore, escorted by chariots and horsemen of Pharaoh, they carried Jacob's body up into the land from which he had come and buried him there.

Now, after the funeral, when they all went down into Egypt again, Joseph's half-brothers began to be troubled. "Now that our father is dead," they said, "Joseph will hate us, and he will certainly pay back all the evil that we did to him." They were afraid to go and talk to Joseph themselves, but they sent a messenger and told him to say: "Before our father died, he left this command, 'Forgive, I pray you, your brothers' trespasses and their sins; for they did you evil.' That is what he said, and now we beg you, forgive these wrongs."

When Joseph heard this, the tears came to his eyes.

Presently his brothers drew near and fell down before his face. "Behold," they said, "we are your servants." Joseph said: "Do not be afraid. Am I in the place of God? As for you, you thought evil against me; but God made it into good at last, so that it should result, as it has this day, in saving many people alive. Fear not; I will nourish you and your little ones." Then he comforted them, and spoke to them with kindness.

So ends the story of Joseph, for no more is told of him, save that at the end of his days he died, and his body was embalmed, and laid, perhaps, somewhere among the royal tombs of Egypt.

CHAPTER VIII

THE STORY OF THE BIRTH OF MOSES, AND OF HOW THE DAUGHTER
OF PHARAOH FOUND HIM BY THE RIVER; AND OF HOW HE KILLED AN
EGYPTIAN AND FLED TO THE DESERT; AND OF HOW HE CAME BACK TO
COMPEL PHARAOH TO LET THE PEOPLE OF ISRAEL GO FREE.

HE FIRST book of the Bible, the book of Genesis, closes with the death of Joseph. Then follows the book of Exodus. As the ancient legends had recounted how Abraham came into Canaan, and how his descendants lived there after him, so the book of Exodus tells how the tribes of Israel came back into Canaan out of Egypt, to which their ancestors had gone down in Joseph's time. The story still is dealing with far-off years, the traditions of which were handed down in saga and song from generation to generation. And no one can tell exactly where the facts leave off and the magnifying of tradition begins. But one thing is certain: forever afterward the Jews looked back to one great figure to whom they attributed not only the deliverance from Egypt but also the formulation of the law by which increasingly the whole life of the nation was ordered. His name was Moses, and the story of Moses is the story of one of the heroes who most greatly have mastered the imagination of this world.

With the beginning of the book of Exodus there is a shifting of the scenes. The kings who belonged to the time of the story of Joseph had disappeared. Many years went by, and the Hebrew people, the descendants of the sons of Jacob, were no longer popular in Egypt. The Egyptians thought that these aliens were crowding them out of their best land. Moreover, they were different, as the Jews have always been different. They seemed to the Egyptians to form a stubborn little party of their own among the general population. What would happen, men began to ask, if Egypt should be at war? And what if the Jews should side with Egypt's enemies? So the Egyptians began to fear and hate the Israelites. A new Pharaoh was on the throne. He made up his mind that he would rid Egypt of these Israelites. He would crush their spirits with slavery. If that were not enough, he would gradually kill them off.

The kings of Egypt had always been great builders. The gigantic pyramids which to this day look out across the desert sands had been built by the labor of innumerable slaves who quarried and shaped the huge stones, floated them down the Nile, dragged them up the river banks, and hoisted them into place by engineering methods now forgotten. That was in far earlier centuries. Before this time also the temples at Thebes and Karnak and Memphis had been built. But still the restless energy and ambition of the Pharaohs had other things upon which men could be put to work—new temples and treasure-houses, palaces for the living, and tombs for the royal dead, embankments for the river, and canals, and roads. The new Pharaoh drafted the Israelites, therefore, into his forced labor. He put hard taskmasters over them, and he made their lives bitter with bondage. Even then he grew afraid to see these people go on multiplying; so he issued an order that all their boy children, as fast as they were born, should be drowned in the Nile.

Among the Israelites there was a man named Amram, whose wife was named Jochebed. They already had one son whose name was Aaron, and a daughter whose name was Miriam. And then another boy was born. For three months his mother tried to hide him, but a baby is not an easy thing to hide. Frightened lest Pharaoh's servant should discover him, and, knowing because of the house where they found him that he was an Israelitish baby, should carry him off and kill him, his mother wove a little basket out of bulrushes and made it water-tight with pitch, so that it floated like a boat; and in it she placed the baby and left it among the reeds by the edge of the river.

Moreover, she put Miriam to watch by the river-bank, to see what might happen.

Down to the Nile at this spot which the baby's mother had chosen, who should come but the daughter of Pharaoh—coming with her maidens to bathe in the river. There among the tall, green flags that grew by the water's edge, she spied something floating. "What was this?" she wondered; and she sent one of her maids to get it. When she opened the top of the basket, she saw the baby, and the baby cried.

That melted her heart. "It is one of the Hebrews' children," she said. Then as she stood there wondering what she should do, up came the little Miriam. She asked the princess whether she would not like her to go and find a nurse from among the Hebrew women so that she could take care of the child, and Pharaoh's daughter told her to go. So Miriam went and called her own mother and the baby's mother; and when Jochebed came, the princess said, "Take this child away and nurse it for me, and I will give you wages."

So Moses' mother had her own baby back to nurse under the protection of the daughter of the king. But the princess adopted him and treated him as her own son. She gave him the name "Moses," which may have been derived from a Hebrew word meaning "drawn out," "because," she said, "I drew him out of the water."

So Moses, instead of being in danger of his life, grew up with opportunity and privilege. It appeared that he might have everything which one could desire for himself; but he could not forget his own people. How could he be content when they were suffering?

One day as he went about and saw these men of his own blood straining under their burdens, he caught sight of an Egyptian taskmaster striking a Hebrew with his whip. He looked this way and that way, and when he saw that no one else was near he struck the Egyptian, struck him so hard that he killed him. Then he hid his body in the sand.

None of the other Egyptians knew what had happened; but of course the Hebrew who had first been struck by the

Egyptian against whom Moses' anger had blazed knew what had happened. The whisper of it spread among the Hebrews, and the next day, when Moses was passing by and saw two of them quarreling and said to the one who he thought was in the wrong, "What are you striking this other man for?" the one whom he rebuked retorted: "Who made you a prince and a judge over us? Do you want to kill me, as you killed the Egyptian?" And Moses said to himself, "Surely this thing is known." Shortly thereafter the report of it came to Pharaoh, and when he heard of it, he said that Moses should be put to death.

There was nothing left then for Moses but to escape as quickly as he could. Out of Egypt, therefore, he fled, and he went into the land of Midian, which is in Arabia. There in the desert country he found a well, and sat down beside it. Now, in that region there lived a priest who had seven daughters, and they came and drew water and filled the watering troughs for their father's flock. But some shepherds came and drove the girls away, until Moses saw it and drove off the shepherds, and helped the girls water their sheep. Their father knew about the trouble which they were always having with the shepherds at the well. And when they came back with the sheep, he said, "How is it that you have come so soon to-day?" Then they told him how an Egyptian had taken their part against the shepherds, and drawn water for them and watered the flock. He asked them where the Egyptian was, and why they had left him behind and had not brought him to their tents and given him something to eat. So they did bring him, and Moses stayed there a long time, and he married one of the sisters, whose name was Zipporah; and in due time they had a son.

There in this country Moses lingered, leading the life of the nomads, and he kept the flock of his father-in-law, Jethro. (But here there is another sign of how various traditions are woven together in the story, for in another place the name of his father-in-law is given as Reuel.) He drove the flock hither and thither according to the pasturage, and one day he came to the slopes of Horeb mountain, or as it is named in another strand of the narrative, Mount Sinai.

Meanwhile in Egypt the woes of the Hebrew people were worse than ever. Pharaoh had redoubled his oppression, and the people cried out to God for deliverance. Moses was far away from Egypt, but he was not far away from the memory of what he had seen when he was there. It troubled his heart with the sense that God had something for him to do; and one day the fire burning in him flamed into a vision before his eyes. There on the desert, where the red sun poured like fire, he saw a bush that burned, and in the midst of it there appeared to him an angel; but though he saw that the bush was burning, it was not consumed. Then as Moses drew near in awe, he heard a voice that said: "I am the God of thy father, the God of Abraham, the God of Isaac, and the God of Jacob"—and the voice went on to say that God had heard the cry of the people of Israel in Egypt, and that he would deliver them and bring them out into a land which they should inherit for their own. "Come now therefore, and I will send you unto Pharaoh, that you may bring forth my people the children of Israel out of Egypt."

"But who am I," said Moses, "that I should go to Pharaoh, and that I should bring forth the children of Israel out of Egypt?"

Then came the voice again, telling him that it was he who should be the deliverer, and that when he had brought the people out they should worship God at this mountain. Then Moses asked how he should convince the Israelites that he was commissioned by God to lead them. What should he tell them was the name of God? And this is the answer which he received: "I AM THAT I AM. Thus shall you say unto the children of Israel, I AM hath sent me unto you." Down into Egypt and into the presence of Pharaoh Moses should go, and in God's name he should demand that the Israelites should be allowed to come out of Egypt and up to Horeb mountain, that they might worship God there together.

This seemed to Moses a very formidable commission. He himself had fled from Egypt to escape the anger of Pharaoh. What would happen when he went and stood before the king with any such demand as that the people of Israel should be set free? He wanted signs that God was really with him, and various signs were given; but still he was troubled. It looked as though a very persuasive man would be needed if anything were to be done with Pharaoh, and Moses said: "Lord, I am not eloquent. I never was before, and I am not now. I am slow of speech, and of a slow tongue." In his heart, however, he knew that this was no excuse, since, when God wishes to use men, he can make them sufficient for his use. So he heard a voice replying to him: "Who hath made man's mouth? or who maketh the dumb, or deaf, or the seeing, or the blind? is it not the Lord? Go, therefore, and I will be with thy mouth, and teach thee what thou shalt say."

But Moses was still dismayed. He prayed that God would send his message by somebody else. Then, to his own misfortune, Moses' prayer was partly granted. Aaron, his brother, was to go with him to be the spokesman. Aaron did so, and half the time he did things wrong, and was a thorn in Moses' flesh from that day forward.

When he had taken leave of his father-in-law, Moses set out for Egypt with his wife and family, and on the way Aaron met him. So into Egypt they went, and they sent word among the Israelites that they wanted to see all their chief men together. The leaders assembled, and Moses and Aaron told them of the experience Moses had had in Horeb, and how they had come down in the name of God to demand of Pharaoh that he let the people go. When they heard that, they were all very glad, and they bowed their heads and said a prayer of thanksgiving.

Then the day came when Moses and Aaron were to confront Pharaoh. Into the royal presence they went and announced their errand. They said that the Lord God of Israel demanded of Pharaoh that his people should be allowed to go up into Arabia and hold a great service of worship there.

Pharaoh was furious. "Who is this God of yours?" he said, "that I should obey his voice? I do not know him, and I shall not let these Israelites go."

The more Pharaoh thought about it, the angrier he grew. What talk was this of letting his laborers off from their work?

Instead of that, he would give them more work than ever. He ordered his overseers to drive the laborers harder than before. They had been making bricks, and they had been furnished the straw which was mixed in with the clay for brick-making. Hereafter they should be required to make no fewer bricks, but they should have to go out and gather the straw for themselves. He would show them what was the result of this idle talking of Moses and Aaron.

Then the poor people were in a desperate case. The Egyptian taskmasters drove them cruelly. They had to scour the ground everywhere to find stubble in place of the straw which was no longer given them. Their chief men came and appealed to Pharaoh, but he was merciless. As they came out of Pharaoh's court, they met Moses and Aaron, and they complained bitterly at what Moses and Aaron had brought to pass.

Moses went away and prayed, and as he prayed his heart was strengthened, and his confidence revived. He and Aaron would go and make their demands on Pharaoh again. This time they would threaten him with dire results which would happen if he did not listen to the message they had brought him from the Lord. So when they stood before him, Aaron threw his shepherd's rod down on the floor and the rod turned into a snake. But Pharaoh looked at that contemptuously. There were plenty of magicians in Egypt, he thought, who could match that exhibition. He sent for some of them, and they cast down their rods on the ground, and they turned into snakes also; and even when Aaron's snake swallowed up the others, Pharaoh was not impressed.

But Pharaoh could not get away from this unyielding Moses who, however reluctant he had been to begin God's work, would not let it fail when once he had begun. The next morning he met Pharaoh as Pharaoh came out to the bank of the river. "The water of this river shall be turned as red as blood," said Moses. "The fish in it shall die, and the water shall be so foul that all the people of Egypt shall loathe to drink it."

Then what Moses had said happened. The river was thick with red slime. Fish suffocated and died. Nobody could drink the water any more, and men began to dig wells everywhere to try to get water which was fit to use.

But presently the river cleared again, and Pharaoh shrugged his shoulders and said that the Nile might do that now and then when mud poured into it from its tributaries. He was not going to let the Israelites go.

Moses prophesied another plague. He said frogs would come up out of the river and out of all the ponds and swarm all over Egypt. They did. Out of the slime and overflow of the river they were spawned by the millions, until Pharaoh and the people grew sick of seeing frogs hopping and squirming everywhere. It was too much, and Pharaoh said that now he would let the Israelites go. Then Moses said he would pray God to take away the frogs, and by the next morning the frogs were disappearing. But no sooner had that happened than Pharaoh said to himself that probably the frogs would have disappeared anyhow, and he hardened his heart and would not listen to Moses when Moses reminded him of his promise.

Next came a plague of lice. The very dust of the earth seemed to be full of them, and they tormented man and beast. But Pharaoh was still stubborn.

Again there came another plague. This time it was flies. They swarmed into all the houses. They buzzed about men's faces and crawled over their food. It got to be more than Pharaoh could put up with; so once more he sent for Moses and told him that if the people of Israel would not go very far away, he would let them take their journey into the desert country for a religious pilgrimage. The flies began to disappear, and Pharaoh immediately plucked up confidence again and decided that he was not beaten after all. He had changed his mind. The Israelites should stay where they were.

It appeared that Moses had to use sterner measures. The next day, therefore, he and Aaron went in before Pharaoh, and took a handful of ashes and scattered it in the air before Pharaoh's eyes. It was a sign of what was going to happen. Wherever dust should blow throughout the land of Egypt, it should make the skin of cattle and of people break out with boils. Thus it came to pass, and everybody was sore and miserable. Pharaoh sent for his magicians to see what they could do in this emergency; but the magicians were so sick that they could not come. Pharaoh was waging a lonely battle; but he was still stubborn.

Another plague then had to follow. This time it was hail. Such a storm broke as nobody could remember having seen or heard of since Egypt was Egypt. It thundered in the sky, and the hail came down so that it sounded like thunder on the earth. Lightning blazed between the clouds and ran like bolts of fire along the ground. The hail broke the limbs of trees. It beat down all the growing crops. It killed the cattle in the field. Even Pharaoh was frightened. He sent for Moses and Aaron. "I have sinned," this time he acknowledged. "God is righteous, and I and my people are wicked." He urged them to pray that this thundering and lightning and this deluge of hail might stop. So Moses, though he was still distrustful of Pharaoh, prayed that the storm might cease, and presently it did stop, and the sun came out again.

After all, a storm is only a storm, thought Pharaoh. This one was worse than most, but storms had to be expected now and then, and, besides, it was over. So he retracted everything he had said. Let the people of Israel stay at work.

After the hail came another visitation. This time it was locusts. Pharaoh had due warning, for Moses told him that if he kept on refusing to let the people go, the locusts should come into his coasts, and they should cover the face of the earth, so that no one could see the ground. Whatever was left from the hail, they should eat, and they should fill his palace and the houses of all his servants and all the houses throughout Egypt. By now Pharaoh's retinue had become weary of these calamities. They begged him to get rid of Moses and Aaron before the whole country should be destroyed. So Moses and Aaron were brought in, and Pharaoh said that the people of Israel could go; that is, some of them could. Whom did they expect permission for? "Everybody," said Moses, "we will go with our young and with our old, with our sons and with our daughters, with

THE SELLING OF JOSEPH

THE FINDING OF MOSES

our flocks and with our herds." "You will not," said Pharaoh.
"The grown men can go, for that is what you asked for, but
no others." (Because Pharaoh knew, of course, that in that
case they would not go.) And Moses and Aaron were driven
out from Pharaoh's presence.

Then came the locusts. The east wind blew from the
desert, and Egypt was familiar with the kind of locust swarms
that the east wind could bring in a bad year. They came in a
cloud that darkened the sky. They came like a beating rain.
They covered the houses and the trees and the ground, and
then they covered themselves until a thick mass of them was
struggling everywhere. So now they swarmed as Moses had predicted, and presently there remained not one green sprig on any
tree or field of Egypt. Once more Pharaoh made ready to surrender. Once more he appealed to Moses to take the locusts
away. There came a change in the wind, and the locusts vanished. Whereupon Pharaoh concluded that it was only the
wind which was wrong in the first place. Locusts had to be
expected once in so often, especially in a locust year.

Then there came a sand storm with its thick curtain of
stinging darkness. But Pharaoh, though he wavered, was once
more not only sullen but dangerous. "Get you away from me,"
he cried to Moses, "take heed to yourself, and see my face no
more; for on the day that you shall see my face again, you shall
die." Whereupon Moses answered, "I will see your face no
more."

Then came the last plague. It is recounted in the book of
Exodus with the proud elaboration of a long and fierce tradition. This was the way in which the children of Israel liked
to believe that their fathers had been delivered. In after-years
of defeat and disaster, they looked back to what they thought of
as their time of triumph. In many a dramatic telling and retelling, they drew their own picture, not only of Moses, but of God
himself, whom they regarded as belonging to themselves. "Are
we not the chosen people?" they asked themselves. And in the
crisis of the chosen people, was not whatever happened justified?

So the last plague, as it related to the Egyptians, should be merciless. Moses said to Pharaoh: "Thus saith the Lord, 'About midnight will I go out into the midst of Egypt; and all the first-born in the land of Egypt shall die, from the firstborn of Pharaoh that sits upon his throne, even to the firstborn of the maidservant that is behind the mill; and all the firstborn of beasts. And there shall be a great cry throughout all the land of Egypt, such as there has been none like it before, nor shall there be one like it any more. But not so much as a dog shall wag his tongue against any of the children of Israel, in order that you may know that the Lord puts a difference between the Egyptians and Israel.' " With that, he turned his back on Pharaoh and went out in great anger.

If we ask to what period in the calendar of history all this belongs, it is not possible to answer surely. It was not earlier than the year 1400 B. C. It may have been a century or more later than that. According to the book of Exodus, the final determination of Moses to lead the people of Israel out of Egypt came in the month Nisan, the first month in the Jewish year; and in this month Nisan there is celebrated now, and has been celebrated through many centuries, the feast of the Passover. Thus it was that the Jews believed the Passover to have begun: God spoke to Moses and told him to tell the people that on the tenth day of the month every man should take an unblemished lamb, and keep it until the fourteenth day of the month, and then all the people should sacrifice the lamb in the evening. They were to take its blood and strike it on the two side posts and the upper door post of each man's house. Then secretly and hurriedly each family should eat its lamb. They should have their sandals on, their staffs in their hands, and they were to be girded for a journey. "For the angel of God will pass through Egypt this night," said Moses, "and he will take the life of the first-born in every family of the Egyptians; but when the angel sees the sign of blood upon any house, he shall pass that house by."

So it happened. The plague fell upon Egypt, and in every family there was death and mourning. But the Israelites rose up to follow Moses. They took whatever they could beg or borrow from their Egyptian neighbors, and out from Egypt toward the north they began to move.

They went toward the Red Sea and the Straits of Suez, while the Egyptians were in confusion behind them. But it did not take the embittered Pharaoh long to determine what he would do. He had his own chariot made ready and six hundred chariots of his army, and out of Egypt toward the north their wheels began to roll. There were squadrons of horsemen also, and the thunder of their hoofs and the sound of the rolling chariots were borne across the wilderness to the Israelites as they were halted before the arm of the sea. Then the frightened people began to blame Moses. "Is it because there were no graves in Egypt that you have taken us away to die in the wilderness?" they cried. "Why did you deal with us thus to bring us out of Egypt? We told you to let us alone and let us go on serving the Egyptians, for it was better to serve the Egyptians than to die in the wilderness."

But Moses answered: "Fear not, stand still, and see the salvation of the Lord, which he will show you to-day: for the Egyptians whom you have seen to-day, you shall see them no more forever. The Lord shall fight for you, and you shall hold your peace." Moreover, the voice of God came to Moses saying: "Why do you cry unto me? Speak to the children of Israel that they go forward." Moses should lift up his rod and stretch it out over the arm of the sea, and the people of Israel should go through the midst of the sea.

All that night a strong east wind was blowing. It blew and blew, and so strongly that the shallow waters were driven before it, and there was a road across the straits. Along that way the Israelites went, and after them came the Egyptians. But in the wet sands the heavy chariot wheels cut deep ruts, so that the horses could not drag them, and the whole army of Pharaoh floundered in confusion. The wind went down, and back the waters flowed, and the Israelites, looking back from the farther shore, watched the Egyptians drowning in the sea.

With that grim picture the story of the deliverance from Egypt comes to its climax, except that there follows in the book of Exodus what is probably a much older writing than the prose account. It is one of the ancient songs, which celebrates the tradition of the triumph. Its religion, colored by its tribal passion, is the product of a far-off time. Old ferocities surge through it, but it represents the way men thought and felt, and the throbbing rhythm of their drums is in it still. It is called the song of Moses:

"Then sang Moses and the children of Israel this song unto the Lord,

"I will sing unto the Lord, for he hath triumphed gloriously;
the horse and his rider hath he thrown into the sea.

"The Lord is my strength and my song, and he is become my salvation;
he is my God, and I will prepare him an habitation;
my father's God, and I will exalt him.

"The Lord is a man of war: the Lord is his name.

"Pharaoh's chariots and his host hath he cast into the sea:
his chosen captains also are drowned in the Red Sea.

"The depths have covered them:
they sank into the bottom as a stone.

"Thy right hand, O Lord, is become glorious in power:
thy right hand, O Lord, hath dashed in pieces the enemy.

"And in the greatness of thy excellency thou hast overthrown them that rose up against thee:
thou sentest forth thy wrath, which consumed them as stubble.

"And with the blast of thy nostrils the waters were gathered together,
the floods stood upright as an heap,
and the depths were congealed in the heart of the sea.

"The enemy said, I will pursue, I will overtake, I will divide
 the spoil;
    my lust shall be satisfied upon them; I will draw my sword,
    my hand shall destroy them.

"Thou didst blow with thy wind, the sea covered them:
    they sank as lead in the mighty waters.

"Who is like thee, O Lord, among the Gods? who is like thee?
    glorious in holiness, fearful in praises, doing wonders. . . .

"The Lord shall reign forever and ever.

"For the horse of Pharaoh went in with his chariots and with
 his horsemen into the sea,
    and the Lord brought again the waters of the sea upon them;
    but the children of Israel went on dry land in the midst of
    the sea."

CHAPTER IX

THE PEOPLE OF ISRAEL, HAVING ESCAPED FROM EGYPT AND CROSSED
THE RED SEA, SET OUT TOWARD CANAAN THROUGH THE WILDERNESS;
AND AT SINAI MOSES RECEIVES THE TEN COMMANDMENTS.

THUS THE people of Israel were delivered from their slavery in Egypt. But they still had a long way to go to reach the promised land. The next part of the story tells of their journeyings.

When they had crossed the arm of the Red Sea and had escaped the pursuing chariots of the Egyptians, they had had their hour of fierce exultancy. But soon their mood changed. For generations they and their fathers had been living in a civilized land. They had roofs over their heads. They could draw water from the great stream of the Nile, or from numberless wells in the level plains near the river. There was food to be had from the near-by storehouses. Now, instead, they were out in the empty spaces where there was little to eat, and sometimes even less to drink. In the daytime the blistering sun poured down upon the sandy desert and was reflected again in its wide and shadowless glare; and when the sun dropped down at evening, a sudden cold came with the night. As city dwellers, they felt helpless in this wilderness. They did not know how to shift for themselves, or what to do. They began to think that even slavery in Egypt was better than this.

But Moses was not daunted. He knew this desolate peninsula which had to be crossed before the desired land of Canaan could be reached. He set the march in motion, and, in spite of their complainings, the people followed him.

From Egypt, Canaan lay to the northeast; but it was not possible to take a straight route in that direction. Instead, the way which Moses chose led at first southeasterly along the shore of the Gulf of Suez, and then toward the great mountains which tower in the east. The story of the journey in the form in which it is preserved in the book of Exodus comes from a later time. It seems most probable that it was finally compiled in the ninth century B. C. The historians who did their work in that period doubtless added their colors to the stories which had come down to them. Religious fervor and patriotic pride made them see this migration of their ancestors in magnified dramatic grandeur. Just as later painters of great battles or other high exploits of history fill their canvases with gorgeous color, so these writers of the Hebrew chronicles wove the purple of their interpretation into the threads of the old accounts which from generation to generation had been handed down. They saw the figure of Moses looming greater and greater against the mists of time. They tell of acts of his which may have had originally some simple explanation in his knowledge of the region and in his own sagacity, but which they describe in amazing fashion as though they were immediate miracles of God. And especially they exalt Moses as the supreme lawgiver of Israel, and attribute to him and to his voice as a spokesman direct from God the whole body of the moral and ceremonial law which doubtless came gradually into being. Nevertheless, the record conveys its clear message of the central reality of this great leader, Moses. And it does more. It outlines the journey of the Israelites and the background of its hardships and dangers as these must essentially have been. Travelers in the Sinaitic peninsula may still recognize marks of the route which the book of Exodus describes.

So let us take up again the thread of the story as the Bible gives it.

After the crossing of the Red Sea, the Israelites went for three days along the bordering desert. It is a long expanse of flat sand and gravel, lying between the arm of the sea to the west and the grim mountains farther inland to the east, where the sun beats down with blistering heat throughout the day, and there are no trees or anything else to cast a shadow. For the three days of marching the Israelites found no water, and at the end of the three days, when they came to a pool in the sands, they found that the water was so strong and so disgusting to the taste that they could not drink it. They named the place Marah, which means "bitterness," and they demanded of Moses, "What shall we drink?" Then Moses, after he had lifted up a prayer for guidance from God, found a certain kind of shrub which, when he had put it into the water, made the water sweet enough for the people to drink. After that he led the people to Elim, where there were twelve springs and a circle of palm trees, and at that oasis, a slender refuge in the midst of the terrible desert, but seeming, doubtless, at that moment to the Israelites like a gift from heaven, they encamped.

But they could not stay there, for they had nothing to eat; so they moved on farther. By this time they were growing sullen again. They talked together against Moses and Aaron, and they said: "Would to God we had died by the hand of the Lord in the land of Egypt, when we sat by the flesh pots, and when we did eat bread to the full; for ye have brought us forth into this wilderness, to kill this whole assembly with hunger."

When they had finished complaining so bitterly of hunger, Moses told them that he had a message from God, and that the Lord said, "Behold, I will rain bread from heaven for you." Then Moses spoke to Aaron and told him to say to the congregation of the children of Israel, "Come near before the Lord: for he has heard your murmurings." So while Aaron was speaking, the people looked toward the wilderness, and there was a cloud in the sky. It was a cloud of quails blowing in from the Mediterranean islands upon the coast, and when they fluttered to earth, the people caught as many of them as they chose. Moreover, the next morning there lay upon the face of the wilderness a small round thing like hoarfrost, which the people had never seen before. But Moses said, "This is the bread which the Lord has given you to eat." They called it manna, and in that region people still gather what they call manna, a gum that falls from the tamarisk bushes and must be picked up before the sun rises, for after that it melts and disappears.

From the place where they were fed with the quails and

where they first found the manna, the Israelites moved farther down along the sea, and then in toward the mountains. Again they began to be tormented with thirst, and again they shouted furiously at Moses: "Give us water. Why have you brought us all up out of Egypt to kill us and our cattle with thirst?" But Moses again was equal to the emergency. From his previous sojourn in this region he knew, as the Arabs know to-day, how to discover water in forbidding and unlikely places. He led the people to a rocky cliff in Horeb, and there his rod found water and the people drank. Moreover, they were coming to one more garden spot before they struck deeper into the mountains. They arrived at the oasis of Feiran, which is called "the Pearl of Sinai," and is the fairest spot in all that otherwise grim peninsula, with row after row of palm trees growing green and luxuriant above the springs which bubble so abundantly from the ground that the water murmurs as it flows.

There the people of Israel might have been tempted to stay and pitch their camp indefinitely, but it was a dangerous place in which to tarry. An oasis was the one spot most sought after, and therefore most fought for by all the restless desert tribes. The Israelites had not been there long when a band of Amalekites fell upon them. Moses stood on the top of a hill, and held in his hand the rod which the people had begun to believe had in it divine power. He had commanded a young leader named Joshua to select the best fighting men from among the people, and Joshua led his followers against the Amalekites. As long as Moses held up his hands, Joshua and his men drove the Amalekites before them; but whenever Moses' hands fell, their spirits fell too, and the Amalekites beat them back. So Aaron and a man named Hur stood by Moses, and they held up his hands, one on one side, and one on the other, and kept them steady until the going down of the sun. Thus by the inspiration of Moses and by the sword of Joshua the Amalekites were routed.

But they were not to stay at the oasis. It was perilous to risk the continuous attacks of all the restless tribesmen of the desert, and besides their ultimate objective lay farther on. So they began to climb toward the gorges and ravines which open into the mountains. In Egypt they had lived in a flat country. When they had first come over the arm of the Red Sea, they had marched along the flat and arid desert which borders the shore. But the desert of Sinai is not all flatness, like the desert of Sahara. On the contrary, some fifteen miles in from the coast, and clearly visible from the sea, great granite mountains rise gigantically. To heights of eight or nine thousand feet they tower, and into them the narrow, rocky passes lead. It was there that Moses wanted to lead the people, there where he himself had hidden when he fled first as a fugitive from Egypt and where he had seen his vision of the burning bush, and where he had received in his soul that commission from God which sent him back to confront Pharaoh and to bring the oppressed people out of Egypt.

Somewhere in a valley among the mountains the Israelites came to a halt. Round them towered the sheer and precipitous crags, barren of vegetation but clothed with a kind of stern beauty in the many-colored strata of their rock. It was an awesome region, particularly to men whose eyes had never looked on heights like these before.

In the camp there at Sinai Moses began to give the people the ordinances which were to govern their daily life and conduct. It was necessary that a migrating multitude like this should be governed with care and wisdom if they were to survive at all. In the book of Exodus, therefore, there are long chapters containing the regulations which Moses is said to have laid down for the people. These set up the elemental laws of justice between man and man. They describe the punishments for crimes of dishonesty and violence. They lay down laws of what in our modern terminology would be called sanitation. They give too the elaborate description of the religious worship which the people were to practice under the leadership of Aaron as their priest.

Undoubtedly many of the laws which are ascribed to Moses belong to a later time. Here in one long record is gathered the accumulated legislation, civil and religious, which grew out of the experience of succeeding generations. But as the beginning of it was associated with Moses, so the whole development was validated by his name. The historians of later centuries looked back through the traditions which they had inherited to Moses as the first and great lawgiver, and all the law of Israel was considered as the Mosaic code.

In this whole body of law, the part which seemed to the Jewish nation to be most important was that part which had to do directly with men's relationship to God. This was the interest which in that great race was always dominant, and it was this interest which has made their contribution to human history unique. In the religion of Egypt there were aspects not much different from idolatry. The Egyptians worshiped many gods, and some of them they worshiped in the form of birds and animals—the hawk, the ibis, the crocodile, the bull. But somewhere in their history the people of Israel attained the conception that for them there was one God only, a God whom no earthly form could represent, and a God whose will was righteousness. For them, above all the peoples of the earth, religion became a matter, not mainly of ceremonial, but of character and of conduct. God was to be worshiped by a life of moral obedience attuned to the holy will of the Most High.

This religion and the morality which flowed from it deepened and widened with the years; but it was through the mediatorship of the great spirit of Moses that the people of Israel believed that the best of it began. It was Moses to whom God spoke. It was through Moses that the Commandments were given, those Ten Commandments which were accounted as not of human but of divine authority.

Of course it is not possible to separate the misty veils of far-off legend, or to see straight through the prismatic colors of this story of the sunrise of a religion, and to know exactly what happened there at Sinai. What we must do as well as we can is to trace the human figure moving through the picture where the immense shadows of tradition also move. It seems that Moses left the people in one of the valleys between the mountains while he climbed up alone into the heights. There he meditated in that solitary communion in which, as in all ages, a great soul makes its contact with the infinite. Then suddenly he *saw*—saw, as with the light of God's own certainty—the moral imperatives which must govern the people's life. These he must carry back to them as God's commandments. These he must chisel on tables of stone in order that their eternal authority should be expressed.

There are two records in the book of Exodus of what the Commandments were which thus were chiseled upon the tables of stone, but there is no doubt as to which of these the people of Israel in after years accepted as having been the Ten Commandments and attributed to the mediation of Moses there in Sinai. Thus they ran:

"I am the Lord thy God; Thou shalt have none other gods but me.

"Thou shalt not make to thyself any graven image, nor the likeness of any thing that is in heaven above, or in the earth beneath, or in the water under the earth; thou shalt not bow down to them, nor worship them.

"Thou shalt not take the name of the Lord thy God in vain.

"Remember that thou keep holy the Sabbath-day.

"Honor thy father and thy mother.

"Thou shalt do no murder.

"Thou shalt not commit adultery.

"Thou shalt not steal.

"Thou shalt not bear false witness against thy neighbor.

"Thou shalt not covet."

Meanwhile as Moses was alone in the mountain, there came the sound of a gathering storm. A storm in the rocky grandeur of those Sinaitic mountains is an awesome and tremendous thing. Through the granite gorges the wind comes roaring. Round the jagged summits of the great cliffs terrific lightning blazes, and the warmer air rising from the valley swirls into a mist that volleys upward round the mountain like smoke from a volcano. Such was the storm that broke when Moses was on the heights. The people shrank back from the foot of the mountain, terrified. They thought that God must dwell on the top of the mountain, that this was why Moses had gone there. The thunder and the lightning were the awful signs that God

had come. When Moses descended they would be ready to bow
down before him in submissive reverence.

But the hours went by, and a long time went by, and Moses
did not come. Then the minds of the people began to turn
backward. They were afraid to follow Moses up into the mountain, and they were afraid of what might have happened to him
there. This terrible God of the heights dismayed them. They
began to think of the more familiar gods of Egypt. They wanted
the sign of a god who would be near at hand. So they suggested
to Aaron that he make them an image like the image of one of
the sacred bulls. They brought him all the bits of jewelry
and scraps of metal they had, and Aaron melted these as best he
could into an image that looked like a calf. When they saw
it, they said, "These be thy gods, O Israel, which brought thee
up out of the land of Egypt;" and they ate and drank, and
danced about the golden calf.

But now it was time for Moses to come down from the
mountain. There his soul had received the Commandments,
and there also he had received a promise: "Thus shalt thou say
to the house of Jacob, and tell the children of Israel: Ye have
seen what I did unto the Egyptians, and how I bare you on
eagles' wings, and brought you unto myself. Now therefore, if
you will obey my voice indeed, and keep my covenant, then you
shall be a peculiar treasure unto me above all people: for all the
earth is mine: and ye shall be unto me a kingdom of priests,
and a holy nation." As he came down from the mountain his
face was shining.

Joshua was with him now. Either he had met him as he
was coming down or he had been with him before. The two of
them drew nearer to the valley where the camp of Israel was.
They could begin to hear the sounds which came up from it.
There was a great shouting. Joshua the warrior was instantly
alert. "There is a noise of war in the camp," he said. But
Moses thought not. He said it did not sound to him like that
kind of shouting. It sounded to him like singing. When they
drew near, they saw that Moses was right. The people were
singing and dancing around the golden calf.

Moses was a man who could be very patient and long-suffering, but there were times when he could blaze with a righteous anger which was terrific. This was such a time. He flung down the tables of stone which he had in his hands, and broke them to pieces on the ground, then swept into the camp and took the image of the calf, flung it into the fire, ground it to pieces, threw the dust of it into the spring of water in the valley, and made the people of Israel drink it.

"What did this people do to you, that you have brought so great a sin upon them?" he demanded of Aaron, and Aaron made his frightened and shuffling answer. "You know the people," he said, "that they are set on mischief. They said to me, 'Make us gods which shall go before us: for as for this Moses, the man that brought us up out of the land of Egypt, we do not know what has become of him.' And I replied to them, 'Whoever has any gold, let them break it off.' So they gave it to me: then I cast it into the fire, and there came out this calf."

But Moses did not listen to Aaron. According to one account, which may reflect the tradition cherished by the later priestly writers, who wanted to make idolatry and the punishment for it seem as terrible as they could, Moses sent certain men of the tribe of Levi through the camp to put the ringleaders of this profanation to the sword. But another account says that Moses went away himself to try to make atonement before God for the people's sins, and he cried, "O Lord, this people hath sinned a great sin, and now, if thou wilt forgive their sin—; and if not, blot me, I pray thee, out of thy book which thou hast written." After that he went again into the mountain, and came back a second time with the Commandments engraven anew upon two tables of stone, and with this message in his heart, that the same God who "will by no means clear the guilty," nevertheless is "merciful and gracious, long-suffering, and abundant in goodness and truth."

CHAPTER X

BUT THE time came when Israel could linger no more in the valley among the mountains. They could not find there any subsistence which would last long. They wanted a land of their own where they could settle, "the promised land," which was yet a great distance to the north. So they broke their camp in Sinai and started again on their march.

In those days everybody believed that a god had a particular habitation. This God of Sinai whom they would take now as their Deity, dwelt, they thought, among the clouds upon the mountain. How, then, should their God go with them when they had left the region where he dwelt? They answered that by making an ark, a shrine of wood cut from trees that grew about the mountain; and in this shrine, which was carried on the shoulders of four men, they believed that the presence of God would go. They were still on the borderland between a new religion of the spirit and the old, crude ideas which all primitive people shared.

Later priestly writers cultivated the tradition that there must have been an ordered worship even in the wilderness; and in the book of Exodus is their description of the tabernacle which afterward existed, and which they assumed to have been established in their distant forefathers' time. It was partly like a building and partly like a tent. For its central shrine it had walls made of wooden panels and a roof made of badger skins and sheep skins, and the large outer court was enclosed by

109

curtains. In the central shrine, which was called the "Holy of Holies," the ark rested, and in the forecourt of it there was an altar where the incense was burned, and a seven-branch candlestick which was always lighted, and a table where there were offerings of sacred bread. On an altar in the outer court sacrifices of sheep and goats and bullocks, according to the immemorial tradition of many ancient peoples, were offered up and burned in the sacrificial fire. When the Israelites struck their camp, they took down the tabernacle and folded up its curtains; and men of the tribe of Levi, who were set apart for this particular responsibility, carried the various parts of the tabernacle and its furnishings in the march and set them up again when they came to a halt. In the books of Exodus and Leviticus and Numbers the tabernacle is described as though it were a gorgeous thing, with its panels overlaid with gold and its curtains made of beautiful linen and other richly woven stuff. It is difficult to imagine how the people of Israel could have got any such amount of gold and other beautiful things in the wilderness, or that they could have brought these out of Egypt. Probably the picture of the tabernacle has been gilded by the long light of tradition, and the original tabernacle may have been the very simple creation which was the best that could have been expected from people beset by the hardships of a desert march. However that may be, the tabernacle has become a symbol of worship from that time to this, and it was the forerunner of the magnificent temples which afterward were to arise when Israel had attained its promised land.

But the way to the promised land was long and arduous, and often to the Israelites it seemed endless as well. They had scant patience and short tempers. Moses liked to think of them as the people of God, but there were times when he must have wondered whether they were not possessed of Satan. They complained and they grumbled. They said they were sick of eating manna all the time. They were sick of going thirsty on long journeys when there was not even so much as a water hole in the desert. They kept thinking of Egypt, and wishing they were back there. When they *were* there, they had wanted desperately to come out, and they had groaned under their slavery; but they forgot that now, and what they remembered was what they used to have to eat. "We remember the fish," they said, "the cucumbers and the melons." In Egypt there was the Nile with fish for anybody's taking, and there were fresh vegetables and fruits. Here there was nothing but sand and blistering sun and emptiness. Once or twice they nearly rebelled. Some of them did actually try rebellion. One day a man named Korah, and a group of men who gathered round him, sent back a sullen answer of defiance to Moses when they were bidden to assemble with the rest of the people for the morning worship. "You take too much upon yourself," they said to Moses and to Aaron. "Why do you lift yourselves up above the rest of the congregation?" And two other leaders of discontent named Dathan and Abiram joined themselves to Korah. "Is it a small thing," they said to Moses, "that you have brought us up out of a land that flows with milk and honey to kill us in the wilderness, and then must you go and make yourself a prince over us? This is no land which flows with milk and honey which you have brought us into, and where is any inheritance of fruits and vineyards here?" But this rebellion was suppressed (according to the book of Numbers) by an earthquake in which Korah and Dathan and Abiram were swallowed up.

This, however, was not the end of Moses' trials. His own sister Miriam and his brother Aaron began to be disaffected. They were jealous of Moses' authority. "Has the Lord indeed spoken only by Moses?" they said. "Has he not spoken also by us?" They put their heads together in what looked like a conspiracy against their brother. But this also failed. Aaron, looking at Miriam, was horrified to see what appeared to be the signs of leprosy upon her. He interpreted it immediately as the judgment of God, and he begged Moses to forgive them both and to intercede for Miriam, that it might not be the leprosy which was upon her. Moses did forgive them, and in parenthesis the story puts these surprising words, "Now, the man Moses was very meek, above all the men who were upon the face of the earth." Moses meek? Pharaoh would not have thought so

People in the camp at the foot of Mount Sinai would not have thought so on that day when Moses came back from the mountains and found them dancing about the golden calf, and in terrible anger ground the image to powder and threw the dust into the water which he made the people drink. Korah, Dathan, and Abiram would not have thought so. But it was true nevertheless. Moses could be awful in his wrath when the purpose of God was at stake, but he could be infinitely patient and self-effacing in matters which concerned only himself. He was not overbearing nor aggressive. He could suffer long and still be kind.

It was true that sometimes his fortitude was taxed almost to the breaking point, but when that happened he did not complain before the face of the people. He went apart and poured out his soul before God. When night came and he heard all the people lamenting around the doors of their tents, he cried to God, "Why hast thou afflicted thy servant, and why have I not found favor in thy sight, that thou hast laid the burden of all thy people upon me? Have I conceived all this people? Have I begotten them, that thou shouldest say unto me, Carry them in thy bosom as a nursing father carries a child? I am not able to carry all these people alone. It is too heavy for me." But strength came to him to carry the heavy burden of his responsibility, nevertheless.

So from Sinai northward in the direction of the land of Canaan, with Moses encouraging them, disciplining them when it was necessary and holding them firm, the people of Israel moved slowly. They were drawing near enough now to the borders of the country in which they wanted to establish themselves for Moses to make preparations for attack upon the desert tribes and the hill tribes which would certainly resist them. He wanted to know exactly what the land ahead was like, and what sort of people were inhabiting it. So he selected twelve scouts, one of whom was Joshua and one of whom was a young man named Caleb, and these men he sent on secretly in advance. "Go see the land," he told them, "and the people who dwell there, and note whether they are strong or weak, few or many.

Is the land good or bad, fat or lean, and is it wooded or not? What sort of places do the people dwell in—in tents or in strongholds? Be of good courage; and bring back with you some of the fruits of the land."

On ahead, therefore, the scouts went to spy out the region along which the people generally would have to advance. From the midst of the peninsula of Sinai, from which they started, it was some hundred miles or more to the southern shores of the Dead Sea. Past that they went over the heights of Moab and up along the valley of the Jordan. Then they came south again and into the country to the east of the river where Abraham had gone with his flocks long before; and then they came back and made their report to Moses. These reports, however, did not agree. There was a majority of ten and a minority of two. The whole twelve of them agreed that the land they had seen was good land. In comparison with the desert it seemed like a paradise, for there were fields of grain in it and olive trees, vineyards, and springs of water in the hills. They brought back a great cluster of grapes which they had taken from a valley which they called Eshcol, and they brought also pomegranates and figs. They used the picturesque phrase which is always used as an expression of great fertility, and said that the land "flowed with milk and honey." But at this point their agreement stopped. The ten said that the people living up that way were so formidable that there was no use hoping to drive them out. They said that they lived in walled cities, very great cities. Moreover, they said the people themselves looked like giants. Caleb and Joshua, on the other hand, said that this was all nonsense. There was nothing extraordinary about the people. It did not matter if there were a few walled cities. These, and the people in them, were nothing to be afraid of. "They are bread for us," said Caleb and Joshua. "The Lord is with us, and we do not need to fear them."

If the people had been as strong-hearted as Caleb and Joshua and had been able to believe what Joshua and Caleb said, they might have gone forward then and there and opened their way into the land of Canaan. But instead they believed the majority, and they turned on Caleb and Joshua with a fury which men show sometimes to the great leaders who bid them do something they do not want to dare. They tried, unsuccessfully, to stone Caleb and Joshua; and, except for small groups who went ahead alone and were promptly cut to pieces by the hostile tribes they encountered, the great body of the Israelites came to a stubborn halt.

"Would God that we had died in the land of Egypt," they said, "or would God we had died in this wilderness! Why has God brought us into this land, to fall by the sword, and to see our wives and children become a prey? It is better to return into Egypt!" So they told one another, and they said, "Let us choose a captain and return to Egypt." But they had no leader, so all the angry muttering came to nothing.

According to the book of Numbers, there fell then upon the people the judgment of God, pronounced through the voice of Moses, that, because of their refusal to follow the lead of Caleb and Joshua, they should wander in the wilderness for forty years; and for forty years they did so wander before the time came when at last they entered into Canaan. But forty years is a round number which the old chroniclers repeatedly used; and the wandering is not likely to have been for any such extended period as that. Nevertheless, it appears that the Israelites were stopped in their advance for a period long enough to make a great change among them. Some of the older generation who never could get quite free from the slave-mind of Egypt were dropping off, and a younger and hardier generation was arising. When presently they appeared at the borders of Canaan, they were a more formidable force than the one which had crossed the Red Sea. They moved northward at length toward the borders of Edom, the country which lies to the south of the Dead Sea. They asked for peaceful passage through the land of the Edomites; it was refused. But they circled round Edom and came out upon the tableland of Moab, that great plateau of towering red rock which is the bulwark between the wide desert to the east, and, on the west, the deep gorge of the Dead Sea. Somewhere about the middle of this plateau, where

the brook Arnon flows through it, they came into collision with
the Bedouin warriors of the Amorites under their chief Sihon.
The Israelites had sent a message to Sihon, saying: "Let us pass
through your land. We will not turn into the fields, nor into
the vineyards. We will not drink from your wells. But we
will go along the highroads until we have passed your borders
again." But Sihon would not let them go peaceably through;
and, instead, he led his warriors to the attack; but the Israelites
defeated him, and captured the Amorite towns. And this was
their taunting song of victory:

> "Come to Heshbon and rebuild it!
> Repair the capital of Sihon, if you can!
> For the blaze began at Heshbon,
> at the capital of Sihon,
> till Ar of Moab was consumed,
> and Arnon's heights devoured.
> Poor Moabites!
> O forlorn folk of Kemosh!
> The god has left his sons to flight,
> his daughters to a prisoner's plight,
> their children have perished
> from Heshbon to Dibon;
> and we ravaged till war's fire
> was blown to Medeba."[1]

Another tribal chieftain, Og, king of Bashan, was encountered,
and the Israelites "smote him, and his sons, and all his people,
until there was none left him remaining, and they possessed
his land."

The Israelites were growing confident now of their power,
and in the book of Numbers there has come down a curious
story. The beginnings of the story, perhaps, were told around
the camp fires, as the Israelites were moving into Moab; but
the story was enlarged in a later time, when men had come to
have such a great idea of the glory of the nation that they could

---

[1] Moffatt translation of Numbers 21. 27-30.

solemnly tell of how even a dumb beast could break into speech because of it.

This is the story of Balak, king of Moab, and of the enchanter, Balaam.

Balak had heard of the defeat of Sihon and the defeat of Og, and he was afraid of the oncoming of the Israelites. He called together his chief men, and he said, "These people will lick up everything around us, as an ox licks up the grass of the field." And then, in his desire for help, he remembered that, off in the region of the Euphrates, there lived a man who was supposed to have unearthly power to work charms. Balaam, the son of Beor, was his name, and to him Balak sent this message: "There is a people come up out of Egypt, and they have spread over the face of the earth, and now they are confronting me. Come, I pray you, and curse this people, for they are too strong for me. If you curse them, perhaps I shall be able to strike them, and drive them out of the land; for I know that any one whom you bless is blessed, and any one whom you curse is cursed."

So an embassy of the chief men from Moab and from Midian set out with payment in their hands, and they came to Balaam and told him the words of Balak.

Balaam told them to lodge there with him for the night, and he would bring them back word as to what instructions he got when he had said his prayers. In the morning he came to them, and he said that they had as well go back to their own land, for he had received a revelation not to curse the people of Israel, and that he could not go with them.

Back, then, the embassy went to Balak and told him that Balaam refused to come. Then Balak sent out another group, more numerous and more honorable than the first; and when they came to Balaam, they told him that Balak had said: "I pray you, let nothing hinder you from coming now, for I will promote you to very great honor, and I will do whatever you ask. Come, then, and curse this people for me."

But Balaam said: "If Balak will give me his house full of silver and gold, I cannot go beyond the word of my God, to do less or more. But stay here this night also, so that I may see."

This time Balaam came back and said that he had permission to go. So he rose up in the morning and saddled his ass, and went with the men of Moab. He was trying now to win the reward which Balak had offered, if by any means he could put a curse upon the people of Israel; but among the Israelites, this was the story of what happened to Balaam then:

An angel of the Lord came and stood in his way to block it, as Balaam, mounted on his ass and with two servants accompanying him, was riding on toward Moab. The ass saw the angel standing in the way with a drawn sword in his hand. Out of the road, then, the ass wheeled, and went off into a field; but Balaam violently beat the ass, and tried to turn her back into the road.

Then the angel went and stood in a path that led between vineyards, with a wall on either side; and when the ass saw the angel this second time, she plunged against the wall and crushed Balaam's foot against it, while he beat her again.

On beyond the angel moved again, and stood this time in a narrow place, where there was no room to pass either on the right hand or on the left; and when the ass saw the angel there, she fell down under Balaam, and Balaam, greatly angered, beat her with a stick. Whereupon the ass began to speak. "What have I done to you," she said, "that you have beaten me these three times?"

Balaam answered: "Because you have mocked me. I wish I had a sword in my hand; for if I had one, I would kill you!"

"Am I not your ass," said she, "upon which you have ridden ever since I belonged to you until now? Have I ever done this way before?"

No, the ass had not done that way before, Balaam admitted; and with that, suddenly his eyes were opened, and he too saw the angel standing in the way with the drawn sword in his hand; and Balaam bowed his head, and fell flat upon his face.

Then the angel rebuked Balaam, and Balaam, frightened, said: "I have sinned, for I did not know that you were standing in the way against me. I will go back home again."

But the angel permitted Balaam to go forward, charging

him, however, to speak no other word than such words as he should be inspired to speak.

On, then, Balaam went until he met Balak, and Balak said: "Did I not send an earnest message to call you here? Why did you not come? Have I not the power to promote you to honor?" But Balaam answered: "See, I have come to you. But what power have I to say anything? The word that God puts into my mouth, that must I speak."

So to the heights of Moab Balak led Balaam, and three times they offered sacrifices, and then Balak waited for Balaam to pronounce a curse on Israel. But three times, so the tradition of Israel said, Balaam, instead of cursing Israel, blessed them, and into the mouth of Balaam, as a prophecy, the book of Numbers puts this splendid chant of Israel's greatness which they wanted to believe.

"Surely there is no enchantment against Jacob
   neither is there any divination against Israel:
According to this time it shall be said of Jacob and of Israel,
'What hath God wrought!
Behold, the people shall rise up as a great lion,
   and lift up himself as a young lion:
He shall not lie down until he eat of the prey,
   and drink the blood of the slain.' "

And to the impatient and angry Balak, desiring a curse on Israel, and not a blessing, Balaam said:

"How shall I curse, whom God hath not cursed?
   or how shall I defy, whom the Lord hath not defied?

"For from the top of the rocks I see him,
   and from the hills I behold him:
Lo, the people shall dwell alone,
   and shall not be reckoned among the nations.
Who can count the dust of Jacob,
   and the number of the fourth part of Israel?
Let me die the death of the righteous,
   and let my last end be like his!"

Finally, Balak beat his hands together in anger, and said to Balaam: "I called you here to curse my enemies, and look, you have blessed them these three times. Go back now, while you safely can, to where you belong! It was in my heart to promote you to great honor; but it seems the Lord has kept you back from honor."

But Balaam, in a climax of the story now which completely satisfied the ideas of Israel, reminds Balak that he had said he could not go beyond the commandment of the Lord, even if Balak should give him a house full of silver and gold; and then he launches into this prophecy:

"There shall come a Star out of Jacob, and a Scepter shall rise
    out of Israel,
  and shall smite the corners of Moab, and destroy all the
    children of Sheth.
And Edom shall be a possession, Seir also shall be a possession
    for his enemies;
  and Israel shall do valiantly.
Out of Jacob shall come he that shall have dominion,
  and shall destroy him that remaineth of the city."

After that, it was no wonder that Balak had no more use for Balaam, and the king turned his back on this enchanter whose spells had been reversed, and he went one way while Balaam went another.

After the story of Balaam, there comes in the book of Numbers the account of various plagues and other sufferings which came upon the people of Israel because they worshiped the gods of the heathen peoples round about, and here again, as usual, it was Moses who turned them to a better way.

Meanwhile both Miriam and Aaron had died; and at length the end drew near for Moses also. He was not to enter into the promised land, but he was to see it. From the valley of the Dead Sea, the huge cliffs of Moab rise in a towering wall, from the summit of which, across the valley, nearly the whole length of Palestine lies revealed. Moses went up alone to the top of

Mount Nebo, four thousand feet above the waters of the Dead Sea, glimmering in its vat below. There on the mountain's crest he stood, a grand old figure, whose "eye was not dim, nor his natural force abated." Across the Jordan he could see the walled city of Jericho, situated alongside its beautiful gushing fountains, fed by the hidden streams that flow from the hills behind it, surrounded with its date-palms and all the greenness of its oasis, which seemed the more fair to eyes which so long had been accustomed to the desert. Beyond Jericho the steep ascents climbed up toward Jerusalem, and farther to the north were the hills and fertile valleys round Samaria. All this he could see, this "land of promise" which had beckoned to him like destiny from the day when he confronted Pharaoh in Egypt. And there, gazing from the mountains, Moses appears for the last time in the story, outlined against the sky. Then presently he is dead, and his body is buried "in a valley in the land of Moab, over against Beth-peor: but no man knoweth of his sepulcher unto this day."

CHAPTER XI

JOSHUA SUCCEEDS MOSES AS THE LEADER, AND HE CAPTURES JERICHO,
WHERE RAHAB, WHO HAD RECEIVED THE SPIES, IS SPARED; AND WITH
MUCH OTHER FIGHTING JOSHUA TAKES POSSESSION OF THE LAND OF
CANAAN.

BEFORE MOSES died he had chosen Joshua to be his successor. "Be strong and of a good courage," he told him. "You shall bring the children of Israel into the land which the Lord promised them, and he will be with you. He will go before you. He will not fail you, nor forsake you. Fear not. Be not dismayed."

So down from the mountains of Moab Joshua led the Israelites into the valley of the Jordan north of where it flows into the Dead Sea, and opposite Jericho. Some of the tribes, Reuben and Gad and half the tribe of Manasseh, had already taken possession of land which had been conquered on the plateau of Moab. They were content to stay there without crossing the river. Joshua told them that their wives and their children and their cattle could remain in the territory they had conquered, but the fighting men should come with him and with the other tribes in the advance. "You shall pass before your kinsmen under arms, all the mighty men of valor, and help them; until the Lord has given your kinsmen a settlement as he has given you." They said to Joshua that whatever he commanded they would do, and wherever he sent them they would go.

Then Joshua sent forward two men as spies into the vicinity of the walled city of Jericho, which lay beyond the river. Secretly they got into Jericho, and they went to the house of a woman named Rahab, who was a harlot—a house which, because it was not too careful of the company it entertained, would not throw any suspicion upon strangers. They hid there, seeking information about Jericho, its people, and its defenses. But the report was brought nevertheless to the king of Jericho that two men had come into the city that night who might be spies, and he sent to Rahab, demanding that these men be handed over. But she denied that they were there. "When it was dark," she said, "the men went out, and where they went I do not know. Pursue them quickly, and you will overtake them." Meanwhile, she had brought them up to the roof of the house and hid them under some piles of flax which were drying there. The guards whom the king of Jericho had sent went out from the city, shutting the gate after them; and they searched all the ground as far as the fords of the river, but, of course, they found no one.

Then Rahab came up to the two spies whom she had hidden on the roof. "I know," she said, "that the Lord God has given you this country, and how the terror of you has fallen upon us, till all the natives are faint before you. For we have heard how the Lord dried up the waters of the Red Sea before you when you left Egypt, and what you did to the two Amorite kings on the east of the Jordan, Sihon and Og, whom you wiped off the earth. As soon as we heard it, our hearts sank and there was no courage left in any man because of you, for the Lord your God is God in heaven above and on the earth beneath. Now, then, since I have showed you kindness, swear to me by the Lord that you will deal kindly with my family, and give me a sure sign of it; swear that you will spare the lives of my father and my mother and my brothers and my sisters and all they have and save us from death." The men replied, "Our lives for yours—only you must not breathe a word about our errand; then we will deal kindly and truly with you when the Lord gives us the country."

They told her: "We will be free from this oath to you, which you have made us swear, unless, when we enter the country, you tie this cord of scarlet thread outside the window through which you let us down. You must gather your father and mother and brothers and all your family inside your house;

anyone who crosses the door of your house into the street, his blood be on his own head, we are not to blame; but if a hand is laid on anyone inside the house, then his blood be on our head! But, remember, if you breathe a word about our errand, we will not be bound by the oath you have made us swear."

"As you say," answered the woman, "so be it." Then she lowered them by a rope out of the window, for her house was on the town wall. She told them, "Get away to the hills, lest the pursuers find you; hide yourselves there for three days till the pursuers return, and then go on your way."

So away they went, while she tied the scarlet cord to the window. They went into the hills and stayed there for three days, till the pursuers returned, having looked for them all along the road and never finding them. Then the two men came down from the hills and crossed over to Joshua, the son of Nun, telling him all that had befallen them. They said to Joshua: "The Lord has put all the country into our hands. The natives are all shivering before us."

So with the ark ready to be borne by the priests before them, Joshua prepared to go over the Jordan.

The chronicle in the book of Joshua tells of what happened next as though it were a miracle: "when they that bare the ark were come unto the Jordan, and the feet of the priests that bare the ark were dipped in the brink of the water (for the Jordan overfloweth all its banks all the time of harvest), the waters which came down from above stood, and rose up in one heap, a great way off, at Adam, the city that is beside Zarethan; and those that went down toward the sea of the Arabah, even the Salt Sea, were wholly cut off: and the people passed over right against Jericho." But the sonorous old words may mean a simple thing. Above the fords of the Jordan the river runs in a crooked course through cliffs of clay. Now and then one of these cliffs collapses where it has been undercut by the stream, and the river for the time is dammed back until the waters break through in a new channel. It may be that some such thing happened when Joshua's army came to the river. At any rate, the Israelites passed over, and they encamped on the arid plain which lies between the west bank of the Jordan and the oasis of Jericho.

As the men of Jericho looked down from their walls upon these invaders there on the plain, and as other dwellers upon the rim of Moab, or upon the heights toward Jerusalem, saw the glimmer of their camp fires in the darkness, they doubtless thought that this was merely another one of the forays which repeatedly swept in from the untamed spaces of the desert. Outwardly these Israelites did not seem much different from all the other fierce Bedouin folk who now and again launched their assault out of Arabia upon the more fertile lands of Canaan. Nor were the methods of fighting which the Israelites under Joshua adopted different from the familiar tribal warfare of that time. Theirs was to be a campaign of conquest, destructive and ruthless. Religious art and poetry have invested the story of the invasion of Canaan with other colors. It has become the epic of the armies of God, a struggle of light against darkness, the high drama of religion and romance. In the ultimate meaning of what was happening there has been a reason for this interpretation. These Israelitish tribesmen did bring with them the germ of a new religion, a religion which already was conceived as the worship of one God rather than of many, and a God whose will was righteousness. And this religion of theirs was to flower in that mighty development of the spirit which should lead on through kings and prophets to its far fulfilment in the figure of Christ. But in order to understand vividly the story which develops in the books of Joshua and of Judges, it is necessary to remember that the spiritual significance of these invaders camped by the banks of the Jordan was something not yet evident. They were a people sharing the tribal ethics of their times and taking for granted a world where force and violence were familiar, and where men got what they wanted by the sword. Of them it might have been written what T. E. Lawrence wrote of his Arabs in *Revolt in the Desert*. "They could be swung on an idea as on a cord. . . . Their mind was strange and dark, full of depression and exaltation, lacking in rule, but with more of ardor and more fertile in belief than

any other in the world. They were a people of starts, for whom
the abstract was the strongest motive, the process of infinite
courage and variety, and the end nothing. They were as un-
stable as water and like water would perhaps finally prevail."

The book of Joshua and the book of Judges, therefore,
can be read for the sheer interest of their story without having
one's religion fettered by their old forms, as used unhappily
to be the case with readers of the Bible who were very devout,
but "not according to knowledge." One's idea of God and of
the ways of God, and one's estimates of the conduct proper to
full-grown spiritual men are not to be shaped from these old
books. It is a long way from Joshua, son of Nun, to Jesus, son
of Mary. It is a long way from the manner in which the invading Israelites dealt with the people of Canaan to the parable
of the good Samaritan. When we perceive this, and are delivered, therefore, from any imagined necessity of defending
these old books as though they represented a fulfilment of
religion, we can go forward to enjoy them with a free mind.
It is not necessary even to endeavor at every point to separate
the actual elements of history from the purple banners with
which they have been adorned. Here are the sagas of a people's
early history as they were told and retold in song and chronicle,
and only long afterward put into writing. The great events
are represented sometimes in symbol and in poetry. The mud-
brick walls of Jericho collapsing before the furious charge of
the Israelites, become the walls of a city which at the sound of
a trumpet dramatically tumble down. A song of victory adjur-
ing the sun and moon to join in Joshua's triumph, becomes a
statement by the chronicler that in the valley of Ajalon, in
order to prolong the day for Joshua's triumph, the sun and the
moon stood still. It is not necessary in every instance to stop
and analyze the story. The drift of general fact is plain. The
Israelites set out to conquer Canaan by the methods of conquest
which were familiar in that day. They believed that God was
with them, and to the best of their conception they were being
faithful to the knowledge of God they had. And later generations, looking back and listening to the tradition, passed on to

their children the stories which still preserve the unspoiled vividness of an uncritical time.

So let us see the picture as they drew it.

The gates of Jericho were shut. Nobody went out of the city and nobody came in. The people of the city were arranging themselves for a siege.

Joshua called the priests, and gave these orders: "Take up the ark of the covenant, and seven of you with seven trumpets of rams' horns will go before the ark." He said that all the armed men should march as the advance guard, and all the rest of the people should follow in procession behind the ark. They should circle the walls of Jericho, but except for the sound of the trumpets they should march without a sound. When the people of Jericho, looking from their walls, saw this army circling the city, they regarded it doubtless with a kind of superstitious foreboding because it was so curiously silent.

The next day, and the next, and so on for six days, Joshua had the city encircled in this same way. On the seventh day his army arose early, about dawn, and marched about the city, not once only but seven times. Then all the priests simultaneously blew a mighty blast upon the trumpets, and all the people shouted the war cry. On toward the walls of Jericho they rushed, each man straight before him, to where the garrison of Jericho, off their guard through the many days of silent marching when nothing happened, perhaps were taken unawares. Down fell the wall flat before the charge, and the Israelites, rushing in, proceeded to exterminate the population of the doomed city. But Joshua had commanded that Rahab should be spared, and she and all her family were saved and brought into the camp of Israel. Whatever silver and gold and vessels of brass and iron were found in Jericho were also saved; but the torch was put to the rest of the city, and it went up in flames. Moreover, Joshua pronounced his anathema over it: "Cursed be the man before the Lord who riseth up and builds this city Jericho," he said. "At the cost of his only son shall he lay its foundation, and at the cost of his youngest son shall he erect its gates."

"So the Lord was with Joshua; and his fame was noised throughout all the country," says the chronicler—the first half of which statement was primitive religion, but the second half of which was doubtless very present fact.

In the hill country to the northwest of Jericho, there was a town called Ai. Joshua sent scouts up into that region to bring back information about this town and its defenses. They came back and reported that it was not necessary that all the fighting forces should be sent against Ai. A small detachment could go up and capture it, because the town had only a few inhabitants. So Joshua sent up a part of his forces; and the next thing he knew, to his astonishment and disgust, the detachment came back routed. The men of Ai drove them back from the town gates, killed a number of them, and chased them headlong down the hills. Joshua rent his clothes and fell to the ground on his face before the ark, and he and the others of the leaders poured dust upon their heads. "Lord Eternal," he cried, "why didst thou ever bring this people across the Jordan only to hand us over to the Amorites to be killed? Would that we had been content to stay on the other side of Jordan! O Lord, what can I say after Israel has turned its back before its enemies! The Canaanites and all the natives will hear of it and surround us and wipe us off the earth."

Then there came to Joshua what seemed to him a sudden revelation. This was no time for him to be lying on the ground. There must be some reason why the men of Israel had been defeated and humiliated in this fashion. What was the reason? Perhaps there had been some offense against God. The next day he marshaled all the tribes before him and separated them out one by one according to the sacred lots. His lot indicated the family of Judah; from that he took a clan, and from that a particular family, and from that a single man whose name was Achan. "My son," said Joshua, "give glory to the Lord God of Israel and make confession to him; and tell me now what you have done; do not hide it." Then Achan answered Joshua, and confessed that, in spite of the order which had been laid upon the army against any private looting in Jericho, he had taken a goodly Babylonian mantle and a quantity of silver and a wedge of gold, and he had hid them in the earth underneath his tent. So Joshua sent messengers to Achan's tent, and there in the ground they found the things hidden as Achan had said. Whereupon Joshua and the men of Israel, in a very summary judgment, took Achan to a valley outside the camp, and there they stoned him to death. It was a merciless proceeding, in keeping with the rude justice of those times; but after that example, private looting was not likely to be tried again.

Later Joshua led his full forces up against Ai. Up they went by night, and Joshua laid an ambush behind the city. In the morning, with the rest of his men, Joshua advanced in a valley in front of the city gates. When the men of Ai saw him, they issued out, and Joshua led his forces backward as if they were defeated. Out streamed the whole garrison of Ai in pursuit and were drawn away from the city, leaving the gates open. Then the Israelites who had been in ambush saw Joshua lift up his spear as a signal, and they immediately rose up and ran toward the gates of Ai, entered them without resistance, and set fire to the city. The men of Ai, looking behind them, saw the smoke of their city pouring up toward the sky, and they had no chance to flee this way or that, for Joshua's men who had pretended to be pursued, now turned upon their pursuers, and the men of Ai, caught in a trap, were slain. Joshua then destroyed the city, as he had already destroyed Jericho, and he hanged the king of Ai upon a tree.

Then into the savage old chronicle there comes another story which is like a glint of wry humor. The fear of Joshua and his men spread in every direction. It reached the town of Gibeon, not many miles away; and the men of Gibeon, with their wits put to work by sharp necessity, bethought them of a shrewd idea. They selected certain ones from among themselves, and put old clothes on them and old, patched shoes on their feet. They gave them provisions in old sacks on their asses, and old mended wine-skins and dry crumbling bread, and they sent this deputation down to Joshua.

When the Gibeonites reached Joshua's camp at Gilgal, they said to him, "We have come from a distant country," and they begged Joshua to make a treaty with them.   He said to them, "Who are you, and where do you come from?"

"From a very far country," they answered; and they went on to tell Joshua that they had heard the fame of his God and of all that he had done in Egypt, and of how he had smitten the kings of the Amorites; Sihon, king of Heshbon; and Og, king of Bashan."   "Look," they said, "at this dry and mouldy bread.   When we set out from our home, we took this hot out of our houses.   These skins of wine which we filled were new, and now they are old and torn, and our clothes and our shoes are worn out through the length of our journeying."   To Joshua and the men of Israel it seemed on the face of it that these men must be telling the truth.   No one could look as they looked unless he had come a long way.   So without further ado they made a treaty with these men on behalf of Gibeon.

Three days after that they learned that these Gibeonites actually lived in the neighborhood, and that their town was only a little distance over the hill.

Of course Joshua and all the rest of the Israelites were mortified at that discovery.   Most of the people wanted to break their oath and destroy Gibeon anyhow; but the leaders refused. "No," they said; "we have sworn to them by the name of the God of Israel."   So they spared the town and spared the lives of the people; but they made them servants, to cut wood and carry water at their bidding.

The news of what had happened at Ai, and the news concerning Gibeon, spread dismay among the other towns near by. Adonizedec, the king of Jerusalem, sent out to Hebron in the south and Eglon in the west, and to other towns, and urged them to come up and join in a league with him to punish the Gibeonites for their disaffection.   When the men of Gibeon heard that, they sent a message of distress to Joshua.   "Do not abandon us," they said.   "Quick, come up to rescue us.   All the kings of the Amorites in the hill country are gathered together to attack us."

So Joshua marched up from Gilgal with his army, which by this time was becoming a force of seasoned fighting men. He defeated the allies with great slaughter, and he pursued them as far as the valley of Ajalon. In the narrative of the book of Judges, there is quoted from an old, lost "Book of the Upright" a poem which sings of the prayer of Joshua:

"O Sun, stand thou still over Gibeon,
    and Moon, over the vale of Ajalon!
And the sun stood still, and the moon stayed,
    till the people were avenged on their foes."

Then, turning the poetry into literalistic prose, the chronicle goes on to say: "So the sun stood still in the midst of the sky and did not hasten to go down for about a whole day. And there was no day like it before or afterward." No doubt the day seemed tragically long to Adonizedec and the chiefs who were allied with him. They fled and hid in a cave, and when Joshua heard it, he told his men to roll great stones across the mouth of the cave and set a guard in front of it until he had finished the pursuit of the fleeing remnants of his enemies. After that he came back, brought out Adonizedec and his confederates, had his army commanders come forward and put their feet on the necks of the prostrate foes, and then he hanged them as he had hanged the king of Ai. All the while, like other warriors even in more enlightened times, he thought that he was the servant of the Lord, and that he was carrying on a holy warfare when he exterminated these people who were the enemies of Israel, and therefore the enemies of Israel's God.

After this, there follows in the book of Joshua a long list of other battles which Joshua won and of other towns which he captured.

Joshua gathered together all the tribes at Shechem and divided the country into districts which they were to occupy. They were to take possession within their several boundaries and consolidate the victories which had already been gained. The tribes of Judah and Simeon were to be in the south, the tribe of Benjamin north of Judah in the hill country above

Jerusalem, Ephraim in the fertile country north of that, and, beyond Ephraim, Manasseh and the other tribes up to the borders of Mount Hermon, where the tribe of Dan held the outposts farthest to the north. (Which is the reason why the phrase "from Dan to Beer-sheba" signifies the utmost distance which it is possible to travel in the land of Israel, and has become in the Bible almost like a proverb to signify from one end of a thing to the other, for as Dan is at the extreme point in the north, so Beer-sheba is at the extremity of the territory of Judah and Simeon, next to the desert in the south.) In this division of the country there reappears a fine figure who has already played his part in the earlier story. Caleb, who had been one of the scouts sent out by Moses when the Israelites were halted in the wilderness many years before, had long since ceased to be a young man; but he came to Joshua now and said that Moses had promised that some day he should have an inheritance in the land of Canaan. He asked Joshua to give him one; and when Joshua asked him what part of the land he wanted, Caleb said that he wanted the hill country round Hebron. This was part of the land which the scouts had seen before, the very land concerning which a majority of them had said that it was populated with giants and could never be possessed. Caleb reminded Joshua of that. Let him take care of these so-called giants. "I am as strong this day as I was the day that Moses sent me," said Caleb: "as my strength was then, so my strength is now, for war or any enterprise." He would show now who had been right, the timorous majority of the spies or he himself and Joshua. So Joshua gave him the country he asked for, and before long Caleb had taken possession of it.

By this time it seemed to Joshua that tribes whose country was to be on the other side of the river, but who had followed him over the Jordan to help in the conquests there, could go back to their own district. So the tribes of Reuben and of Gad and half the tribe of Manasseh marched off homeward. As they came near the Jordan River, they stopped and built a large, conspicuous altar. When the other tribes heard of this, they were greatly surprised and outraged. They said that a central altar had already been built at Shechem for the worship of Israel's God, which was supposed to be the sanctuary for all the people. The men of Reuben and Gad and Manasseh, they thought, must be building an altar to one of the gods of the surrounding pagan peoples. So they sent post-haste a deputation down to inquire what these fellow tribesmen were about. But the men of Reuben and of Gad and of Manasseh said that to build an altar to another god was the last thing in their minds. They were going back across the river into a separate land. The time might come when the people on the west of the Jordan would think that they, the smaller group to the east of it, had no part in the life and religion of Israel. They wanted to set up an altar, they said, to show that they did, and always would worship the God of Israel. So they went home in peace.

Meanwhile, from the lists of Joshua's conquests, from the long roll of captured towns and slain populations, it would seem as though no one could have been left in all Palestine except the invading Israelites; but, as a matter of fact, there creep into the record little evidences that the victory was not as sweeping as the enthusiastic old chroniclers liked to make it appear. Scattered through the country were towns which the Israelites were never able to take. Jerusalem, for example, on its height, was the stronghold of the Jebusites, and never did fall until generations afterward. And some of the Canaanitish people who lived in the plains had iron chariots which made them able to resist the utmost force which the Israelites could bring against them. Gradually the men of the different tribes settled down into such parts of the country as they were able to occupy; but there was a long period of restless and uncertain struggle still ahead.

Even in times of relative peace life had its dangerous aspects. One of the customs of the country and the time was the blood feud. If a man were killed, it was the business of his nearest relative straightway to go out and hunt down the killer. There was often scant effort to find out the reason for the killing. When blood was shed, blood must be shed again in vengeance for it. Even if a man were killed by accident, the man who killed him might have to reckon upon a sword in his back next day from one of the man's kinsmen. By this atmosphere of hot clan vengeance the Israelites were surrounded; and Joshua, by way of tempering this frontier so-called justice with mercy, set up five towns of refuge. Any fugitive fleeing to these towns had sanctuary, and could not be delivered up to his pursuers.

By this time Joshua was growing old, and he knew that the end of his leadership was at hand. So he sent and gathered all the tribes together at Shechem, and he and the tribal chiefs had a service of worship. Then he addressed the whole multitude of the people and gave them a review of the history of the recent years. There before their remembrance he unrolled the record of the eventful years—the deliverance from Egypt, the march across the wilderness, the crossing of the Jordan, the conquest of the country. It had not been due either to their strength or their deserving, he said. It had been due to the fact that their God had been with them, who "did those great signs in our sight, and preserved us in all the way wherein we went, and among all the people through whom we passed." "Be very courageous," he said, "to keep and do all that is written in the book of the law of Moses, that you turn not aside therefrom to the right hand or to the left." He warned them not to become involved in any of the idolatries of the people round about. They must choose, he said, whom they would serve, whether the God whom their fathers had believed in or the gods of the surrounding tribes; "but as for me and my house," the old warrior said, with a bold decisiveness, "we will serve the Lord." So all the people cried that they too would keep the religion of their fathers, and Joshua took a great stone and set it up under an oak at Shechem as a mark of the covenant between him and them that day.

Not long after that he died, and they buried him in the hill country of Ephraim.

CHAPTER XII

HEN JOSHUA was dead, the people of Israel had no leader great enough to take his place. There was no other man with sufficient moral authority to hold all the tribes together. Palestine is an exceedingly broken land. The mountain ridge which runs through the center of it from north to south falls away toward the plains in many lesser ridges, between which the valleys lie like little pockets isolated from one another. The tribes had settled in the different parts of the territory north and south, and now they began, as best they could, to establish themselves against the Canaanites, who had been there before and who still clung to the strongholds from which they had never been completely dislodged.

In the south the tribes of Judah and Simeon, with the help of stout old Caleb, conquered Hebron and the hill country around it; and it is even recorded that they took the cities of Gaza and Askelon and Ekron down toward the coast of the Mediterranean in the country of the Philistines. But even the tribe of Judah could not extend its conquest far into the plains, since the plainsmen had iron chariots against which the Israelites could not stand.

The tribe of Benjamin consolidated its position in the hills which lie about Jerusalem, and so did the tribes of Ephraim and Manasseh in the more fertile country farther north; but beyond that, the other tribes of Zebulun, Asher, Naphtali and Dan were sorely beset, and only with difficulty maintained themselves against the attacks of the hostile peoples round about.

134

Moreover, by this time the people had begun to fall away from the religious loyalties which Joshua had enjoined. They were worshiping the Baalim, which were the local gods of the Canaanite people, and their morale began to suffer. They no longer had the old solidarity of religious passion which they had had in the days of their great leaders, and so they could no longer stand before their enemies; and they were greatly distressed.

Then began the period which is told of in the book of Judges, a period which can be only roughly estimated in its dates. It covers the years from about 1200 B. C. through the century beginning then, and most of the century following. One after another some figure would emerge from the midst of this tribe or that to rally the people round him and to assume, for the time-being at least, the authority which the strong man can always exercise. The book of Judges is the chronicle of these warriors as that chronicle was compiled from many fragmentary sources. The oldest strands in the book of Judges are perhaps as old as 1000 B. C., but the book did not take its final form until more than four centuries later. It includes traditions as they had been handed down in the memory of the generations. It includes old songs of victory which doubtless date in almost the very words we have them in from the times of the judges themselves; for ballads are easily memorized, and they come down unchanged through the years. It is a strange and mingled tale which the chronicle presents, starred with heroism and sacrifice, dark also with shadows of startling cruelty, which were, however, not startling to that old time. Tradition has probably woven here and there an ampler pattern from the threads of the original fact. Figures of angels as well as of men appear within its drama. It is like a great tapestry into which men of a later time have brought together the color and movement of what they conceived life in the time of the judges to have been.

It is not necessary, therefore, to attempt to analyze too closely the elements which have entered into the particular stories. It is enough to listen to them as they were told, and to hear through them again, sometimes the shouting and the confusion, and sometimes the high note of heroic purpose, both of which belong to that time of strife.

Of these figures of the deliverers, these men who became arbiters in the discussions and the disputes of their neighbors, and from time to time became soldiers also, these "judges," as they were called, the first three were not of great significance. The earliest of them was named Othniel, who was the son of a younger brother of Caleb. "The Spirit of the Lord came upon him, and he judged Israel, and went out to war," says the record; and apparently he drove off an invading army out of the east, and the land had rest for a generation.

Next came Ehud, whose method of delivering his people was one that fitted better into that more savage age than into our own conceptions. Eglon, the king of Moab, had made war on Israel, conquered the city of Jericho, and spread desolation in that region when this Ehud, of the tribe of Benjamin, emerged. He, as it so happened, was left-handed. The reason why his left-handedness is mentioned grows plain later in the story. Men in those days who were accustomed to quick, personal encounters would watch the hand of another man who might be a foe, but ordinarily it would be a man's right hand that would be watched, and it was on his left side that his dagger, if he had one, would be hidden. But Ehud came to Eglon in the camp of Moab and sent in word that he had brought a present to the king. He was ushered into Eglon's summer house and, having given his present, he said that he had a secret errand for Eglon, so that all the Moabite bodyguard withdrew. Then Ehud drew near and before Eglon was aware what he was doing, Ehud's left hand whipped out the dagger which was hidden in the right side of his robes, thrust it into the body of Eglon—who was a very fat man—and with the dagger left there so that it could not be drawn out again, Ehud coolly went out through the porch of Eglon's house, shut the doors and locked them after him, and escaped before the servants and soldiers of Eglon knew what had happened. Then he sounded a trumpet in the mountain country of Israel, rallied the Ephraimites around him, seized the fords of the Jordan, thus cutting off the escape of the Moabites who were on the hither side of the river, and overcame them with a great destruction.

After Ehud, the next leader was Shamgar, of whom the only thing told is that he led the attack upon the Philistines and that he was armed with an ox goad; which gives a hint of how meagerly the Israelites were equipped in those days when it was only the Canaanites and the Philistines who had mastered the use of iron.

After these terse stories of the first three judges there comes a longer and a more vivid one, told with a kind of barbaric vividness that is unforgettable. There was a king of the Canaanites named Jabin, who became a terror to the Israelites because of the iron chariots which he possessed. "Nine hundred chariots of iron" the book of Judges says he had, and though that number is probably an exaggeration into which the tradition has expanded the ancient tale, the chariots which he did have were enough to make him seem invincible. For twenty years, it is recorded, he mightily oppressed the children of Israel.

But now, for the first time, a woman appears upon the scene. That warlike stage of Israel seemed a place unfitted for a woman's leadership. But this woman was of heroic breed. Her name was Deborah, and she had become so influential that people resorted to her to have their controversies judged. She could judge men as well as things, and pick out the rare person who had in him the qualities that made him greater than the crowd. Barak, the son of Abinoam, she had seen and marked, and she sent a messenger to him to tell him that she had a revelation from the God of Israel that he, Barak, was to go to Mount Tabor and take with him the men of Naphtali and of Zebulun. "And I," she said, "will draw unto you to the river Kishon Sisera, captain of Jabin's army, with his chariots and his troops, and I will put him in your power."

Barak was willing to obey, but not alone. He wanted Deborah herself—this Old Testament Joan of Arc—to go with him. "If you will go with me, then I will go," said Barak. "But if you will not go with me, then I will not."

"Yes," said Deborah, "I will go with you. Nevertheless the glory of the expedition will not be yours, for the Lord shall sell Sisera into the hand of a woman."

Then Barak gathered together all the fighting men he could from the tribes of Naphtali and Zebulun, and Sisera with his iron chariots rolled up into that plain of Esdraelon which for years without end had been, and would be almost perpetually, a battlefield. Said Deborah to Barak, "Up, for this is the day in which the Lord puts Sisera in your power! Is not the Lord marching in front of you?"

So Barak launched his attack from the slopes of Mount Tabor, and he routed Sisera and his chariots and his army, so that Sisera alighted from his chariot and fled on foot.

On the heels of the army of Sisera streamed Barak's victorious soldiers, until the rout was complete; but Sisera had not yet been overtaken. He had fled away and come to the tent of a man named Heber the Kenite, and Jael, the wife of the Kenite, was there.

"Turn in, turn, my lord," said Jael to Sisera. "Turn in unto me and do not be afraid." So into the tent went Sisera, and Jael covered him with a mantle.

Sisera was all but spent from the fighting and from his flight. "I pray you," said he, "give me a little water to drink, for I am thirsty."

So Jael, seeming to be more generous than his request, brought some milk and gave him that.

"Stand in the door of the tent," he begged, "and if anyone comes and asks you is there any man here, say no." And he lay down wrapped in his mantle on the floor of the tent, exhausted.

Then Jael took a tent peg and a mallet in her hand, and creeping silently near, she drove the tent peg through the temples of Sisera as he slept, and fastened it into the ground.

Presently came Barak hunting for Sisera, and out of the tent door came Jael.

"Come," she said, "and I will show you the man whom you are seeking!" When Barak came into the tent, there on the ground lay Sisera, dead.

It is a savage story, but told with all the gusto of a generation to whom savage exploits in war were nothing strange; and a ballad which is ascribed to Deborah and Barak is one of the most ringing poems which has come down from any ancient literature.

Thus they sang:

"Because the leaders took the lead in Israel,
    because the people freely volunteered,
        bless ye the Lord!

"Hear, O ye kings; ye princes give ear!
    I will sing to the Lord,
        I will sing praise to the Lord, the God of Israel.

"Lord, when thou wentest forth from Seir,
    when thou marchedst from Edom's field,
The earth trembled, the heavens also swayed,
    yea, the clouds poured water,
        the mountains quaked at the presence of the Lord God of
            Israel.

"In the days of Shamgar the son of Anath,
    caravans ceased,
        and wayfaring men took roundabout ways.
The rural population had ceased,
    in Israel they had ceased,
Until thou didst arise, Deborah,
    didst arise a mother in Israel. . . .

"Rouse thee, rouse thee, Deborah:
    rouse thee, rouse thee, utter a song:
        arise, Barak, and lead forth thy captors, thou son of
            Abinoam.

"Then marched down for him the nobles,
 and the people of the Lord marched down for him as heroes.
From Ephraim they came down to the valleys,
 after them Benjamin with his hosts;
From Machir came down commanders,
 and from Zebulun they that wield the marshal's staff.
And the princes of Issachar were with Deborah;
 as was Issachar, so was Barak,
  into the valley they rushed forth at his heels.

"Among the tribal divisions of Reuben
 were great searchings of heart.
Why didst thou sit still among the sheepfolds,
 to hear the flute calls of the flocks?
Gilead remained beyond the Jordan:
 and Dan sought the protection of ships!
Asher sat still on the shore of the sea,
 and abode by his landings.
Zebulun is a people that jeoparded their lives to the death,
 Naphtali also, upon the heights of the field.

"The kings came and they fought;
 then fought the kings of Canaan,
In Taanach by the waters of Megiddo:
 they took no gain of money.
From heaven fought the stars,
 from their courses they fought against Sisera.
The river Kishon swept them away,
 that onrushing river, the river Kishon.
O my soul, march on with strength.
 Then were battered the hoofs of the horses
  by the furious galloping of their chargers.

"Curse ye Meroz, said the angel of the Lord,
 curse bitterly its inhabitants,
Because they came not to the help of the Lord,
 to the Lord's help among the heroes.

"Blessed above women be Jael,
  blessed above women in the tent.
Water he asked, milk she gave;
  she brought him curd in a lordly bowl.
She put forth her hand to the tent pin,
  and her right hand to the workman's hammer;
And with the hammer she battered Sisera, she crushed his head;
  yea, she shattered and struck through his temple.
At her feet he sank down, he fell, he lay still,
  where he sank down, there he lay slain.

"Out of the window leaned Sisera's mother
  and looked through the lattice,
'Why is his chariot so long in coming?
  why tarry the hoof-beats of his horses?'
The wisest of his princesses answered her,
  yea, 'tis she that made reply to her,
'Surely they are finding, dividing the spoil,
  a damsel or two for each man;'

"Booty of dyed garments for Sisera,
  booty of dyed garments, embroidered,
.   .   .   .
"So let all thine enemies perish, O Lord,
  but let them that love thee be as the sun when he rises in
    his might."[1]

After Barak and Deborah had played their parts in the
history of the time and had gone their way, the next figure
who appears is Gideon. This time it was the Midianites who
had become the invaders and the oppressors of Israel. Conditions had grown so bad that the Israelites were hiding in dens
of the mountains and in caves, and in whatever other almost
inaccessible places they could find among the rocks. If they
sowed a little grain in the pockets of the land, the Midianites

---

[1] Reprinted, with slight alterations, from the translation of Julius A. Bewer, in *The
Literature of the Old Testament.* By courtesy of Professor Bewer and of the Columbia
University Press.

came up and seized it as soon as it was ripe. The sheep and the cattle were carried away. It seemed as though these invaders were "as grasshoppers for multitude, for both they and their camels were without number, and they entered into the land to destroy it."

One day a young man whose name was Gideon was threshing wheat by a winepress, and trying to hide it there lest the Midianites should find it. And Gideon had a vision; and unto him there came an angel, who said, "The Lord is with you, O mighty man of valor." And Gideon answered: "If the Lord be with us, why, then, is all this befallen us? and where be all his miracles which our fathers told us of, saying, 'Did not the Lord bring us up from Egypt?' but now the Lord has forsaken us, and delivered us into the hands of the Midianites."

Back to Gideon came the answer: "Go, in your might, and you shall save Israel from the hands of the Midianites. Is it not I who send you?"

Yet Gideon, hesitating, said: "How shall I save Israel? My family is poor in Manasseh, and I am the least in my father's house."

But the angel of God said to him, "Surely I will be with you and you shall smite the Midianites as one man."

Then it is written that Gideon asked for a sign. He put the flesh of a goat which he had prepared and cakes of unleavened bread upon a rock underneath an oak, and an angel touched the rock with the end of his staff and fire consumed the sacrifice. Then Gideon was afraid, because he said, "I have seen an angel of God face to face."

After that, Gideon destroyed an altar which had been built near by to the god Baal. And when the Baal worshipers in the adjacent town heard of it they would have killed Gideon, but he escaped.

Another sign Gideon then asked from God, and he had an answer which satisfied him; so that he determined the time had come to call all the fighting men whom he could rally against the Midianites. To his summons then they came, a great company of them—according to the book of Judges, thirty-two thou-

sand. But Gideon was not a man whose eye was upon numbers. He wanted something more important. He made to
this hastily gathered army of his an extraordinary proclamation.
"Whoever is fearful and afraid, let him return and depart early
from Mount Gilead." Then out of the thirty-two thousand,
twenty-two thousand presently had disappeared.

Still Gideon had not finished with his sifting. He set his
followers in order and led them forward as though he were
going out now to battle. But he arranged it so that the march
led across the bed of a flowing brook. There, on the bank, he
stopped and watched to see how his men behaved. Nearly all of
them, being thirsty, did exactly what most thirsty men would do.
Down on their knees they went at the edge of the stream and
drank their fill. But a few were of a different temper. Here
and there was a man so eager about the advance against the
Midianites that he did not halt, but only scooped water up in
his hands and lapped it with his tongue. Gideon separated
these men from the others. They were only three hundred
out of ten thousand; but Gideon said these three hundred were
enough, and all the rest of that so-called army could go home.
He said that God had revealed to him this, "that by the three
hundred men who lapped will I save you and deliver the
Midianites into your hands."

Nevertheless, the attack which Gideon was about to launch
against the Midianites seemed a forlorn hope. From his camp
on the slopes of a hill he could look down into the valley
beneath and to the opposite hill, and there on the level ground
stretched what seemed to be the endless black tents of the
Midianites, with their camels tethered beside them. But Gideon
was not disturbed by numbers. He had the imagination and
the daring which make great leaders, and he was to use both.

When night came and the camp of the Midianites lay in the
deep shadow between the hills, Gideon took one of his men
and together they went down silently and under cover of darkness came near to the Midianite tents. They stopped outside
one of them and listened. Two men were talking inside. One
of them said to the other: "See here, I had a queer dream

recently. I dreamed that a cake of barley bread came tumbling into our camp. It rolled into a tent and upset it so that the tent lay flat on the ground."

The man with him answered, "Yes, and that means nothing less than the sword of Gideon, the Israelite."

When Gideon heard that his heart leaped. The Midianites were uneasy, and they might be thrown into a panic. It was plain that they had some sort of suspicious dread of him. That being so, the stratagem he was planning would be the more likely to be a success.

Back he hurried to his own camp.

"Get up," he said, "the Lord has delivered Midian into your hands." Quickly he divided his soldiers into three companies, a hundred men in each. He gave to every man a trumpet, a lighted firebrand and an earthen pitcher, and their swords were hung upon their thighs. The firebrands were to be covered with the pitchers, so that the flame of them would be almost smothered and the light not seen as they advanced. The night drew on. All the men in the camp of Midian, except the watch which had just been changed for the middle of the night, were asleep as the three companies of Gideon surrounded the camp in the darkness. "Wait for my signal," Gideon said, "and do as I do. When I blow upon my trumpet, let every man blow a blast on his trumpet also. Smash the pitchers and let your firebrands blaze and then rush in to the attack."

In and around the camp of Midian all was silence. Then, suddenly, in front of the camp a trumpet blew, and a torch flamed in the midst of the shadows. Instantly all around the camp other trumpets blared. There was a crashing noise and other fires leaped out everywhere, and the men of Midian, shocked out of their sleep, seemed to see the whole earth full of fire and tumult. Before they could collect themselves or know what was happening, the soldiers of Gideon, with their drawn swords, were pouring in among the tents. The Midianites were swept in upon themselves in wild confusion. In that panic they began to turn their own weapons against one another. Then they broke and fled, and Gideon and his men followed them as they streamed away for the fords of Jordan in disordered rout.

Over the Jordan Gideon and his men followed. Still there were only three hundred of them, and they were growing faint now and were nearly exhausted; but they kept on with the pursuit. To the town of Succoth they came, and Gideon halting for a moment at the gates of the city said to the chief men of the town, "Give some loaves of bread to these men who follow me; for they are faint, and I am pursuing Zebah and Zalmunna, kings of Midian." But the chief men of the town said, "Have you captured Zebah and Zalmunna yet? And how do we know whether you will finally win this battle or not, that we should take the chance of the Midianites' revenge by helping your army?"

Then Gideon's anger flared. Here he was with this little force of heroic men trying to drive back once and for all these enemies of Israel, and this cowardly town would not run the risk of being on his side. He looked at those men of Succoth. "When the Lord has delivered Zebah and Zalmunna to my hand," he said, "I will tear your flesh with the thorns of the wilderness and with briers."

He came to another town, the name of which was Penuel, and the men there answered him exactly as the men of Succoth had answered before. "When I come back again," said Gideon, "I will break down the tower of this town."

On he went then with his soldiers until he overtook Zebah and Zalmunna. He scattered their army and captured the two kings. He said to Zebah and Zalmunna, "When you came up into the country around Mount Tabor, what sort of men were they that you killed there?" The Midianite chieftains, trying perhaps to flatter Gideon, said "They were men like you, they were royal looking as though they were kings' sons." "Yes," said Gideon. "They were my brothers, the sons of my mother. As the Lord lives, if you had saved them alive, I would not slay you, but now"—he said to his oldest son—"up and slay them." But the youth was afraid. Then Zebah and Zalmunna, facing what they saw was their doom, said, with a bold defiance, "Get up yourself and come against us, for as a man is, so is his strength." So Gideon slew them with his own hand.

The picture of that, though familiar enough in that fierce time, can hardly be regarded now without a shudder. But there is a more satisfying sense of justice connected with what happened next. Back went Gideon to the towns of Penuel and Succoth. He broke down the tower of Penuel as he had said he would; and when he came to Succoth, he said, "You see what has happened to Zebah and Zalmunna, and now let us see what will happen to you. You remember that you said, 'Are Zebah and Zalmunna yet in your hands, that we should give bread to these men of yours?' Well, they are in my hands, and so are you." And thereupon he took thorns and briers; and with them, as the story in the book of Judges puts it in one quaint and effective phrase, "he taught the men of Succoth."

After the death of Gideon there came another period of confusion. The men of Israel went back to their old intermittent hankering after the gods of the surrounding tribes, and began to indulge in pagan practices. There was a general anarchy and civil strife which involved the descendants of Gideon himself. One of Gideon's sons, named Abimelech, hired a number of men as assassins, and with them he went into his father's house at Ophrah and killed the entire families of his brothers, all except one of them, Jotham, the youngest, who hid himself and escaped. Then Abimelech became ruler of the town of Shechem.

When Jotham heard that, he went and stood on one of the high slopes of Mount Gerizim and shouted down to the men of Shechem below. He intended to express his opinion of Abimelech and of the men who had followed him, and he did it by means of a parable.

"Once upon a time," he said, "the trees went forth to anoint a king over them. They said to the olive tree, 'Reign over us.' But the olive tree answered, 'Should I leave my fatness on account of which men honor God through me and go and be promoted over the trees?'

"Then the trees said to the fig tree, 'You come and reign over us.' But the fig tree said, 'Should I forsake my sweetness and my good fruit and go and be promoted over the trees?' "Then the trees said to the vine, 'You come and reign over us.' And the vine said, 'Should I leave my wine which cheers gods and men and go and rule over the trees?'

"So then the trees resorted to the bramble. 'Will you, bramble, come and reign over us?' they said. And the bramble said, 'If you do truly anoint me king over you, then come and put your trees in my shadow. If not, let fire come out of the bramble and burn up even the cedars of Lebanon.' "

Then Jotham went on to apply his parable. "My father fought for you and risked his life and delivered you out of the hand of Midian, and you have risen up against my father's house and slain his sons and made this Abimelech, the son of a maid-servant, king over the men of Shechem. Now, if you think that this is well done to choose this bramble, then rejoice in Abimelech and let him rejoice in you; but if not, may fire come out of Abimelech and devour Shechem, and fire come out of Shechem and devour him." Having said that, Jotham turned and escaped across the mountain before the angry men down below could lay their hands upon him.

Then followed a time of cruel fightings back and forth. After Abimelech had reigned over Shechem for three years, most of the men of Shechem concluded they had had enough of him. A certain Gaal with a band of men came up to Shechem, and most of the people of Shechem went over to his side. They cursed Abimelech and drove him out of the town. But one of the soldiers who still sided with Abimelech sent word to Abimelech secretly to attack Shechem again in the early morning. So the fighting raged back and forth, until at last Abimelech captured Shechem again, killed all the inhabitants who fell into his hands, beat down the city and sowed it with salt. Those of the men who were left from Shechem went and fortified themselves in a near-by temple of one of the tribal gods. Abimelech captured that also and burned it, and then he laid siege to another town near by.

In the town there was a tower, and all the men and women of the town were driven back into this. Up to the tower Abimelech came, and he and his men flung themselves against the tower door and tried to set it on fire; but from the top of the tower a woman threw down a piece of millstone upon Abimelech which broke his skull. "Draw your sword," he said to his armor bearer, "lest men shall say of me that a woman killed me." So his armor bearer thrust him through; and Abimelech was dead. The end of Jotham's parable had come true. The bramble had lit a very deadly fire, both for the trees that chose it to be their king and also for itself.

CHAPTER XIII

IN WHICH ARE MORE STORIES FROM THE BOOK OF JUDGES; OF JEPH-
THAH AND HIS VOW BECAUSE OF WHICH HE SACRIFICED HIS DAUGH-
TER; OF SAMSON AND DELILAH; AND OF THE MAN WHO LOST HIS
GODS.

HUS FAR all the stories recounted in the book of Judges, like the grim old time to which their events belong, are mainly harsh and pitiless. But now comes a story which has in it a wistful pathos which has been wafted like a breath of perfume down all the long years between. It is the story of Jephthah and of Jephthah's daughter, and of Jephthah's disastrous vow.

Jephthah was a man of Gilead, and the tribe of Gilead was one of those which had settled in the territory east of the Jordan River. Farther still to the east, beyond their borders, lay the desert, and from that desert the hostile tribes were always launching their incursions. The Ammonites especially were nearest to this region of the men of Gilead, and the Ammonites had a particular satisfaction in assailing this country, since long ago in the former times their own ancestors had lived there.

In they swept upon the Gileadites, therefore, and the men of Gilead were sorely distraught. They had no leader capable of resistance, and they cast about to find one. "The man we need," they said, "is Jephthah." But Jephthah was not in Gilead. His half-brothers, of whom he had several, had been jealous of him, and, conspiring together, had driven him away from his father's house, so that Jephthah had become an outlaw, living in the bordering country as the leader of a band of men whom his own strength and daring had attracted round him.

The elders of Gilead went to find Jephthah; and when they

did find him, they said, "Come up and be our captain, that we may fight with the people of Ammon."

Jephthah reminded them of how hatefully he had been treated, and of how he had been expelled from his own father's house. "Why are you come out to me now," he asked, "when you are in distress?"

The spokesmen of Gilead answered frankly enough: "That is the very reason why we do turn to you now. We are in distress, and we need you to go with us and fight against the Ammonites, and be our head over all the inhabitants of Gilead."

"If you bring me home again to fight against the Ammonites, and the Lord gives me victory over them, shall I be your head?" demanded Jephthah.

And the elders of Gilead answered, "The Lord be witness between us, if we do not do as you have said."

Then Jephthah started homeward with them, taking command of all the soldiers who were available, and on the way he stopped at a shrine in Mizpeh and had a service of worship.

The next thing he did was to send a message to the king of the Ammonites. He wanted to know what the Ammonites meant by coming and invading this land of Gilead. The king of the Ammonites sent back a reply which from his point of view seemed quite sufficient. He said that the land in which the men of Gilead were belonged by right to the people of Ammon. Their forefathers had lived there before the people of Israel were ever heard of in those parts. "Now, therefore," he said, "restore these lands again peaceably."

But Jephthah had another reading of history. He said that it might be true that the Ammonites once had possessed this territory, but they had been driven out long before the Israelites took it. The Amorites had defeated the people of Ammon and seized their lands, and it was from the Amorites and not from the men of Ammon that Israel had captured it. Besides, he said, the Israelites had been there for these three hundred years. What had the Ammonites been doing all that time? And why were they making this belated challenge now?

Of course the argument got nowhere on either side, as arguments never do when the passion of war is already aroused. It was evident that the issue would have to be fought out, and Jephthah, knowing that the battle would be a fierce one, wanted all the help that he could get. He was a religious man according to the ideas men had then of religion. He believed that the God of Israel would come to his aid if he could show his devotion, and the best way, he thought, to show devotion was to promise a costly sacrifice. So he made a vow that if he should defeat the Ammonites, he would offer up as a sacrifice whatever living thing first came forth out of the door of his house on that day when he should come back in peace.

Out then he went to the clash with the Ammonites. There was a brief but bloody battle. He and his forces won it. The Ammonites were put to rout.

Home then came Jephthah, home from exile and home also from the danger of the fight. He had had his triumph, and now he would have his reward of peace. But the impetuous vow which he had made was still to be reckoned with.

When he drew near to his house, the first living thing he saw was not a herd of goats nor a flock of sheep in his fields, as he had thought it might be. Instead, out from his house there came a group of girls singing and dancing, and in front of them was his own daughter. She was his only child. When Jephthah saw her, his heart sank like a stone, for she was the first person to meet him in this homecoming, and he remembered his vow that whatever came out to meet him first he would offer as a sacrifice.

He clutched his clothes and tore them. "Oh, my daughter!" he cried. "You have brought me very low, and you are one of them that trouble me: for I have opened my mouth unto the Lord, and I cannot go back!"

She understood presently what he meant, but she made no complaint. "My father," she said, "if you have promised, then you must do with me according to that promise." Only she asked that for two months she might go up and down upon the hills with the other maidens and lament the life that never would be hers. So Jephthah, in dumb fidelity to what he thought religion required of him in his vow, sacrificed his daughter; and ever since then the story of Jephthah's daughter has come down through literature like a parable of youth and tragic loss.

After that, of course, there was bitterness in Jephthah's soul. He was a dangerous man to deal with, as some of the tribesmen of Ephraim were to find to their cost. They sent a message to Jephthah, demanding to know why they had not been summoned to join in the battle against the Ammonites. Now that it had resulted in a victory, they resented the fact that they had had no share in the glory of it. They said that they were coming down to set fire to Jephthah's house. They did come over the river, but what happened was very different from what they planned. Jephthah rallied the men of Gilead and drove the Ephraimites back. Moreover, his men seized the fords of the Jordan over which the Ephraimites had to retreat. When a man appeared at the fords, the Gileadite guards challenged him. "Are you an Ephraimite?" they demanded. If he said "No," then they ordered him to say "Shibboleth"; but people of the tribe of Ephraim could not say "Shibboleth." They said "Sibboleth" instead. When a man said that, he did not pass over the river; he fell before the swords of the Gileadite sentinels. "Shibboleth" was a password to life or death, and "Shibboleth" has come down in proverbial language from that day to this.

As the Israelites had their enemies among the desert tribes to the east, so also they had a still more formidable enemy in the country to the west. Along the narrow coastal strip between the Mediterranean and the high ridge of hills that runs from north to south in Palestine, lay the Philistines. They were a powerful people, supposed to have been the heirs of the Minoan civilization of Crete, with strong cities by the seacoast and a civilization further advanced in the arts both of peace and war than the rude culture of the men of Israel. It was from the name of the Philistines that the familiar name for the whole country, Palestine, arose, and over the whole country the power of the Philistines continually threatened to expand. Although the tribes of Israel held the strongholds of the hills, for century after century they had good reason to fear these aggressive neighbors of the plains.

No heroes, therefore, in the chronicles of Israel, were quite so glamorous as the ones whose victories were won over this arch-foe. That is the reason why the longest and most vivid story in the book of Judges is the story of Samson; for it was against the Philistines that Samson made his herculean war.

Somewhere among the hills in the territory of the tribe of Dan there lived a man named Manoah. Beneath the hills stretched long slopes of grain fields and olive groves, and farther down lay the sunny, coastal plain which was rich with orange groves and palm trees, and beyond it the glimmer of the sea. This was Philistia; and Ashdod and Gaza and Askelon lifted their walls and gates there near the Mediterranean shores.

One day Manoah's wife had a vision; and when she told her husband about it, she said that an angel had appeared to her and announced that she should have a son. From his birth he should be a Nazarite, a dedicated man, and the sign of his dedication should be that he must never drink any strong drink, and that he should never cut his hair. "It was a man of God who came to me," she told her husband, "and his countenance was like the countenance of an angel of God; but I did not ask him whence he was, and he did not tell me his name."

Then Manoah prayed to God, and begged that the angel who had appeared to his wife might come again and tell them further what they should do about the child who was to be born.

So on another day when Manoah's wife was in the field, she saw again the angel, and she ran and brought her husband, and he saw him too. He received also exactly the same message which his wife had received before, namely, that a son should be born to them, and that he should be a Nazarite. And then as Manoah hastened and built a fire, so that he might offer up a sacrifice, the angel and the fire seemed to blend, and Manoah and his wife fell on their faces to the ground, and said to one another that the angel had ascended in the flame.

In the course of time Manoah's wife bore a son, and she called his name Samson. He grew up presently into a sturdy, thick-haired boy, and then into a man whose strength had no match anywhere. Nobody could compel him to do this, or to refrain from that; and since he was so impetuous and fearless and strong, it was evident that the Philistines would find him a dangerous neighbor.

One day Samson went down to the town of Timnath, and there he saw a Philistine girl with whom he fell in love. He asked his father and mother to go and see if they could get her to be his wife; but they had no liking for a Philistine daughter-in-law. They wanted to know why, if Samson wished to get married, he could not find a wife among his own people.

Then Samson decided to take matters into his own hands. He started down for Timnath; and as he came through the vineyards suddenly he encountered a young lion. The lion roared, but that did not trouble Samson. He caught the lion with his bare hands, and rent him as he would rend a kid, and after that he continued on his way to Timnath, and visited his Philistine sweetheart.

Some time after that he went again, and there by his path was the body of the lion which he had killed, and between the bones of it a swarm of bees had hived and made their honey. Samson took some of the honey in his hands, and ate it as he went along. Not long after this he was married, and he invited all the young men of Timnath to a wedding feast.

"I am going to ask you a riddle," he said, "and if you can give me the answer in seven days, I will give you thirty shirts and thirty changes of clothes; and if you cannot answer it, then you shall all give thirty of these to me."

"Very well," they said, "put forth your riddle; let us hear it."

"Out of the eater came forth meat, and out of the strong came forth sweetness," said Samson; "that is the riddle; now, find the answer to that."

They cudgeled their wits that day and the next two days, but they could not think of the answer. As the final day drew near, the young men went to Samson's wife, and they said: "Entice the answer to this riddle from your husband. If you do not, we will set your father's house on fire, and burn you in it. Do you invite us to a wedding feast to take away everything we possess?" So Samson's wife came to Samson and began to cry. "You hate me," she said, "instead of loving me. You put forth a riddle to these men of my people, and you have not told the answer of it to me."

"No," he said, "I have not told it even to my father and mother. And why should I tell it to you?"

She kept on weeping and pleading; and at last, when Samson could stand it no more, he told her the answer to the riddle, and she immediately told it to the men of Timnath. At sundown on the seventh day, therefore, they said they had guessed the answer to his riddle.

"What is sweeter than honey?" they said, "and what is stronger than a lion?" They had the answer, but Samson could guess where they had got it.

"If you had not plowed with my heifer," he said to them, "you had not guessed my riddle."

But Samson was not a good man to try to outwit. He went down to the neighboring city of Askelon, knocked in the heads of the first thirty men he met, took their clothes, and brought them back to give to the men of Timnath. After that he went angrily back to his father's house.

Later there happened something which roused his resentment to a still hotter pitch. His father-in-law took his wife and gave her to be the wife of another man; and when presently Samson, at the time of the wheat harvest, came down again to Timnath, he found that his wife was gone; and he was met by the cool suggestion of his father-in-law: "I thought that you had hated her, and so I gave her to a friend of yours: but her younger sister is fairer than she. Why not take her in place of your former wife?" Then Samson, whose idea of moral justice was to do to your enemy as much evil as he had done to you—and, if possible, a little more—considered that, no matter what he devised now against the Philistines, it would hardly even up the score. So the first thing he did was to go out diligently and catch three hundred foxes. He tied the foxes together two by two, and tied a firebrand to their tails, and set them loose in the fields where the ripe corn of the Philistines was shocked. The foxes dragged the firebrands far and wide, and they not only burned up the standing grain, but the vineyards and olive trees also.

The next rejoinder of the Philistines, since they could not get hold of Samson, was to seize his wife and her father, pen them in their own house, and then burn the house down; after which Samson, in his turn, went raging out against the Philistines, and smote them hip and thigh, and, having made a great slaughter in their ranks, retired to a sort of rocky eyrie in the territory of Judah.

Up across the borders of Judah, therefore, which being next to Philistia, was constantly being invaded, came the Philistines, demanding that the men of Judah deliver Samson over into their hands; and a large force of these men of Judah climbed up to the rock where Samson was. They said that it was his fault that the Philistines had invaded their territory, against which Samson made his usual reply: "As they did to me, so have I done to them."

The men of Judah told him that they had come to bind him and hand him over to the Philistines. That was all very well, Samson said, provided they would swear one thing. Would they swear not to fall upon him themselves? Yes; they swore that they would do him no violence. So he submitted to be bound, and they tied his arms with two new ropes and brought him down from his rock.

When the Philistines saw Samson being led toward them bound, they set up a great shout. But they rejoiced too soon. "The Spirit of the Lord came mightily upon Samson." All the wild anger of his strength was roused, and the ropes on his arms became like flax in the fire. He wrenched his hands loose, and picking up the first thing he saw on the ground as a weapon, which happened, so the chronicle says, to be the jawbone of an ass, he fell upon the Philistines and put them to flight.

Shortly afterward, as though to show his contempt for anything the Philistines could do against him, he went down into one of their own cities, the city of Gaza. He went by night, and for a purpose which did him no credit; but there he was. The Philistines heard that he was there. They surrounded the house into which he had gone, and set a watch at the city gate. "In the morning, when it is day," they said, "we shall kill him." But Samson did not wait until morning. He rose up at midnight, and went out toward the gate. Since the gates were shut, he pulled them down and the gate posts with them, and dragged them after him up to the hills.

But even Samson could be reckless once too often. He fell in love with another Philistine woman, whose name was Delilah, who lived in the valley of Sorek.

The chief men of the Philistines came to Delilah, and they said: "Entice him. Find out what is the secret of his great strength, and how we may prevail against him and be able to seize him. If you do that, every one of us will give you eleven hundred pieces of silver." Delilah listened with interest. Eleven hundred pieces of silver seemed to her very desirable.

So when occasion offered, she said beguilingly to Samson, "Tell me, I pray you, what your great strength consists in. How could anyone ever bind you so as to hurt you?"

"Oh," said Samson, "if they should bind me with seven green withes which had never been dried, then I should be no stronger than any other man."

Delilah passed that word on to the Philistines, and they brought her seven green withes which had never been dried, and she persuaded Samson to let her try what the withes would do, and she tied him with them. Meanwhile, men were lying in wait in her house. "The Philistines are upon you, Samson!" she cried. But he broke the withes with which she had tied him as though they were thread.

Then Delilah pretended to be very much offended. "Look how you have mocked me, and told me lies," she said. "I ask you again to tell me, and to tell me this time truly, how you might be bound."

"Well," he said, "if they bound me fast with new ropes with which no work has ever been done, then I should be weak and like any other man."

So Delilah bound him with new ropes, and this time surely, she thought, her treachery would be successful when the Philistines poured in upon him; but this time again he broke the ropes like thread from his arms.

A third time she tried to get his secret, and a third time she failed. Then she beset him with her entreaties. "How can you say you love me," she said, "when your heart is not with me? You have mocked me these three times, and have not yet told me the secret of your strength."

So every day she pressed him, and urged him until his very soul was vexed almost to death, and at last one day he told her all his heart. He said: "No razor has ever come upon my head, for I have been a Nazarite, vowed to God from my birth. If I should be shaven, then my strength would go from me, and I should become as weak as any other man."

Then when Delilah saw that this time he really had told her the truth, she sent to the leaders of the Philistines this message: "Come up this once more, for Samson has showed me all his heart." So they came, bringing their money in their hands. And she took Samson's head upon her lap, and lulled him to sleep, and beckoned to a man to come and cut off the locks of his hair. Then she cried, this time exultantly, "The Philistines are upon you, Samson!" And he cried: "I will go out this time as before and shake myself." But he wist not that the Lord was departed from him. Then the Philistines took him, and put out his eyes, and brought him down to Gaza, and bound him with fetters of brass. And they put him in a prison house, and harnessed him to millstones to grind their corn.

They forgot that his hair would begin to grow again; but it did grow, and, as it grew, Samson began to feel like his old self once more. There came a day when the Philistines had gathered a great assembly for a sacrifice to Dagon their god, and to hold a public rejoicing; for they said: "Our god has delivered Samson our enemy into our hands." So when they were all merry at the feast, someone suggested that they call for Samson, "that he may make sport for us"; and they had Samson brought out of the prison house, and they stood him between the pillars which held up the roof of the banqueting hall, and believed it was fine sport to mock him, as he stood there blind, and, as they thought, helpless. A boy had led Samson by the hand from the prison, and, as the boy stood by him, Samson said: "Let me feel the pillars on which the house is supported, that I may lean upon them." The house inside was full of men and women, and on the flat roof above were others.

Then Samson cried: "O Lord God, remember me, I pray thee, and strengthen me, I pray thee, only this once, O God, that I may be at once avenged of the Philistines for my two eyes!" And he took hold of the two middle pillars by which the house was borne up, of the one with his right hand, and of the other with his left. "Let me die with the Philistines!" he said; and he bent his great shoulders with all his might. The pillars crumpled, and the house fell in upon all the lords of the Philistines, and upon all the people that were therein. "So"—the chronicle ends—"the dead which he slew at his death were more than they which he slew in his life."

The next story in the book of Judges is very different from the story of Samson, and has a curious interest of its own. It is the story of a man who thought in that time, as many men have thought in other times since, that if he could make the right arrangements, religion could be a very convenient and simple matter.

In the country near Mount Ephraim lived this man, whose name was Micah. The first thing we know of Micah was that he had stolen eleven hundred shekels of silver from his mother, about which she had naturally made a considerable outcry when she discovered that it was gone. Afterward his conscience smote him, and he brought his mother's money back. But she took two hundred shekels of it and gave it to a metal worker, who made the silver into little sacred images according to the custom of the pagan peoples round about, which custom the men of

Israel were always slipping into; and Micah set these images up in his house, and considered that he had a little church all his own. He said to one of his sons that he would have to be a priest to carry out the proper ritual in the image-church, and with this arrangement Micah felt very much satisfied.

But presently there came what seemed an opportunity to improve upon it. There came along the road one day a young man from the town of Bethlehem-judah who belonged to the tribe of Levi, the tribe which as far back as the time of Moses had been set apart to take care of the worship of the tabernacle and to be a sort of ordained ministry of the Israelites' church. As he was going on his way, he arrived at the house of Micah. "Where did you come from?" said Micah.

"Oh, I am a Levite of Bethlehem, and I am looking about for a place to live in," was the answer.

"Come live with me," said Micah; "you can be my priest. Every year I will give you ten shekels of silver and a suit of clothes and your food."

So the young Levite said he would stay, and Micah had a consecration service to make him his own particular household chaplain, and was exceedingly pleased with himself and with the situation generally. "Now I know," said Micah, "that the Lord will do me good, since I have a real Levite to be my priest."

But trouble was brewing in a way of which Micah had little thought. Those were days, as the history says, when "there was no king in Israel, but every man did that which was right in his own eyes." Not only individual men did as they chose, but the several tribes did it too. The tribe of Dan had had its share in the division of the country, but it was of the opinion that it had not had enough, and so it determined that it would go and annex the land of some of its neighbors. Consequently, it sent out five men as scouts, and these men happened to come into the neighborhood where Micah lived. They turned in to Micah's house to spend the night, and to their surprise they heard a voice they knew. It was the voice of Micah's young Levite priest, who in his various wanderings had gone through the country of Dan. "Who brought you here?" they inquired.

"What are you doing in this place, and what is it that you have here?"

He told them how it was thus and so that he had come, and how Micah had hired him to be his priest.

They asked him to consult the images and tell them whether they were going to have good luck on their venture, and he came back and told them that they would. On they pressed, therefore, farther to the north and came presently up near the headwaters of the Jordan, and arrived at a town named Laish, where people were dwelling very serenely. In the country round Laish there was no strong authority to preserve law and order. The scouts went back, therefore, and told the rest of the men of Dan that here was a chance to migrate into a country easy to take and well worth having.

So six hundred Danites armed themselves with their weapons and marched north.

On their way toward Laish they passed by Mount Ephraim and came to the house of Micah. The five scouts who had been that way before said to the others: "Do you know that in that house there are some sacred images? Consider then what you have to do."

What they did do was to stand guard at the gate to Micah's property while the five scouts went into his house and appropriated all his silver images.

"What are you doing?" said the priest. "Hold your tongue," said they. "Put your hand over your mouth, and go with us. You can be our priest. Which is better, to be the priest in the house of one man, or to be a priest for a whole tribe?"

The priest thought that question, especially under the circumstances, answered itself; and so he went along with the Danites and Micah's stolen images.

When they had gone a good way on their road, Micah discovered what had happened, and, gathering his neighbors round him, he set out after the Danites and overtook them. When they saw the Danites ahead of them, they shouted.

Then the men of Dan turned round and said to Micah,

"What ails you, that you have come with such a company as this?"

Micah cried in answer: "You have taken away my gods which I made, and my priest too, and are gone away with them. What more have I? And then you ask me, 'What ails you?' "

The men of Dan replied, "You had better not let your voice be heard so loud, lest some hot-tempered fellows here run upon you, and you lose your life and the lives of your whole household."

So they turned their backs and marched off, and Micah, seeing that they were too strong for him, turned and went back to his own house. So Micah lost his priest and his gods, and thought, no doubt, that he had lost his religion, and went back home without any of them.

CHAPTER XIV

THE STORY OF NAOMI AND OF RUTH, AND OF HOW RUTH GLEANED
IN THE FIELDS OF BOAZ NEAR BETHLEHEM, AND OF HOW BOAZ LOVED
RUTH AND MARRIED HER.

AFTER THE stories of Jephthah and Samson, the book of Judges ends with another story which shows again how rude and violent were the times from which these old narratives have come down. Its climax is in a ferocious struggle between most of the tribes of Israel and the town of Gibeah in the tribe of Benjamin, with so much wild killing that one grows tired of reading it. It is a dark climax to the book of Judges, which, indeed, all through is a book which tells of warfare and of fierce passions of various sorts.

But after Judges comes a story of a very different kind. Following the tumultuous chronicles of the earlier book, it is like the contrast of some lovely, still day which follows a storm, or like a sunlit, fragrant valley into which one comes after having been buffeted by winds on the rocky slopes of savage hills. It is the book of Ruth, and it tells the idyllic story of what happened to a young girl, from whom long afterward as one of her descendants the great King David was to come.

In the town of Bethlehem, in the country of Judah, there was a man named Elimelech married to a woman named Naomi, and they had two sons. One year the crops failed, and there was a famine in Bethlehem and all the territory round about. So Elimelech decided that he and his family had better migrate somewhere else. To the east they went, over the River Jordan and up into the high plateau country of Moab, where there was food. In Moab they lived ten years. Their two sons married two girls of the neighborhood. The name of one was Orpah and the name of the other was Ruth.

But meanwhile Elimelech had died, and afterward the two sons died also, and Naomi and her daughters-in-law were left alone. Then Naomi grew homesick for her own country. She had heard besides that the famine was now over in Bethlehem, and so she decided that she would go back among her own people. She said to Orpah and to Ruth, "You had better each one go back to your own mother's house. May the Lord deal kindly with you, as you have dealt with the dead and dealt with me." She said that now that their husbands were dead, they would perhaps each one of them fall in love with someone else and be married again; and if they did, she hoped that God would give them happiness. So she kissed them good-by, and they both wept to think of parting with her. They said they would rather go back with her into her country and live among her people.

But Naomi said: "No, my daughters, turn again. Why should you go with me? I have no more sons who can be your husbands." It was better, she said, that they should stay in their own land.

So Orpah kissed Naomi, but Ruth clung to her. Orpah returned again into her own mother's house in the land of Moab; but Ruth said she would never go back.

"Look," said Naomi, "your sister-in-law has gone back to her people and to her gods. You also should return with her."

Then Ruth said to her: "Entreat me not to leave thee, or to return from following after thee: for whither thou goest, I will go; and where thou lodgest, I will lodge: thy people shall be my people, and thy God my God: where thou diest, will I die, and there will I be buried. The Lord do so to me, and more also, if aught but death part thee and me." Then when Naomi saw that Ruth was steadfastly purposed to go with her, she did not try to dissuade her any more.

On their way then the two of them went until they came to Bethlehem. When they arrived there, all Naomi's own old neighbors in the little town came flocking about. "Can this be Naomi?" they said.

And she answered, "No, do not call me Naomi any more. Call me Mara [which means "bitterness"]; for the Almighty has dealt bitterly with me indeed." She was still grieving for Elimelech and her two sons, and she did not know yet that happier days were in store for her.

They settled again in Bethlehem, and then the question was as to how they should live. There was a merciful custom in all the country which was said to have traced back to the law of Moses, that whenever men who owned land reaped their ripe grain they should not glean the fields too carefully when they shocked it, but leave some of the scattered grain on the ground for poor people to come and gather up.

Near the place where Naomi and Ruth were living there was a field which belonged to a rich and kindly man named Boaz. Ruth said to Naomi, "Let me go now out among the fields and glean grain on the land of someone who may look favorably upon me as I come."

So it happened that it was to Boaz' field that she came, and she followed behind his reapers, picking up the stalks of grain which they left behind.

While she was there Boaz himself walked out from Bethlehem among his fields. "God be with you," he said to the reapers; and the reapers answering said to him, "May God bless you."

Then Boaz saw Ruth, and he said to the reapers, "What girl is that?"

And the man in charge of the reapers answered and said: "It is the Moabitish girl that came back with Naomi out of the country of Moab. She asked us to let her glean after the reapers among the sheaves, and she has been here since the morning."

Then Boaz said to Ruth: "My daughter, have you been hearing what we said? You are not to go glean in any other field. You are to stay in the company of the girls who are harvesting for me. Nobody shall trouble you. When you are thirsty, go to the water jars and drink of what the young men have drawn."

Ruth bowed in grateful thanks to Boaz, and she said, "I do

not know why I have found grace in your eyes or why you should take notice of me, for I am a stranger."

But Boaz answered that he had heard more about her than she knew; because it had been fully reported to him how good she had been to her mother-in-law, and how she had left her own father and mother and the land of her birth and had come with Naomi to live among people whom she had never known before. "May God recompense your work," said Boaz, "and may you have a full reward from the Lord God of Israel under whose wings you have come to trust." So Ruth said that she hoped she would find favor in Boaz' sight, and she thanked him again for all the gentle and friendly way in which he had spoken to her.

At meal-time Boaz said, "Come sit here with the rest of us and eat your bread, and dip it in this vinegar we have here." So she did come and sit beside the other reapers, and Boaz gave her some of his own parched corn; and when she had finished it, she left.

Boaz watched her as she went back to her gleaning, and he said to his reapers, "Let her glean even under the sheaves of grain, and do not hinder her. Moreover, let some handfuls of grain fall on purpose, and leave them on the ground that she may glean them." So all day long Ruth gleaned in the field, and at evening when she winnowed out the grain she had, it amounted to a bushel of barley. She took it up and went back into Bethlehem and showed it to Naomi. "Where could you have gleaned all this to-day?" cried Naomi. "Where have you done so much? Blessed be he who has let you do it!"

Then Ruth described to Naomi the man in whose field she had been gleaning, and Naomi said, "Why, that is Boaz! May God bless him," went on Naomi, "for he has not ceased his kindness to the living and to the dead. This man," she said, "is one of our very nearest kinsmen."

"Yes," said Ruth, "and he told me that I could go with his reapers until they had finished all the harvest."

And Naomi told Ruth to stay with the girls among the reapers and not to venture into any other field. So Ruth did so, and until the end of the wheat harvest she gleaned in the fields of Boaz, and dwelt with her mother-in-law.

Then Naomi began to think of Ruth and Boaz. Ruth had no husband and Boaz had no wife, and it seemed to Naomi that they were suited one for the other. She did not tell Ruth all that was in her thought, but she counseled Ruth as to what to do when she met Boaz and how to bear herself when she saw him. And Ruth very trustfully did what Naomi told her to do.

So it came about that Boaz fell in love with Ruth and determined that he would marry her if he could. But though he was a kinsman of Ruth's husband who had died, there was another man of the town who was a kinsman also, and, according to the law and custom, this other man, because of his particular kinship, would have the first right to ask Ruth to marry him if he chose to do so. So Boaz went and sat down by the gate of Bethlehem. Now, in Israel the gates of the town were the places where people resorted for public business. Markets were held there and people made their agreements there in the presence of witnesses, as though it were a town court of law. So Boaz asked ten of the leading men of Bethlehem to come and sit down beside him. Then he said to this other kinsman: "Naomi, who has come back again out of the country of Moab, is going to sell a parcel of land which belonged to our cousin Elimelech. Now, you and I as the kinsmen have the first right to buy it, and my thought is to advertise to you that, if you choose, you can buy it now before the people of the town and before the elders."

"Yes," he said, "I will buy it."

"But note," said Boaz, "also that when you buy the land of Naomi, you buy with it also the right to marry Ruth the Moabitess, who was the wife of Naomi's dead son."

When he heard that, the other man changed his mind. He said he did not want the land after all. Then said Boaz, before all the representatives of the town's people, "You are my witnesses this day that I have bought everything that belonged to Elimelech and to his sons, and I have bought the right to marry Ruth."

"Yes," said the people, "we are witnesses, and may the Lord make her like Rachel and like Leah, who built the house of Israel."

So Boaz and Ruth were married, and presently a boy was born, to the great joy of Naomi and of everyone else who knew them. They called his name Obed, and years afterward, when Obed himself was grown up and married, he had a son whose name was Jesse; and Jesse in his generation was to be the father of David the king.

CHAPTER XV

ANY OF the men of whom the earlier records of the Bible tell were men of war. Their greatness consisted in their prowess with the sword. Now arises a man whose greatness was of another sort. His power was in his soul. He was a forerunner of a new line of leaders of which Moses also had been a prototype—a man whose dominance was due, not to the might of weapons but to the moral authority with which he lived and spoke. He was the son of a man named Elkanah and of Hannah, his wife.

Elkanah loved Hannah dearly, but for years she had been childless. Another woman who had a grudge against her mocked her because she had no children, and Hannah wept, and did not eat. Elkanah tried to comfort her. "Hannah, why do you weep?" he said, "and why won't you eat? Why is your heart grieved so? Am I not better to you than ten sons?"

But Hannah, who had gone up with Elkanah to carry a sacrifice to the temple at Shiloh, was in bitterness of spirit, and she prayed to the Lord and wept grievously. She made a vow also, and said, "O Lord of hosts, if thou wilt indeed look upon the affliction of thine handmaid and remember me, and wilt give me a man child, then I will give him unto the Lord all the days of his life."

And it happened, as she kept on a long time praying, that Eli the priest noticed her. Now, Hannah was speaking in her heart; only her lips moved, and her voice was not heard. So Eli thought she had been drinking. He spoke to her roughly: "How long will you be drunken?" he asked. "Put away your wine."

169

But Hannah said: "No, my lord, I am a woman of a sorrowful spirit. I have not drunk either wine or strong drink, but I have poured out my soul before the Lord."

Then Eli answered, gently, "Go in peace: and the God of Israel grant you your petition which you have asked of him."

"May your handmaiden find grace in your sight," she said; and she went away and had something to eat, and her face was no longer sad.

The next morning Elkanah and Hannah rose up early, and worshiped in the temple, and returned to their house in Ramah. Not long after that, Hannah knew that she was going to have a child, and in the course of time a son was born, and she called his name Samuel, which meant, "asked of God."

A few years went by, and then, when Samuel had grown old enough to be separated from his mother, Hannah, remembering her vow, took him up with her to the temple. She brought him to Eli the priest. "My lord," she said, "as your soul lives, I am the woman who stood by you here, praying to the Lord. For this child I prayed; and the Lord has given me my petition which I asked. Now, therefore, I have lent him to the Lord; as long as he lives he shall be lent to the Lord." And while the little boy Samuel worshiped in the temple, Hannah poured out her heart in thanksgiving.

Then Elkanah and Hannah went home again, and Samuel was left to serve Eli the priest in the temple.

Now, Eli had two sons, Hophni and Phinehas, who were exceedingly wicked men. They bribed the people who came to the temple of Shiloh with their sacrifices, and exacted tribute from them. They were immoral in their relationships generally. Eli expostulated with them, but never with firmness. He was too indulgent and too weak to curb them. They paid no attention to what he said, and went on with their evil practices as before.

One day a certain God-fearing man came to Eli, and said he had a message from the Lord. He reviewed the long and honorable history of Eli and his family in the priesthood, and then he recited the dishonor of Hophni and Phinehas. He predicted that these two sons of Eli should both die in one day, and that thus the priesthood would come to an end in Eli's line, and that all who might be left in his family would be so impoverished that they would come and crouch to the new priest for a piece of silver and a morsel of bread. Poor old Eli —for he was growing old in years now as well as feeble in will— listened and said nothing; for he knew his own weakness, and there was nothing that he could say.

Nevertheless, the old man had a gentle and a generous heart. The boy Samuel was growing up with him in the temple, gaining favor in the eyes both of God and man, while his own sons were going their way to destruction. He loved Samuel, and did everything he could to help him learn and grow.

As Eli grew older, he was also becoming blind. His eyes were so dim that he needed the help of Samuel more and more. One night he had lain down to go to sleep, and Samuel had gone to bed also. Only the lamp of God was still burning in the temple.

Then Samuel heard a voice which startled him wide awake. "Here I am," he said, and ran to Eli. "Here I am, for you called me."

But Eli said, "No, I did not call you; lie down again."

So Samuel went back to bed and lay down.

The same thing happened a second time. Again Samuel heard a voice and got up and ran to Eli; and again Eli said, "I did not call you, my son; go and lie down."

A third time this happened, and then Eli said that it must be the voice of God which Samuel was hearing. He said to the boy, "If he calls you again, then you shall say, 'Speak, Lord; for thy servant heareth.' "

Once again the voice came, "Samuel, Samuel!" And Samuel answered, as Eli had told him, "Speak; for thy servant heareth." Then Samuel had a revelation, a revelation of what all good men in Israel had begun to see must come true. The voice said to him: "Behold, I will do a thing in Israel, at which both the ears of every one that heareth it shall tingle. In that day I will perform against Eli all things which I have spoken concerning his house. When I begin, I will also make an end." And still the voice went on with its judgment of doom against the old priest and his wicked sons.

Samuel lay there until the morning, and then he got up and opened the doors of the temple. He did not want to tell Eli anything about his vision in the night; but Eli called him. "Samuel, my son," he said. "Here I am," said Samuel; and Eli asked: "What is the thing that the Lord has said to you? I pray you not to hide it from me. God visit his judgment on you if you hide anything from me of all the things he has told you."

So Samuel told him everything; and the old man said, "It is the Lord: let him do what seems to him good."

Soon after that war broke out between the Israelites and the Philistines, and the Philistines, as often happened, began to be victorious. Then some of the elders of Israel bethought them of the ark, the same sacred ark which their fathers had brought with them on the march from Sinai, and which had been kept in the shrine at Shiloh. "Let us fetch the ark out of Shiloh," they said, "for when that is in our midst it may save us from our enemies." Then the people went up to Shiloh and brought the ark out of the shrine, and Eli's sons, Hophni and Phinehas, came with it. When the ark arrived in the midst of the camp of Israel, all the army shouted with a great shout, so that the earth rang with it.

In the camp of the Philistines men heard the noise and wondered what it was about. "What does this great shout in the camp of the Hebrews mean?" they asked one another. They did not know that it was the ark which had come. But some of them began to be uneasy. They had a superstitious fear of what they had heard about gods who had smitten the Egyptians with plagues and delivered the fathers of these Israelites in other times. But others among them were of a different temper. "Be strong, Philistines," they said, "quit yourselves like men, and fight." So they fought, and Israel was beaten, and the army fled toward their tents, with heavy loss in the battle. Moreover, the ark of God was captured, and Eli's two sons were slain.

Then a man from the tribe of Benjamin ran from the army and came that same day to Shiloh, with his clothes torn and with dust upon his head. When he came, Eli was sitting on a seat by the roadside, watching, for his heart trembled for the ark of God. As the man came into the city, he panted forth the news, and all the city cried out to hear it.

When Eli heard the noise of the crying, he said, "What does this tumult mean?" Then the man came hurrying in and told Eli. "I am he that came out of the army," he said, "I fled to-day out of the army." "What is done there, my son?" asked Eli. And the messenger said: "Israel is fled before the Philistines, and there has been a great slaughter among the people. Your two sons also, Hophni and Phinehas, are dead, and the ark of the Lord is taken."

As soon as the messenger spoke those words, "The ark of God is taken," Eli collapsed on his seat, and fell from it dead. Also his daughter-in-law, the wife of Phinehas, heard the tidings that the ark was taken and that her husband and her father-in-law both were dead. On that same day her baby was born, and when the women who were with her said, "Do not be afraid, you have borne a son," she did not answer; but she named the child Ichabod (which means, "Where is the glory?"). "For," she said, "the glory is departed from Israel, for the ark of God is taken."

Down into their own country then the Philistines carried the ark in triumph. To the city of Ashdod they brought it first, and set it up in the temple of Dagon, their god. But the next morning when the men of Ashdod came early into the temple, there was the image of Dagon fallen upon its face on the ground before the ark. They took Dagon and set him up again, but on the second morning when they came again the image once more was flat on its face before the ark; and, moreover, Dagon's head and both the palms of his hands lay broken off upon the threshold. Only the stump of the image was left, from which a superstition arose among the Philistines so that neither the priests of Dagon nor any of the worshipers coming into the temple would step upon the threshold.

Moreover, a plague broke out in Ashdod. The inhabitants of the city and of the surrounding country began to be afflicted with boils, and they attributed this to the dangerous magic of the ark. "The ark of the God of Israel shall not abide with us," they said, "for his hand is sore upon us, and upon Dagon our god." So they gathered together all their chief men of Ashdod, and they said, "What shall we do with this ark of the God of Israel?"

They suggested that they get rid of it by sending it on to Gath. To Gath, therefore, they sent it, and presently the same plague of boils broke out there. Gath passed it on to Ekron, but the Ekronites had already heard of the blight which the ark had seemed to spread, and they lost no time in gathering the chief men of Philistia and urging that the ark be sent out of the country altogether. So after the ark had been in Philistia seven months, the local priests and soothsayers were called upon for their advice. They likewise urged that the ark should be sent back to the country of Israel, but they counseled also that it should be accompanied by a gift. According to the old conceptions of sympathetic magic by which an image of the affected part of the body was supposed to have power to carry away with itself the disease which was represented, they advised that there should be sent with the ark five pieces of gold made in the shape of boils, and five golden mice (which may have represented an idea that rats and bubonic plague went together). So the Philistines made a new cart and yoked two cows to it, and on the cart they put the ark, and upon the ark the golden images which were to placate the anger of the Israelites' God. They turned the cows out into the highway toward the nearest point of the borders of Israel, and the cows went off, lowing as they went.

In the valley of Beth-shemesh some of the men of Israel were reaping their wheat harvest, and as they looked up, what should they see but a cart drawing near and on it, to their amazement, the ark! Into the field of a man named Joshua the cows drawing the cart came, and stopped there near a great stone. So the men who were in the field broke the cart to pieces and sacrificed the cattle as a burnt-offering on the stone. And the Philistines who had followed the cart to see whether it would pass over the border returned to their own country, relieved that the ark was gone.

All this narrative reveals, perhaps, the hand of a later priestly writer who has had part in shaping the narratives which now compose the book of Samuel. His impulse was to magnify the awe which clustered round the ark, and he adds a note that the men of Beth-shemesh, because they had looked into the ark, were "smitten with a great slaughter." "Who is able to stand before Jehovah, this holy God," they said, "and to whom shall he go up from us?" So they sent messengers to the people of Kirjath-jearim, and they came down and took the ark and carried it to the house of a man named Abinadab, and there for many years it remained.

Meanwhile Samuel, who once had been the little boy in the temple, had grown up and become the successor of old Eli, the priest, as the chief moral authority in Israel. Before this time there had been men who were called seers. By various signs and omens they claimed to foretell events and to predict their destined outcomes. To these religious fortune-tellers the people resorted and listened to their directions, in which both truth and superstition mingled. But with Samuel, for the first time, appears the name not of seer but of prophet. He was the forerunner of that great line of men in Israel who, with immense and growing moral authority, spoke for God. The old paraphernalia of divination and magic was passing away, and there appeared the new directness of men whose consciences dwelt with the thought of the Eternal and spoke directly to men the truth their souls perceived.

Samuel went about through the various territories of Israel, hearing controversies among the people and giving judgment on all cases submitted to him. Bethel and Gilgal and Mizpeh were the places in which he conducted his hearings; then he would return to Ramah, where he lived. He had two sons who, like the sons of Eli, were men of a different stamp from their father. They took bribes and perverted judgment. Obviously, neither of these could succeed Samuel, and now that Samuel was growing old, a new desire woke in Israel. It was for a king.

Jewish historians looking back from later times saw the desire for a king as a wicked relapse from piety. Their idea was of a nation directly governed by God through his representatives, the priests. That is why there has come into the story this comment:

"The Lord said, 'Hearken unto the voice of the people in all that they say unto thee: for they have not rejected thee, but they have rejected me, that I should not reign over them. According to all the works which they have done since the day that I brought them up out of Egypt even unto this day, wherewith they have forsaken me, and served other gods, so do they also unto thee. Now therefore hearken unto their voice: howbeit yet protest solemnly unto them, and show them the manner of the king that shall reign over them.' "

After he had heard this dark warning, it is no wonder that Samuel is said to have given the people a thoroughly forbidding prediction of what a king would be like. He said that a king would take their sons and make them his own retainers, to drive his chariots and tend his horses and be the soldiers in his armies; that he would put them to work sowing his fields and reaping his harvests and hammering out his weapons; that he would take their daughters and make them his cooks and his servants generally, and that he would take a tenth part of all their seed and their vineyards and their flocks to pay his own retinue. "Ye shall cry out in that day because of your king which ye shall have chosen you," this comment concludes, "and the Lord will not hear you in that day."

Nevertheless, it was a natural instinct which moved the people to desire a king. Israel had been split into tribal units. The various war chiefs who had arisen, like Barak and Gideon and Jephthah, were at best only local deliverers. The nation wanted a leader who would consolidate its strength, especially against the always menacing Philistines. "We will have a king over us, that we also may be like all the nations," they said; "and that our king may judge us and go out before us and fight our battles." So Samuel listened to the people's appeal, and he began to look about to find a fit man for this new time.

It was not long before the man of destiny appeared. In the tribe of Benjamin there was a substantial person by the name of Kish, and he had a son whose name was Saul, "a choice young man, and a goodly." A tall and impressive figure he was, for from his shoulders up he stood above the average of the people.

One day a herd of asses belonging to Saul's father wandered off. "Take one of the servants," said Kish, "and go and hunt for those asses." So Saul went to the country of Mount Ephraim, and on farther afield he went until he had gone past the borders of Benjamin; but he still had not discovered them. At length he said to the servant, "Come, let us go back, for my father will stop thinking about the asses and begin to be anxious about us." But the servant said: "In this town near by there is a man of God who is held in much honor; whatever he says surely comes to pass. Let us go there; perhaps he can tell us the way we ought to go."

"Yes," said Saul. "But if we go, what shall we bring him? Our bread is spent, and we have no present to bring to this man of God." But the servant replied: "I have here the fourth part of a shekel of silver, and I will give it to the man of God to tell us our way." (For he had in his mind the old idea of a sooth-sayer, who would give his divinations for money.)

Saul decided that his servant's advice was good. "Come, then, and let us go," he said; and they went into the city where was the man of God of whom the servant had heard, and who was no other than Samuel himself.

As they went up the hill to the town they found some girls going out to draw water, and asked them, "Is the seer here?" They said: "He is. Look, there he is before you. Make haste, for he is come to-day to our town, for there is a sacrifice of the people to-day in the high place. The people are waiting there, for they will not eat until he comes to bless the sacrifice. Go on up, for about this time you will find him."

Now, Samuel, of course, had been thinking much of the question of a king, and as he prayed, he had had an answering intuition that the man he wanted to find would come to him. When he saw Saul, the voice of God spoke in his heart, "Behold the man I spake to thee of! The same shall reign over my people." Saul had never seen Samuel before; and as he met him, he said, "Tell me, I pray thee, where the seer's house is." And Samuel answered, "I am the seer. Go up before me to the high place; for you shall eat with me to-day, and to-morrow you shall go, and I will tell you all that is in your heart."

As for the asses, he said that Saul could dismiss them from his mind, for they had been found. There was something more important to consider now. "On whom," he said, "is all the desire of Israel? Is it not on you, and on all your father's house?"

Saul was astonished. "I am a Benjamite," he said, "of the smallest of the tribes of Israel, and my family the least of the families of the tribes of Benjamin. Why then do you speak to me in this fashion?"

But Samuel took Saul and his servant and brought them to the place where the sacrificial feast was to be held, and made them sit in the chief place. That evening Samuel took Saul to his own house, and he talked with him upon the flat roof under the stars. The next morning both of them rose early, and Samuel took Saul again up to the housetop when the day was breaking, and then he led him out toward the gates of the town. "Tell your servant to go on ahead of us," he said; and the servant went on out of hearing. "And now," said Samuel, "I will show you the word of God." Then he took a vial of oil and poured it upon Saul's head, and kissed him, and said, "It is because the Lord hath anointed you to be captain over his inheritance." Then he told Saul what should happen to him on his way home, and what he should do. He said that as he came to a certain hill he would meet a company of prophets, singing and chanting (for in those days there were companies of men who lived together as religious devotees, and who by music and ritual worked themselves into ecstatic utterance). So Saul did meet this company of prophets; and in the exalted mood in which he had taken leave of Samuel, he also began to join in their chantings, so that the people said: "What is this that is come upon the son of Kish? Is Saul also among the prophets?"

After that Saul went home, and when he reached there, he met his uncle. Said he to Saul and to the servant, "Where did you go?" And Saul answered, "We went to look for the asses; and when we could not find them anywhere, we came to Samuel." Then said the uncle, "Tell me, I pray you, what Samuel said to you." But all that Saul replied was that Samuel had told him plainly that the asses were found. As to what Samuel had said and done about the kingship, he told his uncle nothing.

That is one story, and evidently an early and simple one, of the way in which Saul was anointed king. The final compiler of the book of Samuel had evidently found it among his sources, and had incorporated it into the history. But there follows also another account which reflects more definitely the later priestly idea that having a king at all was an act of apostasy on the part of Israel from its proper trust in God alone. According to the second account, Samuel sent out a solemn call for all the people to assemble themselves at Mizpeh. Then he said to them: "Thus saith the Lord God of Israel, I brought up Israel out of Egypt, and delivered you out of the hands of the Egyptians, and out of the hand of all kingdoms, and of them that oppressed you: and you have this day rejected your God, who himself saved you out of all your adversities and your tribulations; and you have said to him, Nay, but set a king over us. Now therefore present yourselves before the Lord."

Then as the various tribes of Israel passed before Samuel, he chose the tribe of Benjamin; and when he had sifted out the tribe of Benjamin, he came to the family of Kish, and he called for Saul. But when men looked for him, he could nowhere be found; he had gone and hidden himself in the camp. But someone discovered him, and then fetched him out. And Samuel said to all the people: "Look now at him whom the Lord has chosen; there is none like him among all the people." And all the people shouted, "God save the king!"

CHAPTER XVI

AUL THEN, whether in one way or in the other, had been anointed king of the tribes of Israel. But to be anointed king and to exercise kingship were as yet different matters. The rule which had been conferred by the anointing had to be turned by the man's own courage and authority into fact.

Saul went to Gibeah; and with him there went a band of men whose hearts had been warmed toward him. But there was another group, men who were antagonistic to Saul, who said, contemptuously, "How is this man going to save us?" They despised him, and brought him no gifts. But Saul held his peace.

Presently came the occasion which was to show the manner of man he was. Nahash, chief of the Ammonites, had made a raid upon the town of Jabesh-gilead, which lay exposed to forays of this sort from the eastern deserts. The men of Jabesh-gilead begged for a treaty, naming the terms under which they could surrender, and the only terms which Nahash would give were that he should put out the right eyes of all the men of the town, as an insult to the power of Israel generally. "Give us seven days," said the Jabesh-gileadites, "and at the end of that time, if there is nothing else to do, we will surrender the town." Meantime what they meant to do was to send messengers throughout all the borders of Israel; and they did send a message which reached Saul in Gibeah and told him what was happening. The people who had heard the news first began to lament with one another as to how terrible it was. But Saul did not stop for lamentations. His anger was greatly kindled. He took the yoke of oxen with which he had been plowing, cut them in pieces, and sent these pieces as tokens to all the territory of Israel. Whosoever did not rally to him quickly, he said, should have his own oxen treated in this fashion. So the graphic result was that "the fear of the Lord fell on all the people, and they came out with one consent."

The fighting men of the tribes then gathered about Saul, and he sent the messengers back to Jabesh-gilead to say, "To-morrow, by the time the sun is hot, you shall have help." His deed was as good as his word. By the next day at noon he had fallen upon the Ammonites and routed them completely, and relieved the siege of the town.

Then in the exultancy of victory, someone remembered the men who previously had been contemptuous of Saul. They came and said to Samuel: "Who was it who said, 'Shall Saul reign over us?' Produce those men, that we may put them to death." But Saul himself interfered. "There shall not a man be put to death this day," he said, "for to-day the Lord has wrought salvation in Israel."

After that Samuel brought the people to Gilgal, and they had a great service of reconsecration, and Samuel spoke there to them all. He laid his own record before them: "For," he said, "I am old and gray-headed; and my sons are with you; and I have walked before you from my childhood unto this day." He inquired of them whether any man could witness to any wrong he had done. Had he taken any man's ox or ass? Had he defrauded any man? Had he received from any man a bribe to blind his eyes from justice? And they all cried that he had never done so, and called God to be his witness and theirs. Then Samuel reviewed their desire for a king and how it had led to the choice of Saul. He warned them of the dangers that this might lead to. But he concluded: "Moreover, as for me, God forbid that I should sin against the Lord in ceasing to pray for you, but I will teach you the good and the right way. Only fear the Lord, and serve him in truth with all your heart; for consider how great things he hath done for you. But if you shall still do wickedly, you shall be consumed, both you and your king."

Two years went by, and the men of Israel were sorely pressed by the Philistines. Their worst handicap was that there were no ironworkers in their country. The Philistines had an abundance of swords and spears; but the Israelites in the main were armed only with such rude weapons as mattocks and axes. Nevertheless, Saul summoned the Israelites to gather round him in Gilgal. He waited for a while impatiently for Samuel to come, in order that he might offer up a sacrifice; and when Samuel was delayed, Saul offered the sacrifice himself, to Samuel's great disfavor when later he arrived and learned it.

Meanwhile the forays of the Philistines were growing worse and worse. The Israelites were driven into the fastnesses of the hills, and hid in thickets, and in caves, and in holes among the rocks.

When things were at this pass, there appeared a new and gallant figure. It was Jonathan, Saul's son. By him, for the first time, the tide of the Philistines' triumph was arrested.

On a certain day Jonathan looked over toward the camp of the Philistines on a rocky hill opposite to where the men of Israel were hidden. He said to the young man who was his armor-bearer, "Come, let us go over to the Philistines' garrison which is on the other side." But he had said nothing of his intention to his father, Saul. Saul was camped under a pomegranate tree in the borders of Gibeah, with about six hundred men around him. "There is no restraint with the Lord to save by many or by few," said Jonathan to his armor-bearer; and he replied, "Do what is in your heart; I am with you."

So through a defile between two great rocks Jonathan and his armor-bearer went forward until they were in sight of the Philistines. "If they say, 'Stay there until we come to you,'" said Jonathan, "then we will stand still in our place, and will not go up; but if they say this instead, 'Come up to us,' then we will go up. We shall take that as a sign that the Lord will deliver them into our hands."

So they went out into the open where the Philistines caught sight of them, and the Philistines called to each other, "See there, these Hebrews have come out of the holes where they had hid themselves;" and they shouted tauntingly to Jonathan and his armor-bearer, "Come up to us, and we will show you a thing or two."

So Jonathan said to his companion: "Come on after me. The Lord has given them into the hand of Israel!" Up the side of the hill, therefore, Jonathan went on his hands and knees, and his armor-bearer after him; and the Philistines, seeing these two dare-devils whom they had to deal with, and supposing, doubtless, that it was impossible that they should be alone, but that they must be supported by some other hidden assault about to come from another direction, lost their stomach for the fight and fell back before Jonathan's attack. As they began to retreat, a panic grew, and men began to turn their weapons wildly one against the other. When Saul and his soldiers heard the noise in the Philistines' camp, they advanced to join the battle; and a number of the Hebrews whom the Philistines had taken captive and incorporated in their army, turned against them, so that there was great slaughter and rout, and the Philistines fell back toward their own country, and over their own border as far as Beth-aven.

It seemed as though there could be nothing but rejoicing for the Israelites that day. But it appeared that Saul, whose growing success was tending to make him dictatorial in a way which he had formerly not been, had given an order against any man in his army touching anything to eat that day. He had said with an oath that any one of his soldiers should be put to death if he so much as stopped to touch food until the evening, "in order," he said, "that I may be avenged on my enemies."

The army in general obeyed him to the letter. Not a man touched food that day. Even when they came through a wood and found honey dropping from the trees, none of them touched it, for they had a dread of Saul and of his threat.

But Jonathan had heard nothing of all this. He had not

been with the main body when Saul gave his order. Consequently, when he saw some honey, he thrust the rod which he had in his hands into it, and sucked the honey from that, and felt much refreshed.

A man who saw him came up to him and said, "Your father strictly commanded all the people with an oath, and said, 'Cursed be the man who eats any food this day.'" And the thought of that oath of Saul, and the thought of Jonathan, made men faint.

But Jonathan answered: "My father has troubled the land. Look now and see how I have been refreshed because I tasted a little of this honey. How much better it would have been if the people had eaten freely to-day of the spoil of their enemies which they have found! Would there not have been then a far greater destruction of the Philistines?" So on went Jonathan and the men with him, and they harried the Philistines from Michmash to Ajalon. But by this time the people were faint, not only from apprehension, but from hunger. When they came in among the fields of the Philistines and among their herds, they fell upon the sheep and oxen and calves, and killed some of them and began to eat part of the meat raw.

Then the report was brought to Saul of what the army had done, and he was outraged, not now because the people had eaten, for the day was over, and the battle was done, and his prohibition of food no longer held, but, rather, because that in eating meat with the blood still in it the people had violated a ritual law which had all the force of religion. Saul sent out an order, therefore, for all the people to bring the animals which they had taken up to a great stone, where he built an altar and made a sacrifice to avert what he thought might be the wrath of God.

Having done that, Saul wanted to press the pursuit of the Philistines. He wanted to renew the battle and continue it all night. He tried to get some assurance from God that he would be successful, but he could not seem to get anything that satisfied him.

Then he came to the conclusion that something was wrong. Perhaps his order had been violated and the oath which he made ignored. If so, he was grimly resolved upon correction. "As surely as God lives," he said, "even if it should be Jonathan, my son, who has offended, the man shall surely die." The whole army stood struck into silence. Not a man answered.

Then said Saul, "Stand all the rest of you on one side, and I and Jonathan my son will be on the other side." Then Saul threw lots, and according to the lot the people escaped, but Saul and Jonathan were taken. "Let the lot be cast between me and Jonathan," said Saul. It was done, and Jonathan drew the fatal lot.

"Tell me," said Saul, "what you have done."

"All I did," said Jonathan, "was to taste a little honey with the end of the rod that was in my hand, and so for that I must die."

"If not, may God do so to me and more also," said Saul; "you, Jonathan, shall surely die."

But then the army broke into a tumult. "Shall Jonathan die," men cried, "Jonathan, who has won this great victory for Israel? God forbid! As the Lord lives, there shall not one hair of his head fall to the ground, for he has wrought with God this day." So the people rescued Jonathan from being put to death.

There had been enough fighting and enough bloodshed, and there came a brief time of quiet.

But before long Saul was at war again, against the Moabites and the people of Ammon, and against the Edomites and various other people, and wherever he fought he seemed to succeed.

Seeing this, the prophet Samuel conceived of a particular work for Saul to do. Samuel, although he was in many respects a great man and the forerunner of men still greater than he, was yet possessed by many of the ideas which were a part of the still crude moral conceptions of the time. He believed in that spirit of vengeance above which even the greatest minds had not then risen. He believed in an "eye for an eye, and a tooth for a tooth"; and since the Israelites were the people of God, he believed that it was the will of God that Israel's enemies should be exterminated when the opportunity offered. Particularly, he remembered the Amalekites, a tribe which had been especially determined in their resistance to the Israelites when they were on their march toward Canaan.

So Samuel told Saul that it was the will of the Lord that he, Saul, should lead an expedition against the Amalekites and destroy the whole people, root and branch. Saul had no question of the propriety of what Samuel said. He did lead an expedition against the Amalekites, and conducted it with the same sort of fierce slaughter which had marked some of the campaigns of Joshua. But he took Agag, the king of the Amalekites, alive. Moreover, he kept the best of the sheep and lambs and oxen and calves—everything, in short, that was good among the flocks and possessions of the Amalekites. Whatever was not worth preserving he put to the sword, but the rest he brought back with him as the army's spoil. This he did, of course, not because he was moved to mercy, but because it seemed the practical and profitable thing to do.

When Samuel heard of this, he was deeply perturbed. He had meant this warfare against Amalek to be what he conceived as impersonal justice. He wanted the Amalekites destroyed because he thought of them as the enemies of God. According to a more developed religion, that appears, of course, as a crude and barbaric idea; but it was honest. Samuel regarded the war against Amalek as a consecrated public policy. He had no mind to see it turned to private plunder, and his moral insight told him that this was what Saul had done. Saul's character and ruling motives had crossed a fatal watershed. Formerly he had been willing to serve what he believed to be the will of God. Now he had begun to serve the interests of Saul.

The conviction began to force itself upon Samuel that Saul's days as king were over. Saul had violated his destiny. The acknowledgment of this grieved Samuel bitterly. He prayed all night, and wrestled against his convictions.

Early in the morning he rose up to meet Saul, and the report was brought to him that Saul, having come to Carmel and set up an altar, had turned and passed on again to Gilgal.

There Samuel overtook him, and Saul greeted him very smoothly. "Blessed be thou of the Lord," he said; "I have performed the commandment of the Lord."

But Samuel was not to be flattered or trifled with that day. "What means," he said, "this bleating of the sheep in my ears, and this lowing of oxen which I hear?"

"Oh," said Saul, with a wave of his hand toward his soldiers, "they have brought them from the Amalekites; for the people spared the best of the sheep and of the oxen for a sacrifice unto the Lord your God. All the rest we utterly destroyed."

Then Samuel answered: "Stop, and I will tell you what the Lord has said to me this night."

"Say on," said Saul.

Then Samuel continued: "When you were little in your own sight, were you not made the head of the tribes of Israel, and did not the Lord anoint you king over Israel? Then the Lord sent you on a journey, and said, 'Go, utterly destroy those sinners the Amalekites, and fight them until they are consumed.' Why, then, did you not obey the voice of the Lord? Why, instead, did you go hurrying after plunder, and do evil in the sight of the Lord?"

Still Saul tried to brazen his situation through. "Yes, I have obeyed the voice of the Lord," he said, "I have gone the way which the Lord sent me; I have brought Agag, the king of Amalek, and have utterly destroyed the Amalekites. But the people, the people took of the spoil, sheep and oxen, the best of the things which should have been utterly destroyed, to sacrifice unto the Lord your God in Gilgal."

Then Samuel answered: "Does the Lord have as great delight in burnt-offerings and in sacrifices as in obedience to the voice of the Lord? Behold, to obey is better than sacrifice, and to hearken than the fat of rams. For rebellion is as the sin of witchcraft, and stubbornness is as iniquity and idolatry. Because you have rejected the word of the Lord, he has rejected you from being king."

Before that dire judgment Saul quailed. "I have sinned," he confessed, "for I have transgressed the commandment of the

Lord, and your words, because I feared the people, and obeyed their voice. But now, I pray you, pardon my sin, and turn again with me, that I may worship the Lord!"

But Samuel replied, "I will not return with you, for you have rejected the word of the Lord, and the Lord has rejected you from being king over Israel."

As Samuel turned about to go away, Saul caught hold of the border of his mantle, so that he tore it, and Samuel said: "The Lord has rent the kingdom of Israel from you this day, and has given it to a neighbor of yours, who is better than you. The Strength of Israel will not lie nor repent. He is not a man that he should change his mind."

But Samuel himself had so far softened that he would not reject Saul publicly. He went with him to the great service of worship and thanksgiving which was to be the climax of the victory over the Amalekites. Yet the old prophet's grim conviction as to the destined punishment of Israel's enemies was not abated. He sent for Agag, and with the sword in his own hand he cut Agag down.

There was a long way yet to go between the tribal religion of Samuel and the religion of the later prophets and the religion of Christ; but Samuel was sternly true to what he believed, and no element of self-seeking had entered into his inflexible decisions. Saul, on the other hand, had sold what he believed to be his duty for the double price of plunder and of popularity. From henceforward his life was to descend into the shadows. He went back to his house at Gibeah, while Samuel went to Ramah, and no more until his death did Samuel come to see Saul. Nevertheless, in his heart he mourned that Saul was fallen.

CHAPTER XVII

THE BEGINNING OF THE STORY OF DAVID, SON OF JESSE, AND SHEP-
HERD OF BETHLEHEM, WHO SLEW GOLIATH; WHOM SAUL BEGAN TO
FEAR AND HATE, BUT WHOM JONATHAN LOVED AND DEFENDED.

OW BEGINS one of the most vivid and impor-
tant parts of all the Old Testament history.
It is perhaps the oldest contemporary narrative which has come down to us from the literature of Israel. The preceding books of the
Old Testament are made up, as we have seen,
of fragments of very ancient songs and sayings and traditions,
woven with later material which reflects the point of view of
writers of centuries much subsequent to those of which the
stories tell. But in the books of Samuel, beginning with some
of the account of Saul and going on to the account of Saul's
successor, there is history so vivid, so detailed, and so consistent,
that it seems certainly to have been written by one who himself
lived in that time, and intimately knew the happenings which
he recounts. The story is the story of David, and its author was
one who knew David well. There is reason for thinking that
it may have been Abiathar the priest, and that he wrote in the
tenth century B. C., either while David was living or immediately after his career had come to its end.

Thus the narrative proceeds:

After Samuel had rejected Saul, the time came when he
saw that he must no longer mourn for what was irretrievable.
He must discover another leader to take Saul's place. So the
inward moving prompted him; and it directed him also as to
where he should go to make a choice.

To the little town of Bethlehem, in the borders of the tribe
of Judah, he went. When the elders of Bethlehem saw the stern
old prophet coming into their midst, they trembled. "Are you

come peaceably?" they asked. "Yes, I am come peaceably," he said. He was there to have a religious sacrifice, and the people were bidden to assemble.

Among those who came were a man named Jesse and his sons, the eldest of whom was Eliab. Eliab was a tall, strong man; and when Samuel saw him, he thought that here surely was the person destined to be anointed in God's name. But a more authoritative voice seemed to speak in his heart, correcting him, as though the Lord were saying, "Do not look on his countenance, or on his height; I have refused him. The Lord does not see as man sees; for man looks on the outward appearance, but God looks on the heart."

Then the other sons of Jesse passed before Samuel—Abinadab, Shammah, and four others—and Samuel was convinced that God had chosen none of them. "Are these all the children you have?" he said to Jesse.

Jesse answered, "No, there is still the youngest, but he is keeping the sheep."

Then Samuel said, "Send and fetch him: we will not sit down until he has come."

So Jesse sent and had his youngest son brought. He was ruddy, with great beauty in his face, and good to look at every way. Then it was as though Samuel heard the voice of God himself, "Arise, anoint him: for this is he." So this youngest son of Jesse, whose name was David, Samuel did anoint with the sacred oil, and from that day David bore himself like an inspired man.

Meanwhile it was otherwise with Saul. The spirit of the Lord had departed from him, and an evil spirit troubled him. He fell into dark moods of somber melancholy. His servants were distressed, and they began to wonder what they could do. Perhaps music would help Saul. They would find someone who could play the harp. It might be that the soothing of this would break the spell of the evil spirit which held Saul in its oppression. They begged Saul to let them go and find a harpist, and he consented. Then one of the servants said that he knew the very man. There was a son of Jesse the Bethlehemite, who

RUTH AND NAOMI

DAVID SUMMONED BEFORE SAMUEL

could play skillfully. "Besides," he said, "he is brave and trustworthy and handsome, the sort of man who seems to be marked with the favor of God." So Saul sent a messenger to summon this man of whom the servant had spoken. It was none other than David; and so David came, and for the first time stood in the presence of Saul. He became Saul's armor-bearer; and Saul loved him. Moreover, when the evil spirit came upon Saul, David took his harp and played, and Saul was refreshed, and the dark cloud would lift from his soul.

But not for long. David himself, who by his music gave Saul's spirit peace, was to become an object of Saul's jealousy and to cause the king's black moods to become more deadly than they had been before.

It came to pass in this wise:

War had broken out again with the Philistines. Up into the territory of Judah the Philistines had come in another one of their invasions, and their army was encamped on an hillside by the valley of Elah, and on the other side of the valley was the camp of Israel. Out into the valley every day there came a huge Philistine warrior from Gath, named Goliath. On his head he had an helmet of brass. He was armed with a coat of mail, with greaves of brass upon his legs. He carried a spear with a staff like a weaver's beam; and his armor-bearer went before him with his shield. Toward the army of Israel, he flung his challenge. "What are you come out for?" he said. "Am I not a Philistine? and you are servants of Saul. Choose a man, then, on your part, and let him come down to me. If he can fight me and kill me, then will we be your servants: but if I beat him, and kill him, then you shall be our servants and serve us. I defy the armies of Israel this day," he shouted; "give me a man, that we may fight together."

Even Saul, when he heard that taunt, was dismayed, and all the rest of the men of Israel with him.

Now, the three elder sons of Jesse, the brothers of David, were in Saul's army; but David, meanwhile, had gone back from the service of Saul to take care again of his father's sheep at Bethlehem. One day in this period, when the armies of Israel and the Philistines lay watching one another, and Goliath was hurling his repeated challenge which no man yet had answered, Jesse was thinking of his soldier sons, and he determined to send them a present—some parched corn and bread and cheeses. He came to David and told him to take these to the camp and find out how his brothers were.

So David rose up early the next morning and left the sheep in charge of someone else and went, as his father had bidden him. As he came to the camp there was a great stir in both armies and a noise of shouting as though a battle were about to begin.

David ran ahead until he found his three brothers. Then as he stood there talking with them, out came Goliath, uttering his accustomed defiance, and David heard him. The ranks which were nearest to him drew back, being afraid. Some of the men said to David: "Do you see this man who is coming up? It is to defy Israel that he comes. If any man can kill him, the king will reward him with great riches, and give him his daughter, and make his father's house free in Israel."

But David looked toward Goliath with anger and contempt. "Who is this Philistine," he said, "that he should defy the armies of the living God?"

Eliab, his eldest brother, who was standing by, overheard him, and his resentment flared. "What did you come down here for," he demanded, "and who have you left to keep those few sheep in the wilderness? I know your pride, and your bad heart. You have come down here to look on while we fight this battle."

David wanted to know what he had done that Eliab should take offense at it. There was a reason for what he had been saying, and he would show it presently. He was not afraid of Goliath, and the men in the ranks saw that he was not. Presently the report of this newcomer was passed on to Saul, and Saul sent for him.

Said David, "Let nobody be troubled about this Goliath; I will go and fight with the Philistine."

Saul answered: "You are not able to go against this Philistine to fight with him. You are only a youth, and he has been a man of war from his youth up."

But David had a different conception. "I kept my father's sheep," he said, "and once there came a lion, and another time a bear, and took a lamb out of the flock. I went out after those beasts and slew them, and delivered the lamb. Both the lion and the bear I killed, and this uncircumcised Philistine shall be as one of them, seeing that he has defied the armies of the living God. The Lord who delivered me out of the paw of the lion, and out of the paw of the bear, he will deliver me from the Philistine."

There was a pause, and Saul said to David, "Go, and the Lord be with you." He armed David with his own armor, put an helmet of brass on his head, and girded him with a coat of mail, and gave David also his sword. But David said he could not go in that fashion. He had never tested himself with armor, nor with a sword. He put the armor off, and laid the sword by.

What he did take was his staff and five smooth stones which he chose from the bed of the brook that ran through the valley. These stones he put into the shepherd's bag which he wore at his waist. In his other hand he took his sling, and with these he drew near to the Philistine.

On came Goliath until he was near to David, and the man who bore his shield went in front. And when Goliath caught sight of David, he scoffed. This was nothing but a boy, he thought, and coming against him, so far as he could see, with nothing but a stick. "Am I a dog," he demanded, "that you come to me with staves?" And he cursed David by all his gods. "Come on," he said then, "and I will give your flesh to the birds and the beasts!"

But David answered: "You come to me with a sword, and with a spear, and with a shield: but I come to you in the name of the Lord of hosts, the God of the armies of Israel, whom you have defied. This day the God of Israel will deliver you into my hand; and I will smite you, and take your head from your body; and the carcases of the host of the Philistines I will give this day to the birds and the beasts, that all the earth may know that there is a God in Israel. Yes, this assembly shall know that the Lord does not save with the sword and spear: for the battle is the Lord's, and he will give you to-day into our hands."

Then when the Philistine moved out toward David, David ran toward him. Putting his hand in his bag, he took out a stone and fitted it into his sling. His arm drew back and whirled with a deadly aim. Out from the sling the smooth stone shot whistling through the air. It caught Goliath as he came forward, between the eyes, and sank into his forehead; and the huge fighter pitched over on his face.

As Goliath fell David ran forward and stood over him. He drew Goliath's own sword out of its sheath and cut off his head. When the Philistines saw that, they fled in panic, and the Israelites, shouting, poured after them along the valley and down across the countryside as far as the gates of Ekron. The army took much spoils from the Philistine tents; but the spoil which David was content with was the armor of Goliath.

At first, as the fruit of David's victory, it seemed as though all were well. Saul sent for David, and insisted that he should not go back any more to his father's house. He gave him a post of command in his army. Moreover, Saul's son Jonathan was drawn to David in a great affection. Jonathan gave David his own robe, his sword, his girdle, and his bow. He covenanted with him in a friendship which was never to be broken, for he loved David as he loved his own soul.

But danger was at hand, and it came suddenly. When the campaign was over and the army was coming home from the rout of the Philistines, the women came out of all the cities of Israel, singing and dancing, to meet King Saul and his soldiers. They had a hymn of victory which they chanted: "Saul hath slain his thousands, and David his ten thousands."

Saul heard that, and his pride was wounded. "They have ascribed to David ten thousands," he said, "and to me they have ascribed only thousands." A new suspicion and a swift hatred flared in him savagely. So this was what the crowd thought of

David! "What can he have more but the kingdom?" he brooded, and he eyed David malignantly from that day forward.

Then began a series of attempts by Saul against David's life.

The first of these was on a day when Saul was plunged in one of his black moods of despair. David came and played the harp in his presence, as he had often done before. But this time Saul's javelin was by his hand. As he watched David, and as his eye fell on the javelin, his crafty madness seemed to find its opportunity. "I will smite David to the wall," he said to himself, and he hurled the javelin; but David avoided the weapon as it whistled by.

Then Saul was the more afraid of David, for he knew in his soul that God had departed from himself. His next attempt against David's life was less direct. "See," he said to David, "I will give you my daughter as your wife, provided you will be valiant in my cause and will fight the Lord's battles." That was what he said outwardly, but inwardly he said, "So it will not be my hand that is upon him, but let the hands of the Philistines deal with him."

Then David answered: "Who am I? and what is my life, or my father's family in Israel, that I should be son-in-law to the king?"

Meanwhile, either Saul changed his mind or his eldest daughter changed hers, for she was married to another man. The youngest daughter, however, whose name was Michal, fell in love with David, and Saul was told of it. "I will give her to him," he reflected, "that she may be a snare to him, and that the hands of the Philistines may be against him." Then he instructed his servants, that they were to seem to talk confidentially to David and tell him how much favor Saul had toward him, and how that he could be the king's son-in-law. So Saul's servants poured these words into David's ears; but David asked, "Does it seem to you a light thing to be a king's son-in-law, that you should talk this way to me, a poor man and lightly esteemed?"

Back to Saul, therefore, the servants went and told him what

David had said, and presently Saul had sent them to David once more. They were to suggest to David that the fact that he was a poor man did not matter. Saul was not concerned with having a rich bridegroom for his daughter. What he wanted was a man who should have won new distinctions in battle. Let David go out single-handed against the Philistines and bring back the evidences of men he had killed. Saul knew the mettle that David was made of. He believed that David's reckless courage would fall into the trap which he was setting, and he hoped that, instead of David killing the Philistines, he would be killed himself.

In the first part of his calculations Saul was right. David did go straightway down into Philistia, but he was not killed, as Saul hoped he would be. Instead of that, he brought back double as many trophies as Saul had suggested from Philistines who had fallen before his sword.

There was nothing for Saul to do then but to carry out his terms and to give Michal his daughter to David as his wife.

When David was married thus to Saul's own daughter, and Saul saw that his daughter loved him, Saul was more filled with hatred against him even than before. He began now openly to tell Jonathan his son and all the retinue around him that they were to kill David. But Jonathan loved David, and one day he took him aside and said to him: "Saul, my father, is trying to kill you. Now then, take heed to yourself to-night; stay in some secret place and hide. I will draw my father into conversation about you, and what I find out I will let you know."

Then Jonathan went to his father and appealed to the old, better self that was not yet quite dead in Saul. "It is not fitting for a king to sin against his servant," he said, "David has not sinned against you. Instead, everything he has done in regard to you has been good. He took his life in his hand and slew Goliath, and God wrought a great salvation through him for all Israel. You saw it then and rejoiced; why, then, will you sin against innocent blood and kill David without a cause?"

Saul hearkened and was moved, and he swore to Jonathan, "As the Lord lives, David shall not be slain."

But this change in Saul was only for a moment. When David had come back, Saul began to eye him again with the same smoldering jealousy as before. One day when David was playing the harp before him, he made a second attempt to kill him with his javelin, and for the second time David escaped with his life only because he was quick enough to avoid the javelin which flew past him and quivered in the wall beyond.

David fled away by night, but Saul immediately sent some of his men to stand guard around David's house in the dark and to kill him when he came out. Michal, David's wife, heard what was afoot, or else saw the shapes of men moving outside the window, and she whispered to David, "If you do not save your life to-night, to-morrow you will be slain." She took a rope, therefore, and let him down through the window on the side of the house that seemed unwatched, and so he escaped.

But David needed to gain time. When Saul's men came into the house, they must not know that David had gone. So Michal took an image in the shape of a man and laid it in David's bed, put a pillow under its head, and then drew the bedclothes over it.

Presently Saul's men came knocking at the door. They wanted to see David. But Michal said they could not see him; he was sick.

Instead of forcing their way in, they went back and told Saul. "Go back and bring him, bed and all," said he, "and let me kill him." So this time the would-be assassins beat upon the door of David's house until the door fell in, and they went into his room to find him; but instead of finding him, all that they found was the image which Michal had put in his bed.

David, meanwhile, was miles away. He went and found Samuel in Ramah, and told him all that Saul had done. Saul heard of it, and he sent men in pursuit, and presently he followed in the pursuit himself. But on the way he met a company of prophets, chanting in their ecstatic fashion, and Saul's strange turbulent spirit fell into an ecstasy too, and he stripped off his clothes like a man possessed, and lay naked on the ground all that day and night.

It was hard for David to understand all this. He could not yet see why Saul should hate him. So after Saul had recovered from his frenzy and had gone home again, David came back secretly and sought out Jonathan. "What have I done? What is my sin in your father's sight, that he should seek my life?" he asked.

Jonathan answered: "God forbid that it should be as you think. You shall not die. See now, my father does not do anything either great or small without discussing it with me. Why should he hide this thing from me? It is not so."

But David said, "Your father certainly knows that I have found grace in your eyes, and he does not want you to understand his purpose against me: but as truly as the Lord lives, and as your soul lives, there is but a step between me and death."

Then said Jonathan, "Whatever you want and whatever you ask, I will do."

"To-morrow," said David, "is the new moon. At that time I should not fail to sit at the king's table; but let me go and hide in the fields until evening of the third day. If your father should miss me, then say, 'David earnestly asked leave of me to go to his city, Bethlehem, for there is a yearly sacrifice there for his family.' If he should say, 'Very well,' then I shall have peace; but if he is angry, then be sure that he is planning some evil. If there is evil in me, kill me yourself rather than bring me to your father."

"That shall never be," said Jonathan; "if I surely knew that any evil had been determined by my father against you, would I not tell you of it?"

But anywhere in Saul's house was a dangerous place for that sort of conversation, and a dangerous one for David to be seen. "Come, let us go out into the field," said Jonathan, and out into the field they went.

Then Jonathan, after he had vowed in the sight of God never to break faith with David, and had made David promise that he would never break faith either with him or with his sons after him, went back to the question which David had asked.

"Yes," he said, "to-morrow is the new moon, and it is true that you will be missed, because your seat will be empty. When you have stayed away three days, then come back and hide yourself in this field by that great stone yonder. I will come out and shoot three arrows to the side of it, as though I shot at a mark. And note this: I will send a boy and tell him, 'Go, find the arrows.' If I expressly say to him, 'Look, the arrows are on this side of you, pick them up,' then you can come back, for there will be peace for you and no harm. But if I say to the boy, 'See, the arrows are beyond you,' then flee. The Lord will be sending you away."

As Jonathan had suggested, so David did. He went into hiding out in the fields. When the feast which marked the time of the new moon was ready, the king sat down at his table. Abner was by his side, but David's place was empty.

That day Saul said nothing. He thought some accident had kept David away.

Next morning he saw that David's place was still empty. "Why is the son of Jesse not come to meat either yesterday or to-day?" he demanded of Jonathan, and Jonathan answered as he had arranged with David: "David earnestly asked leave of me to go to Bethlehem. He said: 'I beg of you, let me go, for our family has a sacrifice in the town, and my brother has ordered me to be there.' That is the reason why he is not at the king's table."

At that Saul's anger blazed against Jonathan. "You son of a perverse, rebellious woman!" he cried, "do I not know that you have chosen this son of Jesse to your own confusion? As long as Jesse's son lives on earth, you shall not be established, nor your kingdom. Send and fetch him then, for he shall surely die!"

"Why should he be slain?" asked Jonathan. "What has he done?"

Then Saul's fury so possessed him that he hurled his javelin at Jonathan his son, and Jonathan arose from the table in fierce anger, and ate nothing all that day; for he was grieved for David, and grieved at the shame that his father had done him.

The next morning, at the time appointed, Jonathan went out into the field and took a small boy with him.

"Run," he said to the boy, "and look out for the arrows which I shoot." And as the boy ran, he shot the arrow beyond him. When the boy was come to the place of the arrow which Jonathan had shot, Jonathan cried after him, "Is not the arrow beyond you?" And he cried again, as though to the boy but really to the hidden David: "Go as fast as you can. Do not linger." Meanwhile the boy was gathering up the arrows to bring them to Jonathan. He did not know the meaning of what was happening. So Jonathan handed over to him his bow and arrows, and told him to go and carry them back into town.

When the boy was gone, David rose from the place where he was hidden and saluted Jonathan, and then they kissed each other and wept. "Go in peace," said Jonathan, "for we have both sworn in the name of the Lord, 'The Lord watch between me and thee, between my sons and your sons forever.'" Then David departed, and Jonathan went home.

CHAPTER XVIII

DAVID IS HUNTED AS A FUGITIVE BY SAUL, BUT TWICE REFUSES TO
TAKE SAUL'S LIFE; GATHERS A BAND OF OUTLAWS, QUARRELS WITH
NABAL, BUT IS KIND TO NABAL'S WIFE; IS HUNTED AGAIN BY SAUL,
UNTIL SAUL IS SLAIN AT MOUNT GILBOA.

OR THE last time, now, David had left the king's house. He was never again to go in and out of Saul's presence. He should be an exile, hunted by Saul through strange fortunes, till Saul himself was dead.

When he left Jonathan, David took his way to a place called Nob, where there was a shrine served by a priest name Ahimelech. When Ahimelech saw David, he became uneasy. "Why are you alone," he said, "and no man with you?"

"The king gave me a commission, and told me to let no man know the business on which I was sent," said David. "He told me of his servants who had been appointed in this place and that. Now therefore what have you here? Give me five loaves of bread, or as much bread as you have."

"But this bread in my charge is no common bread," said Ahimelech; "it is holy bread." He wanted to know this and that about David and the men who were with him, to see whether they were fit to be given bread which had been in a shrine, and finally he did give David what he asked.

But there was a man there at Nob that day who belonged to Saul's retinue. He was an Edomite, named Doeg, and he saw and heard what David said and did.

Said David to Ahimelech, "Have you here no spear nor sword? You see, I have brought neither my sword nor any other weapon with me, because the king's business required haste."

201

Yes, there was a sword there. It was the sword of Goliath the Philistine, that very Goliath whom David himself had slain in the valley of Elah. There it was, Ahimelech said, wrapped in a cloth behind the altar. If David wanted this, he could take it. Then David said, "No other sword is like that; give it to me."

When David had gone, Doeg the Edomite lost no time in going back to Saul and telling him what had happened. So Saul sent for Ahimelech and for all his family. "Listen to me, you son of Ahitub," he said.

Ahimelech answered, simply, "Here I am, my lord."

"Why have you conspired against me?" Saul demanded, "you and the son of Jesse, for you have given him bread and a sword; and you have prayed God on his behalf, in order that he should rise against me, and lie in wait, as he is doing this day."

Ahimelech was amazed. "Who among all your servants is as faithful as David?" he asked. "Is he not the king's son-in-law, obedient to your bidding, and honored in your house? Should I begin to ask God concerning him? Far be it from me to have any question concerning him. I would not have the king impute anything to me or to my father's house. I knew nothing of all this that the king has said, nothing either small or great."

"You are going to die, Ahimelech," said Saul, "you and all your father's family."

Then Saul ordered the footmen who stood about him to slay Ahimelech and all his kinsmen; but not a man lifted his hand to do Saul's bidding. Then Saul turned to Doeg. "You come and fall on them," he said, and Doeg did murder Ahimelech and his family. But one of Ahimelech's sons, Abiathar, escaped and fled after David; and when he told David what had happened, David said: "I knew it that day, when Doeg the Edomite was there; I knew that he would surely tell Saul. I have occasioned the death of all the persons of your father's house. Stay here with me, and do not fear. The one who seeks my life seeks yours also; but here with me you shall be safeguarded."

But the whole country of Israel had seemed so full of

menace for David that he fled into the enemy's country, Philistia itself, and into the city of Gath. He feigned to be mad, and went about scrabbling on walls like a man who had lost his wits; but the Philistines found out who he was, and he dared not stay there.

Then he came back across the border into the hill country and took shelter in a cave called Adullam. His brothers and his kinsmen heard that he was there, and they went thither to join him; and, moreover, all sorts of men who were in distress, men who owed debts, and men who were discontented generally, gathered round him. He became the captain over this growing band of outlaws, which amounted presently to four hundred men.

Some of these men who gathered round David were fighters whose exploits were long remembered. One of them was Eleazar, of whom it was told that in a certain time of war he "smote the Philistines until his hand was weary, and his hand clave unto the sword." Another one was Benaiah, the son of Jehoiada, of whom it is recorded that "he slew two lionlike men of Moab; and he went down also and slew a lion in the midst of the pit in time of snow." In no other land of the world, perhaps, save Palestine, could such a thing have been possible; but in the deep tropical gorges by the Dead Sea lions had their lairs, and occasionally one would find his way up to the hills where on the windswept altitudes the winters are cold enough for snow. This same Jehoiada also is said to have encountered once a certain Egyptian, when he himself had nothing but a staff in his hand, but he went down and wrested the Egyptian's spear from his grasp, and slew him with his own weapon.

They were brave men, these who followed David, and David himself was the type of leader who could command men's great devotion. One day he was in arms against a troop of Philistines. Beyond the country where the enemy moved he could see Bethlehem—Bethlehem where as a boy he had lived, and on the meadows round which he had kept the sheep. He looked toward it with the sudden longing which a man has for the place which is sweet with memories. "O that one would give me drink of the water of the well of Bethlehem, which is by the gate!" he said.

Three men of his company heard him say that. They said no word to David, but they determined together what they would do. Through the lines of the Philistines they somehow made their way. Up the hill to Bethlehem they went, drew water from the well which was by the gate, and brought it back again to David. But instead of drinking it, he did a more impressive thing; he poured it out on the ground to the glory of God. That water, he said, was like the blood of men who went in jeopardy of their lives. It was water too holy for any man to drink.

Meanwhile Saul's pursuit was closing in. At length David was nearly caught in the town of Keilah, into which he had entered with his men; but he made his escape and moved farther to the east into the sterile wilderness of Ziph, which plunges downward toward the Dead Sea. Out to him while he was there came Jonathan. "Fear not," he said to David, "for the hand of my father shall not find you; you shall be king over Israel, and I shall be next to you; and that also Saul my father knows." So they renewed the covenant of their friendship before Jonathan went back as secretly as he had come.

But certain men of the region came to Saul and reported that David had his strongholds in the hill of Hachilah. They told Saul to bring his forces down that way, and they, for their part, would help bring David within his grasp. Saul called down upon their heads every blessing he could think of. They were to go and discover exactly where David's haunts were; they were to find out who had sent him there; they were to make sure of every lurking place where he might hide, and then come back to him with certain information, and he would move. He said that if David were in that country, he would search him out if he had to comb through all the population of Judah. So the men who had come to Saul led the way back again, and Saul followed; but David by that time had moved farther south and nearer the shores of the Dead Sea.

To the wilderness of Engedi David went, and thither also Saul pursued. Three thousand chosen men he now had with him, and he hunted David among the rocks where ordinarily only the wild goats moved. So close was his pursuit that he came one day to the mouth of the cave in the shadows of which David and his men were cornered. Unaware, Saul lay down in the mouth of the cave to sleep. It was the day of which the Lord had said, "Behold I will deliver your enemy into your hand," said David's men to him. There was his enemy, and he could stretch out his hand and do with him as he chose. But David stayed his men. He cut off the skirt of Saul's robe as he lay asleep, and even when he had done that, his heart was troubled. "The Lord forbid that I should do this thing unto my master," he said, "to stretch forth my hand against him, seeing he is the anointed of the Lord."

At length Saul awoke, and, unconscious of what had happened, rose and went out of the cave on his way. Then David followed and cried after Saul, "My lord the king!" Saul stopped, looked back, and there was David.

"Why do you listen to the words of people who tell you that David seeks your hurt?" he called. "Look, to-day your own eyes have seen that the Lord had delivered you into my power in the cave. Some bade me kill you; but I spared you, for I said, 'I will not lift my hand against my lord, who is the Lord's anointed.' Moreover, my father, look, look at the skirt of your robe. I cut off the skirt of your robe, and did not kill you; and by that you can know that I have borne you no evil, nor done any wrong against you; and yet you hunt my soul to take it. May the Lord judge between me and you, and the Lord be my avenger; but my hand shall not be upon you. There is an ancient proverb that says, 'Wickedness proceeds from the wicked;' but my hand shall not touch you."

Saul stopped and stared at David, and when David finished speaking, Saul said, "Is this your voice, my son David?" And Saul wept aloud. "You are a better man than I," he said, "for you have returned me good when I had done you evil. You have showed this day how well you have dealt with me. For if a man find his enemy, will he let him go away? But when the Lord had put me in your power, you did not kill me; therefore may God give you a good reward for what you have done this day. And now I know well that you shall surely be king, and that the kingdom of Israel shall be established by your hand. Swear to me by the Lord that you will not cut off my sons after me, and that you will not destroy my name out of my father's house."

So David gave his oath to Saul, and Saul went home. But David went back up into the hills to his stronghold.

Now, in the region where David was there lived a wealthy man named Nabal, who had three thousand sheep and a thousand goats. His wife, whose name was Abigail, was beautiful and of a quick understanding, but Nabal was a churlish man, both in his disposition and in his deeds. David observed Nabal's flocks. His men had been very restrained in regard to them. Moreover, the presence of David's men had served as a protection to Nabal's flocks against possible raiders from the eastern desert, and David decided to send Nabal a suggestion that there was a fitting way by which a rich man could remember these facts.

So he selected ten young men from those who were under him, and sent them up to Carmel, where Nabal lived. They were to greet Nabal in David's name and to bring a peaceful salutation to Nabal and his house. Then they were to speak, as David put it, "to him that lives in prosperity," and they were to say as follows: "I have heard that you are shearing your sheep. Your shepherds were with us, and we did not hurt them. Neither were any of the sheep missing all the while they were in Carmel. Ask your shepherds, and they will tell you so." That was the preliminary statement, and then his messengers were to let Nabal know that any present from him would be very acceptable to this band of free-lances whom thus far David had disciplined very well.

So David's men went up and found Nabal and delivered David's message, and then they waited for an answer. The answer came, ill-tempered and curt: "Who is David? and who is this son of Jesse?" said Nabal. "There are many servants nowadays who break away from their masters. Shall I take my bread and my water and my mutton that I have killed for my shepherds and give it to men as to whom I do not know even where they come from?"

David's men went back and told David what Nabal had said.

Then said David to all his band, "Gird on every man his sword!" And David likewise girded on his sword, and up they went, four hundred of them, to carry a more effective message to Nabal.

Meanwhile somebody in Nabal's household had told Abigail, Nabal's wife, what had happened, told her about David's messengers and Nabal's surly answer, and told her also how it was true that David's men had protected the flocks when they were in the fields. "They were a wall for us both by night and day," the shepherd said, "the whole time we were with them keeping the sheep." Moreover, the shepherd begged Abigail to do something in the situation before it was too late. Neither did he refer very respectfully to Nabal. "He is such a son of the devil," he said, "that a man cannot speak to him."

Abigail lost no time. She took two hundred loaves, two bottles of wine, five dressed sheep, five measures of parched corn, one hundred clusters of raisins, and two hundred cakes of figs, and laid them on asses. She said to some of her servants, "You go on before me, and I will follow." But to Nabal she said nothing at all.

As she rounded the shoulder of the hill, down from the hill-slope came David and his men, and suddenly she found herself confronting them face to face. David was in a dangerous mood. "Evidently it was of no use," he had said, "that I have guarded all that this fellow has in the wilderness, so that nothing was lost of all that belonged to him. For this goodness he has requited me evil." And the thought of that made him so angry that he swore a great oath that he would kill Nabal and every man in his retinue.

When Abigail saw David, she made haste and alighted from the ass on which she was riding, and fell at David's feet, and bowed her face to the ground. "Upon me, upon me, my lord," she said, "is this iniquity. I beg of you, let me speak to you, and give me audience."

Then she went on to tell David how she had known nothing of Nabal's rebuff to his messengers, and she told him of the presents which she herself had brought to him and to his men. Moreover, she showed David that she knew how he had been pursued by Saul, and eagerly she went on: "But your soul shall be bound in the bundle of life with the Lord your God, and the souls of your enemies shall be flung out as in the middle of a sling." She said that some day David would be ruler over Israel, and she begged him now not to shed blood needlessly, nor to do anything which his own heart would be sorry for in time to come.

Then David said to Abigail: "Now may the Lord God of Israel be blessed who sent you to me! Blessed be your advice, and blessed may you be, because you have kept me this day from coming to shed blood, and from avenging myself by my own hand. For in very fact, as the Lord God of Israel lives, unless you had hurried and come to me, certainly by to-morrow morning there would not have been left a single one of Nabal's men." Then he took the gifts which she had brought him and said, "Go up in peace to your house."

But when Abigail came back to Nabal, she found him having a feast in his house, as though he were the king. He was very jovial, for he was drunk; but she told him nothing, either much or little, until the next morning. Then when he had got over his drunkenness and she told him all that had happened, his heart died within him, and he became like a stone. Ten days after that he was dead.

When David heard that, he came to see Abigail, and before long he married her. Saul, in the meantime, had taken away his daughter Michal, who had been David's wife. But David had married also another wife by the name of Ahinoam, for in those times to have more than one wife was a familiar custom, and men had not begun to extend to women the dignity which in later centuries they learned to give.

But David's perils were not yet over. Once again, and for the last time, Saul came out to hunt him in the wilderness. David's scouts brought him word of Saul's approach, and David came along the rocky ravines to the place where Saul's camp was pitched. He said to two of his men, Ahimelech and Abishai, "Who will go down with me to Saul's camp?" and Abishai said he would. So those two crept toward Saul's camp under the cover of night, and there lay Saul, with Abner his chief captain, and the rest of his men around him. Saul's spear was stuck into the ground by the bolster on which he lay. Abishai whispered to David: "God has delivered your enemy into your hand this day. Now I beg you let me drive this spear through him into the earth. I will not need to do it a second time." But David forbade it. He would not do any violence against the man whom the Lord had anointed. When Saul's time came, let him perish in battle, not by any such killing as this. But David took Saul's spear and flask of water that was by his head, and he and Abishai passed out of the camp again without any man having waked or known that they were there.

To the slope of an opposite hill David went; and through the wide spaces of the night between, he shouted. In the camp of Saul there was the sudden confusion of men waking. "Abner," came the voice of David. "Abner, can't you answer?"

"Who are you that cries to the king?" Abner called back.

"What sort of a valiant man are you?" said David, "you who are supposed to have no match in Israel! Why have you not guarded your lord the king? For someone has been there who might have killed the king. As the Lord lives, you deserve to die, because you have not protected your master, the Lord's anointed. Now look and see where your king's spear is, and the flask of water."

Then Saul knew David's voice, and he said, "Is that your voice, my son David?"

And David answered, "Yes, it is my voice, my lord the king.

Why do you pursue after your servant in this fashion? What have I done, and what evil has been in me?" And he went on again to ask what it was, or who it was, that had made Saul drive him out thus and hunt him as one hunts a partridge in the mountains.

"I have sinned!" cried Saul. "Come back, my son David. I will do you harm no more, because my soul was precious in your sight to-day. Look, I have played the fool, and have erred exceedingly!"

"Here is the king's spear!" David said; "let one of your men come over and fetch it. The Lord put you in my power to-day, but I would not stretch out my hand against the Lord's anointed. As your life was regarded by me this day, so may my life be regarded in the eyes of the Lord, and may he deliver me out of this tribulation."

And Saul answered: "May God bless you, my son David. You shall do great things, and you shall still prevail." But David knew better than to trust himself to Saul's uncertain moods, and he withdrew into the darkness of the hill.

Moreover, it seemed to him so hopeless finally to escape Saul's pursuit within the country of Israel that he determined again upon the desperate expedient of flight into Philistia. With six hundred men, therefore, he passed over the border and went to Achish, who was the ruler of the city of Gath. With that many men at his back, he might be of use to Achish, and he asked Achish to give him a town where he could live. There he lived for more than a year, and he made war against some of the hostile peoples who were neighbors of Philistia, so that Achish began to think that David and his men were valuable allies.

The somber career of Saul was drawing now to its end. Once more war flared up between Israel and the Philistines. And this time Saul had a premonition of disaster.

The great old prophet Samuel was dead. All Israel had lamented him, and had buried him in Ramah, from which his influence had swayed the people for so many years.

The army of Saul had gathered on the slopes of Mount Gilboa, and opposite them lay the Philistines. When Saul looked at the enemy, his heart trembled. He tried to find out some sort of token that would give him hope of victory, but there was none. Well, then, he would find someone who would communicate with the spirits. There were people who were supposed to have weird powers of summoning up the dead. Such a one, a witch if necessary, he would discover, and find out what his soul was tormented to know.

He was told that there was a witch at Endor; so he disguised himself, and, taking two men with him, he came by night to this woman. Could she hold commerce with the world of spirits? Would she bring up from the dead someone whom he should name? She did not recognize Saul, but she was wary. "You know what Saul has done," she said, "how he has tried to drive out of the land those who have familiar spirits and those who are wizards; you are laying a snare for my life." But Saul swore to her by the name of God that no punishment should fall upon her for anything she might do. Then said the woman, "Whom shall I bring up for you?" And he said, "Bring me up Samuel."

Suddenly a flash of understanding came to her, and she shrieked, "Why have you deceived me? You are Saul!"

But the king said to her: "Do not be afraid. What were you seeing?"

And the woman answered, "I saw gods ascending out of the earth." Then she went on: "An old man comes up; and he is covered with a mantle."

Saul perceived that it was Samuel, and he stooped, and bowed his face to the ground.

Samuel said to Saul, "Why have you disquieted me, to bring me up?" And Saul answered, "I am sore distressed, for God is departed from me, and answers me no more, neither by prophets, nor by dreams: that is why I called you, that you may tell me what I should do."

But in Samuel's answer there was no comfort for Saul, but only terror. Why should Saul ask anything of Samuel now, since the spirit of God had abandoned him? The kingdom was rent from his hand, and should be given to David. Moreover, by to-morrow, Saul and his sons should be ghosts like the ghost he saw.

When Saul heard that, he fell headlong upon the ground. All his strength collapsed, for he had eaten nothing all day and all that night.

By this time the woman had come out of her trance, and she was frightened, and compassionate also. She brought Saul some bread and begged him to eat, but he refused. Then the woman and his servants together compelled him. They lifted him up from the ground, and sat him upon a bed, and made him eat. At length he rose up and went away, while it was still night.

In the meantime it seemed as though David should be caught in the necessity of fighting against his own people. Achish had wanted to take David and his men with him, as the Philistines went up to the battle against Saul; but the rest of the Philistines remembered David of old, and were not willing to risk his presence in their ranks. So Achish sent David back into Philistia. And there David shortly had fighting of his own, for with the Philistine armies on the march, the Amalekites had attacked the country from the rear, and taken and sacked one of the Philistine cities. But David arrived in time to pursue the invaders, overtake them and destroy them, and rescue all the captives and the spoil which they had taken. This spoil he sent as a gift to the chief men of Judah, where so long he had been a fugitive and an outlaw in the wilderness. And the favor which he won thereby was presently to stand him in good stead.

But to the north a more tragic thing was happening. Under the slopes of Mount Gilboa the battle had been joined. Upon Saul and upon his sons the Philistines pressed hard. Saul's lesser sons were killed, and then the greatest also. There on the battle field of Mount Gilboa, fell Jonathan. Saul only now was left. He was sorely wounded by arrows; the last hour had come, and he knew it. "Draw your sword," he said to his armor-bearer, "and thrust me through, lest these uncircumcised Philistines come and kill me insultingly." But his armor-bearer would not, for he was afraid. Then Saul drew his own sword, and, turning the point of it against himself, he fell upon it. His life, like a parable, had come to its predestined climax. He had destroyed himself.

When the armor-bearer saw that Saul was dead, he likewise fell on his sword, and died with Saul.

Then when the men of Israel saw that Saul and his sons were dead, they fled, abandoning all the cities round about, so that the Philistines entered in and occupied them. Moreover, the Philistines took Saul's armor and set it up in the temple of Ashtaroth, and with cruel and barbarous triumph they fastened his body against the walls of Beth-shan. But valiant men out of Jabesh-gilead went by night and rescued the bodies of Saul and his sons, and burned them with fire, and buried their ashes under a tree.

While the battle in which Saul had come to his death was being fought, David had returned from his pursuit of the Amalekites who had sacked the Philistine city of Ziklag, and into his presence there stumbled a man with his clothes rent and earth upon his head.

"Where have you come from?" said David; and the man answered, "Out of the camp of Israel I have escaped."

"What happened there?" said David; "tell me!"

"The army has fled from the battle," the man replied; "many are fallen; and Saul and Jonathan his son are dead."

Then fiercely David asked, "How do you know that Saul and Jonathan his son are dead?"

And now the man who had brought the tidings proceeded to a lie which he thought would be shrewdly advantageous. Had not Saul hunted David and tried to kill him? Did not David have good reason to be glad that Saul was dead? And if a man should say that he had helped to bring Saul to his death, what would be more natural than that David should reward him? So to the truth of Saul's death, the man added a tale of his own. "It happened by chance," he said, "that on Mount Gilboa I saw Saul leaning on his spear. Chariots and horsemen were rushing toward him. He looked behind him, and saw me, and called me. 'Who are you?' he said. I answered, 'I am an Amalekite.' And he said, 'Stand over me and kill me, for my coat of mail hinders me.' So I stood over him and slew him, because I was sure that he could not live after he was fallen: and I took the crown that was on his head, and the bracelet from off his arm, and I have brought them hither, my lord, to you."

But to the man's amazement, David took hold of his clothes, and rent them, and all the men that were with him followed his example. And they mourned until evening for Saul and Jonathan, and for all the men who had fallen by the sword.

Then David sent again for the man who had told him the story of Saul's death. "Where did you come from?" he asked.

The man answered, "I am the son of a stranger, an Amalekite."

"How is it that you were not afraid to stretch your hand out to destroy the anointed of the Lord?" demanded David. "Your blood be on your own head, for your own mouth has testified against you." And he commanded one of the guards who stood by to put the man to death.

Moreover, David, with the memories of the old days still dominant over all the bitter later memories of Saul, poured out his lament for Saul and Jonathan:

"The beauty of Israel is slain upon thy high places:
How are the mighty fallen!
Tell it not in Gath, publish it not in the streets of Askelon;
Lest the daughters of the Philistines rejoice, lest the daughters
of the uncircumcised triumph.
Ye mountains of Gilboa, let there be no dew, neither let there
be rain, upon you, nor fields of offerings:
For there the shield of the mighty is vilely cast away, the shield
of Saul, as though he had not been anointed with oil.
From the blood of the slain, from the fat of the mighty, the
bow of Jonathan turned not back,
And the sword of Saul returned not empty.

Saul and Jonathan were lovely and pleasant in their lives, and
in their death they were not divided:
They were swifter than eagles, they were stronger than lions.
Ye daughters of Israel, weep over Saul, who clothed you in
scarlet, with other delights,
Who put on ornaments of gold upon your apparel.
How are the mighty fallen in the midst of the battle!
O Jonathan, thou wast slain in thine high places.
I am very distressed for thee, my brother Jonathan: very pleas-
ant hast thou been unto me:
Thy love to me was wonderful, passing the love of women.
How are the mighty fallen, and the weapons of war perished!"

CHAPTER XIX

HE FIELD was now clear for David to press
forward to that kingship which long before
Samuel had prophesied. With the men who
followed him he went into the country of the
tribe of Judah and to the city of Hebron, and
there the Judæans anointed him to be their
king. They told him that it was the men of Jabesh-gilead who
had rescued the body of Saul and buried it. So David sent messengers to these townsmen, invoking the blessing of the Lord
upon them for what they had done, and inviting their fealty,
because, he said, "Your master Saul is dead, and the house of
Judah have anointed me king over them."

But some of the tribes to the north, under the leadership
of Abner, Saul's commander in his army, took Ishbosheth, Saul's
son, and made him king. So there was civil war, and in the first
clash the forces led by Abner were driven back. One of the
brothers of Joab, who was the commander of David's troops,
pursued after Abner himself, and, when Abner tried to dissuade
him from combat, he pressed on until Abner turned against
him and killed him with his spear. Then the men of Joab followed until they overtook Abner's forces gathered on the top
of a hill, but before the fighting was joined again, Abner called
to Joab: "Shall the sword devour forever? Do you not know
that there will be bitterness in the latter end? How long will it
be, therefore, before you bid the people turn from following
after their brethren?" Joab stopped and listened. He blew
his trumpet, and summoned his men back.

But, intermittently, war between the adherents of Saul's

216

son and the adherents of David went on, and the party of Saul grew weaker and weaker. At length there broke out a bitter personal quarrel between Ishbosheth and Abner, and so enraged was Abner that he told Ishbosheth that he would desert him and give his loyalty to David. He sent messengers to David, and told him that this was what he meant to do.

Furthermore, Abner communicated with the chief men of the northern tribes. He said to them, "In times past you wanted to make David king over you. Now, then, do it, for the Lord has spoken of David, saying, 'By the hand of my servant David I will save my people Israel out of the hand of the Philistines, and out of the hand of all their enemies.' " Within the tribe of Benjamin also he spread this same suggestion, and then with a guard of twenty men he went down to David in Hebron. He said to David, "I will arise and gather all Israel unto my lord the king, that they may make a league with you, and that you may reign over all that your heart desires." So he and David entered into an agreement.

But shortly after Abner had left David, Joab and a detachment of men who had been off on a foray returned, and Joab heard the news that Abner had been to David and talked with him, and had gone off in peace. Then Joab said to David, "What have you done? When Abner came to you, why did you send him away? Do you not know that Abner came to deceive you, and spy out your movements, and learn what you mean to do?"

So Joab sent messengers secretly after Abner, and summoned him back to Hebron, and when Abner came unsuspecting, Joab drew him aside to the gate, as though to speak with him there in confidence, and he stabbed him in the side, so that Abner died. Thus, he said, he had revenge for his brother's death at the hand of Abner.

When David heard this, he was outraged. He called God to witness that he and his kingdom were innocent of Abner's blood. "Let it rest on Joab's head, and on the head of his descendants after him!" Moreover, he said to Joab and all his men: "Rend your clothes, and put on sackcloth, and mourn before Abner's body," and he himself followed after Abner's bier; and when they buried Abner, David wept at his grave, and said: "Did Abner die as a fool? Your hands were not bound, nor your feet put into fetters: as a man falls before wicked men, so thou didst fall." When his servants came to summon David to his dinner, he replied, "May God smite me if I taste bread, or aught else, till the sun goes down." When all the people heard that, it pleased them, as, indeed, whatever the king did pleased the people in that time, and they understood that it was not because of David that Abner had come to his death. "A prince and a great man has fallen this day in Israel," David said. And his heart was sore for the hardness of Joab.

Even through the bitterness of civil war there was something great-hearted in David which made him hate all treachery. There were loyalties in his life which he never lost, and two men were to discover this to their cost. In the retinue of Saul's son, Ishbosheth, who still held precariously to his kingship over the northern tribes, there were two brothers by the names of Rechab and Baanah. One day at noontide, when Ishbosheth was lying on his bed in his house during the heat of the day, they walked into the house, pretending that they were carrying in some wheat. But what they did was to break into Ishbosheth's room, stab him to death, and brutally cut off his head. Immediately they made their escape, and when the darkness came, they traveled until they came to David. "Here," they said, "is the head of Ishbosheth, the son of your enemy Saul, who sought your life, and the Lord has avenged the king this day of Saul and of his descendants."

But David was aghast. "As God lives," he said, "who redeemed my soul out of all adversity, when a man came and told me, 'Behold, Saul is dead,' thinking that I would take it as good news, I took hold of him and slew him in Ziklag, when he thought that I would have given him a reward. How much more when scoundrels have slain an innocent man in his own house on his bed shall I not require his blood of you, and wipe you off the earth?" So David commanded them to be killed, and Ishbosheth he buried in the tomb with Abner.

Once again he was to show his magnanimity toward the family of Saul. Saul's son Jonathan, David's most loved friend, had had a child who was five years old when the tidings came of the fatal battle in which Saul and Jonathan died. When the nurse heard of it, she picked up the child and fled, and, as she fled, she stumbled and fell, and the child was hurt so that ever afterward he was lame. One day David asked of those around him: "Is anyone left now of the house of Saul? If there is, I should like to show him a kindness for Jonathan's sake." It happened that there was a man near by who had formerly been of Saul's servants, and someone sent for him to come to David. David asked, "Is there anyone left now of the house of Saul, that I may show the kindness of God to him?" And the man answered, "There is still a son of Jonathan, who is lame." "Where is he?" said David, and the man told him.

Then David sent and had Jonathan's son, whose name was Mephibosheth, brought to him. And the boy came terrified; but David said, "Do not fear, for I will certainly show you kindness for your father's sake, and will restore to you the lands of Saul, and you shall sit at my table constantly." So Mephibosheth lived with David from that time on.

There were no rivals left now of David's kingship, and the civil strife died out. Representatives of the northern tribes came down to Hebron, and they said to him: "We also are of your bone and of your flesh. In times past, even when Saul was king, it was you who led the men of Israel out to war and brought them home again." Now, they said, it was time for David to be the acknowledged king over all Israel, and so they anointed him. David was then thirty years old, and it had been seven years since Saul and Jonathan fell.

With the tribes united behind him, David could begin to make successful war against the hostile neighbors of Israel, and to consolidate and extend his power. He carried out successful campaigns against the tribes along the borders of the desert to the east of the Jordan, in Moab, Edom, and Ammon, and also against the powerful civilization of Syria in the north, as well as against the old enemy, the Philistines, in the west; but the most important thing he did was to direct an assault against Jerusalem. That natural citadel, lifted upon its dominating hill, had never been subdued in all the years since Joshua had led the Israelites into Canaan. The Jebusites held it, and so strong did it seem that they answered David with confident insults when he appeared before their walls. But David captured Jerusalem, and the city which thereafter was to become the center and shrine of the life of Israel was his, and he set up his residence in its fort. Later his growing power led to a contact with Hiram, king of Tyre, and from that richer city carpenters and masons came down to Jerusalem, bringing cedar wood from the Lebanons to build David a royal house of his own.

At this time David bethought him also of the ark. Ever since that time shortly after the death of the old priest Eli, when it had been captured by the Philistines and then sent back by them across the borders of Israel because of an outbreak of the plague which the Philistines attributed to its presence, the ark had remained in the house of Abinadab in Gibeah. David considered that it ought to be in Jerusalem. So David sent for it, and after various misadventures, it was at length successfully escorted into the newly captured city, and there installed in a tabernacle as a symbol of the presence of God.

But now it was to be shown in the life of David, as it has been shown in the lives of other men before him and since, that prosperity may be more perilous than adversity. In the early days of his hardships and his dangers David had been brave, generous, and in the main self-disciplined. Now he had new power, and with that power new temptations.

At a time when his army under the command of Joab was in the field against the Ammonites, David was in Jerusalem. When evening came, he was restless. He got up from his bed where he was lying and walked out upon the roof of his house. From there he looked down, and he saw a woman bathing, and the woman was beautiful.

David had inquiry made about her. He discovered that her name was Bath-sheba, and that she was the wife of a man named Uriah. Uriah was a soldier in David's army, off somewhere in the field against the Ammonites. David sent messengers to Bath-sheba; he persuaded her to come to his house; he was in love with her, and she yielded to his passion.

But what now of Uriah?

David was concerned, of course, about what would happen. He sent a communication to Joab, commander of his army, with orders that Uriah should be sent back to him. He wanted to see whether Uriah could come back without learning anything, and go back to his house as though nothing had happened. But Uriah, a blunt and courageous fighting man, was indignant at having been sent for. "Israel and Judah and the ark of the Lord are in tents," he said, "my lord Joab and the army are camped in the open fields. Shall I go down to my house and to my wife, and eat and drink? As certainly as you live, and as my soul lives, I will not do it." So he turned to go back to the army.

It was plain that Uriah was a more formidable person than David had reckoned. David, being involved in one wrongdoing, moved on to an even deeper one. He must get rid of Uriah. So by Uriah's own hand he sent a sealed letter to Joab, in which he directed that Uriah should be put in the hottest part of the next battle, deliberately isolated there, and then—then let the Ammonites take care of that.

Joab followed his instructions. In the next fight Uriah was put where he would be most likely to be killed, and killed he was. And when David heard it, he sent back to Joab this unctuous and disgraceful message: "Do not let this fact distress you, for the sword devours one as well as another." Shortly afterward, when what seemed to be a decent period of mourning by Bath-sheba for her husband had passed, David sent and brought her to his house, and she became his wife, and bore him a son.

But the chapter was not yet closed. There was a man in Jerusalem whose eyes were not blind to what had happened.

Neither was his heart afraid. His name was Nathan, and he was one of that succession of prophets in whom the moral passion burned like a divinely kindled flame. In this man's soul the voice of God was speaking, and he did not fear the face of any man.

To David he came one day and began to tell David a story. It sounded like a literal recital of fact, and that is what David thought it was. Nathan, it seemed, had come to ask the judgment and the verdict of the king on something which had happened in his kingdom.

This is what he said:

"There were two men in one city, one of whom was rich, and the other poor. The rich man had exceeding many flocks and herds, but the poor man had nothing save one little ewe lamb which he had bought and nourished. It grew up together with him and with his children. He fed it morsels of his own food, and gave it to drink from his own cup. He carried it in his bosom as though it were his child.

"One day there came a traveler to the rich man, and the rich man would not take of his own flock or herd to provide for this wayfarer who had come to him; but he took the poor man's lamb, and killed that for the wayfaring man who had come."

Nathan stopped, and looked at David. As he had expected, David's anger flared swift and hot. "By the living God," he said, "the man who has done this thing shall surely die, and he shall restore the lamb fourfold, because he did this thing, and had no pity!"

Nathan had accomplished his end. Unwittingly but infallibly David had condemned himself. The prophet's voice grew stern. "Thou," he said as he confronted the amazed and defenseless David, "thou art the man!"

Then with terrible directness he went on to lay bare David's sin before his own eyes. He reviewed all the mercies which God had shown to David. He drew in its stark outlines the crime which David had committed against Uriah. He had done this thing secretly; but God's punishment, Nathan said, would

ELIJAH AND AHAB

THE FINDING OF THE BOOK

be before the eyes of all Israel, and as terrible as the clear shining of the sun.

There was nothing for David to reply. In three words he made his unqualified confession. "I have sinned," he said.

Then Nathan told him that the child who had been born to him of Bath-sheba should die.

All that day David fasted, and all night he lay upon the earth. The child was sick, and he besought God for him. The servants of his household tried to raise him from the ground, but he would not let them, and neither would he eat.

On the seventh day the child died.

When the servants in David's house knew that the child was dead, they were afraid to tell David. "He would not listen to us while the child was living. What will he do if we tell him that the child is dead?"

When David saw them whispering together, he understood. "Is the child dead?" he asked, and they answered, "He is dead."

Then David rose from the earth, washed, and changed his apparel, and went into the house of God and worshiped. Then he came back to his own house, and asked for bread, and ate.

Those who were about him were astonished. "What is this that you have done?" they said. "You fasted and wept for the child when it was alive; but now that the child is dead, you rise and eat bread."

But David answered: "While he was living, I fasted and wept: for I said, 'Who can tell whether God will be gracious to me, that the child may live?' But now that he is dead, why should I fast any more? Can I bring him back again? I shall go to him, but he shall not return to me."

CHAPTER XX

ANOTHER TRAGEDY was to come to David, this time not through his own sin but through his irresolution in dealing with the evil of another.

Among his sons the most brilliant and attractive was Absalom. Absalom had a beautiful sister named Tamar. Another one of David's sons, Absalom's half-brother, Amnon, fell in love with his own half-sister, Tamar, and committed a brutal crime against her. When Absalom heard this, he conceived toward Amnon a hatred which hardened into an unwearying determination to take vengeance. Two full years he waited for his occasion to come. He had expected that David himself would deal with Amnon; but David, though he too had been very angry, had done nothing. Then Absalom planned a feast in connection with the time of sheepshearing. He asked his father to come and all his brothers. Particularly he wanted Amnon. David did not go, but the rest of the family did. Absalom saw to it that all his brothers were well supplied with wine; and when the party was at its height, his servants fell upon Amnon and killed him.

There was a great outcry and panic. All the other brothers of Absalom got to their saddles and rode off as fast as they were able. But the report of Amnon's killing somehow ran ahead of them and grew with the excited telling. The message was brought to David that all his sons had been killed by Absalom and that not one of them was left. One of David's nephews who was with him was shrewd enough to disbelieve this. David would find, he said, that only Amnon was dead, for it was against Amnon that for these two years past Absalom had been cherishing his purpose of revenge. It turned out presently to be as he had said. The watchman on the tower of David's house saw a company of people riding round the slopes of the hill, and when these drew near, they proved to be the group of David's sons escaping from Absalom with the tidings of Amnon's death.

Absalom meanwhile had fled; and David missed Absalom more than he missed Amnon. Now Joab, David's army commander, saw his feeling toward Absalom, and he devised a ruse to persuade David to bring Absalom back. He brought in to David a woman clothed in mourning who said she had come from Tekoah, and she told David a story which Joab had put into her mouth. She was a widow, she said, with two sons, and as they fell to fighting one day in the field and no one was near to part them, in reckless anger one of them struck the other and killed him. All her family, she said, had demanded that her living son be delivered up and be put to death for killing his brother. She begged the king to help her shield her son's life. "As God lives," said David, "there shall not a hair of your son fall to earth."

Then the woman admitted why she had come. If the king could promise to shield one man who had killed his brother, then why not another, why not Absalom?

David was not loath to listen. He guessed that it was Joab who had instructed this woman to entrap him with her tale, and she admitted that it was. So David sent for Joab, and he told Joab to go and find Absalom and bring him home.

When Absalom came, however, David would not see him. He had not brought himself to punish Absalom, but neither now could he deal with Absalom in such a way as might have made him into a new man. He merely sent Absalom to his own house in Jerusalem and commanded that Absalom should not see his face.

But Absalom, established now in Jerusalem, was not idle. He saw his chance and he pursued it. The people of the city admired him for his extraordinary beauty. He had a handsome face, surmounted by a magnificent head of hair which he allowed to grow long. Absalom began to be more popular with the crowd than David was. Meanwhile the months went by and Absalom had no speech with his father the king.

He sent for Joab and demanded that Joab do something to restore him again into his father's favor. But Joab did not come when Absalom sent for him, nor did he come when Absalom sent a second time. The arrogant young prince determined that he would rouse Joab's attention in a more effective way. Next to where he lived there was a field belonging to Joab in which a crop of barley was ripening. Absalom had his servant set fire to Joab's field, and when Joab came then to demand why Absalom had done it, Absalom told him. Why had Joab brought him from his exile to leave him in this fashion? He might better have stayed where he was than to have come back to Jerusalem and be shut out from contact with the king.

Joab came to David and told him this, and David allowed Joab to bring Absalom into his presence; and he kissed this son of his with the old affection which he had never lost.

Whatever affection Absalom had, however, was only a small thing in the balances against his ambition. To-day his father was king. To-morrow there might be a different story.

He acquired for himself horses and chariots, and he had fifty runners who went before him when he drove through the streets. In the mornings he got up early and went out to the city gate, the place where the ordinary people gathered for their discussions and where complaints were heard, disputes settled, and agreements made. If any man came who had had a controversy which needed some judgment from the king, Absalom would ask him where he came from, and the man would tell him that he belonged to such and such a one of the tribes. "Yes," Absalom would reply, "this matter of yours is a good one and you have right on your side, but nobody has been deputed by the king to hear you." And then he would add, "Oh, if I were judge in this land, every man who has had any suit or cause for complaint could come to me, and I would do him justice." And when these men to whom he had spoken in this fashion stooped to make obeisance before Absalom, Absalom put out his hand and drew each man to him and embraced him instead.

It was not long before the report was spread through all the tribes of Israel as to the manner of man that Absalom was. Little by little he stole away the hearts of the people from David.

At length the time came when Absalom believed his opportunity was ripe. He asked David's permission to go down to Hebron, because he said he had a religious vow to pay there. But such was not the real reason why Absalom wanted to go to Hebron. It was in Hebron that David first had been crowned king, and it was in Hebron that Absalom proposed that another king should be crowned instead. He sent secret messengers out among all the tribes saying, "As soon as you hear the sound of the trumpet, then you shall know that Absalom reigns in Hebron."

With two hundred men, therefore, but without any display which might cause suspicion, Absalom left Jerusalem. Quickly the conspiracy spread, and the numbers favoring Absalom increased.

When the news came to David, the situation seemed already beyond control. "The hearts of the men of Israel have gone after Absalom," was the message which was brought to him. With Absalom in rebellion and with the people everywhere apparently rising to support him, it seemed to David that he could no longer hold Jerusalem. Remembering what Absalom had done to Amnon, he knew what might happen now. He told his servants to prepare for instant withdrawal.

With six hundred men, therefore, David fled from Jerusalem. There was one of his servants who had been with him only a little while, and David tried to persuade him to go back and remain in Jerusalem. This man had not been sufficiently identified with his own fortunes to be in danger, David thought, and there was no need for him to share his downfall now. But this man answered, "My lord the king, in whatever place you

are, whether in life or death, there also will your servant be."
So he clung to David, as did the others; and the people along
the way wept as they saw the king go out across the brook
Kidron and up over the Mount of Olives and on toward the
wilderness country to the east.

Zadok and Abiathar, the priests, and the Levites had also
come out with David, bringing the ark of God from Jerusalem.
But David bade Zadok and Abiathar to go back and take the
ark with them. The priests would be safe, he said. They
could, if the time should come, send David messages from
Jerusalem. Moreover, David sent back another man named
Hushai to be his secret agent in the city. He told him to go
there, and if Absalom came to Jerusalem to tell Absalom that
he had deserted David and had come to be a servant of the new
king. He was to keep in touch with Zadok and Abiathar, the
priests, and send out to David any news within the city which
he might learn.

But on the road David had two other evidences of the way
in which the general opinion thought that his kingship was at
an end. He met a man with a couple of asses saddled and laden
with loaves of bread and an hundred bunches of raisins, fruits,
and wine. The man was Ziba, the servant who years before had
told David about Mephibosheth, Jonathan's lame son whom
David had then brought into his own household and befriended
ever since. "Ziba," said David, "what do these laden asses
mean?" And Ziba acknowledged that they had been sent for
by Mephibosheth, who was in Jerusalem and who thought that
he himself now was going to succeed to the kingdom of his
grandfather Saul.

Farther along the road a man named Shimei, who was a
relative of Saul's, came out and cursed David as he went by.
"Oh, so you are come out, you man of blood!" he taunted him.
"You have come out, have you, man of the devil! The Lord
has visited on you all the blood of the house of Saul, in whose
stead you have reigned; and now the Lord has given the kingdom to Absalom your son, and you are caught in your own
mischief."

Then spoke Abishai, one of David's men: "Why should this dead dog curse the lord my king? Let me go over and take off his head!"

But David would not permit him. "My own son," he said, "who came forth from my body, seeks my life. How much more may this Benjamite do so. Let him alone and let him curse. It is the Lord's doing. It may be that the Lord will look on my affliction and will requite me good for this man's cursing to-day."

Meanwhile Absalom had entered into Jerusalem, and with him Ahithophel, who had become his chief officer. But Hushai, David's spy, was also in the city. "God save the king," he said when he came into Absalom's presence. At first Absalom was wary. "Is this the sort of kindness you show a friend?" he said. "Why did you not go out with your friend?"

"No," said Hushai, "when the Lord and this people and all the men of Israel have chosen a new king, his will I be and with him I take my stand. I have served your father. Why now should I not serve your father's son?"

Absalom therefore established himself in Jerusalem and took possession of what was left of his father's household. Not long after that, Ahithophel advised Absalom that he, Ahithophel, should gather twelve thousand men and pursue David by night. "I will come upon him while he is weary and weak-handed," he said. If he could kill David himself, the rest of the men around David would not stand. They would come straggling back to Absalom.

Absalom was not loath to do what Ahithophel advised, but it occurred to him to consult Hushai. "Thus and so Ahithophel has advised," he said to Hushai, "but what do you think? If you have any contrary ideas, say so."

"This counsel of Ahithophel is not good now," said Hushai. "Your father and those who are with him are mighty men; and they are bitter of soul, like a bear robbed of her whelps." Furthermore, he went on to remind Absalom that his father was an experienced soldier. David, he said, would not be staying in anybody's house. He would be entrenched in an ambush and ready for any possible pursuit. Any of Absalom's men marching recklessly after him would fall into that ambush before they knew it. When they discovered that they were suddenly face to face with David, they would remember the lion-hearted man that he was. There would be panic and a great slaughter. Therefore the gist of his advice was that Absalom should send out no hasty force under Ahithophel. Instead of that, he should gather together the largest force he could recruit among all the men from Dan to Beer-sheba; and when they went out to battle against David, Absalom should lead them in person.

Absalom listened and was impressed. It seemed to him that the advice of Hushai was better than Ahithophel's idea.

As soon as he could do so, Hushai slipped away and went to Zadok and Abiathar, the priests. He told them what Ahithophel had advised, and what he himself had said to Absalom. He urged the priests therefore to send a messenger immediately out to David, telling him by no means to halt in the plains of Jordan but to press on farther. His purpose was, of course, as it had been when he persuaded Absalom, to give David more time to escape before the pursuit could be organized.

Outside the city, hiding at a place in the fields, were two men who had been stationed there for just such an emergency. The two priests sent a maidservant out through the gates of Jerusalem to give these men the message which they were to carry to David. She reached them and they started on their way. But a boy had seen them, and he came at once and brought the news to Absalom. Absalom knew nothing of what Hushai or the priests had done, but suspecting that these men might be servants of David, he sent armed men out to pursue them. Finding that they were in danger, they came to the house of a man who was a friend of theirs and a friend to David's cause, and in whose courtyard there was a well. Down the well they went, and the man's wife spread a cover over the well's mouth and put ground corn over the covering so that the well was

hidden. When Absalom's men came by, they asked for two
fugitives, and the woman said they had gone yonder "over the
water." Absalom's men, never suspecting the hidden well,
hunted for them in vain, and thought the men had escaped
over the river. When they had given up the chase and gone
back to Jerusalem, the two men climbed out of the well and
carried their message on to David, who immediately rose up,
together with all who were with him, and crossed over the River
Jordan, so that by morning they were all on the farther side.

Ahithophel, in the meantime, had been so angered and so
humiliated because his advice was not taken that he had ridden
away from Absalom to his own house, and deliberately putting
his affairs in order, he had hanged himself.

Shortly thereafter Absalom assembled his troops, and
marching westward, crossed over the river. David, in the meantime, had been kindly received by the tribesmen among whom
he had come, and they had given plentiful provisions to him
and to his men. Against the coming of Absalom, David divided
his forces into three parts, one of them under the command of
Joab, the second under the command of Abishai, and the third
under the command of Ittai the Gittite. Also he said that he
himself was going with them into battle. But his men protested.
"You are worth ten thousand of us," they said. They wanted
him to stay with the reserve troops and be ready to succor any
of his forces who might be hardest pressed.

So David stood by the gate of the town where his men had
rallied, and as his troops went by, he said to their three commanders, "Deal gently for my sake with Absalom," and all the
people heard him say so.

When Absalom and David's forces came into collision, the
battle was in a wood. It turned into scattered hand-to-hand
fighting, so that it seemed as though the wood devoured more
people than the sword. Absalom was riding upon a mule, and
as he rode under the thick boughs of a great oak, his tossing
hair was caught in the branches, and as the mule passed out
from under him, he was left hanging in the tree. A soldier saw

him and went and told Joab. "Look, I have seen Absalom hanging in an oak!"

"Why when you saw him did you not smite him to the ground?" Joab shouted. "I would have given you ten shekels of silver and a girdle!"

But the soldier was aghast. He said that though he had had a thousand shekels of silver he would not touch Absalom, in the face of what David had said. But Joab exclaimed, "I may not be lingering here with you!" and he took three darts in his hands and went and found Absalom alive and struggling to free himself from the tree; and Joab thrust the three darts through Absalom's heart. Then he blew his trumpet and the battle came to an end.

They took Absalom's body and cast it into a pit in the wood, and heaped a great pile of stones upon it.

Then said Ahimaaz, who was the son of Zadok, the priest, "Let me now run and bring tidings to the king, how the Lord has avenged him of his enemies."

"No," said Joab, "you shall not carry a message this day. Another day you may. But no message must you carry this day, because the king's son is dead."

But he said to another man named Cushi, "Go, tell the king what you have seen." And Cushi ran.

But Ahimaaz begged that he also might go, and finally Joab let him. So Ahimaaz started, and presently he outran Cushi.

Now, David was sitting between the two gates of the town, and a watchman on the parapet above the gate looked out and saw a man running alone. He cried to David and told him that a messenger was coming. "If he is alone," said David, "there is tidings in his mouth."

Nearer and nearer the running figure drew.

Then the watchman saw another man also running, and he called to the porter of the gate, "Look, there is another man running alone."

And David said, "He also brings tidings."

Then the watchman said, "I think the running of the foremost is like the running of Ahimaaz, the son of Zadok."

And David said, "He is a good man and comes with good news."

Then came Ahimaaz near enough for David to see his face. He called out to the king, "All is well," and spent with his running, he fell down upon the ground before David and said, "Blessed be the Lord God who has delivered up the men who lifted their hands against thee!"

But David said, "Is my boy Absalom safe?"

It was to protect David from the first shock of that news that Ahimaaz had come. "When Joab sent the king's servant and me your servant, I saw a great tumult, but I do not know what it was," he said.

"Stand aside," said David, "and wait here." So Ahimaaz stood beside him and waited.

Then Cushi came. "Tidings, my lord the king!" he called. "The Lord has avenged you this day of all them that rose up against you."

And again David asked Cushi as he had asked Ahimaaz, "Is my boy Absalom safe?"

But Cushi answered, "The enemies of my lord the king and all that rise to do you hurt, be as that young man is!"

Then was David stricken to the heart. Up to a room above the gate he made his way, and he wept there. And as he went, those who were near him heard him cry, "O my son Absalom, my son, my son Absalom! would God I had died for thee, O Absalom, my son, my son!"

CHAPTER XXI

DAVID RETURNS TO JERUSALEM, AND THERE IS A SETTLING OF OLD
SCORES.

LL THAT day David mourned for Absalom, and there was consternation in the ranks of his victorious army, for the news had gone everywhere of David's grief. Men crept back silently into the town where David was, like men stealing off ashamed after a rout in battle.

When Joab knew of this, he was angered. Into the house where David was he came, and he said to the king: "You have shamed this day the faces of all your servants who have saved your life and the lives of all your family and household. It seems that you love your enemies and hate your friends! Evidently, if Absalom had lived this day, and all the rest of us had died, you would have been well pleased. The thing for you to do is to go out and speak with appreciation to the army: for by the Lord I swear, if you do not go out, not a man will be staying with you by to-night, and the end will be worse for you than all the evil that has befallen you from your youth until now."

So with his rough bluntness Joab spoke, and David did rise and go out to the town gate. Then the report spread among all the people, "Look, the king is sitting at the gate," and they came out before him from their tents to which they had all withdrawn.

But what had happened made another bitter memory to increase the aversion which David had for Joab.

In the meantime, now that Absalom was dead, there was a reaction among all the tribes of Israel. Men were reminding one another that it had been David who had saved them from the hands of the Philistines in times past. They remembered how Absalom had driven him out of the kingdom, and the result was that Absalom was dead. Why now should not David be sent for and brought back?

So the men in the northern tribes were saying, the tribes in which the old loyalty to Saul had been most entrenched. Hearing this, David sent a message to Zadok and Abiathar, the priests who were in Jerusalem. They were to communicate with the leading men in the tribe of Judah. Why was it that they, his own flesh and blood, were the last to seek to bring him back? Moreover, they were to give a message also to Amasa, who had been Absalom's chief lieutenant, to tell him that David proposed to appoint him commander of his troops in place of Joab. So the hearts of all the men of Judah turned toward him as one man, and they sent back an answer to David, bidding him, and all the men with him, to return.

Homeward, therefore, David turned his face, and came to the banks of Jordan. The men of Judah rallied at Gilgal and went down toward the river to meet him. With them also came Shimei, the same man who, when David had come out of Jerusalem, an exile in peril of his life, had walked beside the road, cursing him and calling down upon him all the vengeance of the house of Saul. Ziba also was there, the servant who had met David with the laden asses which he said he was carrying to Jerusalem, where Mephibosheth expected to be made king. Over the river they went, and came before David, where he was waiting on the farther side.

There Shimei fell down on his face before David, and begged for his forgiveness. He admitted his perversity, but now, he said, he was the first one of his tribe to come down and make obeisance to the king. Abishai was standing by David, and he was indignant. On that previous day of Shimei's cursing, Abishai had wanted to go out and kill him, but David had forbidden it. Now certainly he thought that David would let him put this man to death. But again David stayed his hand. He said that no man should be killed in Israel that day, for he was come back again as king; and turning to Shimei, he said, "You shall not die."

The tide was turning fast now. Men who had been ready to revolt against David in the evil day were following on one another's heels to sue for his favor. After Shimei came Mephibosheth, the lame son of Jonathan whom David had received into his own house. "Why did you not go out with me, Mephibosheth?" said David. But Mephibosheth laid the blame on Ziba, the servant. He said that his own real intention had been to go with David, and he had told Ziba to saddle an ass and bring it to him, so that he might ride with David, since, being lame, he could not walk; and that Ziba had slandered him when he told David that the laden asses were for Mephibosheth to make himself at home in Jerusalem. He admitted all David's goodness to him; and "What right have I," he said, "to cry any more to the king?"

But David cut him short. "Why do you speak to me any more of your affairs?" he said. As for the possessions which he had had, he and Ziba could divide them. But Mephibosheth, whether he was fawning upon David with feigned loyalty, or whether all along he had been sincere—and which he was no one can tell—answered that, so far as possessions were concerned, Ziba could have them all. The only thing he wanted was to know that the king had come again in peace to his own house.

One other finer figure was among those who welcomed David. It was Barzillai the Gileadite, an old man of more than eighty years. He was a rich man also, and he had provided for David generously when David, on his flight from Jerusalem, had come to where Barzillai lived. "Come over the river with me," said David, "and you shall live with me in Jerusalem." But Barzillai said he was too old. There would be no use in his sitting at the king's table. He could not taste what he ate or drank, he said, nor hear the voices of singing men and women. He would be only a burden to the king. He would go over the river, but not to Jerusalem; he would escort David a little way, and then return to his own home to finish out his days. And this he did.

All this welcome to David, however, had been monopolized

by the men of Judah.   They had been the last to send him the
message bidding him return, but they had been the first to go
down to the Jordan valley to greet him.   When the men of
the northern tribes heard that, they were jealous and angry.
They came to David and wanted to know why it was that the
men of Judah had taken possession of him.   The Judæans
answered hotly.   They said the king was their kinsman.   What
right did the men of Israel have to be angry at their going out
to greet him?   Were the men of Israel suggesting that they had
gone out to meet David in order to get some gifts from him?
Well, they had not had so much as a meal at the king's cost.
But the men of the ten tribes answered: "We have ten parts
in the king.   We have more right in David than you.   Why did
you make light of us, and not ask our advice about bringing
back the king?"   So they fell into a bitter controversy; but the
men of Judah talked more loudly and more hotly than the
men of the other tribes.

The resentment of Israel, however, was a matter of more
than words.   A man named Sheba sounded the trumpet of a
new revolt.   "We have no part in David," he said, "nor any
inheritance in the son of Jesse.   Every man of Israel to his tent!"
So while David went back to Jerusalem in the borders of Judah,
many of the men of Israel rallied round Sheba.

David proceeded now to carrying out his intention of ap-
pointing Amasa as the commander of his troops.   He told Amasa
to assemble the men of Judah within three days and to be
ready to lead them.   But as Amasa went about to assemble the
troops, he delayed longer than the time which David had
appointed, and David, impatient for action against Sheba, told
Abishai to take command of such forces as he could gather and
carry the attack against the revolting Israelites.   Abishai started,
and with him also went Joab.   They had not gone far before
Amasa followed and overtook them when they had halted by a
great stone in Gibeon.   He had on one of Joab's uniforms, with
a sword in its sheath girded about his waist.   But as he hurried
up to where Abishai and Joab were, the sword slipped out of
its sheath.

"Are you well, brother?" said Joab as Amasa came up; and he made as if to embrace him. Amasa did not heed the fact that in Joab's hand was a sword; but what Joab did was to stab him under the ribs with a mortal wound, so that he fell and lay in a pool of blood in the midst of the highway. Soldiers seeing him there halted until he was carried into a field, and then the force went on, led by Abishai and Joab, in the pursuit of Sheba. At length they hemmed him in a town, and battered against the wall to throw it down. But a woman parleyed with Joab from the walls, and Joab said that he and the men with him had no hostility against the town; the one they wanted was Sheba. The woman promised that presently Sheba's head should be thrown to Joab over the wall; and this which she had said she persuaded the defenders of the town to do. They did cut off Sheba's head and threw it out of the town; and Joab sounded his trumpet for withdrawal, and his soldiers retired from the city, every man to his tent, while Joab himself went back to Jerusalem to see the king.

Two other somber incidents marked the closing years of David's reign. For three years there was a famine, and David was convinced that this was a punishment from God for somebody's sin. He had, as he thought, a revelation that the sin which was being punished was a cruel deed of Saul, who once had made a ruthless slaughter among the Gibeonites. David sent to the Gibeonites and asked what would seem to them a satisfaction for the old evil which Saul had done, and their answer was that they desired that seven of Saul's descendants should be handed over to their mercy. "I will give them," said David. Mephibosheth he spared; but he took two sons of Saul and of Rizpah, and five of Saul's grandsons, and handed them over to the Gibeonites; and these seven men the Gibeonites hanged on a hill at the time of the beginning of the barley harvest.

But Rizpah took sackcloth and spread it upon a rock from the beginning of the harvest until the rainy season began, and there she laid the bodies of her sons, and guarded them night and day. When David heard of it, he sent to Jabesh-gilead, and had the bones of Saul and Jonathan disinterred, and these, with the bodies of the men who had been hanged, he caused to be buried in the country of Benjamin in the sepulcher of the father of Saul.

After that, there was a pestilence in the land, so that from the territory of Dan in the north to Beer-sheba in the south thousands of men died. David believed it was a retribution for the fact that he had made a census of the men of Israel. This again the ill-omened Joab had done, though it was at David's desire. But after he had commanded it, David was afraid. It seemed to him that his numbering of the people might appear as an act of arrogance, and that God was humbling him for his own conceit of power.

When David was in great distress of mind, there came to him the prophet Gad, and Gad told him to go and build an altar on the threshing-floor of Araunah the Jebusite. Now Araunah's threshing-floor was the great rock which formed the apex of the hill above David's city in Jerusalem. This threshing-floor David bought of Araunah, and built an altar there; and it is upon that rock where long ago Araunah threshed and winnowed his wheat that in succeeding centuries there have risen temples and shrines and mosques, so that from David's day until now that ancient threshing-floor has become, and is, one of the sacred places of the earth.

David's life was near its end, and the record of it in the Second Book of Samuel comes to its climax in a magnificent hymn, which, whether or not David wrote it, is vibrant with the glory and tragedy of his strangely varied life.

"The Lord is my rock, and my fortress, and my deliverer," it begins.

"He is my shield, and the horn of my salvation, my high tower, and my refuge."

And it goes on to words which are scarcely matched for beauty in all the literature of Israel:

"As for God, his way is perfect; the word of the Lord is tried: he is a buckler to all them that trust in him.

"For who is God, save the Lord? and who is a rock, save our God?

"God is my strong fortress: and he guideth the perfect in his way. . . .

"Thou hast also given me the shield of thy salvation: and thy gentleness hath made me great."

CHAPTER XXII

IN WHICH IS RECOUNTED THE DEATH OF DAVID, AND THE COMING TO
THE THRONE OF SOLOMON, HIS SON; AND WHAT SOLOMON DID TO
ADONIJAH, ABIATHAR, JOAB, AND SHIMEI; AND HOW HE GOT HIS
REPUTATION OF BEING VERY WISE.

HEN IT appeared that David's days were num-
bered, there happened in the court what often
happens when a king is about to die—namely,
a conspiracy to seize the succession. One of
David's sons was Adonijah, a younger brother
of Absalom. "I will be king," he said, and he
gathered a retinue of chariots and horsemen and other out-
runners to establish his royal supremacy in Jerusalem. He was
a handsome man and had good hope that the crowd would rally
to him, more especially since the pomp and circumstance which
he had affected had brought no rebuke from David. He had
strong supporters at court, including Abiathar, the priest, and
the always formidable Joab.

But the priest Zadok, and Benaiah, one of David's commanders, and Nathan the prophet, were not on Adonijah's side.
He knew this, and he did not invite them when he had a great
feast by the well of En-rogel, at which were gathered a crowd
from David's court.

Nathan went to Bath-sheba, David's wife, whose son was
Solomon.

Said he: "Have you not heard that Adonijah, the son of
Haggith, reigns and our lord David does not know it? Come
now, let me advise you, for it is a matter of saving your own life
and the life of your son, Solomon. Go to King David and ask
him whether he did not swear to you that Solomon your son
should reign after him and sit upon his throne, and why is it
now that Adonijah reigns? While you are still talking with
the king, I will come in after you and confirm your words."

So Bath-sheba went into the room where the old king lay, and as she bowed in his presence, David said, "What will you have?"

She answered him: "My lord, you swore by the Lord your God that assuredly Solomon your son should reign after you and sit upon your throne. Now, instead, Adonijah is reigning, and you, my lord the king, know nothing of it. Adonijah has killed oxen, fat cattle, and sheep abundantly. He has called all the king's sons, and Abiathar the priest, and Joab the leader of your army. But Solomon he has not invited. And now, my lord the king, the eyes of all Israel are upon you, that you should tell them who should sit on the throne after you. Otherwise, it shall come to pass when you sleep with your fathers that I and my son Solomon will be treated like criminals."

While she was still speaking, in came Nathan the prophet. David's eyes were dim, but they told him this was Nathan who had come. Nathan repeated what Bath-sheba had already said, and made it more explicit. He said that that very day the crowd who had gone out to eat and drink at Adonijah's feast were shouting, "God save Adonijah!" He made it plain that he and Zadok the priest and Benaiah had no part in this matter, and he wanted to know whether David would allow such things to go on.

Then David summoned Bath-sheba to come near. He confirmed with a solemn oath the previous promise he had made that Solomon should succeed him on his throne. He sent also for Zadok and Benaiah, and he told them and Nathan that they were to take the royal servants, and the king's own mule, and mount Solomon upon it; and they were to go down to Gihon and there anoint Solomon as king.

"Amen," said Benaiah; "may God confirm what the king has said."

So down to Gihon, the priest, the soldier, and the prophet escorted Solomon; and there Zadok anointed him with holy oil out of the tabernacle, and they blew a trumpet, and the people who were there shouted, "God save King Solomon!"

When Adonijah and his guests had come to the end of

their feast, they heard the clamor of people shouting and blowing on pipes. Then a trumpet sounded, and when Joab heard that, he said, "What is the meaning of this noise, as of the city in an uproar?"

Before he had finished his question, in hurried Jonathan, the son of the priest Abiathar, pouring out the news of the crowning of Solomon, and of how Solomon had come back into the city and of how King David had expressly ratified his succession to the throne. Then there was trepidation among Adonijah's guests. The party broke up unceremoniously, and every man went his own way.

Adonijah also was afraid, and he went to Jerusalem and took sanctuary in the tabernacle, by the altar. It was told Solomon that Adonijah was there and that he was pleading that Solomon should spare his life. If he behaved himself, Solomon said, he should be spared; but if he did anything amiss, he should certainly die. So Adonijah was brought at Solomon's order into the new king's presence, and when he had come and bowed down before him, Solomon told him to go to his own house.

Then David, knowing that his end was come, gave his final charge to Solomon. "I go the way of all the earth," he said. "Do you be strong, therefore, and show yourself a man. Keep the charge of the Lord your God to walk in his way, to keep his statutes, and his commandments, and his judgments, and his testimonies, as these are written in the law of Moses, that you may prosper in all that you do. And whithersoever you turn, so may the Lord continue his word which he spoke concerning me when he said, 'If thy children take heed to my word to walk before me in truth with all their heart and with all their soul, there shall not fail thee (said he) a man on the throne of Israel!'"

One old thorn still rankled in David's remembrance, and even in his dying he passed it on to Solomon. It had to do with Joab.

"You know," he said, "what Joab did to me and what he did to two commanders of the armies of Israel, to Abner the son of Ner, and to Amasa the son of Jether. He slew them. In peace he shed blood as though in war. I leave you to do according to your wisdom. You are not to let his old head go down to the grave in peace."

But Barzillai, the sturdy old Gileadite who had helped David at the time of his flight, and even Shimei, who had cursed him then but who later had been forgiven, David desired that Solomon should protect and favor.

Then, at the end of his reign of forty years, David died, and was buried in Jerusalem.

Solomon was now established on his father's throne. He was a more ruthless man than David. There were for him no long but inconclusive dislikes such as there had been with David for Joab. When Solomon disliked a man sufficiently, that man disappeared.

The first to fall was Adonijah. He came one day to see Bath-sheba. "Are you come peaceably?" she asked, and he answered, "Yes." He had a favor to ask of her. He prefaced it by reminding her that for a while he himself possessed the kingdom, and that all the people had first turned to him. Now the kingdom was his brother's, and he had a petition which he wanted to make through Bath-sheba. Solomon would not say no to anything that Bath-sheba asked. Would Bath-sheba ask Solomon then to let Adonijah marry Abishag the Shunammite?

Now, Abishag was a young and beautiful girl who had nursed King David in his last days and had been more intimately with him than anyone else.

"Well," said Bath-sheba to Adonijah, "I will speak for you to the king." So she went to Solomon and sat down by him and told him she had a small favor to ask. Solomon bade her tell him what it was, and he intimated that there was nothing she could ask to which he would say no. So she requested that Abishag be given to Adonijah as his wife.

Instantly Solomon's mood changed, and he turned upon his mother. "Why do you ask Abishag the Shunammite for Adonijah? Ask for the kingdom also to be given him, since he is my elder brother! Yes, ask for the kingdom for him and for Abiathar the priest and for Joab. God punish me," he went on, "if Adonijah has not spoken this word against his own life!"

Nor was Solomon's action less deadly than his speech. He said that Adonijah should die that day, and that day Adonijah did die by the hand of Benaiah, whom Solomon sent to execute his sentence.

The next on whom vengeance fell was Abiathar the priest. "Get out of Jerusalem," Solomon told him, "to Anathoth and to your own lands. You deserve death, but I shall not put you to death now because you bore the ark of the Lord before my father David, and because you shared my father's hardships." But Abiathar was dismissed from the court, and people generally thought that his humiliation was the last chapter of the old judgment which had been recorded against the house of Eli, from whom Abiathar was descended.

The third to fall was Joab. He heard what had happened to Adonijah and Abiathar and he, as Adonijah had done once before, fled into the tabernacle and took sanctuary by the altar. Solomon sent Benaiah in to fall upon Joab there. "Come out!" said Benaiah. "No," said Joab, "I will die here." Benaiah hesitated to kill a man in the very shadow of the altar, so he went back and told Solomon that Joab clung to the sacred shrine. But Solomon had no scruples. This was the Joab who had slain Abner and Amasa. Benaiah was to kill him where he was. So Benaiah did, and Joab was buried in his own house, which had fallen ere this into a wilderness.

Still another figure was to get in the way of this implacable king. Shimei was instructed by Solomon to build a house in Jerusalem, to stay there, and not go out of the city. If he so much as crossed over the brook of Kidron, Solomon said, then his blood would be on his own head. For a long time Shimei never stirred out of the city. But some three years afterward two of his servants ran away to Gath. So Shimei saddled his ass and rode off to Gath to find them and to bring them back. After Shimei had come back to Jerusalem, it was reported to

Solomon that he had been away. The king was merciless. He had told Shimei that if he ever went out of the city he should die, and die he did, and by the hand of Benaiah, who, by this time, had become less a soldier than an executioner.

Yet this same Solomon who could be so cruel to individuals was a man of great power, and in some respects of great wisdom too. He made an alliance with the Pharaoh of Egypt and took Pharaoh's daughter to be his wife. He was politically sagacious, and he had a vein of religious interest also. The old customs of earlier days still persisted. Here and there through the country were local shrines which perpetuated a very ancient and half-pagan worship, shrines associated with some great tree, with a sacred well, or with some monumental stone. Solomon went about and offered sacrifice at these various shrines. But he was beginning to think of a religious reformation which should focus the people's worship in one place.

One night when he had gone to the shrine in Gibeon, he had a dream; and in the dream he heard the voice of God saying, "Ask what I shall give thee."

Then Solomon answered: "Thou hast showed to thy servant's father great mercy, according as he walked before thee in mercy and uprightness of heart with thee: and thou hast kept for him this great kindness, that thou hast given him a son to sit on his throne, as it is this day. And now, O Lord my God, thou hast made thy servant king instead of David my father; and I am but a little child. I know not how to go out or come in. And thy servant is in the midst of thy people which thou hast chosen, a great people, that cannot be numbered nor counted for multitude. Give therefore thy servant an understanding heart to judge thy people, that I may discern between good and bad: for who is able to judge this thy so great a people?"

Then Solomon heard the voice of God answer: "Because thou hast asked this thing, and hast not asked for thyself long life, neither hast asked for riches for thyself, nor hast asked for the life of thine enemies, but hast asked for thyself understanding to discern judgments, behold, I have done according to thy words: lo, I have given thee a wise and an understanding heart, so that there was none like thee before thee, neither after thee shall any arise like unto thee. And I have also given thee that which thou hast not asked, both riches, and honor; so that there shall not be any among the kings like unto thee all thy days. And if thou wilt walk in my ways, to keep my statutes and my commandments, as thy father David did walk, then I will lengthen thy days."

Then Solomon awoke and knew that it was a dream. But he determined that he would build to the glory of God a new and magnificent Temple in Jerusalem.

In the fourth year of his reign he began to build, and for seven years he was occupied in the work. He sent to Hiram, king of Tyre, and made an arrangement by which Hiram should furnish cedar trees out of the forests of Lebanon. Gangs of men were collected in Solomon's dominions, and sent up into the forests to cut the trees and hew the lumber. Then from the Lebanons the wood was carried to Tyre, or some other nearby seaport, and thence floated down to a point on the coast to the south, from which it was carried up to Jerusalem. The foundations of the Temple were made of hewn stone, and its superstructure and roof were of cedar, and its floors of fir. Also the doors of the Temple and the figures of the cherubim that guarded the ark, and the sacred vessels of the sanctuary, were overlaid with gold.

Moreover, Solomon built a new and ornate palace for himself, and another palace which at first was the house of his queen, the daughter of Pharaoh, and afterwards became the house of the many wives he married; for, as the record in the book of Kings laconically puts it, "King Solomon loved many strange women."

Conditions in the kingdom had changed in surprising fashion since the early days of Saul. Life in Israel then was still bare and primitive, but now a richer civilization was developing. The land of Palestine has always been a natural crossroads for the streams of commerce of the East. From Egypt in the south to Syria in the north, and thence toward the heart of the great continent lying beyond; from Phœnicia on the Mediterranean coast down toward the port of Ezion-gaber on the Red Sea, the routes of the caravans ran. In Solomon's kingdom wealth was accumulating, and he levied heavily upon whatever wealth there was. His own household establishment and his court were maintained in luxurious fashion. The figures—as is often true in the ancient records—may have become exaggerated as tradition handed them down; but even with considerable subtraction they give the picture of easy lavishness which Solomon's court created. Thirty measures of fine flour and three score measures of meal, the records say, were used every day to furnish his table, together with ten fatted oxen and twenty oxen from the pastures, one hundred sheep, besides harts, and roebucks, and fallow deer, and fatted fowl. Moreover, his stables were full of horses and chariots, with other stables for his dromedaries, and he maintained a force of cavalry as well as of foot soldiers at his court.

It was not strange that a king who dazzled the eyes of his subjects by such rich display, and round whom, at the same time, a general prosperity was developing, should have been accounted a man of wisdom. No doubt the crowd admired his success, and gave to his words the weight which the words of successful men have usually commanded beyond their intrinsic merit. If there were any sagacious saying spread abroad, it was usually supposed that Solomon had said it. Many proverbs came to be connected with his name, to such an extent that a whole book of the Bible, which is probably compiled from various sources, is called "The Proverbs of Solomon." Tradition had it that from all the kings of the earth ambassadors came to learn of Solomon's wisdom.

The particular sovereign, however, who is said to have come to visit Solomon was the queen of Sheba, whose realm is supposed to have been somewhere in the great but mostly empty spaces of Arabia. She is reported to have come to Jerusalem with a great train of camels, bringing a gift of spices and also gold. When she had come to Solomon, "she communed with him of all that was in her heart. And Solomon answered all her questions." But though this glowing picture of Solomon the sage is given, the thing which would seem to have impressed the queen of Sheba most particularly was the opulence of Solomon's court. For when she observed the food that was on his table and the ranks of his servants sitting there, and his cup-bearers, and the richness of his servants' clothes, "there was no more spirit in her." She said she would not have believed what had been told her about Solomon unless she had come and seen for herself. And perhaps there was an unconscious climax in the two things she spoke of when she said, "Thy wisdom and prosperity exceed the fame which I have heard."

That Solomon was prosperous appears beyond doubt; and historians of Israel, recounting or remembering his days, reveled in filling in the picture. They said his drinking vessels were gold, that in his court even silver was held cheap. They said he had a fleet of ships which sailed with the navy of Hiram of Tyre, and that the commerce which he and Hiram carried on brought to his court gold, and silver, ivory, and apes, and pea-cocks. Silver was as common to him, they said, as cobblestones, and cedar wood no more rare than the ordinary sycamores that grew in every vale. He had a great throne of ivory overlaid with gold. The throne was mounted on six steps, and each of the steps was flanked with two sculptured lions.

Doubtless Solomon's reputation for wisdom had a genuine basis also. He could cut through the tangled surface of an issue presented to him and pierce beneath it to reality with an intuition which was like a stroke of genius. The most famous evidence of this swift sagacity of his was in the instance of two women, both of them of loose reputation, who came to him claiming the possession of a baby.

Eagerly one of them poured out her story: "I and this woman dwell in one house; and I was delivered of a child with her in the house. Three days after my child was born, this woman had a child born too. There we were together; no other person was with us in the house, only we two. This woman's child died in the night because she laid on it. And she arose at midnight, and took my son from beside me, while I slept, and laid it in her bosom, and laid her dead child in mine. When I arose in the morning to nurse my child, it was dead; but when I looked at it in the morning light, I saw that it was not my son which I had borne."

"No," said the other woman, "the living child is my son, and the dead one is your son."

But the first woman contradicted her. "No; but the dead is your son, and the living is my son." And so their claims and denials flew back and forth.

Solomon considered, and then he spoke: "One of you says, 'This is my son which is living, and your son is the child that is dead': and the other of you says, 'No; but your son is the dead child, and my son is the living.' Now," he said to the servant, "bring me a sword." And the sword was brought.

"Take that living child," said Solomon, "and divide it in two. Give half to the one woman, and half to the other."

Then cried the woman to whom the living child did belong, for her heart rushed out toward her son, "O my lord, give her the living child, and do not slay it!"

"No," said the other one, "let it be neither mine nor yours, but divide it."

Then said Solomon, looking toward the one who had spoken first, "Give her the living child, and in no way harm it: she is his mother."

And when all the people heard of Solomon's judgment, they marveled and admired, as well they might.

Though Solomon, however, was wise in many matters, there were other matters in which he was not. He was much intrigued with women, and he brought into his harem women from Moab, from Ammon, from Sidon, and from among the Hittites. Not only that, but Solomon became indulgent toward the various pagan forms of worship which these women whom he loved brought with them to Jerusalem. He permitted the cult of Ashtoreth, the Phœnician goddess, and of Milcom, the deity of the Ammonites; and he built a high sanctuary for Chemosh, "the abomination of Moab."

Disintegrating forces, therefore, were at work in Solomon's realm. There was no single-hearted religious loyalty to hold the people together. The luxury of Solomon's court also, and the license of its morals, spread disaffection. The wealth of Solomon was tempting, and respect for Solomon and for his authority was growing less.

Three men especially appeared who would be troublesome, and the third of whom would be fatal for the kingdom in the days of Solomon's son. The first of these was Hadad the Edomite, who had been carried as a child into Egypt, and there had found favor with Pharaoh; the second was Rezon; and the third was Jeroboam the son of Nebat, one of Solomon's servants. All these men were antagonists of Solomon; but the third was to be singled out for a greater rôle. He was a man of great courage and also of great industry, and Solomon had made him one of his chief stewards. But one day as he went out of Jerusalem, he was met by one of those figures who now begin to appear with increasing frequency upon the stage of Israel's life and whose moral authority was often more powerful than the armies of kings. It was a prophet named Ahijah who accosted Jeroboam as he crossed a field. Jeroboam had clad himself in a new garment, but Ahijah caught hold of it and tore it into twelve pieces. He said to Jeroboam, "Take ten of these pieces: for thus saith the Lord God of Israel, I will rend the kingdom out of the hand of Solomon, and will give ten of the tribes to you." The reason, said Ahijah, was the apostasy of Solomon, in that he had permitted the worship of Ashtoreth, Chemosh, and Milcom. From him should be taken away all the kingdom except the single tribe of Judah.

When Solomon heard this, he sought to kill Jeroboam; but it was not to be now as it had been in the earlier days when Adonijah, Joab, and Shimei in quick succession had learned the deadliness with which the king could strike. Jeroboam learned of the king's deadly purpose in time. Down into Egypt he fled for shelter. There he remained until presently Solomon died.

CHAPTER XXIII

FTER SOLOMON had been buried in Jerusalem, Rehoboam his son succeeded to his throne. He went to Shechem to be crowned, and Jeroboam, learning that Solomon was dead, had come back to Israel again. Many of the people made him their spokesman, and with him at their head they went to Rehoboam and said: "Your father made our yoke grievous: now make that heavy yoke of his lighter, and we will serve you." The splendor of Solomon's court was all very well, but the nation had groaned under his exactions in order to make that splendor possible. They wanted now to be left alone.

"Go away for three days," said Rehoboam, "and then come to me again." So the people departed.

Then Rehoboam took counsel with the older men who had been Solomon's advisers while he lived, and he asked them, "How do you advise that I should answer the people?"

They replied: "If you will be a servant to the people and answer them with good words, they will be your servants forever."

But he turned his back on the counsel of the elders, and he consulted with the young men who had grown up with him and were now in his inner circle. "What advice do you give," he said, "for my answer to this people who have said, 'Make the yoke which your father put upon us lighter'?"

These young men were not backward in giving the kind of advice which they believed in, and the worst of it was that Rehoboam took it word for word.

When Jeroboam and the people came back on the third day, Rehoboam, ignoring completely the counsel which the elder men had given, echoed the insolent bravado of his young friends. "My father made your yoke heavy," he said, "I will add to your yoke. My father chastised you with whips, but I will chastise you with scorpions."

So he spoke, and did not even understand the nemesis he let loose. The words of Ahijah the prophet, spoken to Jeroboam, were beginning to come true.

For when the men of Israel saw that the king had not hearkened to them, they broke out into angry protest. "What portion have we in David?" they said. "We have no inheritance in the son of Jesse. Israel, to your tents! See to your own house, David."

So except for the men of Judah over whom Rehoboam reigned, all the rest of Israel revolted. Rehoboam was to discover the completeness of that revolt in an unmistakable manner. He sent Adoram, who was his officer in charge of gathering the tribute, out among the northern tribesmen; but they stoned him to death, and Rehoboam hastily climbed into his chariot and fled into Jerusalem.

Meanwhile, Jeroboam had been chosen king over the new northern kingdom, which called itself Israel in distinction from the southern kingdom, which now was only Judah. Rehoboam tried to assemble an army and march against Jeroboam, but a man of God in Jerusalem, a prophet named Shemaiah, warned him not to do so, and Rehoboam gave up his purpose.

Soon afterwards Jeroboam built the city of Shechem in Mount Ephraim and established himself there. It occurred to him that there was a religious custom which had political danger in it, and which he had better set himself to change. The people had become accustomed in Solomon's time to going up to the new Temple in Jerusalem for worship and sacrifice. If they kept on going up there, Jeroboam thought, their hearts would be turning back to Rehoboam as their king. So he made two calves of gold, and he set them up, one in Bethel and the other in Dan. "It is too much for you to be going up to Jerusalem;" he said to the people, "there are your gods which brought you up out of the land of Egypt." Moreover, he made priests, not out of the traditionally sacred tribe of Levi, but out of any common kind of folk which he happened to choose. He arranged a new ecclesiastical calendar of festivals and sacrifices, all of which was a great scandal to those in whose eyes Jeroboam was to stand as a perverter of religion.

In order to understand truly the rest of the story embodied in the books of the Kings, it is necessary to recognize the change of authorship and the new considerations which now begin to pervade the narrative. The rich material for the stories of Saul and David, and for some of the stories in the earlier part of Solomon's reign, come, as we have already noted, from writings which were almost contemporary with the events described, and are therefore of exceptionally vivid and objective accuracy. But in the general framework of the history of Solomon, and in all the other records which begin with the accounts of Rehoboam and Jeroboam, other and later influences have been controlling. Jeroboam's reign was approximately from 932 to 911 B. C., and Rehoboam's almost the same; but the books of the Kings in their complete form were not written until about three centuries later. They represent the work of a school of historians who arose after the great prophets had lived and had spoken their religiously epoch-making messages. These historians belonged to a time of religious reformation, when the dominant passion was for the purifying of the people's worship, the sweeping away of pagan practices, the destruction of all the little local shrines where ancient superstitions clustered, and the centralizing of the worship of Jehovah at the Temple in Jerusalem. As these historians looked back to previous events in the life of the nation, they read them in the light of their own convictions. The apostasy of Jeroboam, and therefore the ultimate fall of Jeroboam, was due to the fact that he had broken the unity of worship which ought to center in the Temple. Every other king was judged for good or evil by this same standard. If he had discouraged worship at the local shrines, he was commended; if he had favored these, then he was condemned, no matter what else his kingship might have stood for. So the books of Kings must be read with discretion, for they cease to be history of an impartial kind. They are, rather, a long series of warning sermons for which the successive kings are texts. Every incident is so colored as to point an unmistakable moral, and into the mouths of various witnesses are put the verdicts which the later historians believed to have been the immediate judgments of God.

This character of the narrative, with its strong bent toward sermonizing and the use of specific events to prove a large conclusion, appears in the account of what happened after Jeroboam had set up his rival sanctuaries. It is the story of three prophets and of what they said and of what they did, and it runs thus:

One day Jeroboam went to the new shrine which he had set up at Bethel, and stood there burning incense on the altar. As he did so, there appeared a prophet who had come up out of Judah, and he cried to the altar itself: "O altar, altar, thus saith Jehovah: Behold, a child shall be born unto the house of David, Josiah by name; and upon thee shall he offer the priests of the high places that burn incense upon thee, and men's bones shall be burnt upon thee."

Then—so the story goes on—when Jeroboam heard those words which were spoken against his own shrine, with an angry gesture of his hand he ordered that the prophet be seized; but his hand was withered as he did so. Moreover, the altar was torn apart, and ashes poured out from it, until the king entreated the prophet for mercy, and that his hand might be restored. So the prophet did pray God, and Jeroboam's hand was healed.

Then said the king, "Come home with me, and refresh yourself, and I will give you a reward."

But the prophet answered: "If you give me half your house, I will not go with you, nor will I eat bread nor drink water in this place. For thus it was charged me by the word of the Lord, 'Eat no bread nor drink water, and do not return by the same

way on which you came.' " So he left Bethel and started homeward by another road.

But in Bethel there dwelt an old prophet, and his sons
came and told him what had happened by the shrine, and about
the man of God who had come up from Judah. So he said to
his sons, "Which way did he go?" And he asked them to
saddle an ass, and he mounted and rode after the man who had
turned back toward Judah, until he overtook him and found
him sitting beneath an oak.

"Are you the man of God who came from Judah?" he asked,
and the other answered, "I am."

"Then," said the old prophet, "come home and have a meal
with me."

But the other answered, "I may not return with you, nor
enter your house, nor will I eat bread or drink water with you
in this place." The word of Jehovah, he said, had forbidden
him either to eat or drink, and had told him to go home by a
different road.

But the old man from Bethel said, "I am a prophet also, as
you are." And then he told him something else, which was a
lie. He said that an angel had spoken to him and had bidden
him bring this man from Judah back to Bethel. So he did go
back, and sat down to dinner in the old man's house.

But while they were there together, the old prophet began
to condemn him. He said that because he had disobeyed the
divine command which he had said he had received, neither to
eat nor drink in Bethel, he should die in some violent fashion,
and that his body should never be buried with his fathers.

Then the story moves on to its appropriate conclusion.

The prophet from Judah started back a second time homeward; but on the way, a lion attacked him and killed him, and a
message was brought to the prophet in Bethel, telling him that
the man from Judah was dead. At that the old prophet rose
up and rode to the place where the body of his recent guest
was lying. The ass on which he had ridden was still standing
there, and so also, quite decorously, was the lion (for in order
that the story should have its fitting climax, it was not proper

that the lion should have carried away or destroyed the younger prophet's body). The old man carried the body back on his own ass, and he mourned and said, "Alas, my brother!" Then when he had buried the body, he said to his sons, "When I am dead, bury me in the sepulcher where this man of God is buried; lay my bones beside his bones; for the saying which he cried against the altar in Bethel, and against all the temples in the high places of the cities of Samaria, shall certainly come to pass."

Thus the writer of the book of Kings had conveyed his condemnation of Jeroboam; but he goes on to make that condemnation still more emphatic in his account of what happened when Jeroboam's son was sick. Obviously, now Jeroboam wanted true religious counsel, and obviously also, from the point of view of the historian, he could not get it from his own shrines.

This, therefore, is what is told as having happened:

Jeroboam besought his wife to disguise herself, so that she would not be known as the wife of Jeroboam, and go to Shiloh, because at Shiloh was Ahijah the prophet, the same one who first told Jeroboam that he should be king. She should take with her presents of bread and honey, and then the prophet would tell her what would happen to their sick child.

But the voice of God whispered in Ahijah's heart and gave him a foreknowledge of what was happening, so that, as soon as Jeroboam's wife in her disguise came to his door and Ahijah heard the sound of her feet, he said: "Come in, you wife of Jeroboam. Why do you pretend to be someone else? I have heavy tidings for you." Then he told her to carry back to Jeroboam the message that God had made him king over Israel and had divided the kingdom of David, but that, because Jeroboam had set up other gods and made images, his dynasty should be destroyed and his descendants should be eaten by dogs in the city and by vultures in the field. She herself was to go back home, and when she got there her child should die.

Then, in the conclusion of the story, Jeroboam's wife went

home, and as she came to the threshold of her house her child did die. Of the particular pathos of that, the historian is not thinking. The death of Jeroboam's child is simply another instance through which he must point his moral of the doom which he believed must always be visited on the evil which he saw running like a dark thread of explanation through all his history.

With the other events of Jeroboam's kingship, over and above those which had served to point his moral, the historian was not concerned. He summed up the remainder of the record in two abrupt sentences. "The rest of the acts of Jeroboam, how he warred, and how he reigned, behold, they are written in the book of the chronicles of the kings of Israel. And the days which Jeroboam reigned were two and twenty years: and he slept with his fathers, and Nadab his son reigned in his stead."

And at nearly the same time Rehoboam, king in Jerusalem, died; and he falls under condemnation by the chronicler for reasons similar to those for which Jeroboam had been condemned. He too had allowed local shrines and images and sacred trees to continue to be worshiped. A Pharaoh of Egypt had come up against Jerusalem and levied upon it a heavy tribute, and this was represented as the judgment of God against Solomon's son. In the days of Solomon there had been golden shields set up among the treasures of the temple of the Lord; but the Egyptians carried all these away. So Rehoboam could put in their places only brass shields. The splendor of the reign of Solomon was gone.

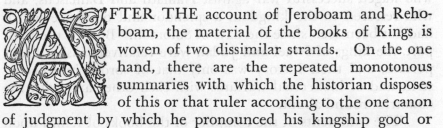FTER THE account of Jeroboam and Reho-
boam, the material of the books of Kings is
woven of two dissimilar strands. On the one
hand, there are the repeated monotonous
summaries with which the historian disposes
of this or that ruler according to the one canon
of judgment by which he pronounced his kingship good or
evil.

Thus, for example, he writes of Rehoboam's successor:

"Now in the eighteenth year of King Jeroboam, the son of
Nebat, reigned Abijam over Judah. Three years reigned he in
Jerusalem. And his mother's name was Maachah, the daughter
of Abishalom.

"And he walked in all the sins of his father, which he had
done before him: and his heart was not perfect with the Lord
his God, as the heart of David his father."

And thus he describes another king of the southern kingdom, the brother of the preceding one.

"And in the twentieth year of Jeroboam king of Israel
reigned Asa over Judah. And forty and one years reigned he in
Jerusalem. And his mother's name was Maachah, the daughter
of Abishalom. And Asa did that which was right in the eyes of
the Lord, as did David his father."

The history is built upon older foundations. Some of the
annals of the Temple are included, and the chronicles of the
kings of Israel and of Judah; but, in most cases, little is taken

259

from these, and the whole record of the kingship is compressed into a formula of praise or blame.

Some of the kings who rose in the three centuries following the time of Solomon were great men. One of these was Omri, of whom we know not only through the records of his own country but through the Moabite stone erected by Mesha, king of Moab, which records in its inscriptions that Omri conquered the whole country east of the Jordan; and for a century after the fall of his dynasty the Assyrians still referred to Israel as "the house of Omri." Another great king was Jeroboam the Second, who waged successful war against Hamath and Damascus, and who restored to the kingdom a splendor and opulence which had not been seen since the days of Solomon. But for the most part, the kings of Israel and Judah were relatively insignificant persons, and their history was only that of sordid internecine strife and of ineffectual warfares with each other and with the countries round about.

The comments of the compiler of the books of Kings upon these rulers, therefore, are one element in the narrative. The other element is a far grander and more significant one. It is made up of the records, which he took from other hands and which he has incorporated into his narrative, of the lives of some of the greatest of the prophets, beginning with the mighty figure of Elijah.

These stories of the prophets were probably written within the schools of their disciples, not long after their time. The accounts bear witness to the tremendous impression which these great figures made upon the popular mind. Their acts quickly grew into legends. The things they did and the words they said were surrounded by an atmosphere of reverence through which the facts were seen in magnified perspective. Extraordinary miracles enter into some of the accounts. It is difficult to know just what the original basis of fact was upon which the accounts as they stand now have been built. Lacking the ability for accurate analysis, it is best to take the splendid old stories as they are. What shines through them indubitably is the immense moral authority of the prophets themselves.

As human figures, they are so great that it is not strange that tradition should have surrounded them with an aura of the supernatural.

It is to the time of the reign of Ahab that the first of these records of the prophets belongs. Thirty-six years after the death of Jeroboam, in the year 875 B. C., Ahab came to the throne of Israel. He was the son of Omri, one of the ablest of the rulers of the northern kingdom. Like Jeroboam, his forerunner, Ahab tolerated the worship at many half-pagan shrines. Moreover, he married Jezebel, the daughter of the king of Tyre, and Jezebel brought with her to Israel the cult of the Phœnician Baal, so that not only the shrines of this alien god but also the Baal-priests were established in Jerusalem.

Then, with no forewarning, there appeared at the court of Ahab a champion of the worship of Jehovah, Elijah, called the Tishbite, because he was a native of Thisbe in Gilead. Of his birth and parentage no word is told. He brought no man's accrediting. Austere and solitary, he stood before the king.

"As surely as Jehovah God of Israel liveth," he said, "before whom I stand, there shall not be in these years dew or rain except according to my word."

Then he disappeared as suddenly as he had come.

The story as it is told in the first book of Kings incorporates now the saga of the prophet as it had been handed down from a time previous to the compiling of the complete book; and as the prelude to the story of Elijah's career there stands the record of three miracles which the tradition associated with his name, to be followed also later by a still more dramatic representation of what happened on Mount Carmel. Thus the story runs:

The word of the Lord came to Elijah, saying, "Get hence and turn eastward and hide by the brook Cherith in the valley of the Jordan." Moreover, the voice told him that there he could drink of the water of the brook and that the ravens would feed him.

So Elijah went and found a hiding place, and the ravens brought him bread and flesh in the morning and bread and flesh in the evening, and he drank of the brook. But after a time the brook dried up because there was no rain.

Again the word of the Lord came to him and said, "Rise, get you to Zarephath, which belongs to Zidon, and dwell there. I have commanded a widow woman there to sustain you." So Elijah arose and went to Zarephath, and when he had come to the gate of the city, a widow woman was there gathering sticks; and he called to her and said, "Fetch me, I pray you, a little water in a vessel, that I may drink." And as she was going to fetch it, he called to her and said, "Bring me, I pray you, a morsel of bread in your hand."

She answered, "As the Lord your God lives, I have nothing but a handful of meal in a barrel and a little oil in a cruse, and I am gathering sticks that I may go home and cook it for me and for my son, that we may eat it and die."

But Elijah said: "Do not fear. Go and do as you have said; but first make a little cake from the meal and oil and bring it to me, and after that, you can make something for you and for your son. For thus saith Jehovah, God of Israel, the barrel of meal shall not waste nor shall the cruse of oil fail until the day that the Lord sends rain upon the earth."

So the woman went and did as Elijah said, and she and he and her household had enough to eat for many days. The barrel of meal did not waste nor did the cruse of oil fail, according to the word of the Lord which he had spoken by Elijah.

After this it happened that the woman's son fell sick, and his sickness was so sore that there was no breath left in him. Then she cried aloud: "What have I to do with you, O you man of God? Have you come to me to call my sin to remembrance and to slay my son?"

But Elijah answered, "Give me your son." And he took him out of her bosom and he carried him up into a loft where he was staying and laid him upon his own bed; and he cried to the Lord and he said, "O Lord my God, hast thou also brought evil on the widow with whom I sojourned by slaying her son?" Three times, then, he stretched himself on the child and cried to the Lord, "O Lord my God, I pray thee let this child's soul come into him again!" And as the answer to his prayer, the soul of the little child did come into him again, and he revived. Then Elijah took him and brought him down to the house and gave him to his mother, and he said, "Look, your son lives." And the woman said to Elijah, "Now by this I know that you are a man of God, and that the word of the Lord in your mouth is truth!"

The days went by, and the months lengthened, and still there was drought in all the land. Then, in the third year, Elijah heard the voice of God commanding him, "Go show yourself to Ahab, and I will send rain upon the earth." Meanwhile in Samaria, Ahab's capital, the famine was sore.

In the court of Ahab was a man named Obadiah, whom the king had made steward of his house. Obadiah was a God-fearing man and, at the time when Jezebel had persecuted and tried to exterminate the prophets of Israel, Obadiah had hid a group of them in a cave and had sustained them there by bread and water which he had brought. To this Obadiah Ahab the king said, "Go through all the land to all the springs and to all the brooks; it may chance that we shall find there enough grass to save the horses and mules alive, so that we do not lose all the beasts." In his desperation, Ahab also set out, he going in one direction through the kingdom and Obadiah in another.

As Obadiah was on his way, suddenly in front of him stood Elijah. Obadiah fell on his face before him. "Are you my lord Elijah?" he said.

"I am," Elijah answered. "Go tell the king, 'Behold, Elijah is here.'"

But Obadiah shrank from the danger of being an intermediary between this dread prophet and the king. "What sin have I done," he pleaded, "that you should hand me over to Ahab to slay? As surely as your God Jehovah lives, there is not a nation or kingdom where the king has not sent to try to find you. And if they said that you were not there, he made them swear an oath that they had not seen you. And now you say 'Go tell the king, behold, Elijah is here!'"

Then he continued: "What if it should happen that as soon as I have left you the spirit of the Lord should carry you away and I should not know where you had gone? Then when I come and tell Ahab and he cannot find you, he will kill me. But I have feared God from my youth. Have you not been told what I did when Jezebel slew the prophets of the Lord, how I hid an hundred of them in a cave and fed them with bread and water? And still you say, 'Go tell the king, behold, Elijah is here!'—when it means that he will slay me."

But Elijah assured Obadiah with a solemn promise that he would certainly show himself to Ahab that day. Obadiah therefore went off to meet Ahab, told him what was about to happen, and Ahab came to meet Elijah. When Ahab encountered the prophet, he said, "So you are he that troubles Israel!"

But Elijah answered: "I have not troubled Israel, but you and your father's house, in that you have forsaken the commandments of Jehovah and have followed the Baalim. Now, therefore, send and gather all Israel to Mount Carmel and all the Baal prophets and the rest of those who eat at Jezebel's table."

Then Ahab sent a message everywhere that the people should assemble, and the priests of Baal were gathered at Mount Carmel.

Then when a great multitude was assembled, Elijah flung out his challenge. "How long," he said, "will you go limping between two opinions? If Jehovah be God, follow him, but if Baal, follow him." The people looked at him in awe and answered not a word.

"I, and only I, remain a prophet of Jehovah," Elijah continued, "but Baal's prophets are four hundred and fifty men. Let them therefore give us two bullocks and let them choose one bullock for themselves, cut it in pieces, lay it on wood, but put no fire yet underneath it. I will dress the other bullock and put it on wood and put no fire under it."

He turned to the priests of Baal: "Call on the name of your gods, and I will call on the name of Jehovah; and the god who answers by fire, let him be God." There was an answering shout from the people. They agreed with what Elijah had said.

"You choose one of the bullocks for yourself and dress it first," said Elijah again to the Baal priests, "for there are many of you. Call on the name of your gods, but put no fire under the sacrifice."

So the Baal priests took their bullock, and prepared it for the sacrifice; and from the morning till noon they offered their prayers and incantations. "O Baal, hear us!" they chanted, "O Baal, hear us!" But there was no voice nor any answer.

When noon had come, Elijah mocked them. "Cry aloud," he said, "for surely he is a god! He may be talking, or he is in pursuit of something. He may be on a journey. Perhaps he sleeps, and must be waked."

Then the priests of Baal cried aloud and, in the fashion of their ritual, cut themselves with knives and lances till the blood poured out upon them. But the day passed and the evening came, and still they had had no answer.

Then Elijah said to all the people, "Come near to me." And the multitude pressed closer. Elijah began to build up the altar of Jehovah which stood there on the mountaintop in ruins.

He took twelve stones, according to the number of the tribes of Israel, and with these stones rebuilt the altar in the name of Jehovah, and made a trench about it. He arranged wood upon the altar, he divided the bullock of the sacrifice and laid the pieces on the wood. "Fill four barrels with water," he said, "and pour it on the sacrifice and on the wood." They did it. "Do it a second time," he commanded. They poured the water on again. "Do it a third time," he said, and a third time they drenched the altar and the sacrifice, so that the water ran down and filled the trench.

Then at the hour of the offering of the evening sacrifice Elijah drew near the altar, and he prayed, "Lord God of Abraham, Isaac, and of Israel, let it be known this day that thou art God in Israel, and that I am thy servant, and that I have done all these things at thy word! Hear me, O Lord, hear me, that this people may know that thou art the Lord God, and that thou hast turned their heart back again."

Swift as a bolt of lightning the fire of the Lord fell, and the wood and the sacrifice burst into flames. The flames streamed out over the stones and the dust, and licked up the water in the trench. And when all the people saw it, they fell on their faces, and they said, "Jehovah, he is God; Jehovah, he is God!"

"Take the prophets of Baal," said Elijah, "do not let one of them escape." So the people seized all the Baal priests, and brought them down, at Elijah's command, to the brook Kishon, and there they slew them.

Elijah turned then to Ahab the king. "Get up, eat and drink," he said, "for there is a sound of abundance of rain." Elijah himself went up to the top of Carmel, kneeled down upon the earth, and put his face between his knees. "Go up now," he said to his servant, "and look toward the sea." The servant went up and looked, and came saying, "There is nothing." "Go back seven times," said Elijah. Then at the seventh time the servant said, "Behold, there rises a little cloud out of the sea like a man's hand;" and Elijah cried then, "Go up, say unto Ahab, 'Prepare your chariot, and get you down, that the rain may not stop you.'" And it came to pass that the heavens were black with clouds and wind, and there was a great rain. Meanwhile, through the storm Ahab drove on the road to Jezreel. But Elijah the prophet, girding up his robe, ran ahead, and came to Jezreel before Ahab could enter there.

In this tremendous fashion the followers of the prophet told the story of his triumph and his exaltation; but a different chapter was to follow.

When Ahab came to the city and told Jezebel the queen what Elijah had done, and told her how the priests of Baal had been slain, then Jezebel sent a messenger to Elijah with this word from her: "So let the gods do to me, and more also, if I do not make your life as the life of one of them by to-morrow about this time!"

Elijah was dealing now with a deadlier foe than Ahab. He arose and fled for his life, and came to Beer-sheba in the country of Judah, and left his servant there; but he himself went a day's journey farther into the wilderness, and sat down at length under a juniper tree, and there he prayed that he might die. "It is enough," he cried, "now, O Lord, take away my life; for I am not better than my fathers." Under the juniper tree he lay down and fell asleep. In his sleep he saw an angel, and twice the angel gave him food and drink, in the strength of which he went on deeper into the wilderness of Horeb.

There he lodged in a cave on the mountainside, and there the word of the Lord came to him and said, "What doest thou here, Elijah?" He answered, "I have been very jealous for the Lord God of hosts: for the children of Israel have forsaken thy covenant, thrown down thine altars, and slain thy prophets with the sword; and I, even I only, am left; and they seek my life, to take it away." But the voice said, "Go forth, and stand on the mountain before the Lord."

Then the Lord passed by, and a great and strong wind rent the mountains, and brake the rocks in pieces before the Lord; but the Lord was not in the wind. After the wind there came an earthquake; but the Lord was not in the earthquake. And after the earthquake, a fire; but the Lord was not in the fire. Then after the fire came a still small Voice.

When Elijah heard that, he wrapped his face in his mantle, and went out and stood in the entrance of the cave. Again there came to him the Voice, and it said, "What doest thou here, Elijah?" Again he answered, "I have been very jealous for the Lord God of hosts: because the children of Israel have forsaken thy covenant, thrown down thine altars, and slain thy prophets with the sword; and I, even I only, am left; and they seek my life, to take it away." The Lord said to him, "Go, return on thy way to the wilderness of Damascus: and when thou comest, anoint Hazael to be king over Syria: and Jehu the son of Nimshi shalt thou anoint to be king over Israel: and Elisha the son of Shaphat of Abel-meholah shalt thou anoint to be prophet in thy room."

So Elijah went back from Horeb down again among the ways of men. As he went, he found Elisha the son of Shaphat, plowing a field with oxen, and as Elijah passed by, he cast his mantle over Elisha's shoulder. Elisha ran after him, and asked that he might go and say farewell to his father and mother, but Elijah abruptly refused to listen. Elisha went with him, and became Elijah's disciple from that day on.

Meanwhile, an evil thing had been happening in Samaria. There was a man named Naboth who had a vineyard close to the palace of Ahab the king. One day Ahab said to Naboth: "Let me have your vineyard, that I may use it for a garden, for it is near my house. I will give you a better vineyard for it; or, if it seems good to you, I will give you the worth of it in money." But Naboth refused. He said the field had come down to him as an inheritance from his fathers. He must not part with it.

Ahab came back to his house heavy and displeased. He flung himself upon his bed, with his face averted, and sulked, and would not eat.

Jezebel his wife came in. "Why are you so dispirited," she asked, "and will eat nothing?" He told her of what he had said to Naboth about the vineyard, and of Naboth's reply. Then said Jezebel the queen: "Do you now govern the kingdom of Israel? Rise up, eat, and let your heart be merry. I will give you the vineyard of Naboth!"

Then she wrote letters in Ahab's name, and sealed them with his seal, and sent them to men who had authority in Samaria. She ordered that there should be a solemn assembly of the people, that Naboth should be accused of blasphemy against God and the king, condemned, and stoned to death.

The commands of Jezebel were obeyed. Naboth was arrested, accused, led out of the city, and stoned until he died.

When Jezebel received the message that Naboth was dead, she came and said to Ahab, "Up, and take possession of the field of Naboth which he refused to give you for money: Naboth is not alive; he is dead."

Down went Ahab toward the field of Naboth to take possession of it. But meanwhile Elijah had heard of what was done, and the word of God was hot within his heart. Suddenly Ahab found himself confronted. "Have you found me, O my enemy?" he said.

And Elijah answered: "I have found you! for you have sold yourself to work wickedness in the sight of God." And as the crime, so should be the judgment. Naboth had been put to death. But in the place where dogs had licked the blood of Naboth, in the time to come dogs should lick the blood of Ahab the king.

The first book of Kings recounts at its due place the death of Ahab; but in Ahab's lifetime the figure of Elijah appears no more. One other story in which he moves belongs to the days of Ahaziah, Ahab's son. Popular traditions concerning the prophet had grown so great, and the legends clustering round him were so full of awe, that more than ever now he is made to appear as superman. Moreover, the historian of the books of Kings found in this last incident a theme exactly suited to re-enforce his one unvarying message—that kings who became opposed to the worship of Jehovah thereby sealed their doom. From the lips of Elijah now he is preaching again upon his impassioned text.

In the days which followed the death of Ahab—so runs the narrative which opens the second book of Kings—Ahaziah his son and successor fell down through a lattice from an upper room of his palace in Samaria, and afterward lay ill. He sent messengers to the temple of Baal-zebub, the god of Ekron, to ask whether he should recover from his hurt. But Elijah met the king's messengers on their way. "Is there no God in Israel," he said, "that you go to inquire of Baal-zebub the god of Ekron?" And he told them to tell Ahaziah that because he had done this he should never come down from the bed on which he was lying, but should surely die.

When the messengers had returned to the king, they told him of what had happened on their road. "What sort of man was he who came up and spoke to you that way?" asked Ahaziah.

They answered, "He wore a mantle of hair, and he had a leather girdle about his loins."

"It is Elijah the Tishbite," said Ahaziah.

Then the king sent one of his captains with fifty men to look for Elijah, and they found him sitting on the top of a hill. "Thou man of God," the captain cried, "the king says, 'Come down.'" But Elijah answered, "If I am a man of God, let fire come down from heaven and consume you and your fifty men." And down the fire came and consumed them. Again Ahaziah sent out another fifty men, and it happened to these as it had happened to the first.

A third captain was sent with a third company of soldiers; but he did not order Elijah to come down. Instead he fell on his knees and prayed that the prophet would have mercy upon himself and upon his men. Then came Elijah down and went back with Ahaziah's captain into the presence of Ahaziah, and to the king's face he told him that, because he had sent a message to the god of Ekron, he should never leave his bed but should surely die.

The writer of the books of Kings adds the same sort of conclusion which has followed his summary of the reign of other kings, and which runs like a roll of drums through the whole long story of what he regarded as repeated religious apostasy. "So he died according to the word of the Lord which Elijah had spoken. And Jehoram reigned in his stead. Now the rest of the acts of Ahaziah which he did, are they not written in the book of the chronicles of the kings of Israel?"

There remains now with reference to Elijah only the description of his final passing from the scene. By this time he had come to be regarded as a figure not belonging to this earth, and as such the story of his departure was handed down.

One day Elijah and Elisha were at Gilgal. Elijah told his disciple to tarry there while he went on to Bethel; but Elisha would not leave his master. On the way to Bethel they encountered a group of men who belonged to the fellowship of the prophets. They said to Elisha, "Do you know that the

Lord will take away your master from your leadership to-day?"
"Yes, I know it," said Elisha; "hold your peace."

Again Elijah sought to leave Elisha behind while he went
on to Jericho, and again Elisha insisted on staying by his side.
At Jericho also another group belonging to the prophets met
Elisha and asked him, "Do you know that the Lord will take
away your master to-day?"

And he answered, "Yes, I know it; you also hold your
peace."

Down by the Jordan then Elijah went with Elisha following, and with the other men who had spoken to Elisha standing
at a distance and watching the two. As they came to the river
bank, Elijah took his mantle, wrapped it together and struck the
waters, so that they parted, and he and Elisha crossed over on
dry ground. Then said Elijah to Elisha, "Ask what you would
have me do for you before I am taken away."

And Elisha said, "I beg you, let a double portion of your
spirit be on me."

Then said Elijah: "You ask a hard thing. Nevertheless,
if you see me when I am taken from you, it shall be as you ask;
but if you do not see me, it shall not be so."

And as they went on and talked together, there appeared
a chariot and horses of fire and divided them, and Elijah went
up in a whirlwind into heaven.

Elisha, gazing after him, cried, "My father, my father, the
chariots of Israel, and the horsemen thereof!" Elijah was gone,
and Elisha saw him then no more.

He took hold of his own clothes and rent them in two.
Also he picked up the mantle which had fallen from Elijah,
and went back and stood by the bank of the Jordan; and taking
the mantle of Elijah, he struck the waters and said, "Where is
the Lord God of Elijah?" The smitten water parted, and
Elisha went over. And when the company of prophets saw
him, they said, "The spirit of Elijah rests on Elisha;" and they
came to him, and bowed before him to the ground.

CHAPTER XXV

HEN ELIJAH vanished, Ahab the king was already dead; but of the manner of his death the story must now turn back to tell. After his encounter with the king at the gate of Naboth's vineyard, Elijah did not appear again in the same scene with Ahab; but the judgment which he had pronounced on Ahab was yet to be fulfilled. This judgment the historian of the books of Kings goes on to recount, though he prefaces it also with another story of the wars of Ahab, in which this time Ahab is victorious, because for the moment it is not Ahab but his enemies who represent in the historian's eyes the sin of defiance against the Lord Jehovah.

Ben-hadad, king of Syria, had gathered all his army and chariots, and with his allies he went up and besieged Ahab's capital of Samaria. He sent a message to Ahab, demanding the surrender of the city, of the women and children, and of all the silver and gold which might be there. Ahab sent back a compliant answer, at which Ben-hadad made his demands more arrogant and insistent. He said that on the morrow he would send his servants to take away whatever they chose. Ahab called his counselors together; and, encouraged by them, he defied this threat.

When Ben-hadad heard that, he sent back a message more insolent than the first. He said he hoped the gods would grind him to powder if he did not so destroy Samaria that there would not be enough dust of it left for each man in his army to take a handful. But Ahab answered, "Tell him, 'Let not him that girds on his harness boast himself as he that puts it off.'"

When that reply came to him, Ben-hadad and his allies were drinking in his pavilions; but he gave the command to his army to set itself in order for assault upon the city. Meanwhile to Ahab there had come an unnamed prophet. He predicted that Ahab should defeat Ben-hadad. And so it happened. For a sudden attack from Samaria, while Ben-hadad and his allies were drinking themselves drunk in his pavilions, routed his army, and Ben-hadad himself barely managed to escape among his fleeing horsemen.

Again came the prophet to Ahab, advising him that he should make his forces stronger and be vigilant in everything he did; "for at the return of the year the king of Syria will come upon you again."

In the meantime the Syrians were saying to Ben-hadad concerning the Israelites: "Their gods are gods of the hills; that is why they were stronger than we; but let us fight against them in the plain, and certainly we shall be stronger than they are. Moreover, do this: Take the kings away, every man of them, and put real captains in their places; and gather a new army, like the army you have lost, horse for horse, and chariot for chariot. Then we will fight against the Israelites in the plains, and we shall win." So Ben-hadad listened, and he did as he had been advised.

The next spring he mustered his army, and went up to Aphek, to attack Israel. The armies of Israel were gathered also; but they looked like little flocks of goats on the mountainside, while the Syrians filled the land.

Then came again the prophet to Ahab, and delivered to him this message: "Thus saith the Lord, 'Because the Syrians have said, "Jehovah is a God of the hills and not a God of the valleys," therefore will I deliver all this great multitude into your hands, and you shall know that I am the Lord.' "

For seven days, the armies lay confronting one another; and on the seventh day when the battle commenced, the Syrians were routed with a great havoc, and Ben-hadad fled to his own city, and went and hid in his palace in an inner room. His servants, gathering round him, said: "Look now, we have heard that the kings of Israel are merciful kings: let us put sackcloth upon our loins and ropes upon our heads, and go out to meet the king of Israel. It may be he will spare your life."

So they did gird sackcloth about them, and put ropes on their heads, and went out to meet Ahab, and said to him, "Your servant Ben-hadad says, 'I beg you, let me live.'"

"Is he still alive then?" answered Ahab. "He is my brother."

A man who listened to him caught at that word "brother," and they all echoed it. "Yes, your brother Ben-hadad," they said.

"Go bring him," said Ahab.

So Ben-hadad's servants carried him the message, and he came out to meet Ahab, and Ahab had him climb up into his chariot.

Said Ben-hadad, "I will restore all the cities which my father took from your father, and you shall have bazaars in Damascus, as my father had in Samaria."

"With this promise," Ahab said, "I will let you go;" so he made a covenant with Ben-hadad, and sent him away.

But Ahab's leniency provoked swift resentment in Israel. A man belonging to one of the companies of the prophets turned to one of his neighbors and said, "Strike me." The man refused, and was direly threatened for his refusal. The prophet went up to another man. "Strike me," he said. This man did strike him, and strike him hard enough to give him a wound. The prophet went off and waited by the roadside for the king, having disguised himself with ashes spread upon his face. As the king passed by, he cried to him and he said: "Your servant went out into the midst of the battle. A soldier stopped and brought a man to me, and said: 'Keep this man. If by any means he should be missing, then your life shall be forfeit for his life, or else you shall pay a talent of silver;' but as I was busy here and there, the prisoner was gone."

Impatiently Ahab answered: "The judgment on you shall be as you have said. You have decided it yourself."

Then quickly the prophet rose and wiped the ashes from

his face, and Ahab discerned who he was. And the prophet said, "Thus saith the Lord, 'Because you have allowed to escape out of your hand the man whom I have appointed to utter destruction, therefore your life shall go for his life, and your people for his people.'"

And Ahab went back to Samaria, heavy of heart, and dispirited.

Three years went by, and in that period there was no war between Syria and Israel; but in the third year, Jehoshaphat the king of Judah came to visit the king of Israel. Ahab already had a reason which made him ready to take up arms again. He had been saying to his men, "You know that Ramoth in Gilead belongs to us, and here we are doing nothing to take it away from the king of Syria." Then when Jehoshaphat had come, he asked him, "Will you go with me to battle for Ramoth-gilead?"

And Jehoshaphat answered expansively that he was altogether at one with Ahab, and his army should be like Ahab's army, and his horses like Ahab's horses. But Jehoshaphat wanted to know what the religious omens might be. He asked Ahab to inquire. So Ahab assembled a whole company of prophets, and asked them whether he should go up to Ramoth-gilead to battle, or whether he should not go up. They all declared that the Lord would deliver the town into Ahab's hands. Jehoshaphat, however, was not satisfied. He wanted to know whether all the prophets had spoken. Was there any one besides who also might be inquired of?

Then Ahab admitted that there was one other man, Micaiah the son of Imlah, by whom the will of God might be sought. "But I hate him," said Ahab, "for he does not prophesy good about me, but always evil."

Jehoshaphat thought that Ahab had better not say that. He wanted to hear what Micaiah might predict. So Ahab sent one of his officers to bring Micaiah; and, meantime, he and Jehoshaphat put on their robes and took their places upon their thrones, which had been set in an open space outside the gate of Samaria. All the crowd of the prophets repeated their predictions before them. One of them named Zedekiah, by way of emphasizing the prophecy, made some horns of iron and exhibited these to the kings. "With these you shall push the Syrians until you have destroyed them," he declared; and the whole chorus echoed what he said.

The officer who had gone for Micaiah, meanwhile, thought to give him safe advice. He told him that all the other prophets unanimously had predicted good for Ahab, and that he had better speak in the same fashion. But Micaiah answered: "As the Lord lives, what the Lord says to me, that will I speak."

So he came to the king. "Micaiah," said Ahab, "shall we go against Ramoth-gilead to battle, or shall we refrain?"

"Go," said Micaiah, "and prosper; the Lord will deliver it into the king's hands."

"How many times," said Ahab, "must I adjure you to tell me nothing but what is true in God's name?"

So it was the truth he wanted. Well, then, he should have it. "I saw all Israel scattered upon the hills as sheep without a shepherd," said Micaiah. "And the Lord said, 'These have no master: let them every one return to his house in peace.'"

Ahab turned to Jehoshaphat. "Did I not tell you that he would prophesy no good about me, but evil?"

Micaiah was not dismayed. He repeated the prophecy which he had already uttered. He said that it was a lying spirit which had spoken from the mouth of the other prophets. Zedekiah, the man who had made himself conspicuous with his horns of iron, went up and struck Micaiah on the cheek. "Which way did the Spirit of the Lord go from me to speak to you?" he taunted.

"You shall see," said Micaiah, "in the day when you shall run from one inner chamber to another to hide yourself!"

"Take this Micaiah and carry him to the governor of the city," said Ahab, "and tell him that the king's orders are to put this fellow in prison, and to feed him with the bread and water of affliction until I come in peace."

But Micaiah said, "If you return at all in peace, the Lord

has not spoken by me." And he called all the people to be his witness.

Up to Ramoth-gilead, then, the kings of Israel and Judah marched, and Ahab said to Jehoshaphat, "I will disguise myself when I go into the battle; but you put on your royal robes." So Ahab did disguise himself.

Meanwhile Ben-hadad of Syria had commanded all the captains of his chariots not to concern themselves with anyone, small or great, except with the king of Israel himself. When they saw Jehoshaphat, they said to themselves that this must certainly be the king of Israel, and they rushed against him until Jehoshaphat cried out, and they saw that it was not Ahab.

Meanwhile an archer in the Syrian army had drawn his bow at a venture, and his arrow struck the king of Israel between the joints of his armor. "Turn," he said to the driver of his chariot, "and carry me out of the army, for I am wounded!" Meanwhile the battle raged more furiously, and Ahab, propped up in his chariot, died at evening, and the blood dripped out of his wound upon the chariot floor. Then when the sun went down, the word ran through all the army: "Every man to his own city, and every man for himself!"

So king Ahab died, and his body was brought to Samaria and buried there; and when at the pool of Samaria his chariot and his armor were washed, dogs came and licked up his blood. The prophecy of Elijah had been fulfilled.

CHAPTER XXVI

THE STORIES WHICH WERE TOLD OF ELISHA, THE FOLLOWER OF
ELIJAH—ESPECIALLY OF HOW HE HEALED NAAMAN, THE SYRIAN, OF
HIS LEPROSY, AND OF HOW HE SAW THE CHARIOTS OF FIRE; AND THE
STORY OF JEHU, AND OF THE DEATH OF JEZEBEL.

THROUGH ALL his career, Elijah had been the
spokesman of the righteousness of God and
the incarnate conscience of his time. When
Elijah had gone, Elisha was left to carry on his
work; but the disciple was a lesser man than
his master. He never attained the heroic
moral stature which had made Elijah's authority so tremendous.
Traditions clustered thick about him, as they had about Elijah;
but they are of a somewhat different kind. The man himself
does not loom so large; the legends of miracles loom larger.
The wonders told of him do not seem to be so directly the out-
growth of moral character as they were with Elijah. Sometimes
they appear to be only the popular embellishments wrought out
of the still crude beliefs of a generation which supposed that a
divine commission must be attested by acts of arbitrary power.

A number of such traditions about Elisha follow one another in the second chapter of the second book of Kings. He
puts some salt into a spring near Jericho, and transforms it so
that the waters, which had been unwholesome before, now are
"healed." He goes up along the road to Bethel; and some
children, coming out of the town, begin to mock him and shout
after him, "Go up, you bald head." Whereupon, Elisha turns
back and curses them; and, as the executors of his curse, two she-
bears come out of the wood and mangle forty-two of the
children.

Jehoram, the new king of Israel; and Jehoshaphat, king of
Judah; and the king of Edom go to make war against the king

278

of Moab, and Elisha is sent for to ask for auguries of victory. He snubs the king of Israel, but for the sake of the king of Judah (where the orthodox worship of Jehovah is maintained) he prophesies victory, and the victory comes to pass, notwithstanding that the king of Moab offers up his own son in human sacrifice on the walls of his beleaguered town. A woman comes to Elisha, telling him she is in debt, and he has her borrow from her neighbors all the empty oil jars she can get, and then these are miraculously filled with oil, so that she pays off her debts, and has money enough left for all her family to live on. He visits a great lady of the town of Shunem, who furnishes for him a prophet's chamber where he may always make himself at home when he comes that way. He promises to her a son, who is duly born. And then the child, after he is grown to be a lad, suddenly falls sick one day in a harvest field, is carried home, and dies on his mother's knees. Elisha raises him from the dead.

He goes to Gilgal, and finds a group of men about to eat some pottage into which had been put herbs that were partly poisonous; and he mixes some meal in the pottage and removes the poison. Also he multiplies food, so that a large company has enough.

Later, when a group of men are building a house by the River Jordan, one man's iron axe-head falls into the water—to his great distress, because it was a borrowed axe. But Elisha cuts a stick and throws it into the river over the place where the axe-head had sunk, and the axe-head swims to the surface, so that the man who has lost it reaches out his hand and grasps it.

But the longest story about Elisha, and the one which has in it most of interest and also most of beauty, is the story of Naaman, the Syrian. Naaman was an army commander of the king of Syria, a great and honorable man in his master's eyes, and a valiant soldier; but he was a leper. Now, it happened that on one of the raids which the Syrians had made into the land of Israel, they had brought back a little maid as one of their captives, and she waited on Naaman's wife.

Said she one day to her mistress: "Would God that my

lord were with the prophet who is in Samaria! He would heal him of his leprosy."

Someone who heard her went and told the king of Syria that a little maid who belonged to the land of Israel had said thus and so; and the king said, "Come, then, I will send a letter to the king of Israel." And the servant to whom the king had spoken set out with the letter and with rich presents of silver and gold and raiment. The letter which he carried to the king of Israel began as follows: "Now when this letter is come to you, behold, I have therewith sent Naaman my servant to you, that you may heal him of his leprosy." But when the king of Israel read that letter, he rent his clothes and cried: "Am I God, to kill and to make alive, that this man should send to me to heal a man of his leprosy? Look now, I pray you, and see how he is seeking a quarrel against me!"

But when Elisha had heard what had happened, he sent word to the king of Israel, demanding to know why he had rent his clothes.

"Let the man come now to me," he said, "and he shall know that there is a prophet in Israel."

To where Elisha lived, therefore, went Naaman with his horses and his chariot, and he stood at the door of Elisha's house. Elisha sent out a message: "Go and wash in the Jordan seven times and your flesh shall be restored, and you shall be clean."

But Naaman was indignant, and went away. "See here," he said, "I thought he would surely come out to me, and stand, and call on the name of Jehovah his God, and put his hand over the leprous place, and heal it. Are not Abana and Pharpar, rivers of Damascus, better than all the waters of Israel? May I not wash in them and be clean?" So he turned and went away in a rage.

But his servants came round him, and they said: "If the prophet had told you to do some great thing, would you not have done it? How much rather then should you do it when all he says is, 'Wash, and be clean'!"

Naaman listened, and his temper cooled. He went down and dipped himself seven times in Jordan, according to the saying of Elisha; and his flesh was restored, like the flesh of a little child, and he was clean.

Glad and marveling, back to Elisha then he went, he and all his company, and stood before the prophet; and he said, "Behold, now I know that there is no God in all the earth, but in Israel. Now, therefore, I pray you, take a present from your servant." But Elisha vowed that he would take none; and, in spite of Naaman's urging, he refused.

Then Naaman made a request for himself. He considered that he had been healed by Elisha's god, the god whose territory was the land of Israel. Every god, he supposed, belonged only to his own land and could be worshiped only there. If, then, he wanted to give thanks to Elisha's god and invoke his continuing aid after he had gone out of Israel and back to Syria, how could he do it? There was one answer. If he could take away with him part of the actual soil of Israel which was the realm of Israel's god and make a shrine elsewhere of that, then the power of that god would still be there. So he said to Elisha: "I beg you, give me two mules' burden of earth, for I will henceforth offer no burnt-offering nor sacrifice unto any other gods except Jehovah. But there is one thing in which may the Lord pardon me! When my master goes into the house of Rimmon to worship there, and leans on my arm, then I have to bow also in the house of Rimmon. When I do that, may your God pardon me."

So Elisha granted him his request, and sent him on his way in peace. But Gehazi, the servant of Elisha, said to himself: "Look how my master has spared this Syrian, Naaman; and has not received any of the presents which he brought. Now, as God lives, I will run after him and get something from him." So he followed after Naaman.

When Naaman saw him running after, he alighted from his chariot to meet him, and asked, "Is all well?"

"Yes, all is well," Gehazi answered. "My master sent me to say that two young men of a company of prophets have just come from Mount Ephraim. He asks you please to give them four hundred pounds in silver and two new robes."

Then Naaman told him to have no uneasiness. He would

give him double what he asked. So back came Gehazi with two servants carrying rich gifts; and when they came near the town, he took these from them and bestowed them in his house. Then he went in to wait upon Elisha.

"Where have you been, Gehazi?" said Elisha.

"I have not been anywhere," Gehazi answered.

But Elisha said, "Did not my heart go with you when Naaman turned back from his chariot to meet you? Do you think this is a time to receive money, to receive garments, and oliveyards, and vineyards, and sheep, and oxen, and menservants and womenservants! Now the leprosy of Naaman shall be visited upon you and upon your children!"

And Gehazi went out from Elisha's presence a leper, as white as snow.

In this story there was friendship between at least one Syrian and the prophet. In the next story the relationship was different. A king of Syria was warring now against Israel. But Elisha sent a message to the king of Israel, saying "Beware that you do not pass such and such a place; for that is where the Syrians will be." So the king of Israel, through the warning of the prophet, escaped the ambush into which he might have stumbled.

Then the king of Syria was greatly irritated. He called his officers, and demanded to know which one of them was playing traitor and selling secrets to the king of Israel. One of them answered: "Not one of us, O lord king. Elisha, the prophet who is in Israel, is the one who tells the king of Israel the very words you whisper in your bedchamber." So the king ordered that spies go to find out where Elisha was, and the message was brought back that he was at Dothan.

To Dothan, therefore, the king of Syria sent a detachment of horsemen and chariots, and a large force, and they, marching by night, surrounded the town. The next morning, when Elisha's servant had arisen early and gone out, he looked and saw the army surrounding the city with horses and chariots. "Alas, my master!" he cried, "What shall we do?"

But Elisha answered: "Do not be afraid: those who are with us are more than those that are with them." And Elisha prayed: "Lord, I pray thee, open his eyes, that he may see." And the Lord opened the eyes of the young man, so that he saw: and, behold, the mountain was full of horses and chariots of fire round about Elisha.

There came another time of danger which revealed Elisha's power still more significantly. Ben-hadad, king of Syria, assembled his army and laid siege to Israel's capital city of Samaria; and the siege was so close that there was a great famine in the town; until the head of an ass fetched ten pounds in silver and the offscourings of food were sold for twelve shillings. To still more horrible straits the people came. One day as the king of Israel was passing by on the wall, a woman cried out and asked his help. What was the matter with her? he asked. And in reply she accused another woman of having entered into an agreement with her to kill and eat their two children; but after she had killed her child the other woman had hidden hers. When the king heard that, he put on sackcloth; and then he began to think that Elisha was somehow responsible for these horrors, and that if he were the right sort of prophet, he would have prevailed upon God to prevent them.

But Elisha said, "Listen to this word of the Lord. Thus saith Jehovah the Lord: 'To-morrow about this time a peck of fine flour shall be sold for only half a crown, and two measures of barley for the same, and that in the gate of Samaria.'"

"Yes," said one of the king's officers, "if the Lord made windows in heaven, then the thing might be."

"Well," said Elisha, "you shall see it with your own eyes, but you shall not eat of it."

Now, near the gate of Samaria, there were four lepers, and they said to one another: "What is the use of sitting here until we die? If we go into Samaria, the famine is in the city, and we shall die there. If we sit still here, then we shall die here. We may as well go and be taken prisoners by the Syrians. If they take us alive, then there we are living; if they kill us, then death would be only what we should have got anyway."

So at twilight they started off for the camp of the Syrians. But when they were come to the outmost fringe of it, to their astonishment they found not a single man there, for a rumor had spread in the Syrian army that the Hittites and the Egyptians were marching against them; and as the darkness came on, they left their tents, their horses, their asses, and the whole camp as it was, and they fled as though for their lives. When the lepers came to the edge of the camp, they went into one tent, ate and drank, and carried out silver and gold and clothes, and hid them. Then they came back and went into another tent, and carried out the contents from that tent also, and hid these too. After that, they bethought them that they ought to be carrying the message of this good news about the Syrian army back to Samaria. So they returned, and called to the guard at the gate, and told how they had been to the camp of the Syrians and discovered nobody there, but only horses and asses tied, and the tents left as though they were abandoned, without so much as the sound of a human voice anywhere among them. So one of the watch called the others, and they sent the news to the king's palace within.

When the king was roused in the night and got up to hear the news which was brought to him, he did not believe it. "I will show you," he said, "what the Syrians have done to us. They know that we are starving, and so they have withdrawn from the camp to ambush themselves in the field, planning that, when we come out of the city, they can capture us and get into Samaria."

But one of his officers urged that a few men should take some of the starving horses that remained in the city, and ride out on these and see what actually had happened. So two men, mounted on two of the chariot horses, went out toward the Syrian camp, and passed the camp on the way leading down toward the Jordan River; and they found the whole road full of weapons and other things which the Syrians in their haste had flung away. Then these men came back and told the king, and the people of Samaria streamed out and looted the tents of the Syrians, so that presently it came true that a peck of fine flour was sold for a shekel, and two pecks of barley for the same.

Meanwhile, the king had ordered the same officer who had questioned Elisha's prediction to take command at the gate; but the crowd ran over him and trod him underfoot, so that he died; and the thing had been fulfilled which Elisha had said, namely, that he should see with his own eyes cheap food instead of famine, but that he should not live to eat that food himself.

Much had been written now in the books of Kings since the prediction ascribed to Elijah of the end of the dynasties of Israel and Judah, and now come the final stories in which that prediction was fulfilled.

Ben-hadad, the king of Syria, fell sick; and while he was lying thus, it was told him that the prophet Elisha had come to Damascus. Ben-hadad sent to Elisha to ask him for some revelation as to whether he should recover from his disease. The man whom Ben-hadad sent as his messenger to Elisha was Hazael; and when Hazael arrived, Elisha told him that he should be king of Syria. Back went Hazael to Ben-hadad, and he told Ben-hadad that Elisha had said that he would certainly recover. But the next day Hazael smothered Ben-hadad with a wet cloth upon his face, and, when Ben-hadad was dead, Hazael seized his throne.

In the meantime Joram, the second son of Ahab, had succeeded to the kingship of Israel; and the new king of Judah, who had the same name as a former king of Israel, Ahaziah, was also of the blood of Ahab, since his mother was Ahab's sister. The king of Judah and his cousin of Israel went to war together against Hazael, the new king of Syria, and in the ensuing battle Joram was wounded and went back to the city of Jezreel to recover, and the king of Judah went to visit him there.

The time had come for the end of Ahab's house, and events moved swiftly. Elisha called to him one of the young neophytes of the prophetic group, and gave him a vial of holy oil, and told him to go to the east of the Jordan to the town of Ramoth-gilead. There he should find a soldier by the name of Jehu. He was to call Jehu out from whatever company he might be in, carry him to another room, and there anoint him king of Israel. Then he was to open the door and flee.

The young man went to Ramoth-gilead, and there a group of army commanders were sitting together, and among them Jehu. "Captain," he said, "I have an errand for you."

"For which of us?" said Jehu.

"For you," he answered.

So Jehu got up and went inside to another room, and the messenger poured the oil on his head, and said, "Thus saith the Lord God of Israel, 'I have anointed you king over the people of the Lord, even over Israel.'" Furthermore, he went on to say that Jehu should smite the house of Ahab, and avenge on Jezebel the blood of all the prophets whom she had slain. The whole family of Ahab was to be destroyed; and, as for Jezebel, she should be eaten by dogs. Having said that, he opened the door and fled.

Jehu went back then to the circle of officers. "Is everything all right?" asked one of them.

"What did this mad fellow want?"

"You know who he is, and what he had to say," said Jehu.

"You lie;" they answered, "tell us what it was."

So Jehu told them what he did say, and how this messenger from Elisha had anointed him king of Israel. They sprang up then, and took their robes and spread them on the stairs for Jehu to stand upon: and they blew a flourish of trumpets, and saluted Jehu as king.

Meanwhile Joram, king of Israel, was still in Jezreel recovering from his wounds, and Jehu's first order was that no one should be allowed to go out of Ramoth-gilead to carry any news to Jezreel. Jehu himself mounted his chariot and drove off toward Jezreel, where not only Joram was but Ahaziah, king of Judah, also. The watchman on the tower of Jezreel looked out and saw Jehu and his escort approaching, and reported that he saw a company drawing near. So Joram said, "Send a horseman out to meet them, and let him say, 'Is it peace?'"

So a soldier on horseback went out to meet Jehu; and when he had come to him, he said, "Thus saith the king, 'Is it peace?' "

"What have you to do with peace?" answered Jehu. "Turn around and come behind me."

The watchman from the wall of Jezreel saw this, and reported, "The messenger came to those men, but he is not coming back again."

So a second horseman was dispatched, who also met Jehu and repeated the message of the first: "Thus saith the king, 'Is it peace?' "

And Jehu answered as before, "What have you got to do with peace? Turn around and come behind me."

A second time the watchman on the wall reported what had happened, and he added that the driving of the man who was approaching was like the driving of Jehu the son of Nimshi, "for he drives furiously."

Joram ordered then that the chariots be made ready, and he and the king of Judah drove out, each one in his chariot, to encounter Jehu; and they met him on the land of Naboth the Jezreelite. When Joram saw Jehu, he said: "Is it peace, Jehu?"

"What sort of peace so long as the villainies of your mother Jezebel and her witchcrafts are multiplied?" he answered.

With that, Joram turned his chariot about and fled, and called to the king of Judah, "There is treachery, Ahaziah!" But as he turned, Jehu drew a bow with his full strength, and the arrow which he shot struck Joram between his shoulders and went out at his heart, and he sank down in his chariot. Whereupon Jehu ordered one of his captains to take the body of Joram and throw it into the field of Naboth, to fulfill the judgment on Ahab and his sons.

Ahaziah, the king of Judah, seeing all this, fled past the garden house of Jezreel, and Jehu, following after him, tried to smite him also in his chariot. Pursuers who overtook him did so, and Ahaziah, though he reached the fortress of Megiddo, reached there only to die. Then his servants carried his body in a chariot to Jerusalem, and buried it in the royal sepulcher there.

Jehu, after his arrow had killed Joram, went on into Jezreel, and the old queen, Jezebel, heard of his entrance. She painted her face, and arranged her hair, and looked out of a window. As Jehu drove into the gate, the queen, who, if she was wicked, was also fearless, called to him, "Did Zimri have peace, when he had slain his master?" (Zimri, who had assassinated one of the former kings of Israel, was burned alive in his own palace by Omri, the father of Ahab, after he had reigned exactly seven days.)

Jehu looked up at the window, and he said, "Who is on my side, who?" And with that two or three palace servants thrust out their heads. "Throw her down," said he, as he pointed to Jezebel. So they threw her down from the window, and her blood was sprinkled on the wall, and on the horses as the chariot of Jehu drove over her body on the ground.

When Jehu had entered into the palace and was sitting down to eat and drink, he said, "Go see about this cursed woman, and bury her; she is a king's daughter." But when they went to bury her, they found nothing left except a few bones, for the dogs had eaten her.

But the grisly tale was still not at an end. In Samaria were many other descendants of Ahab. So Jehu wrote letters to the officials in Samaria and to the guardians of Ahab's family. And he challenged them, inasmuch as they had chariots and horses and a fortified city, to take the best and fittest of their master's sons, set him on his father's throne and fight to maintain him. But these chief men of Samaria, when they received Jehu's letter, were terrified, and they said, "Two kings were not able to stand before him; how then should we stand?" So they sent back to Jehu a message of abject submission. Then Jehu wrote a second letter; and in it he demanded that, if these men wanted to be considered as on his side, they should take the heads of all Ahab's male descendants and send them in baskets to him in Jezreel. In the morning, when Jehu came out, the heads of all these who remained of Ahab's royal family had been laid in two piles by the gate of Jezreel.

After that, Jehu dealt in equally ruthless fashion with the

descendants of Ahaziah, king of Judah; but there was also one more group which he meant to remove. At Samaria he met a man named Jehonadab, the son of Rechab, a man evidently of the sort to be his instrument. Jehu considered himself, as other men also in other centuries have believed themselves to be, a sort of scourge of God; and his idea was that implacable killing of all the opponents of the worship of Jehovah was an act of religious virtue. "Come with me, and see my zeal for the Lord," he said to Jehonadab, and he took him with him in his chariot.

When they had come into Samaria, Jehu assembled all the people and said: "Ahab served Baal a little; but Jehu shall serve him much. Call all the prophets of Baal, and his servants, and his priests, and tell them to come to me; let not one of them be absent: I have a great sacrifice to make to Baal; and no man who is lacking shall live." This he said in deception to cloak his real purpose, which was to bring all the Baal priests together where he could destroy them. At Jehu's command, all the worshipers of Baal did assemble, and they filled the Baal temple from one end to the other.

"Let them put on the vestments of Baal," Jehu commanded; and then he ordered that no one who was not a genuine Baal worshiper should be allowed to stay there. The sacrifice to Baal was begun; and in the midst of it Jehu's soldiers at his orders fell upon the worshipers and put the whole throng to the sword, after which Jehu had the images of Baal dragged out and broken and burned.

All this, so far as it went, brought a grim satisfaction to all the fiercely conscientious religious zealots, who thought then, as men have thought in other times, that fire and sword can somehow cure apostasy; and thus the historian of the books of Kings sums up the story of Jehu:

"Thus Jehu destroyed Baal out of Israel. Howbeit from the sins of Jeroboam the son of Nebat, who made Israel to sin, Jehu departed not from after them, to wit, the golden calves that were in Bethel, and that were in Dan. And the Lord said unto Jehu, Because thou hast done well in executing that which is right in mine eyes, and hast done unto the house of Ahab according to all that was in mine heart, thy children of the fourth generation shall sit on the throne of Israel. But Jehu took no heed to walk in the law of the Lord God of Israel with all his heart; for he departed not from the sins of Jeroboam, which made Israel to sin.

"In those days the Lord began to cut Israel short: and Hazael smote them in all the coasts of Israel; from Jordan eastward, all the land of Gilead, the Gadites, and the Reubenites, and the Manassites, from Aroer, which is by the river Arnon, even Gilead and Bashan. Now the rest of the acts of Jehu, and all that he did, and all his might, are they not written in the book of the chronicles of the kings of Israel? And Jehu slept with his fathers: and they buried him in Samaria. And Jehoahaz his son reigned in his stead."

CHAPTER XXVII

WHICH TREATS OF THE LIFE WHICH PEOPLE LIVED IN THE KINGDOM
OF ISRAEL IN THE EIGHTH CENTURY B. C.; AND OF AMOS, THE
PROPHET WHO CAME OUT OF THE DESERT TO REBUKE THE SINS OF
THE NATION AT THE SHRINE OF THE KING; AND OF HOSEA, THE
PROPHET OF COMPASSION.

AFTER AHAZIAH, king of Judah, had been killed by Jehu, there was confusion in Jerusalem; and Ahaziah's mother seized power, after a ruthless massacre of others of the royal line. Only one little son of Ahaziah's was rescued, and secretly hidden away. Later, through the help of the priest Jehoiada, he was crowned as the boy King Jehoash, and Jehoash gained much favor from the religious group by restoring the Temple, which had fallen into disrepair. But he was killed at last in a conspiracy, and the history of the kingdom of Judah for the next century was for the most part a confused record of intrigue, sordid civil strife, and ineffective foreign wars.

In the northern kingdom of Israel, Jehu reigned from about the year 842 B. C. until 815. The next two kings were inconsequential; but in 784 there came to the throne one of the ablest and most powerful of all the rulers, Jeroboam the Second. As a soldier, he won conspicuous victories, extending the territories of Israel both to the north and south, and being credited even with conquering Damascus. Moreover, in his time there was a great increase of material prosperity. Commerce flourished, and wealth flowed into the kingdom. At Samaria and at Bethel, there arose a kind of opulent and luxurious civilization which surpassed anything which had been seen since the days of Solomon.

But the material wealth of Israel was not accompanied by a parallel increase either in social justice or in religion. Greed

291

was rampant. The rich were growing richer, but the poor were despised and oppressed. The appearance of religion was ostentatiously maintained. Lavish offerings were brought to the various shrines. So-called religious festivals attracted careless crowds; but there was little moral conscience and little real devotion anywhere.

It was at this time, and into the midst of this civilization, that another one of the great prophets came, the first of the prophets whose message has survived in written form. His name was Amos. He was not a native of the northern kingdom, but of Judah. He dwelt in the sterile wilderness of Tekoa, south of Jerusalem. There he lived amid the stark realities of a hard existence, a man of few wants and few possessions, alert, self-disciplined, and unafraid. In this sterile region of moorland, where grew sparse desert broom and a few thin patches of wheat, where Bedouin roved and wild beasts prowled by night, he guarded his sheep. But though he thus lived in the wastes, he was no great distance from civilization. The highroad north from Hebron lay only a few hours' journey to the west. Twelve miles along that road would bring him to Jerusalem, and ten miles farther would carry him over the border to the shrine of Bethel in the kingdom of Israel. This city with its shrine was also a market town, where traders and merchants from all quarters congregated; and thither Amos was accustomed to go up, carrying the wool of his sheep to the market, and carrying also that poorest of fruits, grown on the sycamore trees, which could be cultivated here and there in Tekoa.

Amos, so far as is known, had no formal education. Certainly, he had no commission from any other man; but he was one of those religious geniuses in whom the consciousness of God blazes into a flame of authentic revelation. There in the solitudes of the desert he thought and pondered. His clear eyes had seen, and his clean moral judgment had appraised, the facts of the insolent and godless civilization which flaunted its new wealth at Bethel. And then one day at the shrine at Bethel he began to speak. Solitary and intrepid, like another Elijah, he stood there; but the message which he voiced, and which is written in the book that bears his name, was richer and nobler than the message of Elijah.

Against the opulent self-assurance of those who gathered at the shrine Amos pronounced a message of judgment and of doom. "Seek not Bethel," he said, "nor enter into Gilgal, and pass not to Beer-sheba: for Gilgal shall surely go into captivity, and Bethel shall come to nought. Seek the Lord, and ye shall live; lest he break out like fire in the house of Joseph, and devour it, and there be none to quench it in Bethel." And then he went on to tell of a vision in which he had seen the righteousness of God condemn all the proud structure of the nation's life as one might condemn a tottering wall. "Behold, the Lord stood upon a wall made by a plumbline, with a plumbline in his hand. And the Lord said unto me, 'Amos, what seest thou?' And I said, 'A plumbline.' Then said the Lord, 'Behold, I will set a plumbline in the midst of my people Israel: I will not pass by them any more.'"

The appearance of this self-appointed prophet, this nobody out of the desert, daring to speak thus at the royal shrine, aroused an immediate clamor of indignation. Amaziah, the priest, sent an excited message to King Jeroboam. "Amos," he said, "has conspired against you in the midst of the house of Israel, and the land cannot bear his words. For this is what Amos says, 'Jeroboam shall die by the sword, and Israel shall surely be led away captive out of their own land.'"

To Amos Amaziah said: "You seer, go out of here. Be off into your land of Judah. Eat your bread, and do your prophesying there. But do not ever prophesy again at Bethel, for it is the king's sanctuary, and it is a royal house."

But this priest had no terrors for Amos. "I was no prophet," he said, "neither was I a prophet's son; but I was a herdsman, and a gatherer of sycamore fruit. And the Lord took me as I followed the flock, and the Lord said to me, 'Go, prophesy to my people Israel.' Now, therefore, you shall hear the word of the Lord!" And he launched against Israel and against Amaziah personally a prediction of doom which was terrific.

Three great notes mark the prophecy of Amos and exalt his message to a height of moral and spiritual perception which had never been reached before. In the first place, he swept not one nation only but all nations with the scrutiny of his moral judgment, and arraigned them all alike as accountable to the holiness of God. In the second place, he insisted with passionate intensity that God's will is righteousness, and he identified righteousness, as Elijah had done in the case of Ahab and Naboth, with social justice and fairness and mercy between man and man. In the third place, he proclaimed the unheard-of conviction that the fact that Jehovah had always been Israel's own God, did not mean that he would protect that nation above all the rest. It meant that Israel's responsibility was all the greater, and that, if it were morally delinquent, it should face a more inevitable doom. In the name of God he cried, "You only have I known of all the families of the earth: therefore I will punish you for all your iniquities."

The book of Amos begins with his review of the other nations. They and their cruelties are destined to be punished, and not the less when their cruelties are visited on those who happen to be enemies of Israel. Damascus, Gaza, and the other Philistine cities, Tyre, Edom, and Moab—upon all these he pronounced the certainty of punishment; and then, as the climax, he turned to Judah and to Israel.

"Thus saith the Lord: 'For three transgressions of Judah, yea, for four, I will not turn away the punishment thereof; because they have rejected the law of the Lord, and have not kept his statutes, and their lies have caused them to err. . . . But I will send a fire upon Judah, and it shall devour the palaces of Jerusalem.' "

"Thus saith the Lord: 'For three transgressions of Israel, yea, for four, I will not turn away the punishment thereof; because they have sold the righteous for silver, and the needy for a pair of shoes—they that pant after the dust of the earth on the head of the poor, and turn aside the way of the meek. . . .' "

"Behold, I will press you in your place, as a cart presseth that is full of sheaves. And flight shall perish from the swift;

and the strong shall not strengthen his force; neither shall the mighty deliver himself; neither shall he stand that handleth the bow; and he that is swift of foot shall not deliver himself; neither shall he that rideth the horse deliver himself; and he that is courageous among the mighty shall flee away naked in that day, saith the Lord."

Here in this arraignment of the sins of the nations, Amos has already linked religion with social righteousness; but he goes on to make this still more specific as his indignant spirit flames again against the self-indulgence and the cruelty of the rich.

"I will smite the winter-house with the summer-house; and the houses of ivory shall perish, and the great houses shall have an end, saith the Lord."

"Hear this word, ye kine of Bashan, that are in the mountain of Samaria, which oppress the poor, which crush the needy, which say unto their lords, 'Bring, and let us drink.' The Lord God hath sworn by his holiness, that, lo, the days shall come upon you, that they shall take you away with hooks, and your residue with fishhooks. . . . And because I will do this unto thee, prepare to meet thy God, O Israel. For, lo, he that formeth the mountains, and createth the wind, and declareth unto man what is his thought; that maketh the morning darkness, and treadeth upon the high places of the earth; the Lord, the God of hosts, is his name."

Then his prophecy rises to a pitch of exaltation which makes the rhythm of it beat like a roll of drums:

"Woe to them that are at ease in Zion,
    and to them that are secure in the mountain of Samaria,
The notable men of the chief of the nations,
    to whom the house of Israel come!
Pass ye unto Calneh, and see; and from thence go ye to Hamath
        the great;
    then go down to Gath of the Philistines:
Be they better than these kingdoms?
    or is their border greater than your border?—

Ye that put far away the evil day,
    and cause the seat of violence to come near;
That lie upon beds of ivory,
    and stretch themselves upon their couches,
And eat the lambs out of the flock,
    and the calves out of the midst of the stall;
That sing idle songs to the sound of the viol;
    that invent for themselves instruments of music, like David;
That drink wine in bowls, and anoint themselves with the
        chief ointments;
    but they are not grieved for the affliction of Joseph!"

"I hate, I despise your feasts,
    and I will take no delight in your solemn assemblies.
Yea, though ye offer me your burnt-offerings
    and meal-offerings, I will not accept them;
    neither will I regard the peace-offerings of your fat beasts.
Take thou away from me the noise of thy songs;
    for I will not hear the melody of thy viols.
But let judgment roll down as waters,
    and righteousness as a mighty stream!"

Still the prophet knew that this judgment declared upon a nation which thought itself secure in the favor of its God would rouse an angry disbelief. Was not Israel looking forward to sure prosperity? Did it not expect a "day of the Lord" that would be the culmination of its pride and power?

But this confidence in a day of the Lord Amos turns against itself. There should be a day of the Lord indeed; but it should be a day of condemnation and of doom.

He cried:

"Woe unto you, that desire the day of the Lord!
Wherefore would ye have the day of the Lord? It is darkness,
        and not light.
As if a man did flee from a lion, and a bear met him;
    or went into the house and leaned his hand on the wall, and
        a serpent bit him.

Shall not the day of the Lord be darkness, and not light?
    even very dark, and no brightness in it?"

"Ye who turn judgment to wormwood,
    and cast down righteousness to the earth,
Seek him that maketh the Pleiades and Orion,
    and turneth the shadow of death into the morning, and
        maketh the day dark with night;
That calleth for the waters of the sea,
    and poureth them out upon the face of the earth (Jehovah
        is his name);
That bringeth sudden destruction upon the strong,
    so that destruction cometh upon the fortress."

"They hate him that reproveth in the gate, and they abhor him that speaketh uprightly. Forasmuch therefore as ye trample upon the poor, and take exactions from him of wheat: ye have built houses of hewn stone, but ye shall not dwell in them; ye have planted pleasant vineyards, but ye shall not drink the wine thereof. For I know how manifold are your transgressions, and how mighty are your sins—ye that afflict the just, that take a bribe, and that turn aside the needy in the gate from their right. Therefore he that is prudent shall keep silence in such a time; for it is an evil time.

"Seek good, and not evil, that ye may live; and so the Lord, the God of hosts, will be with you, as ye say. Hate the evil, and love the good, and establish judgment in the gate: it may be that the Lord, the God of hosts, will be gracious unto the remnant of Joseph."

Such was the message of the first of the great prophets whose words have been recorded at any length. What happened to Amos at the end, we do not know: but what Amos said remains as part of the imperishable literature of religion.

About the same time as Amos or a little later, but with his work beginning before Jeroboam died, there arose another prophet equal to Amos in importance. He also prophesied in the northern kingdom of Israel; and he was, as Amos was not, a native of the north. His name was Hosea.

By temperament Hosea was unlike the shepherd of Tekoa. Amos flamed with indignation. He was such a man as John the Baptist was afterward to be, hating iniquity, terrible in condemnation; but Hosea was a more tender and wistful spirit. As clearly as Amos, he saw the sins of his time, but he bore these more directly upon his own heart. He felt the tragedy of the divine purpose seeking human response and not finding it, and in his own soul he shared the sorrows of God.

The book of his prophecy begins with a description of his own wife's infidelity, and of how, after he had put her away, he took her back again as a symbol of God's unwearying love for his people. It was as though, through him, God was saying to Israel: "And I will betroth thee unto me forever; yea, I will betroth thee unto me in righteousness, and in judgment, and in loving-kindness, and in mercies. I will even betroth thee unto me in faithfulness; and thou shalt know the Lord."

As Amos had perceived the iniquities of the time; so also Hosea perceived them:

"Hear the word of the Lord, ye children of Israel: for the Lord hath a controversy with the inhabitants of the land, because there is no truth, nor mercy, nor knowledge of God in the land. By swearing, and lying, and killing, and stealing, and committing adultery, they break out, and blood toucheth blood."

But stronger than the note of condemnation in Hosea is the note of yearning:

"Come, and let us return unto the Lord: for he hath torn, and he will heal us; he hath smitten, and he will bind us up. After two days will he revive us; in the third day he will raise us up, and we shall live in his sight. Then we shall know, if we follow on to know the Lord: his going forth is prepared as the morning; and he shall come unto us as the rain, as the latter and former rain unto the earth."

Then he broke into a dirge of sorrow, as though God himself were sorrowing:

"O Ephraim, what shall I do unto thee?
O Judah, what shall I do unto thee?
  for your goodness is as a morning cloud,
  and as the early dew it goeth away.
Therefore have I hewed them by the prophets;
  I have slain them by the words of my mouth:
  and thy judgments are as the light that goeth forth.
For I desired mercy, and not sacrifice;
  and the knowledge of God more than burnt-offerings."

And again he spoke as though with the lips of God:
"When Israel was a child, then I loved him, and called my son out of Egypt. As they called them, so they went from them: they sacrificed unto Baalim, and burned incense to graven images. I taught Ephraim also to go, taking them by their arms; but they knew not that I healed them. I drew them with cords of a man, with bands of love: and I was to them as they that take off the yoke on their jaws."

This note of compassion in Hosea was to go on echoing in later prophets, and to continue until it found its supreme expression in the cross of Christ.

CHAPTER XXVIII

CONCERNING THE INVASION OF ISRAEL BY THE ARMIES OF ASSYRIA,
AND THE DELIVERANCE OF JERUSALEM AFTER THE ASSYRIANS HAD
BESIEGED IT; AND CONCERNING THE GREAT PROPHET ISAIAH AND THE
PROPHET MICAH, AND WHAT THEY SAID AND DID.

BOUT THE time when Amos and Hosea were prophesying, there appeared a new factor in the history of the kingdoms of Israel and Judah. To the east, in the valley of the Tigris River, the great empire of Assyria was consolidating its strength. Out from its borders its armies of conquest began to move. They threatened Damascus in the north. They had hovered like a stormcloud dark with menace on the horizons of Israel. Menahem, the third of the rulers who, after interludes of violence and assassination, had followed Jeroboam II, sent to the king of Assyria a bribe of a thousand talents of silver as a price to halt the Assyrian advance, and laid a heavy tax on all the kingdom of Israel in order to pay it. Within ten years the Assyrians were back again. Under Tiglath-pileser, they overran much of the north country, invaded Galilee to the west of Jordan and Gilead to the east of it, and carried great numbers of the population back with them to slavery in the east.

Pekah, king of Israel, and Rezin, the king of Damascus, formed a defensive league against this dread menace of Assyria. It seemed to them of the utmost importance that their alliance should be fortified by the strength of the southern kingdom also; but Ahaz, king of Judah, refused to join them. Then Pekah and Rezin turned their arms against Ahaz. If he would not join them willingly in the league against Assyria, they would compel him to come in by force.

In this troubled time and upon this stage where ominous

forces were converging, there appeared now the figure of a
prophet who was to be in many ways the greatest of all those
who bore that name. It was Isaiah, the son of Amoz. He was
as clear an interpreter of moral facts as Amos and Hosea had
been. He surpassed them in the sweep and majesty of his
utterance; and more authoritatively than they or any other
prophet he dared face the immediate dilemmas and decisions of
his time and bring to bear on these the counsels of God, in the
light of which alone he insisted that they should be determined.

Isaiah's description of his call to be a prophet is a witness
both to his own mystic religious temperament and to his perception of those actual evils of his generation to which his religion
should be related.

"In the year that king Uzziah died
I saw the Lord sitting upon a throne, high and lifted up;
And his train filled the temple.
Above him stood the seraphim:
Each one had six wings; with twain he covered his face,
    and with twain he covered his feet,
    and with twain he did fly.
And one cried unto another, and said,
Holy, holy, holy, is the Lord of hosts:
    the whole earth is full of his glory.
And the foundations of the thresholds were moved at the voice
        of him that cried,
    and the house was filled with smoke.
Then said I, Woe is me! for I am undone;
    because I am a man of unclean lips,
    and I dwell in the midst of a people with unclean lips:
For mine eyes have seen the King, the Lord of hosts.
Then flew one of the seraphim unto me, having a live coal in
        his hand,
    which he had taken with the tongs from off the altar:
And he touched my mouth with it, and said,
Lo, this hath touched thy lips;
    and thine iniquity is taken away, and thy sin purged.

And I heard the voice of the Lord,
　　saying, Whom shall I send, and who will go for us?
Then I said, Here am I; send me.
And he said, Go, and tell this people,
Hear ye indeed, but understand not;
　　and see ye indeed, but perceive not!
Make the heart of this people fat,
　　and make their ears heavy, and shut their eyes;
Lest they see with their eyes, and hear with their ears,
　　and understand with their heart, and turn again, and be
　　healed.
Then said I, Lord, how long?　And he answered,
Until cities be waste without inhabitant, and houses without
　　　　man,
　　and the land become utterly waste."

It was an evil time, and Isaiah knew it.　He witnessed the
downfall of the dynasty of Jehu in the north in a welter of
murderous uprisings which destroyed one king to set up another.　He foresaw a revolution also in Judah; and in the
prophecies which form the early chapters of the book which
bears his name there are graphic descriptions of the sins in the
civilization of Judah:

"Woe unto them that join house to house,
　　that lay field to field, till there be no room,
And ye be made to dwell alone
　　in the midst of the land!
In mine ears saith the Lord of hosts,
Of a truth many houses shall be desolate
　　even great and fair, without inhabitant. . . .
Woe unto them that rise up early in the morning,
　　that they may follow strong drink,
　　that tarry late into the night, till wine inflame them!
And the harp and the lute, the tabret and the pipe,
　　and wine, are in their feasts;
But they regard not the work of the Lord,
　　neither have they considered the operation of his hands.

Therefore my people are gone into captivity
    for lack of knowledge;
And their honorable men are famished,
    and their multitude are parched with thirst.
Therefore hell hath enlarged her desire,
    and opened her mouth without measure;
And their glory, and their multitude, and their pomp,
    and he that rejoiceth among them, descend into it. . . .
Woe unto them that draw iniquity with cords of vanity,
    and sin as it were with a cart rope. . . .
Therefore as the tongue of fire devoureth the stubble,
    and as the dry grass sinketh down in the flame,
    so their root shall be as rottenness,
    and their blossom shall go up as dust;
Because they have rejected the law of the Lord of hosts,
    and despised the word of the Holy One of Israel."

Nor was Isaiah alone in the dark picture which he drew of
the life of his people in that day. There was another prophet
who was contemporary with him, whose message also was with
power, though he was not so vivid a figure as Isaiah. He was
Micah, who came from a little Judæan town near the Philistine
border, and of whose origin and of the manner of whose call we
know nothing. Cried he:

"Hear this, I pray you, ye heads of the house of Jacob,
    and rulers of the house of Israel,
    that abhor judgment, and pervert all equity.
They build up Zion with blood,
    and Jerusalem with iniquity.
The heads thereof judge for reward,
    and the priests thereof teach for hire,
    and the prophets thereof divine for money:
Yet will they lean upon the Lord, and say,
    'Is not the Lord in the midst of us?
    no evil shall come upon us.' "

Then Micah went on to this terrific judgment:

"Therefore shall Zion for your sake
    be plowed as a field,
And Jerusalem shall become heaps,
    and the mountain of the house as the high places of a forest."

It was from the voice of Micah also that there came one of the supreme descriptions of the real meaning of religion:

"Hear ye now what the Lord saith:
    Arise, contend thou before the mountains,
    and let the hills hear thy voice.
Hear, O ye mountains, the Lord's controversy,
    and ye enduring foundations of the earth;
For the Lord hath a controversy with his people,
    and he will plead with Israel.
O my people, what have I done unto thee?
    and wherein have I wearied thee?
    testify against me.
For I brought thee up out of the land of Egypt,
    and redeemed thee out of the house of bondage.
And I sent before thee
    Moses, Aaron, and Miriam.
O my people, remember now what Balak king of Moab consulted
    and what Balaam the son of Beor answered him;
Remember from Shittim unto Gilgal,
    that ye may know the righteous acts of the Lord.
Wherewith shall I come before the Lord,
    and bow myself before the high God?
Shall I come before him with burnt-offerings,
    with calves a year old?
Will the Lord be pleased with thousands of rams,
    Or with ten thousands of rivers of oil?
Shall I give my first-born for my transgression?
    the fruit of my body for the sin of my soul?

He hath showed thee, O man, what is good;
   and what doth the Lord require of thee,
But to do justly, and to love mercy,
   and to walk humbly with thy God."

From this background of the iniquities of Judah, which both Micah and Isaiah saw, they perceived that Assyria, terrible as she was, might be the instrument which God should use to break down the pride of his own people and punish their iniquities.

So Isaiah cried:

"And he will lift up an ensign to the nations from far,
   and will hiss for them from the end of the earth;
And, behold, they shall come with speed swiftly,
   none shall be weary nor stumble among them,
   none shall slumber nor sleep;
Neither shall the girdle of their loins be loosed,
   nor the latchet of their shoes be broken;
Whose arrows are sharp,
   and all their bows bent;
Their horses' hoofs shall be counted like flint,
   and their wheels like a whirlwind:
Their roaring shall be like a lion,
   they shall roar like young lions;
Yea, they shall roar, and lay hold of the prey,
   and carry it away safe, and there shall be none to deliver.
And they shall roar against them in that day
   like the roaring of the sea:
And if one look unto the land, behold, darkness and distress;
   and the light is darkened in the clouds thereof."

But what, meanwhile, of the war against Ahaz which had been launched by Pekah and Rezin, kings of Israel and Damascus? Isaiah poured scorn on their conspiracy at the very moment when it was written of the king of Judah that "his heart trembled, and the heart of his people, as the trees of the forest tremble with the wind." "These two tails of smoking fire-brands," Isaiah called the kings of Israel and Damascus, and he said to Ahaz, king of Judah, "Take heed, and be quiet; fear not, neither let your heart be faint." He told Ahaz that the attack of Pekah and Rezin should come to nothing. He was to put his faith in the defenses of God, and he went on: "If you will not believe, surely you shall not be established." But Ahaz would not trust the prophet. He would not stand still, as Isaiah bade him do, and see the salvation of God. He would not trust in "the waters of Shiloah that go softly," by which Isaiah meant the quiet influences of righteousness and faith. He wanted to send to Tiglath-pileser and agree to be his vassal, in order thus to buy the Assyrian off.

In 732 the Assyrian armies besieged and took Damascus. The kingdom of Israel then made war against the new Assyrian sovereign and conqueror, Shalmaneser; but Shalmaneser's answer was to fling his armies against the capital city of Samaria, besiege it and capture it; and with its downfall, the strength and the very existence of the northern kingdom of Israel came to an end. In Judah, the minds of the kings, both of Ahaz and of his successor Hezekiah, and the mind of the people, fluttered here and there, vainly seeking some alliance which might protect them from the oncoming power of Assyria. They would join the Philistines. They would make a league with Egypt. But Isaiah prophesied that all such expedients would be in vain:

"Woe to them that go down to Egypt for help, and stay on horses,
  And trust in chariots because they are many,
    and in horsemen because they are very strong,
But they look not to the Holy One of Israel,
    neither seek the Lord! . . .
Now the Egyptians are men, and not God;
    and their horses flesh, and not spirit:
And when the Lord shall stretch out his hand,
    both he that helpeth shall stumble, and he that is holpen
      shall fall,
And they all shall fail together."

Isaiah called upon Judah for a faith which it was hard for men to rise to:

"As birds flying so will the Lord of hosts protect Jerusalem;
  He will protect and deliver it,
    he will pass over and preserve it."

"For thus said the Lord God, the Holy One of Israel,
In returning and rest shall ye be saved;
    in quietness and in confidence shall be your strength."

And now the Assyrians were drawing near. Sargon had succeeded Shalmaneser, who apparently had died during the siege of Samaria, and after Sargon came Sennacherib. The Assyrian armies were on the march toward Jerusalem. They had swept down through the plains of Philistia, and were about to turn and attack Jerusalem from the west. Then to Lachish, where the king of Assyria was, Hezekiah sent a despairing message. "I have offended;" he said, "withdraw, and whatever you put upon me, I will pay." So Sennacherib exacted of him three hundred talents of silver and thirty talents of gold. And in order to pay them, Hezekiah took all the silver which was in the Temple in Jerusalem and all the treasures of the king's house, and stripped the gold plating from the doors of the Temple, and gave these as his ransom.

But Sennacherib sent his chief officers with an army up against Jerusalem, and they halted outside the city. Hezekiah sent representatives out to meet them. Then the Assyrian legate said, "This is the message from the great monarch of Assyria: 'What confidence is this in which you put your trust?' You say (but they are vain words), 'I have counsel and strength for the war.' Now on whom do you trust, that you rebel against me? You trust in the staff of this bruised reed Egypt, on which if a man lean it will go into his hand and pierce it: that is what Pharaoh king of Egypt is to those who rely on him."

Moreover, in the hearing of the garrisons of Jerusalem, who looked down in silence from their walls, the Assyrian drove home another taunt. Hezekiah had suppressed some of the local shrines, and many of the people were superstitiously ready to think that bad luck might have come from that action. So the Assyrian wanted to know whether Hezekiah's trust was in God, "whose high places and whose altars Hezekiah hath taken away, and hath said to Judah and to Jerusalem, 'Ye shall worship before this altar in Jerusalem.' "

At that, the representatives of Hezekiah said to the Assyrian: "We ask you to speak in the Assyrian language, for we understand it: but do not talk with us in the Hebrew language in the hearing of the people who are on the walls."

But the Assyrian replied the more loudly, deliberately shouting in order that the people who were on the walls might understand: "Hear the word of the great king, the king of Assyria. 'Do not let Hezekiah deceive you, for Hezekiah will never be able to deliver you. . . . Have any of the gods of the nations ever delivered their land out of the hand of the king of Assyria? Where are the gods of Hamath, and of Arpad? Where are the gods of Sepharvaim? Have they saved Samaria out of my hand?' "

Thus, with the record of their ruthless and unbroken conquests behind them, the Assyrians cried their arrogant contempt of the belief that any god could save Jerusalem; and while the people on the wall stood dumb, the legates of Hezekiah went back into the presence of the king and rent their clothes.

To Hezekiah it seemed that the end had come. He dressed himself in sackcloth and went into the Temple, and from there he sent an officer of his household and one of the scribes, also clothed in sackcloth, to Isaiah. They told Isaiah the insults of the Assyrians, and they begged Isaiah to offer up his prayers that Jerusalem might be delivered. Boldly the answer came. "Go and tell your master," said Isaiah: "Thus saith Jehovah, 'Be not afraid of the words you have heard, with which the servants of the king of Assyria have blasphemed me. Behold, I will put a spirit in him, and he shall hear tidings, and shall return to his own land; and I will cause him to fall by the sword in his own land.'

And now, while Jerusalem was ringed round with peril, and at any hour the shock of the Assyrian assault might come, Isaiah had a double message. He saw, as before, the sins of his own people, and he believed that these sins must be atoned for with anguish. He had believed in the awful sureness of a moral justice, which if necessary would use even the Assyrians as its scourge; but he saw also that the Assyrians were brutal and self-confident, and he believed that it was not possible that they should triumph now. His passionate love for Jerusalem, and his hope that God still had a great purpose for a chastened and repentant people to fulfill, gave him confidence that, however hopeless the odds might seem, nevertheless the Assyrians would not capture the city, Jerusalem would not fall.

To his own people, in order that they might realize their own helplessness, and put their trust in God alone, he said:

"Wherefore thus saith the Holy One of Israel,
  Because ye despise this word,
  and trust in oppression and perverseness, and stay thereon;
Therefore this iniquity shall be to you as a breach ready to fall,
Swelling out in a high wall, whose breaking cometh suddenly in an instant.
And he shall break it as a potter's vessel is broken,
  breaking it in pieces without sparing;
So that there shall not be found among the pieces thereof
  a sherd to take fire from the hearth,
  or to take water withal out of the cistern.
For thus said the Lord God,
  the Holy One of Israel,
'In returning and rest shall ye be saved;
  in quietness and in confidence shall be your strength.'
And ye would not: but ye said, 'No, for we will flee upon horses;'
  therefore shall ye flee:
And, 'We will ride upon the swift;'
  therefore shall they that pursue you be swift.

One thousand shall flee at the rebuke of one:
    at the rebuke of five shall ye flee:
Till ye be left as a beacon upon the top of a mountain,
    and as an ensign upon a hill."

But as concerning the Assyrians Isaiah said:

"Thus saith the Lord, the God of Israel,
    'Whereas thou hast prayed to me against Sennacherib, king
        of Assyria,
    this is the word which the Lord hath spoken concerning him:
The virgin daughter of Zion hath despised thee and laughed
    thee to scorn;
    the daughter of Jerusalem hath shaken her head at thee.'"

And again Isaiah said in the name of God:

"I will punish the fruit of the stout heart of the king of Assyria,
    and the glory of his high looks.
For he hath said, 'By the strength of my hand I have done it,
    and by my wisdom; for I am prudent:
And I have removed the bounds of the peoples,
    and have robbed their treasures, and I have brought down as
        a valiant man them that sit on thrones.
And my hand hath found as a nest the riches of the peoples;
    and as one gathereth eggs that are forsaken have I gathered
        all the earth:
And there was none that moved the wing,
    or that opened the mouth, or chirped.'
Shall the axe boast itself against him that heweth therewith?
    shall the saw magnify itself against him that shaketh it?
As if a rod should shake them that lift it up,
    or as if a staff should lift him that is not wood.
Therefore shall the Lord, the Lord of hosts, send among his
    fat ones leanness;
And under his glory there shall be kindled a burning like the
    burning of fire,
And the light of Israel shall be for a fire,
    and his Holy One for a flame."

But, meanwhile, the Assyrian armies had come, and had begun the siege. The defenders of the walls of Jerusalem looked down upon these implacable warriors before whom kingdom after kingdom had gone down, and who had marked their widening conquests on all the roads where their iron chariot wheels had rolled. There seemed to be no hope for Jerusalem. It would be starved out, even if its walls were not carried by assault.

And yet in the end none of these things happened. The unshakable faith of the great prophet was justified. "The angel of the Lord went forth, and smote in the camp of the Assyrians a hundred fourscore and five thousand: and when men arose early in the morning, behold these were all dead bodies."

Evidently, what happened was that a plague broke out in the Assyrian camp; and rumors, moreover, had come to Sennacherib of insurrection back in Nineveh. When the siege was lifted and the Assyrian armies had withdrawn to the east, Sennacherib himself, hurrying ahead, was assassinated as he went into one of the temples in Nineveh, and his son Esarhaddon succeeded him on the Assyrian throne.

Then comes that particular note of prophecy with which the great name of Isaiah is most associated, though it is, perhaps, not most typical of him. He had risen to his greatest heights in his power to trust God, and God only, when the days were dark. Now when the almost incredible deliverance had come, and Jerusalem had emerged from the shadow of the Assyrian menace, Isaiah's faith expanded into a great hope. He believed that the people now might repent of their sins and genuinely begin a new life as in the sight of God. And he trusted that, because this might be so, Jerusalem should be exalted as an exemplar and a torch-bearer of the spirit among all nations; and that there should appear in her a new sort of king whom the spirit of the Lord should call forth.

"Come now, and let us reason together, saith the Lord:
   Though your sins be as scarlet,
      they shall be as white as snow,

Though they be as red like crimson,
    they shall be as wool."

And again his prophecy broke into ecstatic song.

"The people that walked in darkness have seen a great light:
    they that dwelt in the land of the shadow of death,
    upon them hath the light shined.
Thou hast multiplied the nation, thou hast increased their joy:
    they joy before thee according to the joy in harvest,
    as men rejoice when they divide the spoil.
For the yoke of his burden, and the staff of his shoulder,
    the rod of his oppressor, thou hast broken as in the day of
      Midian.
For all the armor of the armed man in the tumult,
    and the garments rolled in blood,
    shall even be for burning, for fuel of fire.
For unto us a child is born, unto us a son is given;
    and the government shall be upon his shoulder:
And his name shall be called Wonderful, Counselor,
    Mighty God, Everlasting Father, Prince of Peace.
Of the increase of his government and of peace there shall be
    no end,
    upon the throne of David, and upon his kingdom,
To establish it, and to uphold it
    with judgment and with righteousness from henceforth
    even forever."

And as the ultimate climax the prophet dreamed of an era of universal peace through that influence which should go out from the new spirit of Jerusalem.

"And it shall come to pass in the latter days,
    that the mountain of the Lord's house shall be established in
      the top of the mountains,
    and shall be exalted above the hills.
And all nations shall flow into it,
    and many peoples shall go and say,

'Come ye, and let us go up to the mountain of the Lord,
to the house of the God of Jacob;
And he will teach us of his ways,
and we will walk in his paths:'
For out of Zion shall go forth the law,
and the word of the Lord from Jerusalem.
And he shall judge between the nations,
and shall reprove many peoples;
And they shall beat their swords into plowshares,
and their spears into pruning-hooks;
Nation shall not lift up sword against nation,
neither shall they learn war any more."

CHAPTER XXIX

THE STORY OF THE TROUBLED TIMES WHICH FOLLOWED THE YEAR 700 B. C., WITH WARS AND TUMULTS, AND KINGS WHO ROSE AND FELL; AND THE REFORMATION WHICH SPRANG FROM THE BOOK OF DEUTERONOMY; AND THE MESSAGES OF THE PROPHETS ZEPHANIAH, NAHUM, AND HABAKKUK.

IT WAS in the year 701 B. C. that the armies of Assyria withdrew from before the walls of Jerusalem, and what had seemed the mortal fate of the city was averted. Although he fell ill with a grievous illness, King Hezekiah was to live nine more years after that time. One notable deed which marks his reign is mentioned in the chronicle after the account of the siege of Sennacherib; but it is probable that this was actually accomplished as a desperate necessity when the Assyrians were drawing near. Outside the walls of Jerusalem, there flows, and has flowed for unnumbered centuries, a spring which is now called the Virgin's Fountain. It is separated by a hill from what was the walled city of Jerusalem in Hezekiah's day; but under his direction, a tunnel was hewn for a third of a mile through the rock, in order to bring the water of the fountain to the pool of Siloam, to which the garrison and the people of the city could have access. The tunnel was chiseled clumsily and roughly, perhaps because it was driven in urgent haste; but accomplished it was, and there under the hill a shaft of it runs to this day.

Hezekiah had also instituted during his reign at least a partial reformation of the corruptions and the pagan practices which had grown up in the worship of the nation; but under his son Manasseh, who was only twelve years old when he came to the throne, and who reigned for fifty-five years, there was to be a deliberate and complete reaction. Manasseh established again the local shrines throughout the kingdom, where old pagan rituals were practiced and where licentiousness flourished under the cloak of religious cults. He built in Jerusalem itself shrines to the gods of Assyria; and, in the courts and on the roofs of the Temple, he set up altars to the sun. He even encouraged the most degraded and brutal of all current forms of worship, that of Moloch with its human sacrifices. And old superstitions and witchcrafts which had come down from more ancient times openly reappeared.

The history as it is written in the books of Kings does not tell what happened at last to Isaiah; but an old legend has it that he was put to death under Manasseh by being sawn in two. The prophets, however, were not silenced. "Thus saith the Lord, the God of Israel," some one of them cried, "Because Manasseh king of Judah hath done these abominations, . . . Behold, I bring such evil upon Jerusalem and Judah, that whosoever heareth of it, both his ears shall tingle. And I will stretch over Jerusalem the line of Samaria, and the plummet of the house of Ahab; and I will wipe Jerusalem as a man wipeth a dish, wiping it and turning it upside down."

Such was the denunciation of a prophet who stands in history unnamed. But there was a prophet who appeared shortly after the time of Manasseh whose name we know. This was Zephaniah. In the year 626 another invasion, as terrifying as the earlier ones of Assyria, swept through Palestine. The army of the Scythians came down by the coast through Philistia, apparently on their way toward an attack on Egypt. In some manner they were halted, perhaps through a ransom paid; but at the time it seemed again as though Jerusalem would be destroyed. Zephaniah, who was himself of royal blood, being a descendant of Hezekiah, believed that Jerusalem was doomed. To him it seemed as though the day of the Lord, that dreadful day of judgment which Amos had proclaimed, was about to break because of the sins of the city and the nation.

"Woe to her that is filthy and polluted, to the oppressing city! She obeyed not the voice; she received not correction;
      she trusted not in the Lord; she drew not near to her God.

Her princes within her are roaring lions;
  her judges are evening wolves;
    they gnaw not the bones till the morrow.
Her prophets are light and treacherous persons:
  her priests have polluted the sanctuary,
    they have done violence to the law.
The just Lord is in the midst thereof;
  He will not do iniquity:
Every morning doth he bring his judgment to light,
  He faileth not; but the unjust knoweth no shame.
I have cut off the nations: their towers are desolate;
I made their streets waste that none passeth by."

Moreover, he chanted his prophecies of doom in words which the great medieval Latin hymn of judgment, *Dies irae*, sent sounding down the later centuries.

"The great day of the Lord is near,
  it is near, and hasteth greatly,
Even the voice of the day of the Lord:
  the mighty man shall cry there bitterly.
That day is a day of wrath,
  a day of trouble and distress,
A day of wasteness and desolation,
  a day of darkness and gloominess,
A day of clouds and thick darkness,
  a day of the trumpet and alarm,
Against the fenced cities,
  and against the high towers."

"Seek ye the Lord, all ye meek of the earth,
  which have wrought his judgment;
Seek righteousness, seek meekness:
  it may be that ye shall be hid in the day of the Lord's anger."

By this time another and a different king was on the throne of Judah. His name was Josiah; and under him took place the greatest religious reformation which Jerusalem had thus far known. It was due to a group of disciples of the great prophets, who, during the dark reign of Manasseh, had hiddenly gone about their work of building what they believed some day might be the basis for a new religious life. They were convinced that the first necessity was the annihilation of all the scattered shrines with the superstitions and paganisms which clustered round them. They believed that, as there was only one God, so his Oneness must be symbolized by the fact that there should be only one great shrine, the Temple in Jerusalem, where his worship centered; and, like the great prophetic line which began with Amos, they saw that religion must be expressed in social righteousness. These ideals they wrought into a book to which they gave the name and the authority of Moses—quite simply and sincerely, because they believed that they were only making explicit the true ideals which had come down from Moses' time. That book was the noble and eloquent setting forth of the law which bears the name of Deuteronomy. In the evil reign of Manasseh they dared not produce it. It was hidden in the Temple, and from the Temple, when Josiah had come to the throne, it was produced.

Shaphan the scribe had come from the king to Hilkiah the high priest with orders for the repairing and beautifying of the Temple, and Hilkiah said to Shaphan, "I have found the book of the law in the house of the Lord." He gave the book to Shaphan, and Shaphan read it.

Back to King Josiah then Shaphan the scribe went, carrying this book of Deuteronomy, and he read it to Josiah. When Josiah heard it, and realized the difference between what this book enjoined and the actual conditions in his kingdom, he rent his clothes; and he commanded Hilkiah, the high priest, and Shaphan and other scribes to go and pray to God to show his will as to what should now be done. "For great is the wrath of the Lord that is kindled against us," he said, "because our fathers have not hearkened unto the words of this book to do according to all that is written concerning us."

The priests and the scribes consulted with an inspired woman by the name of Huldah, and they came back to the king,

telling him that a blessing would be upon him if he carried out
the behests of the book. So Josiah sent an order for all the chief
men of Judah to gather in Jerusalem; and when they were
assembled, the king went up into the Temple and read in their
hearing all the words of the book of the covenant which had
been found in the house of the Lord. There he dedicated himself to the carrying out of what he thought was the newly discovered law. He cleansed the Temple in Jerusalem of all the
pagan altars and all the paraphernalia which belonged to them.
"And he put down the idolatrous priests, whom the kings of
Judah had ordained to burn incense in the high places in the
cities of Judah, and in the places round about Jerusalem; them
also that burned incense unto Baal, to the sun, and to the moon,
and to the twelve constellations and to all the host of heaven."
He destroyed the sculptured horses which had been put in Jerusalem as symbols of the worship of the sun. And the altars
which Manasseh had set up he beat down and had them ground
into dust, which he cast into the waters of Kidron brook. He
sent his agents of destruction especially to Bethel, where Jeroboam, first ruler of the northern kingdom, had long ago begun
his apostasy by establishing forbidden shrines.

One thing there in Bethel he spared, for out of this thing
there came an echo of an earlier history. He saw some
sepulchers on the hill at Bethel, and, supposing that these also
might be the center of some sort of superstitious reverence, he
took the bones out of them, and was about to burn them along
with the altars of Jeroboam. But his attention was attracted by
an inscription on one of these tombs, and he asked what it was.
People in Bethel told him that it was the tomb of that lonely
prophet who had come to Bethel in the days of Jeroboam to
pronounce judgment on Jeroboam for his sin, and whose body,
after he had been killed by a lion on the road, was brought to
his burial by another prophet of Samaria (as the history has
already told). His bones Josiah returned to their resting-place,
that they might remain there in peace.

Moreover, Josiah commanded the observance of the Passover as the law in Deuteronomy had enjoined, and "Surely there

THE CAPTIVES OF BABYLON

BY THE RIVERS OF BABYLON

was not holden such a passover from the days of the judges that judged Israel, nor in all the days of the kings of Israel, nor of the kings of Judah."

To the historian of the books of Kings the reformation of Josiah meant the fulfillment of that purpose for God's people which had run like a thread of hope through all its history, and thus he sums up the meaning of Josiah's reign: "And like unto him was there no king before him, that turned to the Lord with all his heart, and with all his soul, and with all his might, according to all the law of Moses; neither after him arose there any like him."

For this same historian it was a strange dilemma that King Josiah, who seemed to him to have been superlatively good, should come to a tragic end. But he found his explanation in the suggestion that the sins of Manasseh were still not fully expiated. This, he told himself, was the reason for what happened to Josiah; and what did happen was this: The armies of Egypt, under the command of the reigning Pharaoh, came marching up on their way to an attack on Assyria, and Josiah and his forces came into collision with this Egyptian army. Near the fortress of Megiddo on the plain of Esdraelon, Josiah's army was beaten, and he himself was slain. And his body was brought back from Megiddo in a chariot to Jerusalem; and when they buried him, they buried the last of the significant kings.

After him came his son Jehoahaz, who reigned only three months, because an Egyptian Pharaoh dethroned him, took him prisoner into Egypt, and put his brother in his place. This brother was no more than an Egyptian vassal, and he bought his rulership in his puppet kingdom by great tributes of silver and gold which he wrung from his own people by heavy taxes and sent down to Pharaoh.

Meanwhile a more menacing enemy was advancing. In the far East the mighty empire of Assyria had been gradually weakened, both by outward wars and by inner strife. Its capital city of Nineveh, so long a symbol of cruelty and dominion, had declined. Another empire was arising to the south, with its capital at Babylon on the Euphrates. The two empires locked at last in a deadly struggle, and Assyria fell. Nineveh was captured and sacked and set on fire. For many little nations of the world which had been battered by the Assyrian armies, this was a time of fierce exultancy. They thought that the great destroyer was now destroyed. They did not reckon with the fact that another and equally brutal world power had taken its place.

From one of the prophets whose message is preserved in the Old Testament, there sounds the echo of Assyria's fall. It was about the year 612 B. C. that Nineveh was destroyed. In Judah, the prophet Nahum took this as his text for the certainty of the punishment that always must befall iniquity and stubborn pride. His message is not comparable in depth of moral understanding to that of some of the greater prophets; but he could pour out the thing he did believe in a sort of passionate poetry:

"The Lord is slow to anger, and great in power,
   and will not at all acquit the wicked:
The Lord hath his way in the whirlwind and in the storm,
   and the clouds are the dust of his feet.
He rebuketh the sea, and maketh it dry,
   and drieth up all the rivers:
Bashan languisheth, and Carmel,
   and the flower of Lebanon languisheth.
The mountains quake at him, and the hills melt,
   and the earth is burned at his presence,
Yea, the world, and all that dwell therein.
Who can stand before his indignation?
   and who can abide in the fierceness of his anger?
His fury is poured out like fire,
   and the rocks are thrown down by him.
The Lord is good, a strong hold in the day of trouble;
And he knoweth them that trust in him.
But with an overrunning flood he will make an utter end of
    the place thereof,
And darkness shall pursue his enemies.

What do ye imagine against the Lord?   He will make an utter
    end:
Affliction shall not rise up a second time.
For while they be folden together as thorns,
    and while they are drunken as drunkards,
They shall be devoured as stubble fully dry."

    And thus he describes the fall of Nineveh:

"The chariots shall rage in the streets,
    they shall jostle one against another in the broad ways:
They shall seem like torches,
    they shall run like the lightnings.

Where is the dwelling of the lions,
    and the feeding-place of the young lions,
Where the lion, even the old lion, walked,
    and the lion's whelp, and none made them afraid?
The lion did tear in pieces enough for his whelps,
    and strangled for his lionesses,
And filled his holes with prey,
    and his dens with ravin.
Behold, I am against thee, saith the Lord of hosts,
    and I will burn her chariots in the smoke,
    and the sword shall devour thy young lions:
And I will cut off thy prey from the earth,
    and the voice of thy messengers
    shall be no more heard.
Woe to the bloody city! it is all full of lies and robbery;
    the prey departeth not.
The noise of a whip,
    and the noise of the rattling of the wheels,
And of the prancing horses,
    and of the jumping chariots.
The horseman lifteth up both the bright sword
    and the glittering spear:

And there is a multitude of slain,
   and a great number of carcases;
And there is none end of their corpses;
   they stumble upon their corpses.

.   .   .   .

There is no healing of thy bruise;
   thy wound is grievous;
All they that hear the bruit of thee
   shall clap the hands over thee:
For upon whom hath not thy wickedness passed continually?"

But behind Assyria came Babylon. Nebuchadnezzar the king marched with his armies against Jerusalem; and the kingdom of Judah could no longer turn to Egypt for help, for the power of Egypt had been beaten back to its own borders by the oncoming might of Babylon. The king of Judah died presently and was succeeded by his son Jehoiachin; and he had been only three months crowned when Nebuchadnezzar besieged the city and captured it, despoiled the Temple of its treasures, and carried away all the royal family and thousands of the people of Jerusalem as prisoners of war and slaves to Babylon.

It was in this period, when the thrust of the Babylonian peril was first being felt, and before its later and culminating shock, that another prophet, Habakkuk, meditated and preached in Jerusalem. He could understand that the coming of the Chaldeans might be the Lord's way of punishing the stubborn sins of Judah; but his moral sense was troubled by the fact that these Chaldeans were themselves so brutal as to make it seem a dreadful thing that a nation which had supposed itself to be the people of God should be destroyed by them. His prophecy begins as "The burden which Habakkuk the prophet did see." It was the burden of a tragic contradiction through which he sought to behold the light.

"O Lord, how long shall I cry," he said, "and thou wilt not hear!"

Then he hears, as it were, the voice of the Lord answering.

"Behold ye among the heathen,
    and regard, and wonder marvelously:
For I will work a work in your days,
    which ye will not believe, though it be told you.
For, lo, I raise up the Chaldeans,
    that bitter and hasty nation,
Which shall march through the breadth of the land
    to possess the dwelling-places that are not theirs.
They are terrible and dreadful:
    their judgment and their dignity shall proceed of themselves.
Their horses also are swifter than the leopards,
    and are more fierce than the evening wolves:
And their horsemen shall spread themselves,
    and their horsemen shall come from far;
They shall fly as the eagle that hasteth to eat.
They shall come all for violence:
    and their faces shall sup up as the east wind,
And they shall gather the captivity as the sand."

But Habakkuk pleads:

"Art thou not from everlasting, O Lord my God, mine Holy
    One?
    we shall not die.
O Lord, thou hast ordained them for judgment;
    and, O mighty God, thou hast established them for correc-
    tion.
Thou art of purer eyes than to behold evil,
    and canst not look on iniquity:
Wherefore lookest thou upon them that deal treacherously,
    and holdest thy tongue
    when the wicked devoureth the man that is more righteous
    than he?"

Habakkuk does not know what the end will be. He knows
that his own people are sinful, and that the Babylonian menace

is near; but he cannot believe that this is all. Somehow, and at some time, God will reveal a solution for the moral chaos of the world in which he shall be satisfied.

"I will stand upon my watch
  and set me upon the tower,
And will watch to see what he will say unto me,
  and what I shall answer if I am reproved.
And the Lord answered me, and said,
'Write the vision, and make it plain upon tables,
  that he may run that readeth it.
For the vision is yet for an appointed time,
  but at the end it shall speak, and not lie:
Though it tarry, wait for it;
  because it will surely come, it will not tarry.' "

And then Habakkuk advances to the great words which have helped to make religious history in centuries long after his time:

"Behold, his soul which is lifted up is not upright in him:
  but the just shall live by his faith."

And he moves on to that solemn and never-to-be-forgotten summons:

"The Lord is in his holy temple:
  let all the earth keep silence before him."

CHAPTER XXX

URING THE period which covered the latter part of the reign of Josiah and the uneasy reigns of his successors, the period in which Zephaniah and Nahum and Habakkuk prophesied, there arose also another prophet greater than they. In some respects he was the greatest of all those spiritual geniuses who saw and proclaimed the will of God. This was Jeremiah. Born in the little town of Anathoth near Jerusalem about the year 650 B. C., when the degenerate Manasseh was on the throne, he combined to an extraordinary degree qualities which had appeared severally in some of the prophets. He had the moral passion of Amos, something of the tenderness of Hosea, Isaiah's immediate contact with practical affairs, and withal the courage of a consecration which would not let him flinch even when the cost of truth was deadly. His was to be a lot than which no man could have had a harder, namely, to condemn his own country and to pronounce its doom, and to bear all the fury of mingled hate and fear with which so-called patriots in a time of national crisis always assail the man who stands in the way of the crowd emotion.

From his early years Jeremiah was aware of an inescapable spiritual experience which constituted the call of God to a work he could not deny.

"The word of the Lord came unto me, saying, . . .
'Before thou camest forth out of the womb, I sanctified thee, and I have appointed thee a prophet unto the nations.'

325

Then said I,

   'Ah, Lord God, behold I know not how to speak; for I am
     a child.'

But the Lord said unto me, 'Say not, "I am a child;"

For to whomsoever I shall send thee, thou shalt go,

   and whatsoever I shall command thee thou shalt speak.

Be not afraid because of them;

   for I am with thee to deliver thee,' saith the Lord."

The first of his prophecies were delivered in connection
with the invasion of the Scythians, which had called forth also
the prophecies of Zephaniah. In these days Jeremiah was in
Anathoth. Later he went up to Jerusalem, beholding there
the same sins and social wickedness which Isaiah had condemned, and which, in spite of all that had happened since, had
not been repented of. Jeremiah saw that these people were
destined to disaster. What he saw he could describe with a
terrible directness, and with an imagery which pressed his pictures into men's minds as with a red-hot brand. "They were as
fed horses in the morning," he said, "every one neighed after
his neighbor's wife."

He described the cruel greed of the rich:

"Woe unto him that buildeth his house by unrighteousness,

   and his chambers by injustice;

That useth his neighbor's service without wages,

   and giveth him not his hire;

That saith, 'I will build me a wide house

   and spacious chambers,'

And cutteth him out windows; and it is ceiled with cedar,

   and painted with vermilion!"

And the prophet went on to this noble summary of what
men ought to do:

"Thus saith the Lord: 'Execute justice and righteousness,
and deliver him that is robbed out of the hand of the oppressors.
Do no wrong nor violence to the stranger, the orphans, nor to
widows; neither shed innocent blood."

The confidence which Jerusalem had in its imagined safety, Jeremiah proclaimed to be in vain. "Take away her battle-ments," he cried, "for they are not the Lord's;" and as he looked out upon the dark realities of the time, it seemed to him that his whole world was being shadowed by a moral eclipse:

"I beheld the earth, and, lo, it was waste and void;
    and the heavens, and they had no light.
 I beheld the mountains, and, lo, they trembled,
    and all the hills moved to and fro.
 I beheld, and, lo, there was no man,
    and all the birds of the heaven were fled.
 I beheld, and, lo, the fruitful field was a wilderness,
    and all the cities thereof were broken down
At the presence of the Lord,
    and before his fierce anger."

The Scythian attack was not pressed home, but after the Scythians came the greater threat of the Chaldeans, which is another name for the armies that came out from Babylonia. After the death of King Josiah, there was one brief and insig-nificant reign after another until, in 597, when Jehoiachin was king, Nebuchadnezzar captured the city and carried Jehoiachin and great numbers of his people captive into Babylon. After that, Nebuchadnezzar allowed Zedekiah to reign as his vassal; but Zedekiah, in the ninth year of his reign, rashly rebelled. Back again then came Nebuchadnezzar and his armies, and for a year and a half invested Jerusalem with a siege until the whole city was reduced almost to starvation. It was in this period that the great prophecies of Jeremiah were uttered. Constantly he proclaimed that there was only one outcome to these stark facts. Jerusalem would be destroyed, all the national pride of Judah would be humiliated. Even the Temple would vanish. Men had to learn a new religion based upon repentance, and not dependent any more upon any particular sanctuary or any par-ticular place. "Trust not," said Jeremiah, "in lying words, say-ing, 'The temple of the Lord, the temple of the Lord, the temple

of the Lord are these.' " They were not to listen to smooth
prophets who cried, " 'Peace, Peace,' when there is no peace!"
Long ago they had been bidden by the true prophets to "ask
for the old paths, where there is the good way: and walk therein,
and ye shall find rest for your souls." But they had said, "We
will not walk therein." Even the house which was called by
God's name had become "a den of thieves." Therefore the judgment was drawing near:

"For death is come up into our windows,
    it is entered into our palaces;
To cut off the children from without,
    and the young men from the streets."

Not lightly did Jeremiah utter these condemnations. His
prophecies of doom are broken with sudden appeals for forgiveness and for mercy toward the people:

"O Lord, correct me, but with judgment;
    Not in thine anger, lest thou bring me to nothing.
Pour out thy fury upon the heathen that know thee not,
    And upon the families that call not on thy name:
For they have devoured Jacob, yea, they have devoured him
        and consumed him,
    And have laid waste his habitation."

"O thou hope of Israel,
    the saviour thereof in the time of trouble,
Why shouldest thou be as a sojourner in the land,
    and as a wayfaring man that turneth aside to tarry for a
        night?"

Sometimes it seemed to Jeremiah as though the burden of
his prophecies were greater than he could bear.

"O Lord, thou hast deceived me,
    and I was deceived:
Thou art stronger than I, and hast prevailed:

I am become a laughing-stock . . . , every one mocketh me.
For as often as I speak, I cry out; I cry,
  'Violence and spoil!'
Because the word of the Lord is made a reproach unto me,
  and a derision all the day.
And if I say, 'I will not make mention of him,
  nor speak any more in his name,'
Then there is in my heart as it were a burning fire
  shut up in my bones,
And I am weary with forbearing, and I cannot contain."

Inevitably there gathered against Jeremiah a bitter opposition. The son of one of the priests, who was also a custodian of the Temple, took the prophet and put him in the stocks by one of the gates, where all the passers-by could see him. Later he was arrested when he went out to his own town of Anathoth, on the charge that he was about to go and join himself to the Babylonians.

In the reign of Josiah's son he had dictated prophecies to his faithful and intrepid disciple Baruch, and Baruch read the roll which he had written to all the people at one of the Temple gates. A group of the royal household demanded that Baruch read the roll to them, and afterward they took the roll to the king himself; and when the king heard it, sitting in his winter house before a fire, he snatched the roll and cut it with a knife, and threw it into the fire—which only made Jeremiah dictate to Baruch again another roll of prophecies more weighty in judgment than the other.

At a subsequent time, when he was speaking in the courts of the Temple, the priests and others said to all the nobility, "This man deserves to die, for he has prophesied against this city, as you have heard with your own ears." Jeremiah did not deny what he had said; and, "As for me," he continued, "I am in your hands; do with me as seems good to you. But know certainly, that if you put me to death, you shall surely bring innocent blood upon yourselves, and upon this city, and upon its inhabitants." A group of those who heard him were impressed. It was a dangerous thing, they thought, to try to silence a prophet. What if he should be right, and God's authority be behind him? So Jeremiah was released.

But as the Babylonian danger became more imminent and passions ran higher in the city, men again became enraged at Jeremiah. The first assault by Nebuchadnezzar had now been carried through, and Jehoiachin dethroned, and he with many of the people of Judah taken off as prisoners to Babylon. To these Judæan exiles, Jeremiah wrote, advising them to build houses, plant gardens, and establish themselves where they were. They were to seek the peace of the city in which they dwelt, "for in the peace thereof," he said, "shall you have peace." When this was reported back to Jerusalem, the passionate nationalists thought him more than ever to be a traitor. Zedekiah had now come to the throne. Personally, he stood in awe of Jeremiah; but he stood in greater fear of the violent men of his court who hated the prophet. Jeremiah had said plainly that this new king also would presently be humiliated by the Chaldeans. At length the prophet was put into prison again, taken out by the king who sent for him to talk with him secretly, then handed over by the king to the group in his court who now were bent upon the prophet's death. They said to Zedekiah: "He weakens the hands of the soldiers who remain in the city, and the hands of all the people, in speaking such words to them. This man does not seek the welfare of this people, but their hurt." Then Zedekiah weakly answered: "See then, he is in your hands: for the king is not one who can do anything contrary to you."

They took Jeremiah and lowered him into an underground dungeon, where he sank into a filthy mire. It was only through an African servant in the king's house that Jeremiah was dragged out of this dungeon again by ropes which were lowered to him.

Once more the king, frightened and not knowing which way to turn, sent for Jeremiah. Jeremiah urged him to surrender to the Babylonians, and told him that, if he did not, a more dreadful end would come to him and to the city. But Zedekiah was too afraid of the coterie around him to follow the prophet's counsel. He waited too long. At last the city was starved into helplessness, and the garrison tried to escape and was intercepted by Nebuchadnezzar's army. Zedekiah himself and his sons were captured. His sons were put to death before his eyes. Then he himself was blinded and carried away to glorify the triumph of Nebuchadnezzar as he went back to Babylon. Jerusalem itself was ruthlessly destroyed. Its walls were beaten down, the king's house, the Temple itself, and all other great houses wrecked and set on fire, most of the population carried away into slavery, and only a few forlorn remnants of the people left to hide within the ruined walls.

Hostile tribesmen from Edom had joined with the Babylonians in the destruction of Jerusalem, following them as jackals follow wolves; and it was against the Edomites that the prophet Obadiah launched his message of vengeance which forms one of the short books of prophecy in the Old Testament.

Of the awful scenes which attended the fall of Jerusalem and the capture of Zedekiah, there is another picture in the Old Testament besides the picture which is presented in the historical narratives which accompany the prophecy of Jeremiah. This further picture is in the book of Lamentations. The author or the authors of it are not known; but they describe the bitterness of that time, and it is of Jerusalem in the hour of her ruin that the book of Lamentations speaks in the great words so long remembered and so often used: "Is it nothing to you, all ye that pass by? behold, and see if there be any sorrow like unto my sorrow, which is done unto me, wherewith the Lord hath afflicted me in the day of his fierce anger."

Jeremiah was in prison when the city fell. The officers of Nebuchadnezzar's army treated him with respect, and he was let go to Mizpah, where he dwelt among the few people who were gathered there. When the main body of the Chaldean army had withdrawn, they left a man named Gedaliah as governor of the region. He was shortly thereafter assassinated, and the people who remained in Judah then determined that they would go down and seek protection in Egypt. Jeremiah denounced this idea altogether. It was not in Egypt that the people, or any remnant of them, could find a new life. They must find it first through a new birth of the spirit within. Nevertheless, they did go down to Egypt, and they carried Jeremiah there with them, and the great figure of the prophet vanishes from the stage of human history.

The book of his written prophecies closes with prophecies of judgment upon other nations, including an ultimate judgment upon Babylon. It is possible that Jeremiah, after all his long message of doom, still clung to the hope that his people, after chastening, would inherit a brighter future. So he drew this immortal picture of a religion set free from forms and circumstance and dependent only upon the communion of the individual soul with God:

" 'Behold, the days come,' saith the Lord,
  'that I will make a new covenant
With the house of Israel,
  and with the house of Judah.' "

"This is the covenant that I will make
  with the house of Israel;
'After those days,' saith the Lord,
'I will put my law in their inward parts,
  and in their heart will I write it;
  and I will be their God,
  and they shall be my people.' "

And among his prophecies also are these passages, full of the beauty of a far-off hope.

"The Lord appeared of old unto me, saying,
  'Yea, I have loved thee with an everlasting love:
Therefore with loving-kindness have I drawn thee.

"Again I will build thee, and thou shalt be built,
  O virgin of Israel:
Again shalt thou be adorned with thy tabrets,
  And shalt go forth in the dances of them that make merry.

"Again shalt thou plant vineyards
 upon the mountains of Samaria:
The planters shall plant
 and shall enjoy the fruit thereof.

"For there shall be a day,
 that the watchmen upon the hills of Ephraim shall cry,
'Arise ye, and let us go up to Zion
 unto the Lord our God.'

. . . .

"Thus saith the Lord: 'A voice is heard in Ramah,
 lamentation, and bitter weeping;
Rachel weeping for her children;
 she refuseth to be comforted for her children,
 because they are not.'

"Thus saith the Lord. 'Refrain thy voice from weeping,
 and thine eyes from tears:
For thy work shall be rewarded,' saith the Lord;
 'and they shall come again from the land of the enemy.'

" 'And there is hope for thy latter end?' saith the Lord;
 'and thy children shall come again to their own border.' "

CHAPTER XXXI

THE STORY OF THE CARRYING AWAY OF THE PEOPLE AS CAPTIVES TO
BABYLON, AFTER JERUSALEM HAD FALLEN; AND OF EZEKIEL, THE
PROPHET OF THE EXILE, AND OF OTHER LATER PROPHETS OF HOPE;
AND THE NARRATIVE OF HOW NEHEMIAH CAME BACK FROM THE
LAND OF THE CAPTIVITY TO BUILD THE RUINED WALLS OF JERUSA-
LEM, AND OF HOW HE SUCCEEDED IN SPITE OF DANGER AND THE
THREAT OF DEATH.

HE THOUSANDS of Jewish captives whom
Nebuchadnezzar had carried back with him
into the east were settled in colonies round
about Babylon. For the most part they were
not harshly treated. They were allowed to
have houses of their own, to engage in trade,
and to communicate with each other. Some of them gradually
became not only accustomed to their new surroundings, but
content to remain in the midst of these; but among many of
them the homesickness for their own country was never overcome. Both for old affection and for religious loyalty, their
hearts turned back to Jerusalem. The note of their longing
has come down the years in more than one of those wistful chants
which are included in the book of Psalms.

"By the rivers of Babylon,
There we sat down, yea, we wept,
When we remembered Zion.
We hanged our harps
Upon the willows in the midst thereof.
For there they that carried us away captive
Required of us a song;
And they that wasted us required of us mirth,
Saying, 'Sing us one of the songs of Zion.'

334

"How shall we sing the Lord's song
In a strange land?
If I forget thee, O Jerusalem,
Let my right hand forget her cunning.
If I do not remember thee,
Let my tongue cleave to the roof of my mouth:
If I prefer not Jerusalem
Above my chief joy."

Among the people who were carried away after Nebuchadnezzar's first capture of Jerusalem in 597 was the priest Ezekiel.
He was taken to Telabib on the banks of the river Chebar, one
of the great canals which passed by the city of Nippur. He was
a man of patriotic devotion and of great religious passion, a man
of ecstatic moods, whose consciousness of God took the form
of tremendous visions into which his whole being was caught
up. He became the first and most influential prophet of the
exile, a preacher of confidence and hope to the discouraged, and
one also who dreamed great dreams of the restoration of religion
and of the forms which this should take. His prophecy begins
with an appearance of God which he can only describe as a
whirlwind, and a great cloud, and a fire, in the midst of which
were the likenesses of living creatures, the face of a man, the
face of a lion, the face of an ox, and the face of an eagle. In the
cloud also were wings and wheels that flashed and turned, "for
the spirit of the living creature was in the wheels." Ezekiel fell
upon his face; but he heard a voice saying to him, "Son of man,
stand upon thy feet, and I will speak unto thee."

The message which he heard was in part a message of
warning for the continued sins of the remnant of the people who
had been left in Jerusalem, as well as the recital of those past
sins which had produced the exile. But Ezekiel believed that
the scattered people would be reassembled, and the reunited
nation restored to life. And it was as a symbol of this hope that
he described his greatest vision, the vision of the valley of dry
bones.

"The hand of the Lord was upon me, and carried me out

in the spirit of the Lord, and set me down in the midst of the valley which was full of bones, and caused me to pass by them round about: and, behold, there were very many in the open valley; and, lo, they were very dry. He said unto me, 'Son of man, can these bones live?' And I answered, 'O Lord God, thou knowest.'

"Again he said unto me, 'Prophesy upon these bones, and say unto them, "O ye dry bones, hear the word of the Lord. Thus saith the Lord God unto these bones: 'Behold, I will cause breath to enter into you, and ye shall live. And I will lay sinews upon you, and will bring up flesh upon you, and cover you with skin, and put breath in you, and ye shall live; and ye shall know that I am the Lord.' "'' So I prophesied as I was commanded: and as I prophesied, there was a noise, and behold a shaking, and the bones came together, bone to his bone. And when I beheld, lo, the sinews and the flesh came up upon them, and the skin covered them above: but there was no breath in them.

"Then said he unto me, 'Prophesy unto the wind, prophesy, son of man, and say to the wind, "Thus saith the Lord God, 'Come from the four winds, O breath, and breathe upon these slain, that they may live.' "' So I prophesied as he commanded me, and the breath came into them, and they lived, and stood up upon their feet, an exceeding great army."

"Then he said unto me, 'Son of man, these bones are the whole house of Israel: behold, they say, "Our bones are dried, and our hope is lost: we are cut off. . . ." Therefore prophesy and say unto them, "Thus saith the Lord God, 'Behold, O my people, I will open your graves, and cause you to come up out of your graves, and bring you into the land of Israel. And ye shall know that I am the Lord, when I have opened your graves, O my people, and brought you up out of your graves. And I shall put my spirit in you, and ye shall live, and I shall place you in your own land: then shall ye know that I the Lord have spoken it, and performed it, saith the Lord." ' "

But Ezekiel, important though he was, was not so great a spiritual figure as some of the prophets who had preceded him. With him there was a shift of emphasis. The flaming spokesmen of moral righteousness, such as Amos and Hosea and Isaiah and Jeremiah, had identified religion with men's char-acter and conduct in the secular world. They had insisted that elaborate ritual, by which men had supposed that they were honoring God, was as nothing. Hosea's words were typical of them all: "For I desired mercy, and not sacrifice; and the knowl-edge of God more than burnt-offerings." But Ezekiel by tem-perament was the ecclesiastic. Now that he was in exile, with his mournful memories of Jerusalem and its ruined Temple, he believed that religion and the Temple's restoration went to-gether. A great part of his teaching had to do with the way in which he hoped the Temple would be rebuilt, the ritual re-established, and the traditional priestly orders set up again. "The heathen shall know that I the Lord do sanctify Israel," he said in the name of God, "when my sanctuary shall be in the midst of them forevermore."

The hopes which Ezekiel had had for a return of the exiles were destined, in part at least, to be fulfilled. By the middle of the sixth century B. C., the power of Babylon was waning. A new empire was in process of creation farther to the north and east. Cyrus, who began as the king of a petty district in Elam, conquered Persia, and then Media; and on farther to the west his armies began to move.

Meanwhile, among the exiles there arose another prophet, one of the greatest saints and seers of all religious history. We do not know his name, though his prophecies are bound up with those of the great Isaiah and form the latter chapters of that book of the Old Testament which bears Isaiah's name. This prophet, who for lack of further knowledge about him, is called the Second or Deutero-Isaiah, was instinctively a poet, whose words even to this day transmit their rhythm like a song. He believed that Cyrus should be the instrument of God for the restoration of Israel. Cyrus should conquer Babylon, set the exiles free, and let them go back to rebuild Jerusalem. So he brought his exalted message to the people in Chaldea:

" 'Comfort ye, comfort ye my people,'
   saith your God.
'Speak ye comfortably to Jerusalem;
   and cry unto her,
That her warfare is accomplished,
   that her iniquity is pardoned:
For she hath received of the Lord's hands
   double for all her sins.'

"The voice of one that crieth,
'Prepare ye in the wilderness the way of the Lord,
Make straight in the desert
   a highway for our God.
Every valley shall be exalted,
   and every mountain and hill shall be made low:
And the crooked shall be made straight,
   and the rough places plain:
And the glory of the Lord shall be revealed,
   and all flesh shall see it together:
   for the mouth of the Lord hath spoken it.
The voice of one saying, 'Cry.'
   And one said, 'What shall I cry?'
'All the flesh is grass,
   and all the goodliness thereof is as the flower of the field:'
The grass withereth, the flower fadeth:
   because the breath of the Lord bloweth upon it:
   surely the people is grass.
The grass withereth, the flower fadeth:
   but the word of our God shall stand forever.

"O thou that tellest good tidings to Zion,
   get thee up into the high mountain;
O thou that tellest good tidings to Jerusalem,
   lift up thy voice with strength;
   lift it up, be not afraid;
Say unto the cities of Judah,
   'Behold your God!' "

Still more specifically he spoke of Cyrus, and claimed Cyrus as a tool shaped for the using of God.

"Thus saith the Lord to his anointed,
  to Cyrus, whose right hand I have holden,
  to subdue nations before him;
And I will loose the loins of kings,
  to open before him the two leaved gates;
  and the gates shall not be shut.
I will go before thee,
  and make the crooked places straight;
I will break in pieces the gates of brass,
  and cut in sunder the bars of iron;
And I will give thee the treasures of darkness,
  and hidden riches of secret places,
That thou mayest know that I, the Lord,
  which call thee by thy name,
  am the God of Israel.
For Jacob my servant's sake, and Israel mine elect,
  I have even called thee by thy name:
I have surnamed thee,
  though thou hast not known me.
I am the Lord, and there is none else;
  there is no God beside me:
I girded thee, though thou hast not known me:
That they may know from the rising of the sun,
  and from the west,
That there is none beside me.
I am the Lord, and there is none else."

It was this great prophet also who saw the people of Israel as the suffering servant of God, and believed that out of their tribulation redemption would come, not only to them, but also to the other nations of their world. Meanwhile the events which had been hoped for and foreseen were coming true. Cyrus conquered Croesus, king of Lydia. He advanced then against Babylon, and in 539 B. C., that city which had been for two generations of men the symbol of terror and oppression was destroyed. "Babylon is fallen, is fallen!" ran the exultant cry.

Then in somber magnificence he painted the picture of Babylon's fall.

"Hell from beneath is moved for thee
    to meet thee at thy coming:
It stirreth up the dead for thee,
    even all the chief ones of the earth;
It hath raised up from their thrones
    all the kings of the nations.
All they shall speak and say unto thee,
'Art thou also become weak as we?
    art thou become like unto us?'
Thy pomp is brought down to the grave,
    and the noise of thy viols:
The worm is spread under thee,
    and the worms cover thee.

"How art thou fallen from heaven,
    O Lucifer, son of the morning!
How art thou cut down to the ground,
    which didst weaken the nations!
For thou hast said in thine heart,
    'I will ascend into heaven,
I will exalt my throne above the stars of God. . . .'
Yet thou shalt be brought down to hell."

The history of the exiles' return is recorded in what was originally the last part of the book of Chronicles, but which stands in the Old Testament now as the books of Ezra and Nehemiah. The Chronicles were the product of a writer who lived probably at the end of the fourth century B. C. The major part of the history which stands now as the first and second books of Chronicles is a rewriting of the material of the books of Kings, recast according to that later emphasis upon the importance of the Jewish priesthood which had developed among the scribes in the exile. But the books of Ezra and Nehemiah, which were originally part of the continuous narrative of the Chronicles, are of far greater historic value, because they include the first-hand memoirs of two of the great leaders who helped to rebuild the civilization of the Jews in Palestine. Both Ezra and Nehemiah belonged to the fifth century; but the book of Ezra begins with a description of what happened in the century preceding.

With Babylon destroyed and the more tolerant dynasty of the Persian kings in power, the way was now open for the return to their own country of the Jews, who for a half century had been in Chaldea. Shortly after the fall of Babylon, the first little band from the Jews of the captivity went back across the deserts to the country of their fathers; but it was a weary and depressing adventure to which they found themselves committed. They were few in numbers, and they were poor. To rebuild Jerusalem and re-establish a civilization there seemed a forlorn and almost desperate hope. Nevertheless, encouraged by the prophets Haggai and Zechariah, and Joshua the high priest, and under the leadership of Zerubbabel, who was of royal blood, they bent to their task. They set up an altar again within the desolation which had been Jerusalem, and they laid the foundations for the rebuilding of the Temple.

Then came a new danger. The scattered peoples who had been living in the country round about came to Zerubbabel and wanted to have part in the work which he was doing. They said that they also were worshipers of the God of Israel; but Zerubbabel, with that strict idea of religious separateness which during the exile had hardened like a flint, refused to permit their co-operation. Then these people of the surrounding district did their utmost to impede the work. Not only were they in themselves a hostile threat, but they attempted to arouse the suspicion of the Persian overlords against what Zerubbabel was doing. To Artaxerxes, when he had come to the throne, they sent this letter:

"Be it known unto the king that the Jews which came up from thee to us are come to Jerusalem; they are building the rebellious and the bad city, and have set up the walls thereof, and repaired the foundations. Be it known now unto the king, that, if this city be builded, and the walls finished, then they will not pay tribute, custom, or toll, and in the end it will be hurtful to the revenue of the kings. Now, because we have maintenance from the king's palace, and it is not meet for us to see the king's dishonor, therefore have we sent and certified the king; that search may be made in the book of the records of thy fathers. So shalt thou find in the book of the records, and know that this city is a rebellious city, and hurtful to kings and provinces, and that they have moved sedition within the same of old time: for which cause was this city destroyed. We certify the king that, if this city be builded again, and the walls thereof set up, by this means thou shalt have no portion on this side the River."

This letter had its effect. The king sent back an answer which read as follows:

"The letter which ye sent unto us hath been plainly read before me. And I commanded, and search hath been made, and it is found that this city of old time hath made insurrection against kings, and that rebellion and sedition have been made therein. There have been mighty kings also over Jerusalem, who have ruled over all the country beyond the River, and tribute, custom, and toll were paid unto them. Make ye now a decree to cause these men to cease, and that this city be not builded, until another commandment shall be given from me. Take heed now that ye be not slack herein: why should damage grow to the hurt of the kings?"

Armed with this letter, the plotters hurried to Jerusalem, and they forced the builders there to cease their work.

It was at this time that the influence of the prophets Haggai and Zechariah—and perhaps of Malachi also, for it is probable that he too lived about this time—was most significant. The courage of their religious confidence kept the people from being discouraged, and Zerubbabel, notwithstanding the order from Artaxerxes, went on again with the building of the Temple. He said to the Persian governor of the district that the records

would disclose that Cyrus himself had given permission for
what was going forward; and this, when Darius, the new king,
had made a search in the house of rolls in Babylon, he found to
be true; and he confirmed the authority of the Jews in Jerusalem to continue with their building.

So the Temple, even though upon a meager scale, was once
again established in Jerusalem, and there was a great feast of
dedication at which Haggai and Zechariah led the thanksgiving
of the people.

These two prophets, like Ezekiel, were men in whose
preaching the ecclesiastical emphasis was strong; but another
prophet of that time whose prophecies are incorporated in the
book which bears Isaiah's name expressed the spirit of personal
religion and the meaning of God's will for righteousness with
a beauty which had never been surpassed.

"Is not this the fast that I have chosen?
　　to loose the bands of wickedness,
　　to undo the heavy burdens,
And to let the oppressed go free,
　　and that ye break every yoke?
Is it not to deal thy bread to the hungry,
　　and that thou bring the poor that are cast out to thy house?
When thou seest the naked, that thou cover him;
　　and that thou hide not thyself from thine own flesh? . . .
And if thou draw out thy soul to the hungry,
　　and satisfy the afflicted soul;
Then shall thy light rise in obscurity
　　and thy darkness be as the noonday:
And the Lord shall guide thee continually,
　　and satisfy thy soul in drought."

It was about the year 515 B. C. that the Temple thus was
rebuilt. Then follows a period of obscurity; and when next the
curtain lifts and light falls again upon the stage of Jewish history, it is to reveal the noble figure of Nehemiah. Nearly three
quarters of a century had gone by since the time of Zerubbabel

when the career of this new leader begins. Nehemiah, a descendant of a Jewish family of the exile, was the cupbearer of the king of Persia at his palace in Shushan. One day, as he writes, there came back into the East "certain men of Judah; and I asked them concerning the Jews that had escaped, which were left of the captivity, and concerning Jerusalem. And they said unto me, 'The remnant that are left of the captivity there in the province are in great affliction and reproach: the wall of Jerusalem also is broken down, and the gates thereof are burned with fire.' "

When Nehemiah heard that, he wept and fasted. He prayed God to have mercy on his people, and he prayed especially that he himself might be emboldened to ask permission of the king to go to Jerusalem and help restore the city. "O Lord, I beseech thee, let now thine ear be attentive to the prayer of thy servant, and to the prayer of thy servants, who delight to fear thy name: and prosper, I pray thee, thy servant this day, and grant him mercy in the sight of this man. For I was the king's cupbearer."

The next time when he carried the king his goblet of wine, the king, looking at him, said: "Why is your countenance sad, for you are not sick? You have some sorrow at heart."

Then Nehemiah was afraid, but nevertheless he told the king what his sadness was. "The place of my fathers' sepulchers lies waste," he said, "and the gates of it are consumed with fire."

The king desired to know what it was he wanted; and Nehemiah, having breathed a prayer, asked him that he might go to Jerusalem to help rebuild its walls. How long would he be gone, the king inquired, and when would he return? So Nehemiah set a time for his absence, and the king let him go.

Moreover, Nehemiah asked that he might have letters to the Persian governor in the territory to the west, and a letter to the keeper of the king's forests, that he might give him timber; and these things he received.

To Jerusalem then he came. Entering into the city without announcement, he stayed there three days. Then in the night, accompanied by a few men, and telling no one else what he meant to do, he went out and rode around the ruined walls of Jerusalem. Having seen for himself the desolation, he gathered all the chief men of the place together and said to them: "Do you see the distress we are in—how Jerusalem lies waste, and the gates are burned? Come, let us build up the walls of Jerusalem, that we may be no more a reproach." He told them of the encouragement he had had from the king, and also in his own heart from God.

They answered him then, "Let us rise up and build." And they encouraged one another for the work. At least the greater part did so. But there were antagonists with whom Nehemiah would have to reckon.

Sanballat the Horonite, and Tobiah the Ammonite, and Geshem the Arabian, "laughed us to scorn"—so Nehemiah wrote —"and despised us, and said: 'What is this thing that you do? Will you rebel against the king?'"

Nehemiah was not merely a man of creative purpose. He had the power of an organizer also. To different men and families he assigned certain parts of the wall as their responsibilities, and they went to work with a will.

When Sanballat saw this, he tried the weapon of ridicule. "What are these feeble Jews doing?" he said. "Will they revive the stones out of the heaps of rubbish which are burned?"

And Tobiah in answering mockery said, "If a fox goes up against this thing they are building, he will break down their stone wall."

Nevertheless, "we built the wall, and all the wall was joined together unto the half thereof, for the people had a mind to work."

Then Sanballat and the other enemies, seeing that their satire was of no avail, turned to harsher measures. They organized all the hostile tribesmen they could gather in the surrounding regions, and launched attacks upon Jerusalem; but Nehemiah in one brief sentence tells of the double defense which he set up: "We made our prayer unto our God, and set a watch against them day and night."

Yet the builders of the wall were uneasy at the danger in

which they found themselves. They pointed out that outside the new work on which they were laboring were great heaps of ruined stone behind which the enemies could lie in ambush, and from which they could launch their attacks. So Nehemiah divided the forces into two groups. He set half of them, fully armed, upon the walls; and the builders and the men who carried materials did so with swords girded, while Nehemiah himself stood on watch with a trumpeter beside him. He said to all the people: "The work is great and large, and we are separated upon the wall, one far from another. In whatever place therefore you hear the sound of the trumpet, rally there to me: our God shall fight for us." So all day long they worked, and the people who lived outside the walls were gathered within them for defense at night.

Another danger, however, Nehemiah was to face, and this time it came, not from enemies without, but from unrest within his garrison. Some of the people who had farmed the land outside Jerusalem, and had had to leave it because they were working on the walls, said that they had borrowed money to pay the Persian taxes, and they had had to mortgage their lands, their fields, and their houses to the richer men in Jerusalem. "Our flesh is as the flesh of our brethren," they said, "our children as their children." And they said their sons and daughters were being indentured as servants, and they could not redeem them because other men held their lands. Nehemiah immediately called the propertied men together. This thing which they were doing was "not good," he said. "Ought you not to walk in the fear of God, lest you incur the reproach of these heathen our enemies? . . . Leave off this usury. Restore, I pray you, to them even this day their lands, their vineyards, their oliveyards, and their houses, and also part of the money and the produce which you have exacted of them." The men to whom he spoke had nothing to say in rebuttal. They said they would do what Nehemiah had asked, and Nehemiah had them take an oath before the priests.

The same conspirators, however, who had caused Nehemiah trouble before, were still plotting. Sanballat and Tobiah and

Geshem sent Nehemiah a message, asking him to come to a conference with them. He sent them back word: "I am doing a great work, and therefore I cannot come down. Why should the work cease, while I leave it and come down to you?" Four times they sent their message without avail, and the last time Sanballat's servant brought in his hand an open letter which read as follows:

"It is reported among the nations, and Gashmu saith it, that thou and the Jews think to rebel: for which cause thou art building the wall, that thou mayest be their king, according to these words. And thou hast also appointed prophets to preach of thee at Jerusalem, saying, 'There is a king in Judah:' and now shall it be reported to the king according to those words. Come now therefore and let us take counsel together."

Nehemiah's reply was curt: "There are no such things done as you say, but you feign them out of your own heart."

Failing in this effort, Nehemiah's enemies tried once more to frighten him. Nehemiah had gone in Jerusalem to the house of a man who had been hired secretly as the agent of Sanballat, Shemaiah; and Shemaiah, pretending that he was solicitous for Nehemiah's safety, said to him: "Let us go together into the Temple and shut the doors. They are coming here to kill you. Yes, in the night they will come to kill you." But Nehemiah answered: "Should such a man as I flee? Who is there, that, being as I am, would go into the Temple to save his life? I will not go in!"

And now, at length, the wall was finished, and Nehemiah gathered all the people and made a census of them. Then in the street before the water gate he called them together in a great assembly, and Ezra the scribe brought the book of the law of Moses and read it in the hearing of the people. This was the code which had been put into form by the priests and scribes during the captivity in Babylon. It included, not only the moral law, but the ordinances which are found in the books of Deuteronomy and Leviticus, and all the rest of the ritual code which now had been completed as the orthodoxy of

Jewish worship. At the urgent exhortation of Ezra and Nehemiah, and of the other scribes who interpreted the law as it was read, the people took a solemn oath to observe all these injunctions. To the minds of Ezra and Nehemiah, the greatest trespass of the people had been the fact that many of them had entered into marriages with the alien peoples round about. Ezra and Nehemiah insisted that these marriages should be dissolved and that the strict and complete separation of Israel should be established and maintained.

Nehemiah had now finished his main work. He had brought about the rebuilding of the walls. He with Ezra had cemented the population of Jerusalem into a religious unity. Now he returned, as his promise was, to the court of Persia.

But presently, twelve years after his first journey to Jerusalem, he returned. Irregularities had developed, both in the daily conduct and in the religious worship of the people. He came to set these straight, and among other things he enjoined that strict and absolute observance of the Sabbath day which henceforth was to be the unique mark of a faithful Judaism. Most of the people had obeyed the command which he and Ezra had given for the dissolution of marriages with aliens; but he found that the son of one of the priests had married the daughter of his arch-enemy, Sanballat the Horonite. Nehemiah promptly sent this offender into exile; and, according to Jewish tradition, it was through this priest that the priestly succession among the Samaritans, whom the Jews despised, was set up. But Nehemiah, with his unflagging zeal for the law, had done his utmost to see that in Jewry the law was completely obeyed; and doubtless with a quiet conscience he wrote the words which conclude his book: "Remember me, O my God, for good."

Thus the bold figure of Nehemiah passes from the scene, and the history of Jerusalem for succeeding years sinks into relative obscurity. But one of the prophets, whose book appears in the Old Testament, belongs perhaps to the period not long after Nehemiah's work. This is Joel. He lacked the spiritual greatness of such men as Amos, Isaiah, and Jeremiah. His bent of mind, indeed, was rather that of the priest than of the prophet. He had evidently felt the full influence of that great emphasis upon the law and the ritual which developed after the exile. To his mind, the supremely important thing was faithfulness to the religious observances which clustered round the Temple. The most deadly sin that Israel could commit was neglect of the ordinances of worship. If disasters came, it was because the people had been unfaithful in this respect. If they hoped for prosperity, let priests and people perform their obligations. If they did so, then Israel would be blessed; and, unlike the greater prophets, if Israel were blessed, Joel was not greatly concerned with what disasters might fall elsewhere.

But if religiously he was not among the first rank of the prophets, Joel did rise to greatness as a poet. The book of his prophecy contains a magnificent dramatic narrative of a great plague of locusts, which he believes to be a judgment of God, advancing like a destroying army for the people's sins. And it was Joel also who wrote the imperishably beautiful words which have come down across the centuries in litanies of penitence:

"Yet even now, saith the Lord, turn ye unto me with all your
heart,
and with fasting, and with weeping, and with mourning:
And rend your heart, and not your garments,
and turn unto the Lord your God:
For he is gracious and full of compassion,
slow to anger, and plenteous in mercy,
and repenteth him of the evil."

And it was Joel who wrote:

"And it shall come to pass afterward,
that I will pour out my Spirit upon all flesh;
And your sons and your daughters shall prophesy,
your old men shall dream dreams,
your young men shall see visions."

And it was Joel also to whom all thinkers upon the solemn issues of religion owe the great phrase, "Multitudes, multitudes in the valley of decision!"

CHAPTER XXXII

ANY OF the books of the Old Testament are books of history. They show us human beings in action. Through these pages there moves the long pageant of crowded and dramatic life. Thus and so men acted. This and that they did.

But in the Old Testament there are other books which tell, not what people were doing, but, rather, what they thought. The people of Israel had other literature besides history. There were men who were not so much mingling in active life as meditating upon the life they saw. Some of them wrote in prose, and some of them wrote in poetry; and whether in prose or poetry, they achieved not only insight into truth, but great beauty of expression too.

Among these books and collections, all of them probably compiled late in the history of the Jewish nation, there are five which may be remembered together.

One of these is the so-called "Song of Solomon," or the "Song of Songs." At one time it was supposed that Solomon wrote it; but there is little likelihood that he did. Nor did any one man write it, for it is a collection of folk-songs, composed by unknown men, and sung by the people. It is a strange book to be found within the covers of the Bible, and the reason why it still remains there, even in the Bible of the Christian Church, is because it was imagined that the Song was an allegory of Christ as the bridegroom and the church as his bride. But, as a matter of fact, the book deals with very human love in a

NEHEMIAH'S MIDNIGHT SURVEY

ESTHER AT THE COURT

very human, though sometimes in a very exquisite way. In
Oriental countries the marriage feast lasted for as long as a week,
and the bride and groom were set on thrones, while there were
singing and dancing and much festivity before them; and the
Song of Songs is made up of these lyrics which the neighbors, or
the bride and groom themselves, used to sing in these wedding
festivals. Among them are lines of purest poetry:

"I said, 'I will rise now, and go about the city,
In the streets and in the broad ways,
I will seek him whom my soul loveth:'
I sought him, but I found him not.
The watchmen that go about the city found me:
To whom I said, 'Saw ye him whom my soul loveth?'
It was but a little that I passed from them,
When I found him whom my soul loveth:
I held him, and would not let him go. . . .

"My beloved spake, and said unto me,
Rise up, my love, my fair one, and come away.
For, lo, the winter is past,
The rain is over and gone;
The flowers appear on the earth;
The time of the singing of birds is come. . . .'

"My beloved is mine, and I am his;
He feedeth his flock among the lilies.
Until the day be cool, and the shadows flee away. . . .

"Until the day be cool, and the shadows flee away, . . .
I will get me to the mountain of myrrh,
And to the hill of frankincense. . . .

"Awake, O north wind; and come, thou south;
Blow upon my garden,
That the spices thereof may flow out.
Let my beloved come into his garden,
And eat his precious fruits."

Another and different book is the book of "The Proverbs." It is a collection of the sayings of wise men, or sages. They were thoughtful observers of life, and they put down in short and picturesque comparisons what the everyday facts seemed to them to mean. Mostly their observations were shrewd, but also kindly. They had common sense and humorous understanding, and sound judgment as to the foundations which men must build on if their lives would be honorable in the sight of men and God. "The fear of the Lord is the beginning of knowledge; but the foolish despise wisdom and instruction," said one of the first of the proverbs.

And out of the rich collection of them, come these others which show the quality of the book:

"Go to the ant, thou sluggard;
  Consider her ways, and be wise:
    Which having no chief,
    Overseer, or ruler,
  Provideth her meat in the summer,
  And gathereth her food in the harvest.
  How long wilt thou sleep, O sluggard?
  When wilt thou arise out of thy sleep?
    'Yet a little sleep, a little slumber,
    A little folding of the hands to sleep'—
  So shall thy poverty come as a robber,
  And thy want as an armed man. . . .

"As a jewel of gold in a swine's snout,
  So is a fair woman that is without discretion. . . .

"Better is a dinner of herbs where love is,
  Than a stalled ox and hatred therewith. . . .

"Better is a dry morsel and quietness therewith,
  Than an house full of feasting with strife. . . .

"Hope deferred maketh the heart sick:
  But when the desire cometh, it is a tree of life. . . .

"The heart knoweth its own bitterness;
   And a stranger doth not intermeddle with its joy. . . .

"A soft answer turneth away wrath:
   But a grievous word stirreth up anger. . . .

"Pride goeth before destruction,
   And an haughty spirit before a fall.

"Righteousness exalteth a nation:
   But sin is a reproach to any people.

"A merry heart doeth good like a medicine;
   But a broken spirit drieth the bones."

If the writer of the book of Ecclesiastes had ever heard that last quoted proverb, it is certain that he did not take it very seriously, for Ecclesiastes was not written by a man with a merry heart. Rather, it sounds like the message of a "broken spirit," which was in a fair way to dry up his bones.

It is in many respects the most dismal book of the Old Testament. "Vanity of vanities, saith the Preacher; vanity of vanities, all is vanity." That is the way it begins, and it goes on mostly in that same strain. The world to the writer of the Ecclesiastes seemed a dreary place. Life was only one monotonous thing after another. According to his idea, very little happens that is worth happening; "and there is no new thing under the sun."

"The words of the Preacher, the son of David,
      king in Jerusalem.
   Vanity of vanities, saith the Preacher;
      vanity of vanities, all is vanity.
   What profit hath man of all his labor
      wherein he laboreth under the sun?
   One generation goeth, and another generation cometh;
      but the earth abideth forever.
   The sun also ariseth, and the sun goeth down,
      and hasteth to his place where he ariseth.

The wind goeth toward the south,
    and turneth about unto the north;
It turneth about continually in its course,
    and the wind returneth again to its circuits.
All the rivers run into the sea,
    yet the sea is not full;
Unto the place whither the rivers go,
    thither they go again."

So "the Preacher" reviews one experience in life after another. He had applied his heart "to know wisdom and to know
madness and folly"; and he perceived that this also was a striving
after wind. "For in much wisdom is much grief: and he that
increaseth knowledge increaseth sorrow. I said in my heart, 'Go
to now, I will prove thee with mirth; therefore enjoy pleasure':
and, behold, this also was vanity."

He sought for possessions, and for pleasures and luxurious
delights; but neither in these did he find any satisfaction. He
looked at labor; but he could not see that there was any joy in
its fruits. He looked at the course of life, and it seemed to
have no meaning. "For that which befalleth the sons of men
befalleth beasts; even one thing befalleth them. As the one
dieth, so dieth the other; yea, they have all one breath, and the
man hath no pre-eminence above the beasts: for all is vanity."
He looked at old age, and he found it only a mournful wasting
away of strength, for then

". . . the grasshopper shall be a burden,
    and desire shall fail:
Because man goeth to his long home,
    and the mourners go about the streets:
Or ever the silver cord be loosed,
    or the golden bowl is broken,
Or the pitcher be broken at the fountain,
    or the wheel broken at the cistern,
Then shall the dust return to the earth as it was:
    and the spirit shall return unto God who gave it."

When all was said and done, the only conclusion he found himself able to arrive at was that life is inexplicable; and since no one can explain its contradictions, one had best just go on living, and gather such satisfactions as offer by the way.

"In the morning sow thy seed, and in the evening withhold not thy hand: for thou knowest not which shall prosper, whether this or that, or whether they both shall be alike good. Truly the light is sweet, and a pleasant thing it is for the eyes to behold the sun. Yea, if a man live many years, let him rejoice in them all; but let him remember the days of darkness, for they shall be many. All that cometh is vanity.'

Altogether, it is a curious book to be found within the covers of the Bible, for it does not express any religious message of certainty or confidence. Nevertheless, we may well rejoice that it has been preserved, not only because in its form of expression it is often beautiful, but also because it is a real picture of some moods of human life which need to be remembered. It helps to complete the Bible's great picture of man as he really is, and so makes all the more forceful the message in its other books of the grace of God which man needs.

If Ecclesiastes is all on one note, there is another book in the Old Testament which has in it as many different notes as the music of all the instruments in an orchestra. It is "The Book of Psalms." It is the great collection of the lyric poetry of religion. It is compiled from the work of many writers, and it covers many generations in the history of Israel. Some of the psalms are poems of religious meditation, such as the psalm which is printed first of all:

"Blessed is the man that walketh not in the counsel of the ungodly,
  nor standeth in the way of sinners,
  nor sitteth in the seat of the scornful.
But his delight is in the law of the Lord;
  and in his law doth he meditate day and night.

"And he shall be like a tree planted by the rivers of water,
that bringeth forth his fruit in due season.
His leaf also shall not wither;
and whatsoever he doeth shall prosper.
The ungodly are not so:
but are like the chaff
which the wind driveth away.

"Therefore the wicked shall not stand in the judgment,
nor sinners in the congregation of the righteous.
For the Lord knoweth the way of the righteous:
but the way of the ungodly shall perish."

Some of the psalms are outbursts of spiritual joy, such as the eighth psalm, which begins, "O Lord, our God, how excellent is thy name in all the earth! who hast set thy glory above the heavens;" or the twenty-seventh psalm, which begins as with the sound of trumpets,

"The Lord is my light and my salvation;
whom then shall I fear?
The Lord is the strength of my life;
of whom then shall I be afraid?"

Other psalms throb with the deep music of penitence and confession.

"Out of the deep have I cried unto thee, O Lord;
Lord, hear my voice:
O let thine ears consider well
the voice of my complaint.

"If thou, Lord, wilt be extreme to mark what is done amiss,
O Lord, who may abide it?
For there is mercy with thee;
Therefore shalt thou be feared.

"I look for the Lord;
My soul doth wait for him;
In his word is my trust.

"My soul fleeth unto the Lord
  Before the morning watch:
  I say, before the morning watch.

"O Israel, trust in the Lord:
    for with the Lord there is mercy,
  And with him is plenteous redemption.
    And he shall redeem Israel from all his sins."

Some of the psalms have to do with individuals, and some of them have to do with the nation. Many of the most beautiful ones are marching songs which were chanted by the pilgrims on the way to Jerusalem at the time of the Passover or other great festivals of the Jewish year. Such are the one hundred and twenty-first psalm and the one hundred and twenty-sixth.

"I will lift up mine eyes unto the mountains:
  From whence shall my help come?
  My help cometh from the Lord,
  Which made heaven and earth.

"He will not suffer thy foot to be moved:
  He that keepeth thee will not slumber.
  Behold, he that keepeth Israel
  Shall neither slumber nor sleep.

"The Lord is thy keeper:
  The Lord is thy shade upon thy right hand.
  The sun shall not smite thee by day,
  Nor the moon by night.

"The Lord shall keep thee from all evil;
  He shall keep thy soul.
  The Lord shall keep thy going out and thy coming in,
  From this time forth and forevermore."

"When the Lord turned again the captivity of Zion,
  We were like unto them that dream.

Then was our mouth filled with laughter,
And our tongue with singing:
Then said they among the nations,
'The Lord hath done great things for them.'

"The Lord hath done great things for us,
Whereof we are glad.

"Turn again our captivity, O Lord,
As the streams in the South.
They that sow in tears shall reap in joy.
Though he goeth on his way weeping,
Bearing forth the seed,
He shall come again with joy, bringing his sheaves with him."

But when all is said and done, there is no way of describing the book of Psalms. The only way to appreciate its beauty is to go and read it, for as has been truly said, "The psalms are a mirror in which each man sees the motions of his own soul."

In the books of Old Testament literature one other remains to be mentioned, and that perhaps the greatest of all. It is the dramatic poem of Job.

In this book the unknown writer wrestles with the question which men have wrestled with all down the years. Why should the righteous suffer? What is the meaning of calamities which do not seem to be deserved? And in the face of so much suffering and so much sorrow, what shall we think of the justice and the love of God?

In the early Old Testament times the established belief was that happiness and sorrow were given to every life according to its deserts. If a man were good, then he should be blessed. If he were evil, then he should be punished. If life were prosperous, therefore, it meant that a man stood in the favor of God. If disasters came upon him, it meant that he had sinned, and that God punished him for his offenses.

But the drama of Job is built upon the fact that Job was a

good man, and that, nevertheless, upon this good man all sorts of sorrow and bereavement descended. He was "perfect and upright, and one that feared God, and turned away from evil." Yet upon him the evil of affliction fell.

The book opens with a prologue in heaven. The messengers and representatives of God come to present themselves before his face, and among these comes Satan, or "the Adversary."

"Whence comest thou?" the Lord God asks of Satan, and he answers, "From going to and fro in the earth, and from walking up and down in it." Again the Lord God asks: "Hast thou considered my servant Job? For there is none like him in the earth, a perfect and upright man, one that feareth God and turneth away from evil." But Satan answers: "Doth Job fear God for nought? Hast not thou made a hedge about him, and about his house, and about all that he hath on every side? Thou hast blessed the work of his hands, and his substance is increased in the land. But put forth thy hand now, and touch all that he hath, and he will renounce thee to thy face."

Then it is determined that Job shall be tested at Satan's hands; and thick and fast disasters begin to fall. A messenger comes to Job, and tells him that all his five hundred yoke of oxen and his five hundred asses have been stolen, and the servants who guarded them slain. Another messenger comes upon the heels of the first to tell Job that a fire from heaven has burned up his seven thousand sheep. Another messenger brings the news that robbers have driven off his three thousand camels. And finally he learns that all his sons and daughters, gathered together at a feast in the eldest brother's house, have been killed when the house collapsed before a great wind from the desert.

Job rose and rent his clothes, and sat down again mourning; but he said, "Naked came I out of my mother's womb, and naked shall I return thither. The Lord gave, and the Lord hath taken away. Blessed be the name of the Lord." But his distresses were not yet ended. There fell upon him a sore disease, so that all his body was covered with boils; and he went out and sat among the ashes, and his wife advised him to renounce God and die.

And now upon the scene appeared a group of Job's friends, who said they came to be his comforters, but who turned out to be his tormentors, because they kept on insisting that his afflictions must be a sign that he was very wicked, and that the first thing he needed to do was to repent.

Said Eliphaz, one of these so-called comforters:

"Remember, I pray thee, who ever perished, being innocent?
Or where were the upright cut off?
According as I have seen, they that plow iniquity,
And sow trouble reap the same.
By the breath of God they perish,
And by the blast of his anger are they consumed."

And another friend, Bildad, then insists:

"Doth God pervert judgment?
Or doth the Almighty pervert justice? . . .
If thou wouldest seek diligently unto God,
And make thy supplication to the Almighty:
If thou wert pure and upright;
Surely now he would awake for thee,
And make the habitation of thy righteousness prosperous.
And though thy beginning was small,
Yet thy latter end would greatly increase."

But Job answered bitterly:

"No doubt but ye are the people,
And wisdom shall die with you.
But I have understanding as well as you;
I am not inferior to you;
Yea, who knoweth not such things as these? . . .

"Surely I would speak to the Almighty,
And I desire to reason with God.
But ye are forgers of lies;
Ye are all physicians of no value. . . .

"Hold your peace, let me alone, that I may speak;
And let come on me what will. . . .
Behold, he will slay me;
I have no hope:
Nevertheless, I will maintain my ways before him.
This also shall be my salvation,
For a godless man shall not come before him.
Hear diligently my speech,
And let my declaration be in your ears.
Behold now, I have ordered my cause;
I know that I am righteous.
Who is he that will contend with me?"

Then Job goes on with pathetic lament for his own hope-lessness, as it seems to him that he is left alone both by man and God.

"For there is hope of a tree, if it be cut down, that it will sprout
        again,
And that the tender branch thereof will not cease.
Though the root thereof wax old in the earth,
And the stock thereof die in the ground:
Yet through the scent of water it will bud,
And put forth boughs like a plant.
But man dieth, and wasteth away:
Yea, man giveth up the ghost, and where is he?
As the waters fail from the sea,
And the river decayeth and drieth up;
So man lieth down and riseth not:
Till the heavens be no more, they shall not awake,
Nor be roused out of their sleep."

Back come his "comforters," more argumentative and insistent than ever, demanding that Job admit his own perversity, and confess the sins which they think must lie back of his afflictions. But the debate arrives at no conclusion. Still Job asserts his innocence, and still he cries out for some way in which he may plead his cause before God. He cannot understand why he has been smitten, and yet he holds to his trust that God has not forsaken him.   At length, at the climax of the poem, all the argument is swallowed up in a vision.   Job hears the awful voice of God himself, speaking out of a whirlwind, and God asks:

"Who is this that darkeneth counsel
  By words without knowledge?
Gird up now thy loins like a man;
  For I will demand of thee, and declare thou unto me.
Where wast thou when I laid the foundations of the earth?
Declare, if thou hast understanding.
Who determined the measures thereof, if thou knowest?
Or who stretched the line upon it?
Whereupon were the foundations thereof fastened?
Or who laid the corner-stone thereof,
When the morning stars sang together,
And all the sons of God shouted for joy?"

On through many other verses of magnificent poetry continue the questions which Job heard as though spoken by the voice of God.   It is as though God were confronting Job with all the marvels and mysteries of the universe.

"Hast thou commanded the morning since thy days began,
  And caused the dayspring to know its place? . . .

"Hast thou entered into the springs of the sea?
  Or hast thou walked in the recesses of the deep?
Have the gates of death been revealed unto thee?
Or hast thou seen the gates of the shadow of death?
Hast thou comprehended the breadth of the earth?
Declare, if thou knowest it all. . . .

"Canst thou bind the cluster of the Pleiades,
  Or loose the bands of Orion? . . .

"Knowest thou the ordinances of the heavens?
  Canst thou establish the dominion thereof in the earth?"

Job is overwhelmed with awe; but at the same time, his spirit enters strangely into peace. He cannot understand his own affliction; but, after all, that begins to seem to him only a little thing. Why should he understand, when there is so much else that is mysterious? He will be still before the greatness of God.

Thus it is that the drama of Job does not present any smooth answer to the question with which it is concerned. In the end it does not explain why good men suffer. But what it does do is to deny forever the glib arguments of persons like Job's comforters who explain prosperity or calamity as being weighed out exactly according to man's goodness or his sins. And so the book of Job in the Old Testament opens the way for the New Testament and its picture of Jesus, who became the great Sufferer, not for any sins of his own but for the sins of others, and through his suffering helped men in a new way to understand the love of God.

CHAPTER XXXIII

THE BOOK OF ESTHER, WITH ITS STORY OF AHASUERUS AND THE
BRAVE YOUNG QUEEN; AND OF THE GALLOWS WHICH HAMAN MADE,
AND OF WHAT HAPPENED THEN TO HAMAN; AND THE BOOK OF
JONAH, WITH ITS STORY OF THE WHALE.

LTHOUGH a considerable number of the Jewish exiles had gone back from the east with Zerubbabel, and with Ezra and Nehemiah, to re-establish Jerusalem, many of them—and probably most—remained in the countries to which their forefathers had been carried and in which they, the descendants, had been born. Among these Jews of the exile there were two tendencies. Some of them became assimilated more and more to the life of the country in which they were dwelling. They entered into business there, and some of them grew wealthy. They were content to remain where they were, and little by little to drift away from their Jewish separateness.

But among others the exactly opposite influence was working. The exile produced in them not amalgamation with the foreigners, but an intense and growing racial pride. The bitter memories of national defeat rankled in their hearts. Deprived of political independence, they cherished more and more their belief in the unique religious destiny of Israel. They believed that they had been, and that they still were, the peculiar people of God. Consequently, there grew up an almost fanatical devotion to the law and to the ritual as the mark of Israel's separateness. It was during this period following the exile that the books that now form the Pentateuch were finally compiled, and into the older inherited materials were woven the strict ideas of priests and scribes.

Another significant development which began in this period

364

was the formation of synagogues. Jews of the exile could no longer go to the Temple in Jerusalem to worship. They needed, however, a rallying point where they could be instructed in the law, and where they could express their solidarity. The growth of the synagogue was the answer to this need, and the Jews who returned from the exile to Palestine took the institution of the synagogue with them, and it became the vital center of Jewish instruction, and was to remain so throughout the rest of the Old Testament and down into New Testament times.

Moreover, the national pride of the Jews of the exile found expression from time to time in literary work. Some writer who became the spokesman of the passionate hopes and antipathies of his people would embody their emotions in some historical or imaginative work.

Of such an origin and of such a nature was the book of Esther. It is one of the most vivid and interesting, and yet one of the least religious books of the Old Testament. The name of God is not once mentioned in it. It vibrates with an unabashed hatred of the people among whom the Jews felt themselves to be imprisoned. It is an historical romance laid in the reign of Ahasuerus, or Xerxes, in the early part of the fifth century B. C. It is not spiritually edifying, but it is of great importance, as showing how the Jews of the exile felt; and from its story there emerges in Esther one character of great strength and grace.

The story begins with a feast which King Ahasuerus made to all his court and retinue, "when he showed the riches of his glorious kingdom and the honor of his excellent majesty many days, even an hundred and fourscore days. And when these days were fulfilled, the king made a feast unto all the people that were present in Shushan the palace, both great and small, seven days, in the court of the garden of the king's palace; there were hangings of white cloth, of green, and of blue, fastened with cords of fine linen and purple to silver rings and pillars of marble: the couches were of gold and silver, upon a pavement of red, and white, and yellow, and black marble. And they gave them drink in vessels of gold (the vessels being diverse one from another), and royal wine in abundance, according to the bounty of the king."

Now, when the king was merry with wine, he sent his chamberlains to bring Vashti the queen, "to show the peoples and the princes her beauty; for she was fair to look on." Vashti refused to come, which roused the king to fury.

To later times it would seem that Vashti did modestly and well in refusing to come and exhibit her beauty before the half-drunken party; but no such idea was in the mind of the writer of the book of Esther. He believed, with old-world assurance, in the authority of the male. So his story goes on to tell of how the indignant Ahasuerus took counsel of his princes as to what should be done. One of them declared that Vashti had not only wronged the king but the realm generally. "For this deed of the queen shall come abroad unto all women, to make their husbands contemptible in their eyes, when it shall be reported: 'The king Ahasuerus commanded Vashti the queen to be brought in before him, but she came not.' And this day will the princesses of Persia and Media which have heard of the deed of the queen say the like unto all the king's princes. So shall there arise much contempt and wrath." This counselor recommended that Vashti should be discrowned and sent away from the king's palace in disgrace. If that were done, he said, then "all the wives will give to their husbands honor, both to great and small." This advice seemed to Ahasuerus to be excellent. So he divorced Vashti, and he sent a message through the kingdom "that every man should bear rule in his own house."

Now came the matter of filling Vashti's place; and though the competition for this honor was conducted in a peculiarly Oriental and unlovely manner, there did blossom from it a beautiful person to win the king's regard. Esther, the niece of Mordecai, one of the Jews of the exile, won Ahasuerus' love, and she became his queen.

It was not known, however, that Esther was a daughter of the Jewish people, and Mordecai had counseled her not to reveal it. This meant, of course, that Mordecai's relationship to her also was not known. But good fortune now gave Mordecai himself an opportunity to put Ahasuerus in his debt. Sitting one day at the gate of the king's palace, he heard two of the royal chamberlains plotting against the king's life. He told Esther of it, and Esther told the king, and upon examination the two men were found guilty and were hanged.

But now another and a sinister figure appeared upon the scene. The king had taken as his favorite a man named Haman, and had promoted him above all the princes of his court. All the royal servants were commanded to bow down and do reverence to Haman; and they did so—all but Mordecai. Mordecai the Jew stood erect and unregarding when Haman passed by, and it was so conspicuous that other members of the court asked him how he dared to disobey the king's command. They made a daily wonder of it, but he paid no attention. Meanwhile some of them had discovered that he was a Jew, and they went and told Haman how this Jew held him in open disrespect. Haman was so angry that he determined that he would have adequate revenge. It seemed to him not enough to punish Mordecai alone. He would make Mordecai the cause for the destruction of all his people.

So one day Haman said to King Ahasuerus, "There is a certain people scattered abroad and dispersed among the peoples in all the provinces of thy kingdom. Their laws are diverse from those of every people; neither keep they the king's laws: therefore it is not for the king's profit to suffer them. If it please the king, let it be written that they be destroyed: and I will pay ten thousand talents of silver into the hands of those that have charge of the king's business, to bring it into the king's treasuries."

To this Ahasuerus agreed, and he gave his signet ring to Haman as a sign of authority to carry out his purpose. Letters were sent then to the governors of all the provinces, sealed with the king's ring, giving orders that on a certified day all the Jews were to be massacred and their property taken. Meanwhile, "the king and Haman sat down to drink; but the city of Shushan was perplexed."

When Mordecai heard what had been done, he rent his

clothes and put on sackcloth and ashes and came before the king's gate. Some of Queen Esther's waiting-maids came and told her this, and the queen was much troubled. She sent other raiment for Mordecai, begging him to put this on instead of sackcloth and ashes; but he would not. Then she despatched her chamberlain to Mordecai to ask how it was that he was doing this, and Mordecai told him in reply what Haman had done and of the danger which was afoot. He gave him a copy of the royal decree, which now had been despatched everywhere, ordering the extermination of the Jews, and he begged that Esther would go to King Ahasuerus and supplicate him to spare her people.

Back to Mordecai Esther sent her perplexed and troubled message. Did not Mordecai know that the law of the court (a law not without reason among those Oriental dynasties where assassination was frequent) was that anyone who went into the king's presence without having been summoned was liable to be put to death? For thirty days, she said, she had not seen the king's face. How should she dare to go to him now?

But Mordecai sent back word to Esther, "Think not with thyself that thou shalt escape in the king's house, more than all the Jews. For if thou altogether holdest thy peace at this time, then will relief and deliverance arise to the Jews from another place, but thou and thy father's house shall perish: and who knoweth whether thou art not come to the kingdom for such a time as this?"

In this crisis Esther put all thought of herself aside. She told her servant to say to Mordecai: "Go and gather all the Jews together, and fast for me three days, and I and my maids will do the same. So will I go in unto the king, which is not according to the law; and if I perish, I perish."

Mordecai went then and gathered his people together, and fasted, as Esther had said. On the third day, Esther put on her royal apparel and went into the king's inner court, where he was sitting upon his royal throne. When he saw her standing there, she won favor in his sight, and he held out the golden scepter that was in his hand. Esther drew near and touched it. What would she have, the king asked, and what was her request? It should be given to her, even to half of his kingdom; and Esther said, "If it seem good unto the king, let the king and Haman come this day to the banquet that I have prepared for him."

Shortly thereafter the king and Haman went to Esther's banquet. Again Ahasuerus wanted to know what his queen's petition was. Whatever she asked, should be granted. But Esther faltered for a moment before the perilous disclosure she had to make. She asked that the king and Haman would come to another banquet on the morrow. Then she would tell him what was in her heart.

From the queen's table that day Haman went away joyful and elated. Had he not been twice bidden in company with the king to dine with the queen? But in the gate there again was the stubborn figure of Mordecai; and when Haman saw him, his anger blazed. He controlled himself, however, and went home, where he immediately gathered his wife and his friends around him. He told them how rich he was, and how favored. He recited all the promotions which the king had granted him. He told about Esther's invitations. "Yet all this avails me nothing," he said, "so long as I see Mordecai the Jew sitting at the king's gate." His wife and his friends shared his indignation. They advised him to have a gallows built nincty feet high, and to persuade the king to have Mordecai hanged on it. Then, they said, he could go merrily with the king to the banquet; and Haman agreed that in that case he could. He had the gallows made.

But that night King Ahasuerus was restless, and could not sleep. He commanded to have the book of the chronicles of his reign brought and read to him. And as it was read, suddenly the king heard again and was reminded of Mordecai's act in having saved him from the two conspirators who were plotting against his life. He had forgotten all about that. He asked his servants what honor and dignity had been bestowed on Mordecai as a reward for this. They told him, "Nothing." "Who is in the court?" said the king. His servants said that Haman was there; for at that moment Haman had come into the outer court of the king's palace to suggest to him the great advisability of having Mordecai hanged on his new gallows.

"Let Haman come in," said King Ahasuerus. So in came Haman.

"What shall be done unto the man whom the king delights to honor?" Ahasuerus asked.

"He means me," thought Haman. "To whom could the king so much want to do honor as to myself?" But very deferentially Haman said aloud that if there were any man whom the king delighted especially to honor, he should suggest that royal apparel be brought and the horse that the king was accustomed to ride on, and the favored one should have a royal crown put on his head and be arrayed by one of the princes, and one of the princes should lead him on the king's horse through the streets, and proclaim before him that thus it was done to the one whom the king desired to honor.

Thus craftily Haman spoke. Whereupon the king adopted Haman's suggestion, but in a way that left Haman aghast. "You make haste," he said, "and take the apparel and the horse, as you have said, and do all this to Mordecai the Jew, who sits at the king's gate." So Haman went off to clothe Mordecai and lead him in the triumph which he had supposed was for himself.

Home he hurried after that to pour out to his wife and his friends the story of his outrage. But they gave him little consolation. It seemed to them an omen of worse things to come; and while they were still talking, the king's chamberlains came to bring Haman to Esther's banquet.

For this second time, therefore, the king and Haman sat at the queen's table; and now again the king asked of Esther what her petition was, and again he promised that whatever she asked would be given her, even to half of his kingdom. She answered him that the thing for which she made petition, if she had found favor in his sight, was her own life and the life of her people. And she told him that she was of Jewish blood, and that it was her people who had been condemned by the king's edict to be destroyed and slain. Who was it, the king demanded to know, who had dared to suggest this; and Esther reminded him who it was. It was Haman, this same Haman sitting at her banquet now.

Haman shrank in fear, and the king rose up wrathfully and went out to walk up and down in the garden of the palace. Left alone with the queen, Haman began to beg for his life. In the intensity of his pleading he fell down on the couch where the queen was reclining, and the king, coming in suddenly at this moment, was furious. He instantly summoned his servants, and they covered Haman's face. One of them told the king of the gallows which Haman had built near his own house for Mordecai. "Take him out and hang him on it!" said Ahasuerus. So they hanged Haman on the gallows where he had thought that Mordecai would be.

Queen Esther then begged the king to revoke the edict which he had sent out, ordering the killing of the Jews; but this to the author of the book of Esther did not seem a sufficiently vivid climax. The king, therefore, refuses to revoke his order on the ground that the laws of the Medes and Persians, once promulgated, were never withdrawn; but he sent out another edict, giving to the Jews themselves permission to attack and kill, in the first place, all their neighbors who might be plotting violence against them. Thus, therefore, it was done. The people who a little while before had seemed to be doomed, rose up against their non-Jewish neighbors and killed many thousands of them; a conclusion which to the writer of the book seemed wholly right and commendable as a proper triumph of his people over their foes; and he is careful to add that "on the spoil they laid not their hand."

Moreover, to make the matter complete, Haman's ten sons were hanged on the gallows also.

All this, says the conclusion of the book, was celebrated by the institution of a new feast, the feast of Purim; and the whole book may have been intended as an argument for the keeping of this particular feast. For a long time the book of Esther was not regarded with favor among the Jewish people, as, indeed, it could hardly be among those who were conscious of the religion of the prophets; but in later centuries, as the Jews became more and more the victims of persecution, they found food for their pride in this book, and it was adopted at length into the Old Testament canon.

But the mood which dominated the book of Esther was not the only mood which found expression in the literature of the exile. There were those who regarded the greatness of Israel in a completely different light from that in which the writer of the book of Esther thought he saw it. Israel's business among the nations was not simply to protect itself. Its business was to be a preacher of spiritual truth to all peoples. This other and grander conviction found voice in the book of Jonah. It is a book not by Jonah but about Jonah. Neither is it history, but an allegory and a sermon. Jonah himself was a prophet without much spiritual vision who had lived in the period of Israel's history before the downfall of the nation and the Captivity, and who had voiced the same sort of fanatical nationalism with which the book of Esther blazes. But some time, perhaps in the fourth or third century B. C., an unknown writer took Jonah as a figure for his allegory, and showed how the will of God would compel a reluctant prophet to go and carry the message of God's salvation even to Israel's enemies.

This is the narrative of the book:

To Jonah the son of Ammitai comes the word of God, commanding him to go to Nineveh and call upon it to repent. Jonah does not want to go. He flees to Joppa, hoping to escape the compulsion which has been laid upon him. He pays his fare upon a ship and launches out to sea.

But God sent a great storm upon the sea, so that the ship was in danger of being broken to pieces. All the sailors were afraid, and they called every man on his particular god, and flung the cargo overboard to lighten the ship. Jonah, meanwhile, was asleep in the hold. So the ship's captain came and woke him, and told him to join the others in praying to his God. But the sailors concluded that there was someone on board against whom the wrath of the gods was directed. So they threw lots to see who he might be, and the lot indicated Jonah. They wanted to know what wickedness he had done, and Jonah confessed that he was a worshiper of Jehovah, but that he was fleeing from his presence.

Then they wanted to know what they could do to make the storm abate, and Jonah confessed that it was for his sin that the storm was sent, and that, if he were thrown overboard, the sea would grow calm. At first the sailors would not do it, and they did their utmost to row the ship back to land; but the more they rowed, the more tempestuous the sea became. So at last they took Jonah and cast him from the ship, and when they had done that, the sea ceased from its raging.

But the commission of God for Jonah was not to be defeated. A great fish was made to swallow Jonah, and in the fish's belly for three days Jonah remained, saying his prayers and acknowledging his faults; and at last the fish cast him out on dry land.

For the second time the word of God came to Jonah, saying, "Arise, go unto Nineveh, that great city, and preach to it the preaching that I bid thee." So Jonah went and prophesied in Nineveh that after forty days the city for its sins should be overthrown. To that particular preaching Jonah was not greatly averse; but the thing to which he was averse was that Nineveh should act upon it. And Nineveh did. The people put on sackcloth and inaugurated a fast, from the least to the greatest, and even the king of Nineveh rose from his throne and clothed himself in sackcloth and sat down in ashes. He commanded that all the people should pray to God, and cease from all their violence and evil ways. So God saw their repentance, and turned away from Nineveh the judgment which had been proclaimed against it.

At this Jonah was exceedingly displeased. He ventured to express his irritation openly to God. This was exactly what he had said all along when he was back in his own country, he declared; and this was the reason why he had escaped in the ship. He had been afraid that God would be merciful, and that after he, Jonah, had prophesied the punishment which Nineveh deserved, God in his forgivingness would withdraw the threatened doom. So, said Jonah, "I beseech thee, take my life from me, for it is better for me to die than to live." And out of Nineveh he went and built him a booth, and sat there to see what would happen to the city.

But God was content with one question for his answer. "Doest thou well to be angry?" he asked of Jonah. And then he caused to be enacted for Jonah a parable. God created a gourd vine which sprouted and grew, and covered Jonah with the shade of its thick leaves, and Jonah was much pleased with his shelter. But the next morning there came a worm which attacked the vine so that it withered; and when the sun arose with a sultry east wind, and the heat beat down upon Jonah's head, he fainted; and again he requested that he might die. But God's answer came to him: "Doest thou well to be angry for the gourd?" Jonah replied that he thought he did have a right to be exceedingly put out. But then comes the climactic answer which embraces the message and the meaning of the whole book. "And the Lord said: 'Thou hast had pity on the gourd, for which thou hast not labored, neither madest it grow; which came up in a night, and perished in a night: and should not I have pity on Nineveh, that great city, wherein are more than sixscore thousand persons that cannot discern between their right hand and their left?' "

CHAPTER XXXIV

THE LAST YEARS OF THE OLD TESTAMENT, WITH THE CONQUEST OF
JERUSALEM BY THE KINGS OF SYRIA AND THE GALLANT STRUGGLE OF
THE MACCABEES FOR FREEDOM; AND THE FIERY STORIES OF THE
BOOK OF DANIEL, AND THE HOPES WHICH MEN STILL CHERISHED AS
THE OLD TESTAMENT PERIOD CAME TO ITS END.

ALTHOUGH THE history of Jerusalem in the
years following the life and work of Nehemiah
was obscure, it was not ignoble. In numbers
and in material power, the little group of people who clustered there seemed insignificant
among the nations of the world. No glorious
events starred the record of the immediately succeeding years.
Nevertheless, the real thing which was happening was significant far beyond what the ordinary reckoning would have
perceived. For here was a people who, sometimes narrowly and
sometimes fanatically, yet with a steadfast and unbroken loyalty,
were preserving the inheritance of a great religion in the midst
of a pagan world. Though their ecclesiasticism and their customs were exclusive, they were nevertheless bearing an indis-
pensable witness which could not have been borne in any other
way. Not only the ritual, but also the moral law and the great
traditions of the prophets, were being kept alive; and by this
continuing life the later growth which belongs to the New
Testament was made possible.

A little more than a century after the rebuilding of Jerusalem under Nehemiah a new empire arose and a new wave of
conquest swept over Palestine and all the countries round it.
Alexander of Macedon, afterward to be known as Alexander the
Great, having mastered all of Greece, led his phalanxes into the
east and into the Persian Empire of Darius, whose armies he
overthrew at the battle of Issus in 333. Advancing steadily, he
captured Damascus, and, turning along the Mediterranean coast,

375

he came to Tyre, which after a long siege he took, and hanged two thousand of its inhabitants upon its broken walls and led thirty thousand more away into slavery. He turned then against Jerusalem, but Jerusalem surrendered, and Judæa was left unharmed.

Ten years later, at the peak of his world domination, Alexander died, and his empire was divided. Egypt became one independent kingdom, and Syria another, and between these two there ensued an intermittent warfare with Jerusalem as one of the prizes in the struggle. For a time Egypt prevailed; but early in the second century B. C. the Egyptian armies were defeated by the Syrians, and the power of Syria, not only in its military control, but also in the influence of its civilization, now began to dominate Judæa.

The Syrian kingdom had become thoroughly imbued with the spirit of the new Greek culture which had been brought into the east by Alexander. Many in Israel also yielded to the fascination of this culture which seemed so much more beautiful and luxurious than their own. They wanted to be a part of a more cosmopolitan civilization; and both in religion and life they affected a tolerance which to the stricter Jews seemed nothing but indifference and laxity. These stricter ones were made all the more resolute by the disintegrating forces of the time. They exalted the importance of the law which the scribes were forever teaching. They were determined that the life of Jewry should be not less but more distinct from that of their neighbors round about.

For a time there was no open conflict. In Jerusalem there was a high priest who served the interests of Syria and was sympathetic with the Greek culture, but no open insult or violence was offered to the more orthodox group.

The situation changed when Antiochus the Fourth, called Antiochus Epiphanes, succeeded to the throne of Syria. In 172 B. C., angered by an unsuccessful campaign against Egypt, Antiochus returned northward by way of Jerusalem, sacked the city, and plundered many of the treasures of the Temple. Four years later, in 168 B. C., he proceeded in an even more ruthless fashion. He set up heathen altars in Judæa, erected shrines to Zeus in the holy area of the very Temple itself, and there, as the crowning outrage and insult to the Jews, he ordered the sacrifice of a sow.

For the faithful Jews to whom the traditions of their religion were precious, the issue now was one of life and death. They were faced with brutal persecution. To possess a copy of the law was to risk immediate execution. Many people, both old and young, died for their faith. It looked as though they were faced with nothing but despair.

In one of the books of the Apocrypha (which is sometimes bound up as an appendix to the canonical books of the Old Testament), there is a vivid description, written probably in the same century with the events portrayed, of the brutal cruelty which Antiochus caused to be inflicted. "When they had rent in pieces the books of the law which they found, they burnt them with fire. And wheresoever was found with any the book of the testament, or if any consented to the law, the king's commandment was that they should be put to death. . . . They put to death certain women, that had caused their children to be circumcised. And they hanged the infants about their necks, and rifled their houses, and slew them that had circumcised them. Howbeit many in Israel were fully resolved and confirmed in themselves not to eat any unclean thing. Wherefore they chose rather to die, that they might not be defiled with meats, and that they might not profane the holy covenant: so then they died. And there was very great wrath upon Israel."

And with mournful eloquence the history recites: "The city was made an habitation of strangers, and became strange to those that were born in her; and her own children left her. Her sanctuary was laid waste like a wilderness, her feasts were turned into mourning, her sabbaths into reproach, her honor into contempt. As had been her glory, so was her dishonor increased, and her excellency was turned into mourning."

It is to this period that there probably belongs that remarkable book of the Old Testament which bears the name of

Daniel. In the prophecy of Ezekiel, Daniel is mentioned with Noah and Job as a representative of saintliness and courage. It would seem that Daniel lived sometime during the exile; but the book of Daniel in the form in which the Old Testament now contains it belongs to a time much subsequent to that. Its writer is unknown; but after a fashion common in the Orient, he gave to his book the name of a greater figure who had lived before him. Much of the material which he used had probably come down from an earlier period; but however this may be, and whether some of it was written earlier, or all of it was written later, it is certain that the book was circulated during those tragic years when the Jews were battling against the deadly perils to their life and to their religion which followed the dese- cration of Jerusalem by Antiochus. This book of Daniel ap- peared as a trumpet blast of faith and hope. Here were the gathered traditions of heroic men who had lived in ages of persecution and had triumphed; and in the latter chapters of the book, under the cover of symbolism, and in great imagery which is like a mingling of fire and cloud, the writer sets forth those denunciations against Antiochus and those prophecies of his doom which he could not have dared to express except in a cryptic way. His book is one of the first examples of apocalyptic literature, impassioned and dramatic, which is so veiled in mean- ing that the enemies might not be aroused, but clear enough for the initiated to understand—a type of literature which became more and more popular as one tyranny after another, Greek, Syrian, Roman, pressed upon Palestine.

The first of the stories in the book of Daniel is laid in the time of Nebuchadnezzar, king of Babylon. It tells of Daniel and of three of his friends, Hananiah, Mishael, and Azariah, whose names, however, were changed to Shadrach, Meshach, and Abednego.

Daniel and these friends of his would not eat the food of the heathen king, nor drink the wine which he drank. One of the eunuchs of the court, to whom had been committed the charge of these Hebrew captives, was troubled by this fact that they would not eat and drink. He thought that they would

presently begin to waste away, and that he would be held
accountable for their wan appearance. But Daniel urged him
to make a test. Let the eunuch give to him and to his friends
for ten days nothing but water and herbs, and then at the end
he should see what he should see. The eunuch consented;
and when the period was over, these men who had cared nothing for the dainty food and wines of Nebuchadnezzar, on being
brought before the king, were found "in every matter of wisdom
and understanding concerning which the king inquired of them,
ten times better than all the magicians and enchanters that were
in all his realm."

After that Nebuchadnezzar dreamed a dream, and he called
all the soothsayers and other supposed interpreters of dreams
among the Chaldeans to explain his vision to him. He demanded, in the first place, that they should tell him what it was
that he had dreamed, and then tell him the interpretation of
it. They were helpless; but not so Daniel. To him in a vision
of the night the vision of Nebuchadnezzar was revealed, and he
blessed the God of heaven, and he said: "Blessed be the name
of God forever and ever; for wisdom and might are his. And
he changeth the times and the seasons: he removeth kings, and
setteth up kings; he giveth wisdom unto the wise, and knowledge to them that know understanding; he revealeth the deep
and secret things; he knoweth what is in the darkness, and the
light dwelleth with him."

To Arioch, the captain of the king's bodyguard, to whom
Nebuchadnezzar in his anger had given orders to kill all the
so-called wise men of his kingdom, Daniel went, and told him
that he could interpret the king's dream. So he was brought
before Nebuchadnezzar, and he said:

"Thou, O king, sawest, and, behold, a great image. This
image, which was mighty, and whose brightness was excellent,
stood before thee; and the aspect thereof was terrible. As for
this image, his head was of fine gold, his breast and his arms of
silver, his belly and his thighs of brass, his legs of iron, his feet
part of iron, and part of clay. Thou sawest till that a stone was
cut out without hands, which smote the image upon his feet

that were of iron and clay, and brake them in pieces. Then was the iron, the clay, the brass, the silver, and the gold, broken in pieces together, and became like the chaff of the summer thresh-ing-floors; and the wind carried them away, that no place was found for them: and the stone that smote the image became a great mountain, and filled the whole earth."

Under this figure of the dream of Nebuchadnezzar, with its image made up of various elements, the imperiled Jews in the time of the Maccabæan struggle could read the meaning of the different world-empires—Babylonian, Median, Persian, and Greek—and could find their hope and courage quickened by the prophecy of the stone from the great mountain, which meant Israel, breaking the image into pieces and scattering it like chaff.

Then follows the story of Nebuchadnezzar's furnace, with its message of assurance, to men themselves in the midst of the flame of persecution, that marvelous deliverance would come to those who put their trust in God. Thus, suggests this religious dramatist, it was in olden times; thus it can be again.

He tells how Nebuchadnezzar, the king, made an image of gold one hundred and ten feet high, and eleven feet wide, and he set it up in the plain of Dura, in the province of Babylon. Then he sent and caused to be gathered together all the gov-ernors, satraps, and other rulers of the provinces, for the dedica-tion of the image. They came, therefore, and the herald cried aloud:

"To you it is commanded, O peoples, nations, and lan-guages, that at what time ye hear the sound of the cornet, flute, harp, sackbut, psaltery, dulcimer, and all kinds of music, ye fall down and worship the golden image that Nebuchadnezzar the king hath set up: and whoso falleth not down and worshipeth shall the same hour be cast into the midst of a burning fiery furnace."

So when the multitude heard the sound of the music, they did fall down and worship the image of gold.

But not Shadrach, Meshach, and Abednego. They did not make obeisance; and tale-bearers quickly reported the fact to

Nebuchadnezzar. "These men, O king," they said, "have not regarded thee. They serve not thy gods, nor worship the golden image that thou hast set up."

So Nebuchadnezzar in rage and fury commanded the three men to be brought before him. Was it of deliberate purpose that they had refused to bow down before the image? Well, they should have another opportunity; and if this time they did not worship, they should be cast into the midst of the burning fiery furnace. "And who," he said, "is that god that shall deliver you out of my hands?"

Then Shadrach, Meshach, and Abednego replied: "O Nebuchadnezzar, we have no need to answer thee in this matter. If it be so, our God whom we serve is able to deliver us from the burning fiery furnace; and he will deliver us out of thy hand, O king."

"But if not," they went on, "but if not, be it known to thee, O king, that we will not serve thy gods, nor worship the golden image which thou hast set up."

Furiously then Nebuchadnezzar commanded that the furnace be heated seven times hotter than before; and into the furnace Shadrach, Meshach, and Abednego were cast, and fell down bound into the midst of the flames.

But as Nebuchadnezzar looked, he was astonished, and hastily he rose up. "Did not we," he said to his counselors, "cast three men bound into the midst of the fire?"

"True, O king," they answered.

"Lo," he said, "I see four men loose, walking in the midst of the fire, and they have no hurt; and the aspect of the fourth is like a son of the gods!"

The king drew near the mouth of the furnace, and he called to Shadrach, Meshach, and Abednego, "Ye servants of the Most High God, come forth, and come hither." Then out of the furnace these three men came unharmed, and without so much as the smell of smoke upon their garments.

Whereupon the triumphant story ends with Nebuchadnezzar confessing the might of the God of Shadrach, Meshach, and Abednego, and commanding that no one, on pain of death, shall speak a word against the God whom they have worshiped, "because there is no other god that is able to deliver after this sort." And Shadrach, Meshach, and Abednego were promoted in Babylon.

Then follow other stories which were meant to encourage the Jews suffering under the tyranny of Antiochus Epiphanes, and to convey perhaps to the tyrant himself warnings of what could happen to those who set themselves in the way of the righteousness of God.

As the story of the burning fiery furnace had centered round the friends of Daniel, so these next stories center round the great figure of Daniel himself.

Nebuchadnezzar, the king, was in his palace, and there he had a dream which troubled him. To all the astrologers and soothsayers and Chaldeans he sent demanding that they come and tell him the interpretation of the dream, but none of them could fathom it. At last came Daniel, and to him Nebuchadnezzar told his dream. He had seen in the midst of the earth a great tree, the height whereof reached to heaven, and the branches of it shadowed the ends of the earth. Its leaves and fruit were fair to see. The beasts of the field had refuge under it, and the birds of the heaven dwelt in its boughs. But in Nebuchadnezzar's dream, he saw "a watcher and an holy one from heaven." He cried aloud that the tree should be hewn down, its branches cut off, and its fruit scattered; though there should be left in the earth the stump of its roots which should be bound with iron and brass.

This was the vision which Nebuchadnezzar had seen, and Daniel thereupon told him the interpretation of it. The great tree was Nebuchadnezzar himself; and he and his glory, like the tree, should be hewn down. Yet after his pride should have been humbled, he and his kingdom should be kept alive like the roots of the tree, bound with brass and iron. "Wherefore, O king," continued Daniel, "let my counsel be acceptable unto thee, and break off thy sins by righteousness, and thine iniquities by showing mercy to the poor."

After twelve months therefore, Nebuchadnezzar walked in the palace of the kingdom of Babylon and he said, "Is not this great Babylon, that I have built for the house of the kingdom by the might of my power, and for the honor of my majesty?" But even as he thus exulted there came a voice saying, "The kingdom is departed from thee." And Nebuchadnezzar's mind was touched with madness, so that he was driven from among men and ate grass like an ox, and his body was wet with the dew of heaven.

But after a time Nebuchadnezzar lifted up his eyes to heaven, and his understanding returned to him; and "he blessed and honored him who liveth forever, whose dominion is an everlasting dominion, and whose kingdom is from generation to generation."

Then, as the climax of the story, Nebuchadnezzar's kingdom and all the glory of it is restored to him, because he had repented and humbled himself before God.

But another and more fateful story follows.

Belshazzar, the son of Nebuchadnezzar, having succeeded his father on the throne, made a great feast to a thousand of his lords, and commanded the golden and silver vessels which Nebuchadnezzar had taken out of the Temple in Jerusalem to be brought, that these might furnish the revels of his company. "So they drank wine, and praised the gods of gold, and of silver, of brass, of iron, of wood, and of stone."

But in that moment there came forth fingers as of a man's hand, and wrote upon the plaster of the wall of the king's palace; and the king saw the part of the hand that wrote. He was amazed and terrified, and sent for all the soothsayers, demanding that they read the writing; but they could not. But the queen told him of Daniel, and Daniel thereupon was sent for. And Belshazzar offered him great gifts if he would read the writing on the wall.

Then Daniel answered, "O thou king, the most high God gave Nebuchadnezzar thy father a kingdom, and majesty, and glory, and honor. And for the majesty that he gave him, all people, nations, and languages trembled and feared before him:

whom he would he slew; and whom he would he kept alive; and whom he would he set up; and whom he would he put down.

"But when his heart was lifted up, and his mind hardened in pride, he was deposed from his kingly throne, and they took his glory from him. And he was driven from the sons of men; and his heart was made like the beasts, and his dwelling was with the wild asses. They fed him with grass like oxen, and his body was wet with the dew of heaven; till he knew that the most high God ruled in the kingdom of men, and that he appointeth over it whomsoever he will.

"And thou his son, O Belshazzar, hast not humbled thine heart, though thou knewest all this; but hast lifted up thyself against the Lord of heaven. And they have brought the vessels of his house before thee, and thou and thy lords, thy wives and thy concubines, have drunk wine in them; and thou hast praised the gods of silver, and gold, of brass, iron, wood, and stone, which see not, nor hear, nor know. And the God in whose hand thy breath is, and whose are all thy ways, hast thou not glorified:

"Then was the part of the hand sent from him; and this writing was written. And this is the writing that was written, MENE, MENE, TEKEL, UPHARSIN.

"This is the interpretation of the thing:

"MENE; God hath numbered thy kingdom, and finished it. TEKEL; Thou art weighed in the balances, and art found wanting. PERES; Thy kingdom is divided, and given to the Medes and Persians."

Then swiftly the doom which Daniel had prophesied descended. In that night was Belshazzar the king of the Chaldeans slain, and Darius the Mede took his kingdom.

One other story of the inability of earthly tyrants to prevail against a servant of the most high God follows these stories of Nebuchadnezzar and Belshazzar.

Darius, the king, had first promoted Daniel to honor; but presently he issued an order which Daniel would not observe. For at the crafty instigation of men at the court who wanted to destroy Daniel, Darius put forth a decree that no one should make any petition of any God or man for thirty days, save of the king himself.

Daniel knew of this, but not for a moment would he observe it. When the decree was signed, he went into his house, and the windows of his room being open toward Jerusalem, he kneeled down three times a day and prayed, and gave thanks to God as he had done before.

Men spying upon him saw him praying thus, and came and asked Darius: "Hast thou not signed a decree, that every man that shall ask a petition of any God or man within thirty days, save of thee, O king, shall be cast into the den of lions?" He answered that it was true, "according to the law of the Medes and Persians, which altereth not."

Then they went on to tell him that Daniel had despised his decree, and that three times a day he prayed, as he always had, to the God of Israel.

Sorrowfully then Darius was moved to carry out his decree. He sent for Daniel and had him cast into the den of lions, while he himself went to his palace and spent the night, wretched and sleepless.

In the morning early he rose and came with haste to the lions' den and cried with a lamentable voice to Daniel: "O Daniel, servant of the living God, is thy God, whom thou servest continually, able to deliver thee from the lions?" And out of the lions' den came Daniel's voice saying: "O king, live for ever! My God hath sent his angel, and hath shut the lions' mouths, that they have not hurt me: forasmuch as before him innocency was found in me; and also before thee, O king, have I done no hurt."

Whereupon this story too comes to its end, not only with triumph for the righteous, but with a warning for the wicked. The king commanded to take up Daniel out of the den; "and they brought those men which had accused Daniel, and they cast them into the den of lions, them, their children, and their wives; and the lions had the mastery of them, and brake all their bones in pieces or ever they came at the bottom of the den."

After these stories come other accounts of the visions of

Daniel himself, which are written in the five concluding chapters of the book. The interpretation of these visions is an intricate matter, but the message of all of them is alike; namely, invincible confidence for the people who believed themselves to be in covenant with God, and faith in a greater destiny of the spirit over all the tyrannies of this passing world. And among these accounts of Daniel's visions are the words which afterward were to be held as a prophecy of Christ: "I beheld till the thrones were cast down, and the Ancient of days did sit, whose garment was white as snow, and the hair of his head like the pure wool: his throne was like the fiery flame, and his wheels as burning fire." . . . "I saw in the night visions, and, behold, one like the Son of man came with the clouds of heaven, and came to the Ancient of days, and they brought him near before him. And there was given him dominion, and glory, and a kingdom, that all people, nations, and languages, should serve him: his dominion is an everlasting dominion, which shall not pass away, and his kingdom that which shall not be destroyed."

Such was the type of literature through which the Jews in the time of Antiochus Epiphanes sought to keep the flame of their courage and their independence burning. Nor was their faith in vain. Not only in the pages of a book, but upon the arena of their actual affairs, deliverance was coming. It broke upon them sudden as a flame. One of the most heroic chapters of Jewish history was about to begin. It is set forth in the book of Maccabees, already quoted in this chapter; and this book of Maccabees is one of the most heroic chronicles in all the history of Israel.

In the little town of Modin, perched among the hills of Judæa, there lived a man of a priestly family named Mattathias, who had five sons—John, Simon, Judas, Eleazar, and Jonathan. One day when a Syrian officer was offering a reward to a Jew if he would make a pagan sacrifice, Mattathias interposed. He "answered and spoke with a loud voice: 'Though all the nations that are under the king's dominion obey him and fall away every one from the religion of their fathers, and give consent to his commandments, yet will I and my sons and my brethren walk in the covenant of our fathers. God forbid that we should forsake the law and the ordinances. We will not hearken to the king's words, to go from our religion, either on the right hand or the left.' "

So Mattathias spoke, and his actions were as bold as his words. When one of the Jews stepped forward to sacrifice on the heathen altar, Mattathias ran and struck him down. He turned then and killed the king's commissioner and destroyed the pagan altar.

After this, he and his sons fled to the mountains, where other men rallied about them, and a religious war began.

That was in the year 165 b. c. Some twelve months later, Mattathias died. But before he died, he said to his sons: "Now hath pride and rebuke gotten strength, and the time of destruction, and the wrath of indignation. Now, therefore, my sons, be ye zealous for the law, and give your lives for the covenants of your fathers. Call to remembrance what acts our fathers did in their time; so shall ye receive great honor and an everlasting name. Fear not then the words of a sinful man. . . . To-day he shall be lifted up, and to-morrow he shall not be found, because he is returned into his dust, and his thought is come to nothing. Wherefore, ye my sons, be valiant!"

Valiant, without question, they were; and not only valiant. They were men of extraordinary ability as leaders of the people, both in battle and in statesmanship. The first of them to succeed his father was Judas, to whom was given the surname Maccabæus, or the Hammerer. For four years he made war against the Syrians with almost constant success. He restored the Temple, which had been desecrated by Antiochus; and the Jewish Feast of Lights, which from that day to this has been celebrated, dates from that act of Judas Maccabæus. The quality of his spirit is revealed in a reply of his, when, at a moment of great danger, some of his men said: "How shall we be able, being so few, to fight against so great a multitude and so strong, seeing we are ready to faint with fasting all this day?" Judas answered: "It is no hard matter for many to be shut up in the hands of a few! and with the God of heaven it is all one, to deliver with a great multitude or a small company; for the victory of battle standeth not in the multitude of an host; but strength cometh from heaven."

At length, however, Judas, after many victories, dared one too many conflicts in which the odds were heavily against him. He fell on the battlefield; but he had established the independence of his people.

After him came his brother Jonathan, who partly through his own courage and skill, and partly through civil conflicts in Syria and the struggles of different claimants for the Syrian throne, consolidated and extended the power which his brother had built up in Judæa. He reached out also for a treaty of friendship with Rome, and secured it. He conquered most of the cities along the Mediterranean seaboard, and secured from the king of Syria the recognition of himself, not only as military commander, but as high priest in Jerusalem.

It was not through any defeat in battle, but through an act of base treachery on the part of the Syrian Trypho that Jonathan, after eighteen years of leadership, was taken prisoner and presently put to death.

With Jonathan's death, the succession of the sons of Mattathias was, however, not yet finished. After Jonathan came Simon, no less courageous and no less successful than his two preceding brothers; and when he died, in 135, thirty years after the death of his father, the province which Antiochus Epiphanes had insulted and dispossessed had become a nation which, though limited in territory, was independent; and a high-priesthood with supreme military and civil power had become hereditary in the Maccabæan line.

Nor was it only in its history of military struggle that the Maccabæan struggle was important. During this time there were being shaped religious influences which should be conspicuous in the times of the New Testament. There had already appeared the party of the Sadducees, who were the aristocrats among the Jews. They were loyal to the law, but they did not hold it with strictness. They possessed most of the hereditary positions in the Temple worship, and therefore it was to their interest as well as their conviction that all the ordinances of religion should be maintained. But at the same time they were not without sympathy for Greek culture and Greek civilization. They were the ecclesiastical men-of-the-world.

But against them there was another party, never very large in numbers, but exceedingly influential. This was the party of the Pharisees.

The Pharisees were the religious zealots of the nation. They comprised at first the heroic minority who were willing to resist the heathenizing influence of Antiochus Epiphanes, even to the death. As defenders of the law and of life under the law, they would go to any lengths of faithfulness; but it is not difficult to understand how this zeal of theirs gradually stiffened into a narrow legalism. The law, and every jot and tittle of it, became to them an object of intense and fanatical insistence. They should present their bitter opposition presently to One in whom the spirit of a new life was more important than the law.

The times which we think of as belonging to the Old Testament were drawing now to a close. After Simon came his son John Hyrcanus, and after him came the other lesser rulers in whose times the conflict between the Pharisees and the less strict elements in the nation grew bitter. The struggle of various rivals for the high-priesthood led to civil war, and into the midst of their quarrelings came the Romans. There was a wavering policy, first of surrender and then of rebellion, until at length the Roman general Pompey marched against Jerusalem, laid siege to it and captured it with great slaughter. Jewish independence, which had been re-established under Judas Maccabæus almost exactly one hundred years before, had now come to its end. Henceforward, for a long time, the Roman power was to be dominant in all Palestine, though the Romans were content to give local jurisdiction to certain rulers who were amenable to them. In the time of Pompey there arose an Idumean named Antipater, who through his own force and his crafty manipulations of political intrigue, became ruler in Judæa. His son was the equally forceful and equally unscrupulous Herod, afterwards, through his success as a ruler and his lavishness as a builder, to be called Herod the Great. And with Herod we have come to the years when One was born at whose appearing the Old Testament is finished and the New Testament begins.

THE NEW TESTAMENT

CHAPTER XXXV

 HE CALENDAR which nearly all the world uses is dated according to the Christian era. It reckons the years of our present time as nineteen hundred and so many years after the year one; but this year one which the calendar makes the milestone for all its reckoning is not the first year of creation. It is not the first year of the beginning of our knowledge. It is not the first year of history. It is the year in the midst of the long stream of human life in which a new religion was born with the coming of a child whose name was Jesus, and whom afterward men were to follow and adore as Christ. That year has become a turning point with reference to which all history before and after it is reckoned. We enumerate the years which precede it as such and such a year B. C., or Before Christ; and when we speak of any event of the history which has followed it, we say that it happened in such and such a year A. D., Anno Domini, "in the year of the Lord." Whenever we date a letter or draw up a public document, we pay our silent witness to the supreme importance of an event which all Christians remember and of which the New Testament tells.

That period of our calendar's beginning was a confused time in the world's history. There were many outward things to make men proud and content; but there was much inward restlessness and bitterness of soul. Rome had extended her conquests over all the lands bordering the Mediterranean Sea. Her legions held the ancient site of Carthage. They dominated

393

what once had been the empire of Egypt. They had their camps as far north as the Danube; and to the east they were in Syria and beyond. Great buildings, coliseums, theaters, forums, not only in Rome but in the expanding cities of her far-flung provinces, testified to the wealth and magnificence of the empire. Of Augustus Cæsar, the emperor, it was said that he found Rome a city built of brick; he left it built of marble. But in the Roman Empire there was beginning to be a weariness of soul. Old religions were crumbling. In that break-up and mingling of many civilizations which the Roman conquests had brought about, new cults were arising, the so-called mystery religions, which held out to their votaries the promise of salvation through secret rites. But multitudes of people had no real religion whatever, nor any sense of a heavenly meaning in the things of earth. Men and women of that age might have recognized as not exaggerated the lines which a modern poet wrote:

> "On that hard Pagan world disgust
>   And secret loathing fell.
> Deep weariness and sated lust
>   Made human life a hell.

> "In his cool hall, with haggard eyes,
>   The Roman noble lay;
> He drove abroad, in furious guise,
>   Along the Appian way.

> "He made a feast, drank fierce and fast,
>   And crown'd his hair with flowers—
> No easier nor no quicker pass'd
>   The impracticable hours."[1]

The people in Israel were disillusioned in another sort of way. They were not worldlings, as many of the Romans were. They clung with stubborn loyalty to their ancient religious hopes. But to many it seemed as though these hopes were tragically defeated. Their fathers had believed in a nation that

---

[1] "Obermann Once More," from *The Poetical Works of Matthew Arnold*, 1907. The Macmillan Company. Used by permission.

would be great and free; but now the nation, after the last heroic but too brief chapter of the Maccabæan struggle, had sunk into subjection under the rule of Rome. Long ago the prophets had proclaimed that Messiah would come to be God's leader and deliverer. The sense of frustration which the nation felt made men all the more passionately hopeful that Messiah might come soon. In name, these hopes were religious; but often they assumed a very crude political and militaristic form. More than once, shortly before Jesus was born and afterward, sudden rebellions flared in the province of Galilee and were crushed by the Romans and by Herod with cruel punishment. It seemed as though all the old glorious expectations were doomed to be defeated. As a nation Israel had lost whatever pride and rank it had once possessed; and in religion there was danger that the old faith would harden into formalism. The Pharisees and scribes taught with stubborn insistence every jot and tittle of the law of Moses and of the elaborations which the rabbis had woven round these. But there were others who were almost ready to become indifferent. In the confusion of the world's counsels, who knew whether religion mattered? There were plenty of teachers, but where was anyone who in his own personality and in his own life gave authority to what he said?

It was into such a world that the new life entered. And the New Testament is the story of that life itself and of its first flaming consequences. The New Testament, as it stands printed in the Bible, is much shorter than the Old. It has twenty-seven "books" as against thirty-nine, and these different writings which make up the New Testament are in general much briefer than those of the Old. They represent also in their origins a much more compact period. The earliest of them, which are some of the letters of the apostle Paul, were written about the year 50 A. D.; the latest of them probably early in the next century. Of some of them, such as Paul's letters, we know their authorship and almost exactly the time and circumstance of their writing. Some of them we cannot place so precisely. Neither can we always be sure of the relative elements of first-hand observation and of tradition which enter into them. The four Gospels, with which the New Testament opens, bear the names of Matthew, one of the twelve disciples of Jesus; of Mark, a young man who was at one time a companion of Paul and also knew Simon Peter; of Luke, a Greek physician who was with Paul on some of his missionary journeys; and of John, the most beloved among the twelve who were nearest Jesus. Christian scholarship has wrestled with the questions which these Gospels present —questions of authorship and questions of date and of the material which they embody. In the appendix of this volume there is a list of some of the books in which these questions are dealt with in the most understandable and helpful way. It is not our province to enter into them here. What we are listening to now is not a commentary on the Bible but the story of the Bible itself. That story was written by men who gathered together all the knowledge they could command concerning Jesus and concerning the fellowship which grew up in his name. Some of that knowledge was made up of immediate and personal memories. Some of it was arrived at indirectly through the impression which Jesus had made upon others. Some of it, such as the stories of the infancy, rises on great wings of devotion into those realms of expression where poetry takes the place of prose. These men who wrote the New Testament were inspired of God. Their inspiration was not so much in the technique of their writing (for like all historians they wrote within the limitations of their time), but, rather, in the passion of experience which made them write. They had come into touch with the infinite and unexampled personality of Jesus. And it is his personality as the incarnation of the very God come near to men which moves through the New Testament pages.

Let us listen, then, to the story as the New Testament tells it; for through the whole story, regardless of whatever puzzling elements there may seem to be in some parts of it, we come again into the presence of Him who stands at the dividing point of time and in whom history became new.

 HE ACCOUNTS of the birth of Jesus, as these
are written in the Gospels of Luke and of Mat-
thew, are among the loveliest stories of the
world. They were written by men whose souls
were filled with the sense of the wonder of
Jesus; and as they looked back to his birth, it
seemed to them that nothing could be too wonderful to believe
about the manner of it. In what may have been the three-
quarters of a century which had passed between the birth of
Jesus and the time when the Gospels of Matthew and Luke were
written, many traditions had begun to grow. It was easy for
worship to sing of an annunciation by an angel, to sing of the
birth of the Deliverer in such wise as the Greek world into
which Christianity was now going would understand, to sing of
adoring Magi following the shining of their star. These traditions the writers of the Gospels received and wove like golden
threads into their story of the great fact that in Jesus a new life
and a new influence had come into the world. Some of the
things they tell perhaps are not so much objective history as a
lyric effort to account for history. They write as poets write,
expressing the truth sometimes with symbols and with imagery.
But the impression they give is the true impression, namely,
that in the birth of Jesus something happened which could
make both earth and heaven rejoice.

Here, then, is the picture as they drew it:

In the little town of Nazareth there lived a maid whose
name was Mary. Nazareth lay among the hills of Galilee, with

Samaria to the south of it and Judæa to the south of that.   In
Galilee men seemed to be of more ardent temperament than
others of their countrymen.   It was in Galilee that the rebellions against the power of Rome most often flared.   And back
of these rebellions there lay the deeper hope of which they were
only the crude expression, the hope for God's deliverance of his
people.   The highest form which that hope could assume was in
the eternal longing that Messiah might appear.   It may be
that Mary in Nazareth had brooded upon that hope.   Be that
as it may, the hope was to be fulfilled through her in a way
greater than she or any other of her time could dream.

The soul of a woman can be very sensitive to the things of
God; for, to her, the windows of the infinite may be opened
and her eyes may see into those realities which are beyond our
space and time.   We do not know where Mary was at the
moment when her supreme experience came, whether in some
long-since-vanished house in which she dwelt and went about
her quiet ways there in the little village, or whether out among
the fields and flowers, or whether on the hills which encircled
Nazareth and stand there to-day as they stood in those far years
when Mary's feet could walk upon their climbing paths, and
when her eyes could gaze from their summits into the sunrise
or up to the quiet stars.   Where she was we cannot tell, but what
she was we know—a woman pure enough and receptive enough
for an eternal meaning to be brought to her.   One day she
had a vision.   There before her stood the awful figure of an
angel, and the words she heard him speak were these: "Hail,
thou that art highly favored, the Lord is with thee: blessed art
thou among women!"

Before that radiant presence, Mary shrank, amazed, for she
was troubled at the angel's saying, and bewildered as to what his
salutation meant.

But once again she heard his voice: "Fear not, Mary: for
thou hast found favor with God.   And, behold, thou shalt conceive in thy womb, and bring forth a son, and shalt call his name
JESUS.   He shall be great, and shall be called the Son of the
Highest; and the Lord God shall give unto him the throne of

his father David. And he shall reign over the house of Jacob for ever; and of his kingdom there shall be no end."

From the rapture of that experience Mary came back to the everyday realities of Nazareth; but not to anyone in Nazareth did she yet tell what she had seen and heard. Instead of that, according to the story which has come to us in the Gospel of Luke, she set out presently on a journey into the hill country of Judæa to see her cousin Elisabeth; for to Elisabeth also there had come a wonder which was in a measure like her own. Elisabeth was the wife of an old priest named Zacharias, who in the course of his duties had been ministering in the Temple. At the time of the offering of the incense, as the cloud of incense smoke arose, the marveling eyes of Zacharias seemed to see an angelic figure there, and he heard a voice that said, "I am Gabriel, that stand in the presence of God; and am sent to speak unto thee, and to show thee glad tidings." The glad tidings were that he and his wife Elisabeth, though both of them were now growing old, should have a son whose name should be called John, and who should be a messenger to prepare the way for another greater than himself. "And many of the children of Israel shall he turn to the Lord their God. And he shall go before him in the spirit and power of Elias, to turn the hearts of the fathers to the children, and the disobedient to the wisdom of the just: to make ready a people prepared for the Lord."

All this Elisabeth told to Mary, and Mary told the tidings of what had come to her. And as they rejoiced together, Mary's soul was singing. The message of that inward song of hers has echoed down the Christian centuries in the words in the Gospel which are called "The Magnificat" and which are repeated in the services of innumerable Christian churches as every Sunday evening comes:

"My soul doth magnify the Lord,
And my spirit hath rejoiced in God my Saviour.
For he hath regarded the low estate of his handmaiden:
  for, behold, from henceforth all generations shall call me
  blessed.

For he that is mighty hath done to me great things;
and holy is his name.
And his mercy is on them that fear him
from generation to generation.
He hath showed strength with his arm;
he hath scattered the proud in the imagination of their
hearts.
He hath put down the mighty from their seats,
and exalted them of low degree.
He hath filled the hungry with good things;
and the rich he hath sent empty away.
He hath holpen his servant Israel,
in remembrance of his mercy.
As he spake to our fathers,
to Abraham, and to his seed forever."

Mary stayed for a while with Elisabeth, and then went back
to Nazareth.

Not long after that, Elisabeth's son was born; and when, on
the eighth day, he was taken into the Temple according to the
Jewish law, the friends and family supposed that he would be
named Zacharias after his father. But his mother said, "Not so;
but he shall be called John."

Then they made signs to Zacharias to ask how he would
have the baby named; for, since that overwhelming experience
which had come to him in the Temple, Zacharias had been
unable to speak so much as a single word. He beckoned for a
writing tablet, and wrote on it, "His name is John." And as
those who read it looked at him and shook their heads in won-
derment, suddenly Zacharias' power of speech came back to
him; and with his tongue loosed, he praised God and burst into
prophetic utterance concerning what this son of his should grow
up to be:

"And thou, child, shalt be called the prophet of the Highest;
for thou shalt go before the face of the Lord to prepare his
ways;

To give knowledge of salvation unto his people
    by the remission of their sins,
Through the tender mercy of our God;
    whereby the dayspring from on high hath visited us,
To give light to them that sit in darkness
    and in the shadow of death,
To guide our feet into the way of peace."

Meanwhile Mary was back in Nazareth, and there she had
been married to Joseph, to whom before her vision of the angel
she had already been betrothed. It was drawing on toward the
time when her child, who had been promised, should be born;
but according to the story as it is told in the Gospel of Luke, he
was not to be born in Nazareth.

Augustus Cæsar, the emperor of Rome, was devising a new
tax to be collected from every inhabitant in the provinces where
Rome ruled. To this end, all persons were ordered to present
themselves for enrollment; and since Joseph belonged by family
connection to Bethlehem, it was to Bethlehem that he must go.

From Nazareth, therefore, southward toward the hill country of Judæa Joseph started, to be taxed, with Mary his espoused
wife, being great with child. It was not a short journey for
Joseph. For Mary it was very long. At the end of the weary
road they climbed the little hill that led to Bethlehem, seeking
shelter in the village khan; but many others whom the enrollment had compelled to come to Bethlehem had got there before
them, and now at the end of the day the town was crowded.
There was no room for them in the inn, and the only place
where Joseph could find shelter was in a stable, and the only
thing which offered as a cradle was a manger spread with hay.
And there in the darkness, with only the near-by bodies of the
oxen as warmth against the winter's night, Mary brought forth
her firstborn son and laid him in a manger.

Bethlehem did not know. The inn did not know. But the
lovely narrative of the Gospel of Luke tells of those who did
know that something infinite had happened. "And there were
in the same country shepherds abiding in the field, keeping

watch over their flock by night. And, lo, the angel of the Lord came upon them, and the glory of the Lord shone round about them; and they were sore afraid. And the angel said unto them, 'Fear not; for, behold, I bring you good tidings of great joy, which shall be to all people. For unto you is born this day in the city of David a Saviour, which is Christ the Lord. And this shall be a sign unto you: Ye shall find the babe wrapped in swaddling clothes, lying in a manger.' And suddenly there was with the angel a multitude of the heavenly host praising God, and saying, 'Glory to God in the highest, and on earth peace, good will toward men.' And it came to pass, as the angels were gone away from them unto heaven, the shepherds said one to another, 'Let us now go even unto Bethlehem, and see this thing which is come to pass, which the Lord hath made known unto us.' And they came with haste, and found Mary and Joseph, and the babe lying in a manger. And when they had seen it, they made known abroad the saying which was told them concerning this child. And all they that heard it wondered at those things which were told them by the shepherds. But Mary kept all these things and pondered them in her heart. And the shepherds returned, glorifying and praising God for all the things that they had heard and seen, as it was told unto them."

Moreover, through the Gospel of Matthew there comes another rich tradition of those first days in Bethlehem. It tells of others who came to see the Child of Mary. In the ancient East, the study of the stars was for some the gateway of religion. In the march of the constellations, in the conjunctions of the planets, and in other signs which they observed as they searched the skies, men with instinctive poetry of devotion believed that they could read the thoughts of God. It is of such men that the Gospel according to Matthew tells.

"Now when Jesus was born in Bethlehem of Judæa in the days of Herod the king, behold, there came wise men from the east to Jerusalem, saying, 'Where is he that is born King of the Jews? for we have seen his star in the east, and are come to worship him.' When Herod the king had heard the things, he was troubled, and all Jerusalem with him. And when he had gathered all the chief priests and scribes of the people together, he demanded of them where Christ should be born. And they said unto him, 'In Bethlehem of Judæa: for thus it is written by the prophet, "And thou Bethlehem, in the land of Juda, art not the least among the princes of Juda: for out of thee shall come a Governor, that shall rule my people Israel." ' Then Herod, when he had privily called the wise men, inquired of them diligently what time the star appeared. And he sent them to Bethlehem, and said, 'Go and search diligently for the young child; and when ye have found him, bring me word again, that I may come and worship him also.' When they had heard the king, they departed; and, lo, the star, which they saw in the east, went before them, till it came and stood over where the young child was. When they saw the star, they rejoiced with exceeding great joy.

"When they were come into the house, they saw the young child with Mary his mother, and fell down, and worshiped him: and when they had opened their treasures, they presented unto him gifts; gold, and frankincense, and myrrh. And being warned of God in a dream that they should not return to Herod, they departed into their own country another way. And when they were departed, the angel of the Lord appeared to Joseph in a dream, saying, 'Arise, and take the young child and his mother, and flee into Egypt, and be thou there until I bring thee word: for Herod will seek the young child to destroy him.' When he arose, he took the young child and his mother by night, and departed into Egypt: and was there until the death of Herod, that it might be fulfilled which was spoken of the Lord by the prophet, saying, 'Out of Egypt have I called my son.' "

There is a tradition in the Gospel of Matthew that Herod, having heard rumors of a Messiah born in Bethlehem, which roused his superstitious fear and anger, sent soldiers to kill all the children in Bethlehem of two years old and under, and that Joseph, warned in a dream, took Mary and the little child Jesus, and, fleeing into Egypt, remained there until the death of Herod. The Gospel of Luke says nothing of this flight to Egypt, but tells of the presentation presently of the child Jesus in the Temple, where an old man named Simeon, devout and eager, took the child Jesus in his arms and cried:

"Lord, now lettest thou thy servant depart in peace,
   according to thy word:
For mine eyes have seen thy salvation.
Which thou hast prepared before the face of all people;
A light to lighten the Gentiles,
   and the glory of thy people Israel."

And to Mary Simeon said:

"Behold this child is set for the fall and rising again of many
     in Israel;
   and for a sign which shall be spoken against:
(Yea, a sword shall pierce through thy own soul also,)
   that the thoughts of many hearts may be revealed."

Then the Gospels of Matthew and Luke converge in telling that Mary and Joseph, with the child Jesus, came back to Nazareth, where he grew and waxed strong in spirit, filled with wisdom, and the grace of God was upon him.

CHAPTER XXXVII

IN NAZARETH among the hills of Galilee Jesus lived as a little child, and as a boy growing up toward manhood. The Gospels tell nothing of those years, for their whole story is very brief. But from what is known of the background of life in general among the towns of Galilee in that time, it is possible to imagine how the boy Jesus lived and in what ways his interests were expanding. We know that he was not alone. The Gospels indicate that he had four brothers, James, Joses, Juda, and Simon, and at least two sisters. To be the elder brother to little boys and girls growing up with him in the home was one of the experiences through which his own spirit grew. The house of Joseph and Mary was simple and bare, as all the houses in the village were. Its walls were probably of whitewashed stones, with windows high up beneath the flat roof, and a wide door that opened to the street. Its beds were only woven rugs kept on a platform at the inner end of the house in the daytime, and spread upon the earthen floor at night. For furniture there was only a small table or two, a wooden chest to hold clothes, woven baskets for food, tall jars for water, and a stand on which was a stone lamp in the oil of which a floating wick glimmered flickeringly. There was no such thing as a stove, but the fire for cooking burned on an open hearth. Outside the house a stairway led to the roof; and sometimes a room or booth was built there, opening toward the sky and the stars.

There was no luxury in the houses of Nazareth, and only meager comfort, as measured by the conditions of to-day. But the home of Joseph and Mary had something which larger houses sometimes lack. It had religion. In a tiny case fastened upon the doorpost there was a writing from the Scriptures; and whenever anyone came in and out, his fingers touched this in reverence. The songs which were sung to little children were the psalms, and so in their ears from the beginning rang the echo of the name of God. Every weekly Sabbath, and each of the great religious feasts, as these followed one another through the year, had the particular prayers, or the lighting of candles, or the recitation of lovely ancient rituals of family blessing, which had been handed down through the homes of Israel age after age.

The first teachers of a little child in a Jewish home were his own mother and father. They would teach him very early the blessing to be said over food, and words of praise to God, and the great simplicities of what he was supposed to believe and to do. Then when he was old enough, he would go with the other boys of the village on week-days to school in the synagogue; and there he would learn to read, and to memorize long passages from the law and from the prophets. And on the Sabbath to this same building of the synagogue he would come with all the grown-up people of the town to hear again the law and the prophets read, perhaps also to hear them explained by someone who was called upon that day to speak, and to worship God as all the faithful people of his nation, wherever in the world they might be scattered, would also be worshiping him that day. That this worship on the Sabbath was one of the habits which sank deepest into the mind and heart of Jesus we know by the reference in the Gospel of Luke, which tells how one day in the later years Jesus came back to Nazareth and "entered into the synagogue, as his custom was."

While the boy Jesus listened, he thought and wondered. Thus and thus the law commanded; but what was the central meaning of the law? It was written in the book of Deuteronomy that the voice of the Lord said to Moses, "I will speak unto

thee all the commandments, and the statutes, and the judgments, which thou shalt teach. . . . Ye shall observe to do
therefore as the Lord your God hath commanded you: ye shall
not turn aside to the right hand or to the left." The rabbis and
scribes had been busy for generations, and were busy still, in
multiplying their definitions as to what the "commandments
and the statutes and the judgments" were. They had a prescrip-
tion of the law for every imaginable act of every day—for the way
a religious person should wear his clothes, for the manner of
washing his hands before a meal, for how far he could and could
not walk on the Sabbath day; and these prescriptions were as
binding as those which had to do with greater things. They
multiplied rules beyond remembering. Yet it was written in
the prophecy of Jeremiah, "After those days, saith the Lord, I
will put my law in their inward parts, and write it in their
hearts; and I will be their God, and they shall be my people."
It was this that he was seeking—not the law which was learned
by rote in the Sanhedrin school, but the law of the love of God
as the glad emotion of the loving heart. There was a way of
the Father which should "not turn to the right hand or to the
left," and he would know it.

At length the time came when Jesus passed from boyhood
into what was regarded in Israel as the age when the boy could
enter into the full inheritance of the religion of the covenant
people. He was twelve years old; and it was the season for the
greatest of all the holy festivals, that of the Passover. For the
keeping of the Passover, with its exultant commemoration of
the deliverance from Egypt, the Jewish people from all quarters
of the world turned their faces toward Jerusalem. Every year
Joseph and Mary went up from Nazareth; and now Jesus went
with them, for the first time to feel himself a part of the pilgrim
throng that sang together of Jerusalem builded as "a city that
is compact together: whither the tribes go up"; for the first time
to catch sight of the walls and towers of the Holy City; for the
first time to enter through her gates and walk the ancient streets
where the heart of all his people's history seemed to beat.

When the great day of the festival had come, "at even, at the going down of the sun, at the season that thou camest forth from Egypt," every Jewish family kept the solemn ritual of the Passover meal; and there at Jerusalem Jesus kept it with Joseph and Mary. So much in general we know; and then, through the Gospel of Luke, we know also one clear incident which stands out from the otherwise unrecorded days and years of the early life of Jesus. When the Passover festival was finished, Mary and Joseph started from Jerusalem to go home to Nazareth. They were traveling with the same company of their neighbors with whom they had come; and they supposed that Jesus was somewhere in the group. But at nightfall when they inquired for him among their kinsfolk and friends, they could not find him. Anxiously then they turned back to Jerusalem, seeking him. Hither and yon in the city they searched, and found no trace of him. Then at length they went to the Temple; and there in the Temple, where the teachers of the law were accustomed to gather, Jesus was. He sat in the midst of them, listening to them and asking them questions. "Son," said his mother, "why have you treated us so? Your father and I have been searching for you in distress."

"Why did you have to look for me?" he answered. "Didn't you know that I would be in my Father's house?"

They did not understand him; and they were amazed at having found him where they did. But he went with them back to Nazareth, and entered as before into the life of the home; while his mother kept in her heart the memory of what he had said. Meanwhile, as the Gospel of Luke sums up the years that followed, he "increased in wisdom and in stature, and in favor with God and man."

The curtain of silence which veils the life of Jesus in Nazareth does not lift again until it shows him going out of Nazareth as a man to begin the work from which he never came back to make the little town his home. But there, so far as we can infer, he did live for some eighteen years after his first visit to Jerusalem for the Passover, when he was twelve.

The occupations of people in Nazareth were simple ones. Women drew water and filled their jars at the village well, ground corn and baked it into flat bread upon the hot stones of the hearth, wove cloth and dyed it and made it into clothes, swept the house and trimmed the lamps and watched over little children as mothers have done since the beginning of the world. Men sowed and reaped the fields, or pruned the vineyards, herded the sheep and cattle on the hills, or worked as masons and as carpenters; and in his father's shop the boy Jesus learned a man's skill in hand and eye. It may be that from Joseph he learned also conceptions which went far deeper, and that the sweetness of his memories of this human father of his breathed through the instinctive use of "Father" as the word which he used when he spoke of God.

After the description of the early Passover visit to Jerusalem, there is no mention of Joseph in the records of the Gospels, so that it would seem that Joseph died when Jesus yet was young; and it may be that on the shoulders of the boy there fell the responsibility of earning a livelihood for the family in his father's place. Nor was his position in the home an easy one. It is plain from later references in the Gospels that his brothers did not understand him, and that they were sometimes antagonistic to the great interests which filled his soul. He was of a different nature from the rest; and they seemed to have sensed it and to have resented it. When later he began to preach his gospel of a love that does not seek rewards but gives itself unsparingly in service, he was only putting into words the difficult ideal which he himself had clung to in the Nazareth family group.

Meanwhile, though his life still centered in the little town, the thoughts of Jesus must have been going far. Nazareth lay among the hills; but over the hills the wide pageant of the world was spread. From the heights above the town the eyes of Jesus could look upon scenes which were rich with associations of the storied past, and vivid with the throbbing life of the immediate day. Southward lay the plain of Esdraelon, the immemorial battleground where the armies of Israel had fought in many centuries, and where the tides of war from many empires had surged and clashed. Soldiers of the Egyptian Pharaohs had marched there. The iron wheels of the chariots of Assyrians had rumbled there. Philistines from the coast and Bedouin invaders from the desert had fought there. And past it in more recent times the phalanxes of Alexander had moved upon their conquering way. Over that plain the feet of David had gone back and forth, and on it Saul and Jonathan had fallen.

Toward the west rose the great ridge of Carmel, clothed with mighty memories of Elijah; and beneath that and beyond it was the glimmer of the sea, where the triremes came and went from distant Rome. To the east, across the Jordan valley, were the marble walls of the cities of the Decapolis, witnesses to the new sort of civilization which had come to his country with the Roman conquest; and on any of the roads of Galilee might be seen a Roman legion with its golden eagles flashing in the sun. Where was the kingdom of which the prophets of Israel had dreamed? What had become of the fulfilment of the promise that the mountain of the Lord's house should be established in the top of the mountains and exalted above the hills, and that all nations should flow into it, while out of Zion should "go forth the law and the word of the Lord from Jerusalem"? To many in Israel it seemed that those hopes had been bitterly brought to naught. Where was the promised kingdom of the Holy One? Was Cæsar more powerful than God?

Such questionings Jesus must have heard among the restless folk of Galilee; and he himself had seen what the Roman power could be. While he was a boy in Nazareth, there had been a sudden rebellion under a leader by the name of Judas, centering round the splendid new city of Sepphoris which lay only six miles north of Nazareth. Under Varus, a Roman force had moved against the revolutionists; and when after a quick, short struggle, the Romans were the masters, the flames of burning Sepphoris were red against the sky, and along the roads scores of men hung crucified as tokens of the Roman vengeance.

Meanwhile, many in Israel still hoped passionately for a leader and a deliverer, for a Messiah sent from God to set his people free. They sang of him,

"He shall thrust out sinners from the inheritance,
He shall destroy the pride of the sinners as a potter's vessel,
With a rod of iron he shall break in pieces all their substance."

Concerning all these things Jesus must have pondered in the quiet years. He was conscious of powers such as no other man possessed. Within his soul he drew upon the infinite resources of God. He knew that he was born to immortal destiny. He knew that he could lead men. What if God's will for him were that he should set up the sort of kingdom which so many in Israel cried out for? What if he should be a leader and a conqueror stronger than the conquerors who had come from Rome?

When Jesus did at last go out from Nazareth to begin his work, the first words upon his lips were these: "The kingdom of God is at hand!" But he had changed the meaning of the kingdom from what the crowd expected. In the long years of his preparation he had thought through to his own conclusions. He would inaugurate a kingdom that must be built not in the world of weapons but in the inner world of human hearts made new by the love of God.

The occasion for the commencement of his ministry came with the appearance of a new prophet in Israel. It was none other than John, the son of Zacharias. He had been a solitary, brooding man, a dweller in the deserts, as some of the great prophets had been before. And now out of the desert he came, gaunt and formidable, his soul on fire with the message of his moral passion. He had contemplated his nation's life in the awful light of the righteousness of God, and now he spoke to it with an authority which subdued men and held them spellbound.

It was by the fords of the Jordan, not very far from Jerusalem, that he appeared, dressed in camels' skins, with a leather girdle about his waist. It was in the fifteenth year of the reign of Tiberias Cæsar in Rome, when Pontius Pilate was governor of Judæa, and Herod Antipas (son of Herod the Great) tetrarch of Galilee. Listening to him, men heard the echo of the prophecy of Isaiah:

"The voice of one crying in the wilderness.
　'Prepare ye the way of the Lord, make his paths straight.
Every valley shall be filled,
　and every mountain and hill shall be brought low;
And the crooked shall be made straight,
　and the rough ways shall be made smooth,
And all flesh shall see the salvation of God.' "

People flocked to him from every quarter, and people of every sort. He was preaching repentance of sins, and calling on men to be baptized as a sign of their repentance and of their desire to enter the company of the purified ones who should be fit for God's kingdom when it came.

People in the crowd wanted to know what they should do to show their change of mind; and John answered, "Whoever has two coats, let him give one to someone who has none; and whoever has food, let him do the same."

The taxgatherers asked what they should do. "Do not grind out of people more than you are supposed to get," John replied.

Soldiers were there also. "What shall we do?" they demanded, and John answered: "Do not treat people violently. Do not bring any false accusation. Live on your wages."

But to the Pharisees and the scribes John spoke in a fashion which took their breath away. "You offspring of vipers," he said, "who has warned you to flee from the wrath that is coming? Bring forth fruits fit for repentance, and do not imagine that you can say, 'We have Abraham as our father.' I tell you God can raise up children of Abraham out of these stones. Now the axe is laid to the roots of trees, and every tree that does not bear good fruit is chopped down and flung into the fire."

Then he went on to say, "I will baptize you with water; but there is coming one who is mightier than I, whose sandals I am not fit to unloose. He shall baptize you with the Holy Ghost, and with fire. His winnowing fan is in his hand, and he will thoroughly purge his floor, and gather the wheat into the garner; but the chaff he will burn with unquenchable fire."

Among the crowds who flocked to listen to John excitement and expectation grew. He was preaching the coming of the kingdom. Would the kingdom mean the deliverance of the nation? Was Messiah about to come from God, and to come as a conqueror and a deliverer? Or was John himself the Messiah? That was the question which was beginning to be whispered here and there.

Then down from Nazareth to the Jordan valley came Jesus. In his own soul the great hour had struck for him. The preaching of John was the heralding of the sort of kingdom which he knew now that he must fulfill. But he came first to share in John's baptism. He would identify himself with the needs of the nation and this new expression of its desire for God.

John hesitated. He recognized in Jesus a greatness beyond his own. "I have need to be baptized of you," he said, "and do you come to me?"

"Let it be so," said Jesus, "for it is thus that we must fulfill the purposes of God."

So John baptized him, and when Jesus came up out of the river, there was such a shining of the Spirit in his face that men, looking back upon it, said that the Spirit of God had come upon him like a dove descending out of heaven. They said there was a voice, "This is my beloved Son, in whom I am well pleased."

After the baptism Jesus went away from the place where the crowds were. He withdrew into the desolate and desert country to the west of the Dead Sea, the same country in which the prophet Amos had dwelt long before, and from which John himself had come when he began to preach. He must be alone now to face and to settle the alternatives of his life.

There in the wilderness he fasted and prayed, and there he

went through the spiritual conflict which is described with vivid imagery, and in substantially the same form, in the Gospels of Matthew and of Luke. Thus the Gospel of Luke records it. "And Jesus being full of the Holy Ghost returned from Jordan, and was led by the Spirit into the wilderness, being forty days tempted of the devil. And in those days he did eat nothing: and when they were ended, he afterward hungered. And the devil said unto him, 'If thou be the Son of God, command this stone that it be made bread.' And Jesus answered him, saying, 'It is written, That man shall not live by bread alone, but by every word of God.' And the devil, taking him up into a high mountain, showed unto him all the kingdoms of the world in a moment of time. And the devil said unto him: 'All this power will I give thee, and the glory of them: for that is delivered unto me; and to whomsoever I will, I give it. If thou therefore wilt worship me, all shall be thine.' And Jesus answered and said unto him, 'Get thee behind me, Satan: for it is written, "Thou shalt worship the Lord thy God, and him only shalt thou serve." ' And he brought him to Jerusalem, and set him on a pinnacle of the temple, and said unto him, 'If thou be the Son of God, cast thyself down from hence: for it is written, "He shall give his angels charge over thee, to keep thee: and in their hands they shall bear thee up, lest at any time thou dash thy foot against a stone." ' And Jesus answering said unto him, 'It is said, "Thou shalt not tempt the Lord thy God." ' And when the devil had ended all the temptation, he departed from him for a season."

Thus the struggle with the soul of Jesus is represented as a struggle between the devil and himself; and in the light of all we know concerning Jesus' life before and afterward, this is what it would seem that his temptation meant:

The voice of the tempter was the voice of the plausible lower choice which whispered to Jesus and tried to make him listen.

It suggested to him, in the first place, that in the public life which he was now about to begin the best thing he could do would be to win the allegiance of the people by satisfying their

"WIST YE NOT?"

JESUS BLESSING LITTLE CHILDREN

material needs. He had great power, and he could change conditions of life in Israel. There were multitudes who were poor,
heavily taxed, and overburdened. He knew the lot of the poor.
He had lived among them and knew the pathos of their life.
He knew that often it was as though they had nothing but stones
to subsist on. "Turn their stones to bread," said the tempting
voice. "Help make people more prosperous and comfortable.
Then they will be grateful and will follow you, and you can
begin to do God's work among them after that."

But Jesus knew that was not true. He foresaw that those
who would follow for the things they could get would not
necessarily follow on to seek the finer gifts of God. "Man doth
not live by bread alone," he said, "but by every word that pro-
ceedeth out of the mouth of God."

"Well then," came the next suggestion, "if you are not
interested in helping people be more comfortable, then satisfy
their cry for freedom. If you will not be a Messiah concerned
with material ends, then be the Messiah concerned with military ones. The old passion of the nation is crying out for one
of its own blood who shall be a conqueror. It wants a leader
who will rally discontent and defiance against the dominance
of Rome. In God's name, be that leader! Create your own
throne of power, and then you can sway the people as you will."

There in the wilderness Jesus perhaps was seeing in imagination the vision which he had seen from the hilltops of Nazareth, seeing the wide pageant of the world spread out below,
with its tokens of empire and its suggestions of the power which
a leader of men could forge. The voices of ambition were offering him a kingdom if he would accept the methods which are
this world's price of power. But something deeper in his spirit
answered, "Get thee hence, Satan: for it is written, 'Thou shalt
worship the Lord thy God, and him only shalt thou serve.' "

But one temptation more remained. If he had rejected the
suggestions of material favors and military might, and if he were
determined to stake the whole outcome of his life's adventure,
not upon wealth and not upon weapons, but only upon the
power of the Spirit; then, surely, because he had given himself

completely to the guidance of God, God would protect him and defend his obedient life from harm. Angels would bear him up whenever there was danger that he should dash his foot against a stone. He might go into peril, but he would go through it. Was there anything less that should be expected if God were really God? Could he not require of his Father this witness to his favor and protection?

But once again Jesus had another answer. He must not limit his faithfulness by any question of the immediate result. He must not put conditions upon his consecration. It might be that God's will for him would be seeming defeat; it might be that at the end of the road there would wait—a cross. He would not let his faith in his Father's purposes be bound by any question of what might happen to himself. "Thou shalt not make trial of the Lord thy God," he said.

So at length, sure in his own decisions, at peace in his own soul, confident and self-mastered, Jesus came back from the wilderness; and it is no wonder that the Gospel of Matthew says that "angels came and ministered unto him."

CHAPTER XXXVIII

THE BEGINNING OF JESUS' MINISTRY AMONG THE PEOPLE IN GALI-
LEE; HIS CALL TO MEN IN THE FISHING-BOATS TO FOLLOW HIM AND
BE HIS DISCIPLES; AND THE STORIES OF HOW HE HEALED THE SICK,
AND HOW HE TAUGHT THE PEOPLE.

ROM THE Valley of the Jordan, Jesus went
northward into Galilee. He did not return
to Nazareth, but he dwelt instead at Capernaum on the Lake of Galilee, a larger town
than Nazareth, and one through which the life
of the province flowed in a fuller stream.

He was beginning now his public ministry. All that was
in his mind and soul can only be conjectured, but this at least
is plain: that he felt himself to have a relationship with God his
Father such as no other human figure had claimed before, that
he was conscious of unique power over the bodies and the minds
of men, and that he himself should be the center of a new and
redeemed society to be created from above. He began to
preach and to say, "Repent: for the kingdom of heaven is at
hand."

His first act was to gather round him a little group of
picked men who should be with him, learn of him, and share
his spirit. He walked one day along the shore of the Lake of
Galilee and watched fishermen casting their nets into the waters.
Two of them were brothers, Simon and Andrew. Jesus called
them. "Come, follow me," he said, "and I will make you
fishers of men." They left their nets immediately and followed
him.

A little farther along the shore he saw James and John,
the sons of Zebedee. They were in their fishing-boat, mending
their nets. He summoned them also, and they left their father
and the hired crew who were in the boat and went with Jesus.

417

These were the first four of the group which was to grow to twelve and which should be with Jesus from that time on to the end.

It is through these men that directly or indirectly there have come down to us those recollections of Jesus and of what he said and did which have been embodied in the Gospels. An early Christian tradition has it that in Mark, the earliest of the written Gospels, we have the echo of what Peter told. Another Gospel, the one which is printed first in the New Testament, bears the name of Matthew, who was one of the twelve; and the fourth Gospel bears the name of John. It is impossible certainly to know to what extent "The Gospel According to Saint Matthew" traces back in its finished form to the disciple as its author, or to be sure whether "The Gospel According to Saint John" was written by John the son of Zebedee or by another John. These questions have been studied by innumerable scholars, and their varying conclusions have been written in many books; but when all is said and done, this remains clear— that those who did write the three Gospels already named, and Luke, who wrote the remaining one, must have drawn their knowledge of Jesus from the little group of those who were closest to him in his life. They had no written words of his own. He never set down any description or explanation for biographers to use. Consequently, the figure of Jesus which appears in the Gospels is Jesus as he was reflected in these other men's eyes. These men were not scientists. They did not analyze or describe facts and events in the same way or in the same terms which would be characteristic of modern men. They spoke the language of their world and of their time—a time which accounted for particular forms of sickness by saying that the sick folk were "possessed of devils," which interpreted events not understood as "miracles," and which had its own presupposition of the "signs" which must characterize the Messiah.

It is not strange, and it should not be disturbing, that it is sometimes difficult to reach through to the precise fact which lies back of one or another of their descriptions. We cannot always accept, for example, their diagnosis of a particular sickness, or their explanation of the method in which Jesus accomplished this or that; but these things are unimportant. The important thing is to feel the immense personality of Jesus as they felt it. To listen to the swift story of the Gospels, and to catch the full impression of it, are better than to stop and try to translate all its expressions into present-day terms. What we want to do is to see again the Jesus whom these men saw, the figure who drew their affections, commanded their loyalty, and at the same time gave them such an overwhelming sense of power as to make them feel that for him nothing was impossible.

One other thing always must be understood. We speak of "the story of the Gospels," but it is true that this story is not set down in any one unbroken or consistent narrative. The four Gospels give us many separate recollections of what Jesus did and taught, often without exact indication either of time or place. In putting together the materials drawn from the different Gospels into one continuous story it must be a matter of conjecture whether some particular description properly belongs before or after some other one. Nevertheless, even with these uncertainties of detail, the narrative in its main sweep from beginning to end becomes a living thing through which the figure of Jesus moves from the first days of his ministry in Galilee to the climax on the cross.

The group of men in their fishing-boats by the lakeshore, Jesus walking on the beach and calling these men to come with him—that is the first picture which comes down to us through the light of the disciples' recollection. Then the scene changes. It is the Sabbath, and Jesus has gone into the synagogue at Capernaum.

At the point in the service when it was customary to call on somebody to comment on the Holy Scriptures which had been read, they called on Jesus. He rose in the synagogue and began to speak, and the congregation was astonished. They were accustomed to having familiar ideas rehearsed in pious regularity, but here was something different. Jesus taught them as one who had authority, and not as the scribes.

Nor did he teach only. In the synagogue there was a man "with an unclean spirit." He cried out distractedly: "Let us alone; what have we to do with you, you Jesus of Nazareth? Are you come to destroy us? I know you who you are, the Holy One of God!" Jesus looked at this distraught man, and he spoke to something deep within him. "Hold your peace," he said, "and come out of him." The man was convulsed, and gave a great cry, and the congregation said that the unclean spirit was tearing him and coming out. The real man was restored, and all the people were amazed, and they began to ask one another: "What sort of a thing is this? What new sort of doctrine is this? With authority he commands the unclean spirits, and they obey him!"

Meanwhile the report of what had happened began to spread through all the region of Galilee.

From the synagogue Jesus went to the house of Simon and Andrew, and James and John also were with him. The mother of Simon's wife lay sick of a fever, and presently they came and told Jesus of her. He went and took her by the hand and lifted her up. At his touch the fever left her, and she began to wait upon all who were in the house.

The report of this also went abroad, and by the evening of that day at sunset, people who had relatives and friends who were sick or distracted went after them and brought them where Jesus was. It seemed as though the whole city were gathered together at his door. He healed many of these sick folk and "cast out many devils." Then when the long day ended, this day in which the power in him had been drawn upon heavily, he needed something more than sleep. A long while before the next morning dawned he rose up and went out of Capernaum into a solitary place, and there prayed.

Simon Peter and the rest of the little group of his disciples followed after him. When they found him, they said, "All men are seeking you." He answered, "Let us go into the next towns, that I may preach there also; for that is why I have come forth." So in synagogues throughout Galilee he preached, and healed people who were possessed of evil spirits.

One day there came to him a leper, kneeling down before him, and beseeching him, "If you will, you can make me clean."

Moved with compassion, Jesus stretched out his hand and touched the leper. "I will," he said, "you shall be clean." And as soon as he had spoken, the man's leprosy vanished from him, and he was clean. Jesus strictly charged him that he should not spread this tidings. "Say nothing to any man," he said; "go on your way, show yourself to a priest, and for your cleansing make a thank-offering of the thing which Moses commanded."

Jesus was foreseeing already the crowds who would come thronging around him because they wanted to see wonders performed. But notwithstanding what he had said, the leper went out and began to blaze abroad the story of what had happened, so that Jesus could not go openly into any town, but moved in the open country. Nevertheless, there people flocked to him from every quarter.

Perhaps it was about this time that Jesus went back once more to Nazareth. It was the Sabbath day when he was there, and, as his custom was, he entered the synagogue at the hour of worship. He was asked to read the Scripture, and was given the parchment roll which contained the book of the prophet Isaiah. He turned toward the end of it. (It is in the sixty-first chapter of the book of Isaiah, as this book is divided in our printed Bible.) And he read this:

"The Spirit of the Lord is upon me, because he anointed me to preach good tidings to the poor: he hath sent me to proclaim release to the captives, and recovering of sight to the blind, to set at liberty them that are bruised, to proclaim the acceptable year of the Lord."

Jesus rolled up the parchment and handed it back to the minister of the synagogue, while the eyes of all the congregation were fastened upon him.

He began to speak to them. "This day as you listen," he said, "this scripture is fulfilled." That was a gracious beginning, they thought. He was bringing them good news of the near approach of the blessings which Isaiah had promised. They began to whisper to one another, "Is this not Joseph's son?" They were excited to think that the son of a carpenter whom they had known could make such an impression in the synagogue.

But Jesus had not finished. He knew that the report had preceded him to Nazareth of all that he had been doing in Capernaum and in other towns of Galilee. The neighbors would be waiting to see if he would work wonders here as he was said to have worked them in other places. So he said: "You will surely say to me this proverb, 'Physician, heal thyself. Do here in your own country the same sort of things that we have heard that you did in Capernaum.' But a prophet is not without honor except in his own country and among his own kin and in his own house. Moreover, I tell you this truth also: In the days of Elijah, when no rain fell for three years and six months and there was great famine in all the land, there were many widows in Israel; but Elijah was not sent to any of these. He was sent to a woman who was a widow in Zarephath in the region of Sidon. And in the time of the prophet Elisha there were many lepers in Israel; yet none of these were cleansed, but, rather, Naaman the Syrian."

The mood of the congregation had changed. Jesus was implying that the promises of God might not be for them but for the outsiders. As they listened, they were filled with wrath. They rose up and crowded about Jesus, thrust him out of the town, and even took him with them up the pathway that led to the brow of the hill above Nazareth. They were so infuriated that they meant to throw him down from the hilltop, but there was that in him which overawed the mob. He passed through the midst of them and went on his way.

He went back to Capernaum then; and so far as the record of the Gospel goes, he never returned to Nazareth.

In Capernaum and in the country near it he preached to increasing crowds. The common people heard him gladly. They were held by the note of authority which always rang in his voice. They recognized that he was not repeating old traditions, but speaking out of his own knowledge of the living God. They saw that he knew life, the simple homely life they were familiar with; and they heard him speak in language they could understand. Moreover, he had a way of making religion seem a blessing and not a burden. He did not talk mostly, as the scribes and Pharisees did, of the things they had not done. Instead, he talked to them of the glory and goodness of God.

Frequently he taught in parables. That is to say, he would describe some scene of men's everyday surroundings, or tell a story of what had happened, or might happen, in any man's life, and he would make these into symbols of the meaning of God which for him was manifest in all familiar things. One day he told the parable of the sower; perhaps as he was teaching out of doors, where those who were listening to him could see at that moment the figure of a man sowing seed on a windswept hill. "Some seed," he said, "falls on the trodden paths, where birds come down and consume it. Some falls on stony ground, where the earth is shallow; and although it may spring up quickly, because it has no deep roots it will be scorched and withered by the full heat of the sun. Some falls among thornbushes, and the thorns choke the seed so that it will bear no grain. But other seed falls on good ground, where it will yield a harvest of thirty or forty or a hundred times the sowing.

"The word of the kingdom of God is like that," he said. "With some the seed is carried away, or in their hearts it falls on such stony ground that it has no enduring root, or it is crowded out by the cares of this world and the deceitfulness of riches. But there are others into whose hearts the word of God falls like seed on the good ground, to bring forth the harvest of abundant life."

Other parables also he used to describe the way in which the power of God could take hold of human lives and how it could grow. He said that at first it might be like a mustard seed, the tiniest of all the seeds; but one which, when it was planted, grew into a great bush in which the birds of the air found shelter. It was like the little bit of leaven which a woman would take and hide in three measures of meal, till presently the whole was leavened. It was like the growth of grain, which no man himself can bring about, but which goes on in his field by night as well as by day, whether a man works or whether he is sleeping. And the kingdom of God, he said, is like a treasure hid in a field, or like a precious pearl which, when a man has heard of, he may well sell everything else that he has in order to gain it.

The longest record of his teaching is written in the Gospel of Matthew and is called "The Sermon on the Mount." Somewhere on a height not far from the Lake, Jesus sat down one day, and his listeners were gathered in front of him. He began with those encouragements which are called "The Beatitudes."

"Blessed," he said, "are the poor in spirit: for theirs is the kingdom of heaven.

"Blessed are they that mourn: for they shall be comforted.

"Blessed are the meek: for they shall inherit the earth.

"Blessed are they which do hunger and thirst after righteousness: for they shall be filled.

"Blessed are the merciful: for they shall obtain mercy.

"Blessed are the pure in heart: for they shall see God.

"Blessed are the peacemakers: for they shall be called the children of God.

"Blessed are they which are persecuted for righteousness' sake: for theirs is the kingdom of heaven.

"Blessed are ye, when men shall revile you, and persecute you, and shall say all manner of evil against you falsely for my sake.

"Rejoice, and be exceeding glad: for great is your reward in heaven: for so persecuted they the prophets which were before you."

Then the Sermon on the Mount (which as it is written in the fifth, sixth, and seventh chapters of Matthew's Gospel may represent what Jesus said at one time, or more likely may be utterances of his on different occasions brought thus together, but which in any case is made a unit by his unmistakable spirit shining through it) goes on to remind the followers of Jesus that they must be like salt brought into the world to sweeten and preserve it, and like the light of a city set upon a hill. They should represent not the setting aside but the fulfilment of all the best religious knowledge which they had learned from the law and from the prophets. But they were to understand something deeper than the particular commandments of the law. It was not enough that they should merely abstain from evil acts. Their minds and their hearts must be purged from evil. "Unless your righteousness shall exceed the righteousness of the scribes and Pharisees," he said, "ye shall in no case enter into the kingdom of heaven." They had heard the commandment, "Thou shalt not kill." They must go beyond that, and not even give way to anger. They had heard the scribes and Pharisees exhort them as to the gifts they were to bring to the Temple; but if they had come to the very foot of the altar with their gift, and should remember there some human being whom they had offended, they should turn back from the Temple itself to go first and be reconciled. They had heard the commandment, "Thou shalt not commit adultery;" but the lustful desire and the lustful look could be already adultery committed in the heart. The good life must be a matter of self-discipline at any cost. "If your right eye offend you," said Jesus with an illustration so sweeping that no one could mistake the urgency of what he meant, "pluck it out and cast it from you. If your right hand offend you, cut it off: for it is better that one of your members should perish than that your whole body should be cast into hell."

In this same Sermon on the Mount he taught his disciples how to pray; how to keep their speech so straightforward that they had no need of oaths; how to give alms, not in the spirit of display and not for men's applause, but for the sake of the love of God and in his sight alone; how to fast, and still to keep their faces cheerful; how to seek their treasure from the gifts of God and not from the world's riches, and to be free from anxiety because they should learn to put their trust in God; how to treat all men, not grudgingly, but in the spirit of God's unbounded gifts. "You have heard," he told them, "that it has been said, 'you shall love your neighbor and hate your enemy.'

But I say unto you, 'Love your enemies, bless them that curse you, do good to them that hate you, and pray for them which despitefully use you, and persecute you; that ye may be the children of your Father who is in heaven: for he makes his sun to rise on the evil and on the good, and sends rain on the just and on the unjust. For if you love them which love you, what reward have you? Do not even the publicans the same? And if you salute your brethren only, what do you more than others? Do not even the publicans so? Be therefore perfect, even as your Father which is in heaven is perfect.' "

Then as the climax of the Sermon on the Mount stands Jesus' reminder that words and smooth professions do not make up religion, but that God requires reality. "A tree is known," he said, "by its fruits. If a tree bears good fruit, it is a good tree; and if it bears evil fruit, then it is an evil tree, and should be cut down and burned in the fire."

"Not every one who may say to me, 'Lord, Lord,' shall enter into the kingdom of heaven; but he who does the will of my Father who is in heaven. Many will say to me in that day, 'Lord, Lord, have we not prophesied in your name, and in your name done many wonderful works?' But then will I profess to them, 'I never knew you: depart from me, you that work iniquity.' "

"Therefore, whosoever hears these sayings of mine and acts accordingly, I liken him to a wise man who built his house on a rock. When the rain descended, and the floods came, and the winds blew, and beat upon that house, it did not fall; because it was founded upon a rock. But every man who hears these sayings of mine and does not observe them, shall be likened to a foolish man who built his house on the sand. And when the rain descended, and the floods came, and the winds blew, and beat upon that house, it fell; and great was the fall of it."

When they listened to Jesus speaking in this fashion, some of the people were not so sure that they liked his teaching as they thought they were at first. To the best of them, he made God seem so wonderful that they were willing to try anything in order to have God come into their own lives as he evidently was already come into the life of Jesus. But there were others who began to think that religion was too costly a matter. When Jesus talked of plucking out one's right eye and cutting off one's right hand rather than have the whole body perish, they knew well enough what he meant by that illustration. They knew that the kingdom of God which he held out to them as so beautiful and joyous a promise might require that they get rid of some of their cherished sins before they could inherit it, and they were not so sure that this was what they were ready to do.

Moreover, there was another group which was beginning to look askance at Jesus for the things he taught and the things he did. These were the Pharisees; the priests who had business with the Temple in Jerusalem; and other leaders of the church. Their power over the people rested upon their ability to make the people obey the exact letter of the law, and Jesus had a way of setting the letter of the law aside if human need and the mercy of God required it. One day he went through a field of grain; and the disciples reached out and gathered some of the ears of wheat in their hands, and rolled them together to separate the sweet kernel from the husks, that they might eat it. The Pharisees said they broke the Sabbath law, because the Sabbath law forbade work, and what they did was equivalent to grinding wheat, and that was work. But Jesus asked them whether they had never read how once, when David was weary and hungry on his flight from Saul, he had gone into a shrine and taken the holy bread which was there as an offering before the altar, and given this to the men who were with him because they were in need. "The Sabbath," he said, "was made for man, and not man for the Sabbath."

On another day he was in Capernaum, and the report spread quickly that he was in a certain house. Immediately a crowd gathered, filling all the rooms and the street outside, and Jesus preached to them. Meanwhile, four men who had a friend who was sick with palsy brought this palsied man on a pallet in the hope that Jesus would heal him. But on account of the press of people, they could not come near where he was.

So they climbed up the outside stairway to the flat roof of the house, took part of the roof to pieces, and lowered the sick man down to the room where Jesus was. When Jesus saw these men's faith, he said to their palsied friend, "Son, your sins are forgiven." A group of scribes were in the room, and they said, resentfully, "Why does this man thus speak blasphemy? Who can forgive sins but God?" Jesus looked at their lowering faces, and saw what they were feeling in their hearts. "Which is easier," he asked, "to say to this man sick of the palsy, 'Your sins are forgiven,' or to say, 'Arise, take up your bed, and walk'? But in order that you may know that the Son of man has power on earth to forgive sins (he turned and spoke to the sick man) 'I say to you, arise, take up your bed, and go your way to your own house!' " Immediately the man rose, took up his bed, and went out through the crowd, so that they were amazed and glorified God, saying to one another that they had never seen anything on this fashion before.

Other things which the opponents of Jesus considered as grounds of offense were multiplying. One day Jesus, as he passed by the gate of the town, saw Levi the son of Alphæus (the same man who was to be known afterward as Matthew the apostle), collecting customs. He was one of the "publicans," as the Jews called the tax-collecting class, whom particularly they hated and despised. Jesus said to Matthew, as earlier he had said to James and John and Andrew and Simon Peter, "Follow me," and Matthew arose and followed him. Moreover, he made a feast in his house to which he invited many of his publican friends and others whom the pious looked down upon as sinners. And Jesus and his disciples were there as Matthew's guests. The Pharisees and scribes were outraged. "How is it," they said to the disciples, "that he eats and drinks with publicans and sinners?" When Jesus heard it, he answered: "Those that are well have no need of a physician; they that are sick do. I did not come to call the righteous, but sinners to repentance."

From another direction also Jesus was challenged. People said to him one day: "The disciples of John the Baptist used to fast, and the Pharisees fast; but your disciples do not. Why is that?" In reply Jesus asked them whether they thought the friends of the bridegroom at a wedding fasted while the bridegroom was in their midst. If the bridegroom were taken from them, then would be a time for fasting. He meant that he had come to bring a new message of joy in God, and the old gloomy practices which the over-pious made much of were out of tune. Inconsistent things should not be patched together. "No man sews a piece of new cloth on an old garment," he said, "for if he does, the new piece tears out the old, and the rent is made worse than before. Nor does any man put new wine into old wineskins; for if he does, the new wine will burst the skins and the wine be spilled. But new wine must be put into new skins."

The men who clung at all costs to old traditions did not like that teaching. They liked still less what Jesus did on another day. He went into the synagogue, and among the people there was a man who had a withered hand. The scribes and other sticklers for the law watched him to see whether he would heal on the Sabbath day. Jesus looked at the crippled man. "Stand forward," he said. Then he turned to the little group of sullen critics who were watching. "Is it according to the law to do good on the Sabbath day or to do evil, to save life or to kill?" They kept silent. Then Jesus, looking at them with anger because of the hardness of their hearts, said to the crippled man, "Stretch out your hand;" and as he stretched it out, it was restored whole as the other one.

But from that day the Pharisees became increasingly his enemies. They went out and found some of the Herodians— that is to say, the men who curried favor with Herod, the tetrarch of Galilee, who already had his reasons for being afraid of Jesus. And these two groups plotted together as to how they might destroy him.

CHAPTER XXXIX

HILE JESUS was beginning his ministry in
Galilee, the work of John the Baptist was com-
ing to its close. He had denounced Herod
Antipas, tetrarch of Galilee, because Herod
had taken his brother's wife. Herod thereupon had caused John to be arrested, and had
put him in the gloomy prison of Machærus, in the region of the
Dead Sea.

From the prison John sent messengers to Jesus. The great
preacher was distressed and troubled. He had believed that
Jesus would be the Messiah, the deliverer sent from God to
bring in the Kingdom in some tremendous way; but the world
still seemed to go on as it had gone before. Herod and other
evil rulers were still in power. Where were the signs of a new
redemption come from God?

So the messengers from John brought their question to
Jesus, "Art thou he that should come, or do we look for another?"

Jesus pointed to the sick folk who were clustering around
him. "Go back," he said, "and tell John what you have seen and
heard; how that the blind see, the lame walk, the lepers are
cleansed, the deaf hear, the dead are raised, and the gospel is
preached to the poor. And blessed is he who shall not be
offended in me." He knew that it was hard yet for John to
understand that the kingdom of God comes not with observation, and must be created from within rather than from without.

430

When John's messengers had gone, he began to speak to the people about John. What was it that they had expected to see when they went out into the wilderness when John was preaching? A reed shaken by the wind? A man clothed in soft raiment? No, he said, obviously not that; for if one is looking for those who are gorgeously appareled and living delicately, he should look in the courts of kings. Well, what was it that they went out to see? A prophet? "Yes," he continued, "and, I tell you, much more than a prophet, for this is he of whom it is written, 'Behold, I send my messenger before thy face, which shall prepare thy way before thee.' I tell you that of all men born of women there has arisen no greater prophet than John the Baptist." And then he concluded with these surprising words: "Yet he that is least in the kingdom of God is greater than he."

Not long after that, John the Baptist was dead. Herod's wife, on whose account John the Baptist had denounced Herod, cherished a resentment much more bitter than that which Herod himself had felt. She bided her time until she could take revenge on John. Now, on Herod's birthday he gave a great feast, and at this feast the daughter of Herodias, his wife, came in and danced before Herod and his guests, and Herod was greatly pleased. With an oath he promised to give her whatever she should ask. Her mother had already told her what to ask for if the chance should come, and so she replied that what she wanted was the head of John the Baptist on a platter. Herod was dismayed; but because of the oath which he had sworn before all his guests as witnesses, he would not retract his promise. So he sent to the prison where John was, and had him beheaded; and the head was brought on a platter and given to Herodias' daughter, and she took it in triumph to her mother.

Meanwhile the disciples of John took his body and buried it, and came and told Jesus what had happened.

The road ahead would be more dangerous for Jesus now. He began to enlarge the number of those who should be with him and who presently would carry on his work. The men whom he chose to be nearest to him were twelve: Simon, whose surname was Peter, and his brother Andrew; James and John, sons of Zebedee—the four who were called from the fishing-boats on the Lake of Galilee; Matthew, the publican; and in addition to these, Philip, Bartholomew, Thomas, James the son of Alphæus, Thaddæus, Simon the Canaanite, and Judas Iscariot.

His friends and his family were becoming alarmed now about him. The leaders of the church were jealous of his grow-ing authority among the people. A delegation of scribes came down from Jerusalem, and they said that by the prince of devils he was casting out devils. To them Jesus made a crushing reply. They had committed, he said, the utmost blasphemy which men can commit because they had tried to twist goodness and make it into evil. When they said that his works of mercy were works wrought by the devil, they had blasphemed against the Holy Spirit; and that blasphemy, he said, has no forgiveness but is in danger of eternal condemnation.

He was becoming increasingly the center of conflict. His mother and his brothers came one day, and, standing at the edge of the crowd that gathered round him, sent in a message to him. Apparently they wanted to dissuade him from the perilous work on which he was launched—perilous to him, and perhaps they thought to them. But he said to the crowd, "Who is my mother and my brothers?" And as he looked into the faces of those who were nearest to him, he said: "Behold, my mother and my brothers! For everyone who shall do the will of God, the same is my brother, and my sister, and my mother."

For the most part now he had been in the country near Capernaum; but sometimes he went across the lake to escape the pressure of the crowds. One evening he launched out in a boat with the disciples, and other little ships were with him. A great storm of wind fell upon the lake. The waves rose and beat into the ship, so that it was full of water. But Jesus lay in the stern of the boat asleep on a pillow. The frightened dis-ciples woke him. "Master," they said, "do you not care that we perish?" But when he woke and looked at them, they lost their fright. Remembering it afterward, they said that he rebuked the wind and bade the sea be still. The storm which had dropped over the hills upon the dangerous lake ceased as suddenly as it had come, and there was a great calm. "Why are you so fearful?" said Jesus. "How is it that you have no faith?"

On the other side of the lake Jesus went into the country of the Gadarenes. In the hills of that rough region there were caves which were used as tombs, and in the hills roundabout the tombs a man out of his mind had taken shelter. According to the cruel custom of the times, an insane man would ordinarily have been in chains; but this man had such mad strength that he had broken the fetters with which he had been bound and torn chains to pieces, and no one had been able to tame him. Night and day he was in the hills and among the tombs, crying and cutting himself with stones; but when Jesus came up from the lake, the poor, mad creature recognized in him someone different from all the other human figures whose approach would set him wild. He ran toward Jesus, shouting and crying, drawn toward him and yet begging him not to torment him. When Jesus asked him what his name was, he answered wildly that his name was "Legion," for the evil spirits in him were many. But before the steady eyes of Jesus and the compassion in Jesus' face, the miracle happened in the man's distracted mind and soul. The terror and the torment left him. "The unclean spirits" were gone. The madman of the tombs was healed.

Now, on the slopes of the hills there was feeding a large herd of swine. Frightened by the noise of the madman's shouting, they set off in a violent stampede, rushed down a steep slope that ended in cliffs over the lake, and, tumbling down into the water, were choked and drowned. The keepers of these pigs ran back to the town and told what had happened. It was perhaps from their excitement and their desire for an explanation sufficient to excuse themselves that the story assumed the form in which it has come down through the Gospels—that it was the devils cast out of the madman who had entered into the swine, and that Jesus gave them permission to enter. People of the town, and especially the owners of the swine, were much excited. Some of them marveled at the healing of the man who had dwelt among the tombs; but more of them were offended at what had happened to the herd. A human being was healed, but the hogs were lost. They were afraid of Jesus, and they invited him to leave their country.

When Jesus went back to the ship, the man who had been healed followed him, begging that he might go with him. But Jesus told him "No." He was to go home to his friends and tell them what great things the Lord had done for him, and how he had learned the Lord's compassion. So the man went back and spread it far and wide among the cities of the Decapolis, and many marveled at what they heard.

When Jesus had gone back across the lake, there were other needy human beings awaiting him. One of the rulers of the synagogue, named Jairus, hurried toward him and fell at his feet. "My little daughter lies at the point of death," he said. "I pray you, come and lay your hands on her, that she may be healed; and she shall live." Jesus started with him toward his house, and a crowd of people followed, thronging round him.

In the throng was a woman who for years had had a bleeding which none of the physicians to whom she had been could staunch. She had spent everything she had, and was no better, but, rather, worse. When she heard of Jesus, she came in the press behind him and touched his garment. "For," she said to herself, "if I may touch but his clothes, I shall be whole." Instantly there ran through her body a sudden certainty that she was healed. Jesus, quickly sensitive to any human contact, perceived at once the woman's appeal and the power which had gone out from him in answer, and turning about, he said, "Who was it that touched my clothes?" The disciples were astonished.

"You see the multitude thronging you," they exclaimed, "and do you say, 'Who touched me?'"

But Jesus searched the faces of the crowd to see who it was that had done this thing. Then the woman, trembling, came and fell before him, and told him all the truth, and he answered and said, "Daughter, your faith has made you whole; go in peace, and be healed of your plague."

As he was yet speaking to her, messengers came from the house of the ruler of the synagogue, whispering to him: "Your daughter is dead. Why trouble the Master any further?"

But Jesus, when he heard that, said to the ruler of the synagogue, "Do not be afraid; only believe." And he let no others follow him except Peter and James and John. Coming with them to the house of Jairus, and finding there a tumult and all the household weeping and wailing, he entered among them and said: "Why do you weep and make this commotion? The little maid is not dead, but sleeping." They looked at him with scornful disbelief. But when he had put them all out, he took the father and mother of the girl, and his disciples, and entering in where she was lying, he took her by the hand; and he said to her, "Talitha cumi," the Aramaic words which translated are, "Little maid, I say unto you, Arise." And immediately she rose and walked, and all the household were filled with great astonishment. But Jesus told them to go get something for her to eat, and to keep silent about the matter.

Two other healings are told in the Gospel of Luke alone. The first of these is of the illness of a servant of a certain centurion. Having heard of Jesus, he asked some of the elders of the Jews to go on his behalf and appeal to Jesus to come and save this servant, whom he loved. They, when they had come where Jesus was, besought him earnestly, for they said that the centurion was a man worthy of Jesus' favor. He loved the nation of Israel, they said, and had himself built a synagogue in their town. Jesus went with them; but when they were now not far from the centurion's house, he sent out friends, saying to Jesus: "Master, do not trouble yourself, for I am not worthy that you should come under my roof, nor did I think that I myself was worthy to come to you. Only say the word, and my servant shall be healed. I myself," he went on, "am a man set under authority, and I in turn have soldiers under me, and I say to this one, 'Go,' and he goeth; and to another, 'Come,' and he cometh; and to my servant, 'Do this,' and he doeth it." When

Jesus heard this, he marveled, and he said to the throng which followed him, "I tell you I have not found any faith so great as this, no, not anywhere in Israel." And the messengers who had been sent, when they returned to the house, found that the centurion's servant was well.

Not long after that Jesus came to a city called Nain. His disciples were with him, and many others. As they drew near to the gate of the city there was carried out as dead a young man, the son of a widow. Jesus looked upon this mother with compassion, and he said to her, "Do not weep." He drew near to the procession and bade those who bore the young man on his bier stand still. He spoke: "Young man, I say to you, Arise!" Then he that had been carried out as dead sat up and began to speak, and Jesus gave him to his mother.

Awe and astonishment ran through the crowd, and they said, "God has visited his people!"

After this Jesus considered that the time had come for his disciples to begin to learn to do in God's name such things as they had seen him do. So he drew the twelve round him and sent them out two by two, and he told them that they too should have power over the unclean spirits in men. They were not to take anything for their journey except a staff—no food, no money, no scrip. They were to be shod with sandals, and to carry not even an extra coat. "Whenever you enter into a house," he said, "abide there until you leave that place. And if there are any who will not receive you, when you depart, shake off the dust from your feet for a witness against them. For verily I tell you, it shall be more tolerable for Sodom and Gomorrah in the day of judgment than for that city." So out they went, and preached that men should repent, and they healed many distracted and deranged people and many of the sick.

CHAPTER XL

WHICH DEALS WITH THE STORIES OF SOME OF JESUS' MIRACLES, AND
GOES ON TO TELL OF HIS COMPASSION FOR THE WOMAN WHO CAME
TO SIMON THE PHARISEE'S HOUSE; AND OF HIS TRANSFIGURATION ON
THE MOUNTAIN, AND THE LESSON WHICH HE TAUGHT TO HIS DISCI-
PLES FROM A LITTLE CHILD.

BACK FROM their tour of the towns of Galilee, into which Jesus had sent them to preach and to heal, came the disciples, telling him all that they had done. Jesus said, "Come, let us go apart into a desert place, and rest a while." For there were many coming and going, and they had no leisure even so much as to eat. So they launched out in a ship privately to go to lonely countries somewhere on the other side of the lake; but the people saw them setting sail, and many of the throng, recognizing Jesus, ran ahead around the shore of the lake, outstripping the boat, and were on the other shore when Jesus and his disciples landed. The disciples doubtless were annoyed; but Jesus looked on these eager people with compassion. They seemed like sheep having no shepherd, and he began to teach them many things.

But as the day waned, the disciples came to him and urged him to send the people off. "This is a desert region," they said, "and it is late. Let these people go into the country round-about and buy themselves bread, for they have nothing to eat."

Jesus answered, "Go, give them something to eat."

They replied, "Shall we go and buy two hundred penny-worth of bread, and give it to them?"

"How many loaves have you now?" asked Jesus. "Go and see."

When they had looked, they came back and said, "Five, and two fishes."

437

The account of what follows is written in all four Gospels; but it is true nevertheless that we cannot clearly understand it. Here was a throng of people in the wilderness whose hunger Jesus was moved to satisfy. Was it hunger of the body which he removed, or was it the hunger of the soul which had first moved him to compassion? The accounts in the Gospels describe the production of physical food by Jesus in such quantity that all the throng was satisfied. He made the people sit down first on the grass, and not only that, but he divided them into groups. Then he took the five loaves and the fishes which the disciples had brought him, looked up to heaven and blessed these, broke the bread, and gave the broken bread and the fishes to the disciples to distribute to the people. Did individuals here and there in the little groups into which Jesus had divided the people have food of their own, which, in the spirit they had caught from Jesus, they shared with those about them? Or was there some other way beyond our ken in which Jesus added to the five loaves and two fishes, so that there was enough for all? We cannot tell. In any case, the significance of whatever it was that happened there in the wilderness would seem to be best expressed by that which, in the Gospel of John, follows the story of the feeding. The material bread becomes a parable of the spiritual bread. Jesus says, "My Father gives you the true bread out of heaven, for the bread of God is that which comes down out of heaven and gives life to the world." The people who were listening said, "Lord, always give us this bread." And Jesus answered, "I am the bread of life: he who comes to me shall never hunger; and he who believes on me shall never thirst."

In the evening after the feeding of the people, the disciples boarded their ship again and set forth across the lake for Capernaum, but Jesus went instead along the shore. Night fell, and a head wind was blowing. They rowed in distress, and about the fourth watch of the night, when they had rowed some twenty-five or thirty furlongs, they looked up and saw Jesus, walking, as they thought, upon the sea. At first they cried out, supposing that it was an apparition; but Jesus' voice

came to them: "Be of good cheer. It is I. Be not afraid."
Suddenly he was with them in the boat. They had come to
the land to which in the wind and the darkness they had been
rowing.

No sooner was it noised about that Jesus had come back
to the hither shore of the lake than sick folk began to flock to
him again. Friends of those who were too sick to walk brought
them on their beds. In villages and cities and the open country, the sick were led along the ways where Jesus was expected
to come, hopeful that they might touch even so much as the
border of his garment, and thereby be made well.

At length, Jesus passed out of the region of Galilee. He
went farther over the border into the country of Tyre and Sidon,
and entered into a house there, and desired that no one should
know it. But he could not be hidden. There was a woman
whose young daughter "had an unclean spirit," who heard of
Jesus and came and fell at his feet. She belonged to the Greek
population of the Syro-phœnician coast. She besought Jesus that
he would cast the evil spirit out of her daughter. He answered
her in words that seem to sound strangely from his lips: "Let
the children first be filled. It is not fitting to take the children's
bread and to cast it to the dogs." He was speaking as a man of
Israel might have been expected to speak to the foreigner, and
as the foreigner might have expected him to speak.

But something in his eyes must have made this Syro-
phœnician woman understand at once the whimsical compassion
which turned his words to gentleness, for she answered: "Yes,
I know, Lord; but the little dogs under the table do eat of the
children's crumbs."

"For this saying," he replied, "go your way; the evil spirit
has gone out of your daughter."

And when she came to her house, she found her daughter
healed.

Back then toward the Lake of Galilee he came; and on the
way, there met him a man who was deaf and also had an impedi-
ment in his speech, and who begged Jesus to lay his hands upon
him. Jesus drew him aside, and put his fingers into his ears and

touched his tongue, and, looking up to heaven, he drew a deep breath, and said to the man, "Ephphatha," which means, "Be opened." Then the man's hearing came back to him, and his tongue was loosened, and he spoke. Jesus enjoined him that he should tell no one what had happened; but notwithstanding this, the news was published everywhere.

But it was not only to the sick in body that Jesus' compassion went out. One day he was invited by a Pharisee to come to his house to dine. So Jesus went and sat down at the Pharisee's table. Now in that city was a woman who was a sinner; and when she knew that Jesus was sitting at dinner in the Pharisee's house, she brought an alabaster jar of perfume; and, standing back of Jesus, and weeping so that her tears fell down upon his feet, she wiped the tears away with the hair of her head, and kissed his feet, and anointed them with the perfume. When the Pharisee who had invited Jesus saw this, he said to himself, "If this man were a prophet, he would have perceived what sort of a woman this is whom he is touching; he would have known that she is a woman of the streets." But he said nothing out loud, and there was silence until Jesus himself began to speak.

"Simon," he said, "I have something to say to you."

"Teacher," Simon replied, "say on."

"There was a certain lender," Jesus continued, "who had two debtors. One of them owed him five hundred pence, and the other fifty. When they had not anything with which to pay, he forgave them both. Which of them, then, do you think will love him most?"

Simon answered, "I suppose he to whom he forgave most."

Then Jesus said, "You have judged rightly;" and as he turned to the woman, he said to the Pharisee: "Simon, do you see this woman? I entered into your house, and you gave me no water to bathe my feet. But she has wetted my feet with her tears and wiped them with her hair. You gave me no kiss of welcome; but she since the time I came in has not ceased to kiss my feet. You did not anoint my head with oil. She has anointed my feet with perfume. And so I tell you, her sins, which are many, are forgiven because she loved much. But anyone to whom little is forgiven will have little love." Then he said to the woman, "Your sins are forgiven."

And as they who sat at table with him began to whisper among themselves, "Who is this who dares even to forgive sins?" he said to the woman, "Your faith has saved you; go in peace."

But such an incident as this was only one more occasion for the growing antagonism of the Pharisees toward him. They could not tolerate what they considered his ignoring of convention. For them people belonged in classes, and as such were either to be honored or despised. They could not see, as Jesus did, the single soul which called out a love of God stronger than any pre-judgments of the law. One day a group of Pharisees and of Sadducees came and asked him for a sign from heaven. What could he show them that would attest his authority? But he answered: "When it is evening and the sky is red, you say, 'It will be fair weather to-morrow;' but if the sky is red in the morning, you say, 'It will be foul weather to-day.' You know how to distinguish the indications of the sky, yet you cannot discern the signs of these times." If they did not have enough discernment of moral cause and effect to realize the portents of danger for their world and for their generation, they would get no further sign from him. He left them, and went his way. But he knew now that threatening forces were gathering round himself, and the echo of this begins to appear increasingly in what he said to his disciples.

Out of the borders of Galilee he went again. Perhaps it was because he sensed the gathering peril from those who chose to make themselves his enemies in his own nation. Perhaps it was in order to escape again for a while the pressure of the crowds. He went into the country near Cæsarea Philippi. On the way he asked his disciples, "Who are the people saying that I am?" They gave him their various answers. They said that some of the people called him one of the prophets; others said he was Elijah; others believed that he must be John the Baptist. He turned to them. "Who do you say that I am?" he asked.

Then Peter burst suddenly into the expression of what, perhaps, all of them had begun to think. "You are Messiah!" he said.

And Jesus charged them that they should say this to no one else.

Then from that time he began to tell them that presently he must go to Jerusalem and suffer many things at the hands of the elders, the priests, and the scribes. He should be killed; but after three days, he would rise again. Peter was shocked. A Messiah who should be put to death! This seemed to him a wild, incredible thing. He took Jesus aside and began to argue and correct him. But Jesus turned upon Peter with withering rebuke. "Get behind me, Satan!" he said. "Your mind is not on the things of God, but the things of man." Then gathering round him his disciples and all others who were near him, he said: "If any man would come after me, let him deny himself, and take up his cross, and follow me. For whosoever wants most of all to save his life, shall lose it; but whosoever loses his life for my sake and the gospel's, shall save it. What would it profit a man if he gained the whole world and forfeited his soul? If any man is ashamed of me and my words in this wicked and adulterous generation, the Son of man also shall be ashamed of him when he comes in the glory of his Father, and of the holy angels." "Moreover," he said, "I tell you there are some of those who stand here to-day who shall not taste death until they see the kingdom of God come with power."

The time was coming when men must choose what loyalty they would follow, and they must be ready to pay the price of faithfulness. It was of this clear-cut decision that Jesus was thinking when he said: "Do not suppose that I came to send peace on the earth: I did not come to send peace, but a sword. For I am come to set a man at variance against his father, and the daughter against her mother, and the daughter-in-law against her mother-in-law. So that a man's foes shall be those of his household. He that loves father or mother or son or daughter more than me is not worthy of me. Nor he that will not take up his cross and follow me."

Meanwhile in Jesus' own soul a light was burning, the increasing light of his willingness to face the danger which lay ahead. One day he took with him three of the disciples, Peter and James and John, and together they went up into a high mountain. There as they watched him on the heights, it seemed to them that his whole form was bathed in radiance. He stood above them as one transfigured, his face shining and his garments white as light. They were overcome with awe. They said they saw Moses and Elijah there talking with him, and Peter began to cry out about building three tabernacles for Jesus and for them. They said also that out of a cloud that floated across the mountain top they heard the voice of God himself, saying, "This is my beloved Son; hear him." Then this vision passed. Gazing about, they saw that there was no one there save Jesus only with themselves. He had come and had said, "Rise up, and do not be afraid." And as they came down from the mountain, Jesus charged that they should speak of their vision to no one until after he himself had risen from the dead.

But their thoughts were still troubled and confused. They asked Jesus, "Why do the scribes say that Elijah must come back before Messiah comes?"

He answered: "Elijah has indeed come already, but men did not know him, and did to him whatever they chose. So also must the Son of man suffer." Then they understood that when he spoke of Elijah having already come, he was speaking of John the Baptist.

At the foot of the mountain they saw the other disciples and a crowd of people pressing round them. And as soon as the crowd saw Jesus, they began to run toward him. Out of the throng one man came foremost.

"Master," he cried, "I have brought my son to you. There is a dumb spirit in him which seizes him and dashes him down, so that he foams and grinds his teeth, and he is wasting away. I appealed to your disciples, that they should cast the spirit out, and they could not."

Then Jesus answered: "O generation without faith, how

long shall I be with you? How long shall I bear with you?" And to the man he said, "Bring your son to me." Then the boy was brought, and, as he stood before Jesus, a convulsion seized him, and he fell on the ground, wallowing and foaming. Jesus asked the father, "How long has it been since this has happened to him?"

The man answered, "Ever since he was a child." And he went on to tell Jesus how sometimes the boy would fall into the water, and sometimes into the fire. "But if thou canst do anything," he cried, "have pity on us, and help us."

Jesus echoed those first faint words, those doubtful words which had showed how timid was the father's hope. "If thou canst!" he repeated. Then to the man he said, "All things are possible to him who believes."

And the man cried out in answer, "I believe;" and then, "Oh, help my unbelief!"

Then Jesus turned to the boy and commanded the mad spirit in him to depart. The boy gave a wild cry, raved, and fell as though he were dead, so that most of the people crowding round said, "He is dead." But Jesus took him by the hand, and lifted him up, and the boy arose, and Jesus gave him to his father. And later on that day, when the disciples came to him and asked him, "Why could we not cast out the evil spirit?" he answered, "This kind can come out only through much prayer."

Another lesson he taught the disciples on a day not long thereafter. Jesus had come with them to Capernaum; and when they had reached the house where they were going, he asked them, "What was it that you were discussing on the road?"

They fell into an embarrassed silence because they had been disputing with one another who should be the greatest. He sat down and called the twelve around him, and he said to them, "If any man wants to be first, he shall be the last of all and the servant of all." Then he took a little child and set him in the midst of them, and, taking the little child in his arms, he said: "Whosoever shall receive one such little child in my name receives me, and whosoever receives me, receives not me but Him who sent me."

John, perhaps because he wanted to change the subject from the dispute about greatness, concerning which all of them had been much ashamed, said to him: "Master, we saw a man casting out devils in your name, and we forbade him because he does not follow in our company."

But Jesus went on to say: "Do not forbid him, for no man who does a mighty work in my name shall soon thereafter speak evil of me. He who is not against us is for us. Any man who shall give you even a cup of water to drink because you are Christ's, I tell you he shall by no means lose his reward." Then Jesus brought them back to the truth which he had made them listen to when he had set the child in their midst, and he said, "Whoever causes one of these little ones who believe on me to stumble, it were better for him that a millstone were hanged about his neck and he were thrown into the sea." And again he said: "Salt is good; but if the salt has lost its saltness, what will you use for seasoning? Have salt in yourselves, and be at peace one with another."

But Peter came to him and wanted to ask him a question. "How often," he said, "must I forgive anyone who does a wrong to me? Shall I forgive him seven times?"

Jesus answered: "No, I do not tell you till seven times; say rather till seventy times seven." Then he told Peter and the other disciples a story to make plain to them how poor a thing it is for one to be grudging in forgiveness when he himself may have been forgiven so much more. He said: "There was a certain king once who had an accounting with his servants. One of them owed him a vast sum of money; and when it was found that he had nothing to pay, the king demanded that the man and all his family should be sold into slavery, and so the debt be paid. But the man fell down on his knees and begged him to have patience with him, and he would pay all he owed. So the king, moved with compassion, released him, and forgave him all his debt. But that servant, going out, found one of his fellow-servants who owed him a few pennies, and, taking him by the throat, he demanded that he should pay him what he owed. Then this fellow-servant besought him, as he himself before had besought the king, to have patience, and presently he would pay everything that was due. But the man would not. Instead, he had his fellow-servant thrown into prison until the debt was settled. Then when the other servants saw what had been done, they were very sorry, and came and told the king. And he called the first servant before him. He denounced him for his wicked cruelty, because, although he himself had had his debt forgiven, he was willing to have no mercy on the man who owed him a debt. So the king handed him over to punishment until he should pay everything that was due."

When he had finished that story, Peter knew what Jesus meant when he had refused to set limits for his forgiveness. How could he talk now of seven times being enough to forgive some other man by whom he had been wronged, if he remembered how many times God had forgiven him?

THE CENTURION

THE CHILD IN THE MIDST

CHAPTER XLI

CONCERNING "THE GOSPEL ACCORDING TO SAINT JOHN" AND ITS
STORIES OF THE VISIT OF NICODEMUS TO JESUS, OF JESUS' MEETING
WITH THE WOMAN OF SAMARIA BY JACOB'S WELL, AND THE HEALING
OF THE MAN BORN BLIND; AND THE PARABLES OF THE LOST SHEEP,
THE LOST COIN, THE PRODIGAL SON, AND THE GOOD SAMARITAN; AND
WHAT JESUS SAID TO THE YOUNG MAN WHO WAS VERY RICH.

HE STORY of the life of Jesus which we have
been following is woven from accounts which
are written in the Gospels of Matthew, Mark,
and Luke. The fourth Gospel was written
later than these three others. It is further
away, therefore, from a fresh remembrance of
what Jesus had said and done. Moreover, the Gospel often
seems to be more of a meditation than a history. Yet its
accounts must also be included if we are to see the full picture
of Jesus as men remembered him. Here, then, are some of
the glimpses into the spirit of Jesus which this Gospel alone
affords:

The world in which Jesus lived was full of many people
who were sick and sad, and often, as we have already seen, it
was among these sick and sad folk that he moved; but one of
the first pictures in the fourth Gospel is that of Jesus in the
midst of joy. "There was a marriage at Cana of Galilee, and
the mother of Jesus was there, and Jesus also was bidden, and
his disciples, to the marriage." With this beginning the Gospel
goes on to recount its tradition that, during the banqueting
which followed, the wine gave out, and when Jesus' mother
came and told him of it, he caused water-jars to be filled with
water; and that he turned this water into wine. And so, says
the evangelist, he "manifested forth his glory; and his disciples
believed on him."

447

Another early chapter in this fourth Gospel tells of a visit to Jesus in Jerusalem by a member of the Sanhedrin named Nicodemus. To Nicodemus Jesus said that "Unless a man be born again, he cannot see the kingdom of God."

Nicodemus was astonished. "How can a man be born again when he is old?" he wanted to know.

And Jesus answered: "Unless a man be born of water and of the Spirit, he cannot enter into the kingdom of God. That which is born of the flesh is flesh; and that which is born of the Spirit is spirit. Do not be astonished that I have said to you 'You must be born again.' The wind blows where it lists, and you hear the sound of it, but you cannot tell whence it comes and whither it goes. So is every one who is born of the Spirit." Other words also are added in the Gospel as having been part of this conversation between Nicodemus and Jesus; and at the end of it the evangelist adds his own conclusion. "For God so loved the world, that he gave his only begotten Son, that whosoever believeth in him should not perish, but have everlasting life."

On another day, according to the same fourth Gospel, as Jesus was going north through Samaria, he came to the place where there was the ancient well of Jacob. At mid-day Jesus sat by the well to rest, while the disciples had gone to a near-by town to buy food. A woman of Samaria came to the well to draw water. Now, between the Samaritan people and the Jews there was an old suspicion and dislike, and when Jesus asked the Samaritan woman to give him a drink of the water which she was drawing from the well, she was offended.

"How does it happen that you, a Jew, ask a drink of me, a Samaritan woman?" she said.

But Jesus' love of people was too wide to recognize a difference between different names and nations. He began to talk with her about this water which she was drawing from the well. Many a time she had been there. Many a time she would come again. It was weary business forever filling water-jars to slake the thirst of people who would be thirsting again to-morrow. Moreover, Jesus saw that there was in the woman another thirst which the water could not quench. Her soul was thirsty, thirsty for a better knowledge of the living God; and Jesus said: "Every one who drinks of this water shall thirst again. But whosoever drinks of the water that I shall give him shall never thirst; it shall be in him a well of water springing up into everlasting life."

The woman of Samaria still did not understand. She thought that he meant some magic kind of water which would keep her from having to come continually filling water-jars at this well. But gradually as Jesus went on talking with her, she began to be more and more impressed.

"Sir," she said, "I perceive that you are a prophet." Nevertheless, because she considered him as a Jew and therefore alien to her own people, she was on her guard against believing what he said. "Our fathers have worshiped in this mountain," she argued, "but you say that Jerusalem is the place where men ought to worship."

Then he answered: "Woman, believe me, the hour is coming when neither in this mountain, nor yet at Jerusalem, shall men worship the Father. . . . God is a Spirit: and they that worship him must worship him in spirit and in truth."

Of another woman also there is a picture in this Gospel. Once a group of Pharisees and scribes came to Jesus, dragging with them a woman whom they declared they had taken in adultery. They said that the law was that a woman who had sinned in this fashion should be stoned to death; but what did Jesus say? They wanted to lead him into a trap. They knew that his loving-kindness would make him pitiful toward this woman. But if he dared excuse her, he would be guilty of excusing one whom the law condemned. Jesus looked at them in silence, and answered not a word. Then he stooped down, and with his finger he began to make letters in the dust. As they pressed round him, clamoring for an answer, he straightened himself and said: "Whichever one among you is free from sin, let him cast the first stone at her." Then he stooped down again, and began once more to write something on the ground. They, when they had heard what he said, stole away, angry and embarrassed, from the eldest down to the last; and Jesus was left alone except for the woman standing there before him. He rose and turned to her. "Woman," he said, "where are your accusers? Has no one condemned you?"

She said, "No one, Lord."

Then Jesus said: "Neither do I condemn you. Go your way, and from this time forward sin no more."

In this same Gospel which bears the name of John there is another story of the compassion of Jesus. There was a certain man who had been blind ever since he was born, and Jesus saw him sitting by the roadside. He stooped, made clay from the dust of the ground, put it on the blind man's eyes, and told him to go wash in the pool which was called Siloam. The blind man rose, groped his way to the water, bathed his eyes—and suddenly he saw. All his neighbors and the people who had been familiar with him as a roadside beggar, began to ask one another: "Is not this the same man that sat and begged?" Some said, "This is he." Others said, "No, but somebody like him." But he said, "I am the man."

Then they all wanted to know how it was that his eyes had got their sight again, and he told them of Jesus and of what he had done. When they asked him where Jesus was, he did not know. So the people brought this man who formerly had been blind to the Pharisees, and the first thing the Pharisees took note of was that he had been healed on the Sabbath day, at which they took immediate offense. They questioned him as to how he had been given his sight, and he told them of Jesus and of what Jesus had done. But they were still angry about what they said was the breaking of the Sabbath law. Moreover, they did not believe that the man was telling the truth. Accordingly, they sent for his parents. "Is this your son?" they said. "And do you say that he was born blind? How does it happen then that now he sees?"

His parents said that it certainly was their son; but as to how he had been healed, they did not know. So the Pharisees went back again to questioning the man himself. They wanted him to tell them over again what had happened, and they tried to browbeat him into saying that Jesus must be a sinner because he had broken the law by healing on the Sabbath day. But the man stuck stubbornly to his own belief. "We know," he said, "that God does not hear sinners; but if anyone worships God, and does God's will, God does hear him. This man could not have done anything unless he had been of God."

This made them only the more angry. "Give the glory to God," they demanded; "we know that this man is a sinner."

But the man who had been blind answered: "I do not know anything about whether he is a sinner or not. There is one thing I know, which is that I used to be blind, and that now I can see."

Then angrily the Pharisees drove him away. But Jesus heard of this, and came and found him; and when he had talked with him, this man who had been blind turned to Jesus with a great belief, and worshiped him.

It was after this that Jesus began to speak of himself as coming among men like a good shepherd coming among his sheep. "The thief comes," he said, "only that he may steal, and kill, and destroy. I have come that they may have life, and may have it abundantly. I am the good shepherd; the good shepherd lays down his life for the sheep. The man who is an hireling and not the shepherd, who knows that the sheep are not his own, if he sees the wolf, leaves the sheep and flees for safety. He flees because he is an hireling, and does not care for the sheep. But I am the good shepherd, and I know my own, and my own know me. As my Father knows me, so I know the Father, and I lay down my life for the sheep."

Of the same spirit as this teaching of Jesus are three of his beautiful parables which are written in the Gospel of Luke. In two illustrations and in a longer story, Jesus described what the love of God is like. Some of the Pharisees and scribes had been complaining because, they said, he associated with sinners. And Jesus said:

"Which man among you, if he should have a hundred sheep and should lose one of them, would not leave the ninety-nine sheep where they were, and go after the lost one until he find it? And when he had found it, he would lay it on his shoulders, rejoicing, and would call his friends and neighbors together, and say, 'Rejoice with me, for I have found my sheep which was lost.' I tell you that likewise there shall be more joy in heaven over one sinner who repents than over the ninety and nine people, already righteous, who do not need repentance.''

"Or suppose there is a woman who has ten silver coins. If she loses one coin, does she not light a lamp, and sweep the house, and search everywhere until she finds it? When she has found it, she will go and tell the good news to her friends and neighbors also. Like this too is the joy in the presence of the angels of God over one sinner who repents.''

And then he went on to tell the lovely story which is called "The Parable of the Prodigal Son," but might also be called "The Parable of the Loving Father." "There was a certain man," he said, "who had two sons, and the younger of these said to him, 'Father, give me the part of your property which will belong to me.' So the father divided what he had between his two sons. Not many days after that the younger son gathered everything he had together, and set out on a journey to a distant country, and there he wasted his property with riotous living. When he had spent everything he had, there occurred a great famine in that country, and he began to be in want. So he went and hired himself to one of the citizens of that land, and this man sent him into his fields to feed swine. No one gave him anything now, and he was ready to eat the husks which the swine ate. Then when he came to himself, he said: "How many hired servants of my father have food enough and to spare, and I perish here with hunger! I will arise and go to my father, and I will say to him: "Father, I have sinned against God and in your sight also. I am not worthy any more to be called your son. Make me as one of your hired servants." ' So he went back to his father.

But when he was still a long way off, his father saw him and was moved with pity, and ran and fell on his neck and kissed him. Then the son said: 'Father, I have sinned against God and

in your sight.   I am not worthy any more to be called your son.'
But before he could finish what he had meant to say, his father
called to the servants: 'Bring out quickly the best robe and put
it on him.   Put a ring on his hand and sandals on his feet.   And
take the calf which has been fatted and kill it, and let us eat
and be merry; for this my son was dead and is alive again, he
was lost and is found!'

"So they all began to be merry.

"Now, the elder son was in the field, and as he came back
and drew near the house he heard music and dancing.   So he
called one of the servants and asked what this meant, and the
servant told him, 'Your brother has come, and your father has
killed the fatted calf, because he has received him safe and
sound.'   So he was angry, and would not go in; and his father
came out and entreated him.   But he said to his father: 'Look,
for these many years I have served you.   I never disobeyed a
word of yours; and yet you never gave me a kid, that I might
make merry with my friends.   But when this your son came, this
son who squandered your property with harlots, you have killed
for him the fatted calf.'   But his father answered: 'Son, you
are always with me, and everything that is mine is yours.   But
it was right to make merry and be glad; for this your brother
was dead, and is alive again; he was lost, and is found.' "

On another day there came another and seemingly very
eager figure.   A young man who was rich ran to Jesus, and
kneeled before him.   "Good master," he said, "what shall I do
to inherit eternal life?"   Jesus asked him whether he did not
know the Commandments; that he should not kill, that he
should not commit adultery, nor steal, nor bear false witness,
nor covet, and that he should honor his father and his mother.
"Master," he said, "I have observed all these Commandments
since I was a child."

Then Jesus, as he looked at him, loved him; and he said:
"There is one thing you lack, if you would be perfect.   Go and
sell all you have, and give to the poor.   Then your treasure will
be in heaven, and you can come and follow me."   But the young

man's face fell as he listened, and sadly he went away, for he would not leave his great possessions.

Then Jesus said to the disciples, "How hard it is for those who have riches to enter into the kingdom of God!" When his disciples showed in their looks that they were amazed to hear him say so, Jesus said: "You children! Can you not see how hard it is for those who trust in riches to enter into the kingdom of God? It is as easy for a camel to go through a needle's eye as it is for a rich man to enter into God's kingdom." But they were astonished all the more. And they said, "Who can be saved then?" And Jesus answered: "With men it is impossible, but not with God; with God all things are possible."

Then Peter began to remind Jesus that he and the other disciples had left their homes and families for his sake, and Jesus told them that more than all the beautiful things they had left behind them they should have again, though they should have to pass through persecution before they found them. And he added, "There are many who are first who shall be last, and the last first."

Another story also Jesus told to show the sort of pity men ought to have toward one another, and he made it the more striking by choosing as its hero a Samaritan, a man of that race whom the Jews despised. It happened that a lawyer had been trying to ask him questions which he thought Jesus might not be able to answer. "What should I do," he said, "to inherit eternal life?" Jesus asked him whether he knew the Scriptures, and, if so, what he had read there.

The lawyer answered this: "You must love God with your whole heart, with your whole soul, with your whole strength, and with your whole mind; also, you must love your neighbor as yourself."

Jesus told him that he had given the right answer to his own question; if he lived up to it, then he should really live.

But the man, who was seeking an excuse rather than an answer, asked another question. "But who is my neighbor?" he said.

Then Jesus told him this parable: "There was a certain

man once who was traveling from Jerusalem to Jericho, and on the road robbers fell upon him, stripped off his clothes, wounded him, and then fled, leaving him half dead. Now, it so happened that a priest came down that way; and when he saw the injured man, he slipped past on the other side. In the same way a Levite, when he had reached the place, came and looked at the hurt man lying there, but he also then went by on the other side. But then came a Samaritan who was journeying that way; and when he saw the man, he had pity on him, and bound up his hurts, pouring oil and wine upon his wounds, and set him on his own steed, and brought him to an inn, to take care of him. The next morning when he went on his way, he took out two shillings and gave them to the innkeeper, and said, 'Take care of this man, and anything more that you spend I will repay you when I come again.' "

The lawyer had been listening, listening to a very different answer from the one which he thought he would get. "Who is my neighbor?" he had asked. He wanted Jesus to make a definition as to who his neighbors were—his relatives, his friends, the people who lived in the same street. Very well, then. If they made up his neighbors, then the rest of the world were not his neighbors, and he need have no concern with them. But Jesus turned the matter round. It was not a grudging question of who the neighbors were to whom he had an obligation. The question was of where the opportunity opened for him to go and be a neighbor. "Which one of these three," asked Jesus, "was neighbor to the man who fell among thieves?" The lawyer had to answer, "He that took pity on him." And Jesus said, "Then you go and do likewise."

CHAPTER XLII

WHICH DEALS WITH MANY OF THE SWIFT INCIDENTS OF JESUS' LIFE,
AND HIS REPLIES TO MANY PEOPLE WHO CAME TO HIM WITH QUES-
TIONS AS HE WENT ON HIS WAY FROM GALILEE INTO JUDÆA; AND
WHICH TELLS OF THE HEALING OF BLIND BARTIMÆUS AT JERICHO,
AND THE ENTRY AT LENGTH OF JESUS THROUGH THE SHOUTING MUL-
TITUDES INTO JERUSALEM.

THE TIME came when Jesus felt that he must leave Galilee. Galilee was familiar ground. In Galilee were many people who loved him. In Jerusalem he would be counted an outsider, and in Jerusalem were men jealous of his influence and ready to do anything they could to destroy his work. But Jerusalem was the capital of his nation. Jerusalem was the center of its religion and its life. And so to Jerusalem he felt that he must go.

He gathered his disciples, therefore, and they took the road which led south from Galilee. They saw that it was toward Jerusalem that his face was steadfastly set. One evening, as they were drawing near to a village in the Samaritan country, he sent two of the disciples as messengers to ask if they might be received there for the night. But the villagers would have none of them. When this message was brought back to Jesus, James and John were indignant. They asked Jesus whether fire could not be called down from heaven to burn up such a place as that. But Jesus rebuked them. He had not come to destroy men's lives, he said, but to save them. He went on to another village; and the one which had refused to welcome him never knew what it had lost.

At another point on the journey there came a man who said he wanted to join Jesus, and to follow him, no matter where he went. Through the words of Jesus' reply it is as though one could see him smile. "Foxes have holes, and the birds of the air have nests," he said, "but the Son of man has no place in which to lay his head." If a man was ready to follow that sort of master, let him come.

Two other men also were drawn toward Jesus; but both of them had excuses why they must delay a while and do something else first; and Jesus said, "No one is fit for the kingdom of God if he puts his hand to the plow and then looks back."

Increasingly in what he said as he went on his way to Jerusalem, Jesus made those who were round him understand that there was much which they had to bear if they should continue to be his disciples. They were going into danger; and they must be ready to strip themselves of fear and of self-seeking if they were to face the hard things which lay ahead. "I have come to cast fire upon the earth," he said, "and what if the fire be already kindled? I have a baptism to be baptized with, and I am under stress till it is finished!" And he said to the crowd that flocked about him, who thought perhaps, as crowds often do, that they could gain the blessings of the spirit merely by listening to great words and imagining that they were affected: "Any one of you who does not bear his own cross and come after me cannot be my disciple. For suppose one of you should wish to build some great thing—a tower, for example—would you not sit down first and calculate the cost of it, and see whether you have enough to finish? Otherwise, when you have laid the foundation, and are not able to carry the building through, all the onlookers shall begin to mock and say, 'This man began to build, and was not able to finish.'

"Or, again, what if a king marches out to encounter another king in war. Will he not sit down first and take counsel whether he is able with ten thousand men to meet the enemy who comes against him with twenty thousand? If not, while his foe is still a long way off, he sends his representatives and asks conditions of peace. So it is that whichever one of you will not pay the price of all that he has, cannot be my disciple."

Jesus never let the questions or the answers of those who gathered round him drift into empty argument. There were then, as always, plenty of people ready to speculate about God in general; Jesus brought them face to face with the immediate matter of God's particular will for them. Once a crowd was agog with speculation about a group of Galilæans who had been brutally killed by the soldiers of Pilate, the Roman governor of Jerusalem, in a disturbance at the Temple. They wanted to know whether these Galilæans were any greater sinners than the rest of the people, and was that the reason why God had let them thus be slain? But Jesus checked their theorizing. "You will all perish equally," he said, "unless you repent."

On another day somebody asked him, "Lord, will only a few be saved?" And he answered, "You try to enter in through the narrow door, for I tell you there are many who will try to enter and shall not be able." Then he went on to picture those who had talked much about the Kingdom, but had done little to enter it, as being like people who come and knock at the door of a house at nightfall. "When the master of the house," he said, "gets up and shuts the door, then you come and stand outside and knock at the door and call him, asking that he let you in. And he shall answer, 'I do not know who you are or where you come from.' You will begin to say, 'Why, we ate and drank in your company, and you taught in our streets.' But he shall say: 'I tell you, I do not know you. Be off, you doers of evil.' There shall be weeping and gnashing of teeth when you see Abraham, and Isaac, and Jacob, and all the prophets, in the kingdom of God, and you yourselves cast out. For men shall come from the east, and from the west, and from the north, and the south, and shall find place in the kingdom of God. But there are those who are last now who shall be first, and there are some who are first who shall be last."

There were those, of course, who did not understand, or who did not want to hear, this heroic note in Jesus' message. They thought they could use him for their own ends. One day a man came to Jesus and pleaded with him to use his influence to have the man's brother divide with him an inheritance which he had received. "Man, who made me a judge or a divider over you?" Jesus answered. And then he continued: "Take care, and keep yourselves from covetousness. A man's life does not consist in the abundance of things which he possesses. There was a certain rich man once whose land yielded plentifully. So he began to say to himself, 'What shall I do now when I have not room enough in which to put away all my harvest? This is what I am going to do: I will pull down my barns, and build bigger ones; and in them I will store away all my grain and my goods. And I will say to my soul, "Soul, you have goods laid up now for many years; take your ease, eat, drink, and be merry." ' But God said to him, 'O fool, this night your soul is required of you; and all these things you have stored up, whose then shall they be?' Thus it is with every one who lays up treasure for himself, and is not rich toward God."

Yet it was hard for even those who were closest to Jesus to forget themselves and what they hoped to gain. They did not want large barns and stored-up goods like the rich man in the story, but they wanted rank and honor and favored place in the sort of kingdom which they kept thinking Jesus would create. One day there came to him James and John, with the confidential manner of men who do not want others to hear what they are about to say. "Master," they began, "we have something we want to ask of you, and we want you to say you will do it."

"What is it that you want me to do?" he asked.

Then they answered, "Promise us that we may sit, one on your right hand and the other on your left, when you come into your glory."

Said Jesus: "You do not know what this is that you are asking. Are you able to drink the cup that I shall drink, and can you be baptized with the baptism that I am baptized with?"

The matter was taking another turn now; but these men who had come to him with their ambitions nevertheless did have great purpose in them too. They answered, "Yes, we are able."

"Well, you shall drink the cup that I drink of," said Jesus, "and you shall indeed be baptized with my baptism; but to sit on my right hand and my left is not mine to give. That belongs to those for whom it shall have been prepared by my Father."

Presently the word spread among the other ten of the twelve disciples as to what James and John had asked. These others were indignant. So Jesus called the whole group together; and he said: "You know that among the Gentile people those who are made rulers lord it over everyone, and with them, to be a great man is to exercise authority. Among you it is not so. Whoever would become great among you, shall be your minister. Whoever will be the first, shall be the servant of all. For I tell you that the Son of man did not come to be ministered to but to minister, and to give his life as a ransom for many."

Another parable which Jesus told about this time may have made James and John remember what he had said to them. One day at a dinner Jesus watched how some of the guests crowded forward and took the seats of honor, and he said to the disciples: "When you are invited by any man to a marriage banquet, do not sit down in the seat of honor, for perhaps a more distinguished man than you will have been invited, and the host, who invited both you and him, may come and say, 'Let this man have your place,' and you shall go with shame to take the lowest seat. But when you are invited, go and sit down in the humblest place; and then the host who has invited you may come and say, 'Friend, go up higher.' And thus you shall be honored in the presence of all who sit at the table with you."

Another parable also he told. "There were two men," he said, "who went up into the Temple to pray. One was a Pharisee, and the other a publican. The Pharisee stood and prayed by himself: 'O God, I thank thee that I am not as the rest of men, extortioners, unjust, adulterers' (then, with a side glance at the publican standing there also in the Temple), 'or even as this publican. I fast twice every week, and I give tithes of everything I get.' But the publican, standing far off, would not even so much as lift his eyes toward heaven, but he beat upon his breast, crying, 'God, be merciful to me a sinner.' I tell you that this man went down to his house forgiven rather than the other: for every man who exalts himself shall be abased; and he who humbles himself shall be exalted."

Day by day people came to Jesus and asked him questions

and the memory of the answers which he gave has come down
through the Gospels and is written there in the traditions of his
teaching—teaching about marriage, about prayer, and about
perseverance in prayer; about the need of watchfulness for the
great moments when opportunities come from God, about
responsibility for the gifts which God has given, and always
about the love of God which makes every single human soul of
value. It was this latter message which Jesus loved to dwell
upon, and which he was continually exemplifying in his own
attitude to those he met. One day a number of mothers tried
to bring their little children to him, begging that he should
put his hands on them with his blessing. Self-importantly the
disciples tried to discourage them, as though, in their opinion,
Jesus must be concerned about larger matters. But when Jesus
saw what they were doing, he was indignant, and he said, "Let
those little children come to me, and do not stop them. God's
kingdom is made up of such as they. I tell you that anyone who
does not receive the kingdom of God in the spirit of a little
child shall by no possibility enter in at all." Then he took the
children up in his arms and laid his hands on them in blessing.

On another day, as he was entering a village, ten lepers
met him; and, as was the custom of lepers, they dared not come
close to Jesus and those who were with him, but stood at a
distance and cried, "Jesus, Master, have mercy on us!" When
he saw them, he answered, "Go show yourselves to the priests."
And as they went, they were cleansed. One of them, when he
saw that he was healed, turned back, and with a loud voice
began to glorify God. And he threw himself upon his face at
Jesus' feet, and thanked him. Now this man was a Samaritan.
"Were there not ten cleansed?" Jesus said. "Is there not one
who has come back to give glory to God except this alien?" But
to him he said, "Rise up and go your way. Your faith has made
you whole."

He was drawing nearer now to Jerusalem, and had come
almost to the gates of Jericho. There by the road a blind man
was begging, whose name was Bartimæus. He heard the foot-

steps of the crowd, asked what was happening, and learned that it was Jesus of Nazareth who was coming along the way. "Jesus, Son of David," he cried, "have mercy on me!"

The people standing near him, rebuked him. They told him to keep still and leave Jesus alone; but louder and louder he kept crying.

Jesus stopped. "Call that man," he said.

Then some of them passed the message to the blind man. "Courage," they said, "he is calling you."

Flinging off the cloak that was around him, Bartimæus sprang up and made his way toward Jesus.

"What is it," said Jesus, "that you want me to do for you?"

"O Master," he answered, "that I may have my sight!"

Then to him, as to the leper, Jesus proclaimed the answer to his prayer. He could go in peace. His faith had healed him. And the man who had been blind, seeing now, followed Jesus on his way.

Through the gates of Jericho Jesus went into the city itself, and in Jericho there lived a man named Zacchæus, who was the chief tax-collector and was rich. He was curious to see Jesus; but, being a short man, he could not look over the heads of the people who crowded the road. So, running on in advance, he climbed into a sycamore tree to look down at Jesus, for Jesus was to pass that way.

When Jesus came to that place, he looked up. "Zacchæus," he said, "hurry and come down. To-day I shall be staying at your house."

So Zacchæus made haste, and down he came, and went ahead to his house, and joyfully greeted Jesus there.

When the crowd saw this, they began to criticize. "Look," they said, "he is gone in to lodge with a man who is a sinner."

But Zacchæus stood before Jesus, and he said, "Lord, I am going to give half of my goods to the poor; and if I have extorted anything wrongfully from any man, I will restore it four times over."

And Jesus answered, "Salvation is come to this house to-day, for you, Zacchæus, the publican, are also a son of Abraham.

And the Son of man is come to seek and to save that which was lost."

Past Jericho he went, and on to the little town of Bethany, not far from Jerusalem. There he entered the house of a man named Simon, who had been a leper. And as he was at the table there came a woman with an alabaster flask of very costly perfume. This flask she broke, and poured the perfume upon Jesus' head. Some of them who saw this were angry, and they said: "What sense is there in this waste of perfume? It might have been sold for over three hundred shillings and the money given to the poor." So they grumbled against the woman.

But Jesus said: "Let her alone; why do you trouble her? It is a beautiful thing she has done to me. She has done what she could. She has anointed my body beforehand for the burial. And solemnly I tell you that wherever this gospel shall be preached through the whole world, what she has done shall be told in remembrance of her."

In the Gospel which bears the name of John (that Gospel which, as we have already seen, was written much later than the others) there is recorded the tradition of how Jesus raised from the dead a man named Lazarus, whose sisters were Mary and Martha, and to one of whom he spoke the beautiful and never-since-forgotten words, "I am the resurrection, and the life: he that believeth in me, though he were dead, yet shall he live: and whosoever liveth and believeth in me shall never die." No such account as this one of the raising of Lazarus appears in any one of the other three Gospels. The names of Lazarus and of Mary and of Martha do appear, but in different connections. Jesus told this story: "There was once a rich man," he said, "who wore purple and fine linen and ate luxuriously every day. Meanwhile at his gate, full of sores, there lay a beggar named Lazarus, who would have been thankful to be fed with the crumbs that fell from the rich man's table, and the street dogs came and licked his sores.

"The time came when the beggar died, and he was carried by angels into Abraham's bosom. Then the rich man also died, and was buried, and, being in torment, he lifted up his eyes and saw afar off Abraham, and Lazarus in his bosom. 'Father Abraham,' he cried, 'have mercy on me, and send Lazarus, that he may dip the tip of his finger in water, and cool my tongue; for I am tormented in this flame.' But Abraham answered: 'Son, remember that in your lifetime you received your good things, and Lazarus evil things. Now he is comforted, and you are tormented. Moreover, between us and you there is a great gulf fixed: so that they who would pass from hence to you cannot; neither can they pass to us who would come from where you are.' 'Then,' said the rich man, 'I pray you therefore, that you would send Lazarus to my father's house, to warn my five brethren, lest they also come to this place of torment.' But Abraham said, 'They have Moses and the prophets; let them hear them.' 'No, father Abraham,' the rich man cried, 'but if one went to them from the dead, they will repent.' But Abraham answered, 'If they will not hear Moses and the prophets, they will not be persuaded, though one rose from the dead.' "

So it is in a parable here that the name of Lazarus appears, and it may be that the account concerning Lazarus in the Gospel of John is a parable also—a parable of the life eternal.

Of Mary and Martha, who are mentioned as the sisters of Lazarus, there is given in the Gospel of Luke one single picture. When Jesus went one day into the village where they lived, Martha invited him into their house. Mary her sister also was there, and she sat at Jesus' feet and listened to his words. Martha was distracted with all the flutter of her preparations, and when she saw Mary sitting there, she was annoyed, and came to Jesus and said: "Master, have you no care that my sister leaves all the serving to me? Tell her to come and help me." But he answered her: "Martha, Martha, you are anxious and troubled about many things. Only one thing is needful. It is Mary who has made the good choice, and it shall not be taken away from her."

The companionship of Mary's spirit meant more to Jesus than the food which Martha was so busy to prepare. A shadow lay upon the road ahead. He was about to enter Jerusalem, Jerusalem which seemed so beautiful and so sacred, but which for him was dark with peril. He was foreseeing what might happen when he said concerning the woman who anointed him in Simon the Pharisee's house, "She has done this for my burial."

Why was Jerusalem dangerous for him?

Because, in the first place, men who lived in the capital were jealous of one who came from Galilee. There had been a discussion once about Jesus in Jerusalem among some of the men of the ruling council, and one of them, Nicodemus, had spoken in Jesus' favor; but the others turned upon him in contempt. They wanted to know whether he had ever read the Scriptures. If he had, they said, he would find that no prophet had ever come out of Galilee; and in their opinion, none ever would.

Because also the chief men of the church were offended at Jesus for not keeping their traditions. They said he did things such as healing on the Sabbath, which pious people would not do.

Because there were those who whispered that he did not love his own nation enough. He was no patriot, they said. He associated with outsiders. He spoke of Samaritans as though they were as good as Jews.

Because the men who held high office in Jerusalem feared what would happen when so many people followed him. There might be some disturbance, they thought, which they could not control, and then the Roman authority would turn them out of office.

And, above all, because there were men in Jerusalem who pretended to be religious, and were members and leaders of the church, and yet were secretly guilty of mean and cruel things. They knew that Jesus knew; they recognized that he had no fear; and they were sullenly uneasy lest he should expose them to the people. They remembered that once before he had said of some of them that they were like people who washed the outside of a cup and left the inside of it full of all uncleanness. He said they measured off even the insignificant little spices into proper parts when it was a question of the tithing law, but cared nothing for justice and the love of God. He said they were like hollow tombs hidden under the surface, which men walking over them thought to be solid ground.

Men like these were waiting in Jerusalem, with minds suspicious and with bitter hearts. They had already grown so hostile to Jesus that they had begun to plan how they might put him to death. They told themselves high-sounding reasons why they should do so. They said that wherever he went, there was bound to be disturbance; and too much disturbance, with the Romans as watchful as they always were, might bring some punishment down upon the nation. "It is better," they said, "that one man should die rather than that the whole nation perish."

All these things Jesus understood. The clear eyes of his spirit foresaw the future. Some time before, some of the Pharisees had tried to dismay him by bringing the news that Herod, the tetrarch of Galilee, was about to seize him. Jesus waved their threat aside. They were to go and tell "that fox" that he would go forward with his work until it was finished; and he added, "It cannot be that a prophet should perish out of Jerusalem." But then the deeper level of his emotions broke through into words: "O Jerusalem, Jerusalem, thou that killest the prophets, and stonest them that are sent unto thee, how often would I have gathered thy children together, as a hen gathers her brood under her wing, and ye would not! Behold, your house is left unto you desolate: and verily I say unto you, 'Ye shall not see me, until the time comes when ye shall say, "Blessed is he that cometh in the name of the Lord." ' "

He was coming now. He knew what might happen; but he knew also the greater victory which lay beyond. As his Father's appointed Son, he would enter into the sacred city, to bring to men there the gospel of the salvation which they must either choose or reject; but which, whether they should choose it or reject it, would at last prevail.

CHAPTER XLIII

THE NARRATIVE OF WHAT JESUS DID AND OF WHAT HE SAID IN JERU-
SALEM THROUGH THE FIRST DAYS OF "HOLY WEEK," INCLUDING THE
PARABLES OF THE TALENTS AND OF THE JUDGMENT; AND OF HOW
HE DROVE THE TRADERS OUT OF THE TEMPLE; AND OF THE ANGER
AND THE ENMITY WHICH BEGAN TO HARDEN NOW AGAINST HIM TO
BRING HIM TO HIS DEATH.

T WAS on a Sunday that Jesus entered Jerusalem, and he chose to enter it in a way which
all the city would be stirred to see. Hitherto
he had charged his disciples not to speak of
him as the Messiah, for he knew that in the
minds of many of the people the thought that
Messiah might be at hand would rouse passionate expectations
of a new kingdom created by war and tumult—the kind of kingdom upon which in the temptations he had turned his back.
But the hour had struck now when, even at the risk of mis-
understanding, he must make plain to Jerusalem that he had
come in a spiritual authority such as not even the greatest of
the prophets had claimed before.

They should see him, not only as the great preacher from
Galilee, but as the One long promised and appointed by the
living God. In the book of the prophet Zechariah it had been
written: "Tell ye the daughter of Sion, 'Behold, thy King cometh
unto thee, meek, and sitting upon an ass, and a colt the foal
of an ass.'" Jesus remembered that, and the people would
remember it, and so they would recognize the significance of
what he was about to do.

He sent two of his disciples into a near-by village to untie
a colt which was there. They did so; and when the colt was
brought to Jesus, he mounted it, and with the disciples beside
him, he set forward along the road that led over the hill of

Olivet. From the brow of the hill across the narrow intervening valley, Jerusalem, crowned by the gleaming splendor of the Temple, came full into view; and from the streets of Jerusalem men could see and hear what was happening on this road that ran from Olivet. It was the beginning of the week which culminated in the Passover, the greatest of the festivals of the Jewish year, and the pilgrims were already coming to the Holy City. Some of them, doubtless, were Galilæans who recognized Jesus and claimed him as their own. Quickly the throng began to gather round him. Some of them broke off the branches of palm trees and spread them on the road. Others put their cloaks down like a carpet for Jesus' way. Voices began to chant, and other voices took up the refrain: "Hosanna! Blessed is he that cometh in the name of the Lord. Blessed is the kingdom that cometh, the kingdom of our father David. Hosanna in the highest!"

In Jerusalem men stopped and listened. They asked one another what was happening? Who was this who was coming? And the answer ran, "This is the prophet, Jesus, from Nazareth of Galilee."

Within the gates of the city Jesus went, but those who looked for any startling action were to have to wait. He went to the Temple, and quietly he looked at what was there. Deep emotions must have been stirring in his spirit, but his lips were silent. That night he went out again to Bethany. On the morrow he would come again, and in a different way.

The next day he did come. Straight to the Temple he went. In the Temple enclosure were inner and outer courts, and some of these courts were shrill with the noises of a crowded market. Money-changers had their booths there, to change the ordinary money of the people who came to the Temple for the special coins which alone were allowed to be current in the Temple area. Sellers of animals and of birds were there, and pens of sheep and cages of doves—the sheep and doves which people could buy for sacrifices. These traders had their places through the favor of the Temple priesthood. Some of the money they made went to the men who let them make it. In the face of this greedy traffic the indignation of Jesus burned. He threw down the tables of the money-changers, and drove out the sellers of sheep and of doves. "It is written," he said, "that 'My house shall be called the house of prayer'; but ye have made it a den of thieves!"

When the chief priests heard of this, they were so angry that they were ready to destroy Jesus then and there; but they did not dare to touch him, for the crowd, which is always drawn by boldness, pressed round him and hung upon his words. Nevertheless, the forces which were hostile to Jesus were being strengthened against him. These now were not only the Pharisees, who disliked him because they said he did not keep the letter of the law; not only the chief priests, who were embittered by the authority he had dared assume within the Temple, but also the Temple traders and others like them in Jerusalem who resented the idea that business should be disturbed.

In the Gospels are various brief descriptions of what Jesus taught and of what he did in the days immediately following the cleansing of the Temple. Most important were two parables in which he dared to express to the authorities in Jerusalem, to priests and other leaders of the church, the truth that they ought to be the first to welcome the message of God which he was bringing; but that instead they were too dull of heart to hear it, and might find themselves in consequence rejected by God, whom they pretended to worship and to serve.

"There was a man once who had two sons," he said; "and coming to one of these sons, he said to him, 'Son, go work to-day in the vineyard.' He answered, 'I will not.' But afterward he repented, and he went. Then the father came to the second son, and spoke to him as he had spoken to the first one. This son answered, 'I go, sir.' But he did not go. Now which of these two, do you think, did his father's will?"

He waited then for an answer. They thought that was plain enough. These men who listened to Jesus may well have shrugged their shoulders when they answered, "The first." But they were hardly prepared for the application which he gave now to the story. "I tell you," he said, "that the publicans and the harlots will go into the kingdom of God before you. John the Baptist came to you preaching righteousness, and you did not believe him; and when you saw that the publicans and harlots did believe him, not even then did you repent and believe him too."

He went on with another illustration, the point of which struck home among those who listened, and aroused in them an even deeper resentment than the other. For now he was speaking of himself and of the authority which he had from his Father and which these men were rejecting. "Listen to this further parable," he said. "There was a rich man once who planted a vineyard, set a hedge about it, made a winepress in it, and built a tower; and he leased it all to tenants, while he himself went away. When the harvest season had come, he sent some of his servants to the tenants to receive his part of what the vineyard had produced. But these men took his servants, beat them and stoned them, so that one of them was killed. He sent other representatives after these, and the tenants of the vineyard did what they had done before. So then the owner of the vineyard sent his son to them, for 'They will respect my son,' he said. But these men who had possession of the vineyard, when they saw the son, said one to another: 'Here comes the heir. Let us kill him, and take his inheritance.' So they took him, and flung him from the vineyard, and killed him. What do you think the lord of the vineyard will do to men like these?"

Jesus could tell a story with such an overwhelming impression of direct reality that some of those who listened did not at first perceive the hidden meaning in it. They answered instantly: "He will put miserable creatures like that to death, and will let the vineyard out to other tenants who will pay him his dues from the harvest."

Jesus answered: "Have you never read in the Scriptures, 'The very stone which the builders rejected is made into the corner stone: this is the Lord's way, though it is marvelous in our eyes'?" Then he turned directly to those priests and others whose sullen and growing hatred he was well aware of, and he said, "The kingdom of God shall be taken away from you, and be given to a nation which shall bring forth the fruits that belong to it." This was what they might call indeed "a hard saying"; and he went on to add: "He who falls on this stone shall be broken to pieces; but whomsoever it shall fall upon shall be ground into dust."

All of which, when the chief priests and Pharisees heard, they knew he had spoken to them.

After this the priests and some of the Pharisees, and certain also of the politicians in Jerusalem, put their heads together to see how they might trip Jesus in his talk. Insinuatingly some of them came to him and said: "Teacher, we know that you are so sincere that you do not stand in awe of anyone; you do not flinch before men of importance, but honestly teach the way of God. So we should like to ask you, Is it lawful to give tribute to Cæsar or not? Shall we give, or shall we not give?" He saw through the hypocrisy of their purpose, and he said: "Why do you make a test of me? Bring me a penny, and let me see it." So they brought one. He said: "Whose portrait and inscription is this?" "Cæsar's," they answered. "Then," said Jesus, "give to Cæsar the things that are Cæsar's, and give God the things that are God's."

In such wise Jesus spoke to those groups in Jerusalem who had set themselves against him. And he went on to explain further what he felt about them to his disciples and to others who gathered round to listen. "Beware," he said, "of the scribes, who like to go about in long robes, and to be saluted in the market places, and to take the chief seats in the synagogues, and the highest places at feasts. They devour widows' houses, and for a pretense make long prayers. So shall they receive the greater condemnation."

It was the greed and cruelty which he knew was hidden beneath the robe of religion which made the fire of Jesus' spirit leap like lightning; and, on the other hand, his pity was always going out to the poor. One day in the Temple he had sat down opposite the treasury-chest into which the worshipers dropped their offerings. He saw rich men come by, and ostentatiously put in large gifts. Then there came a poor widow, who put in two of the smallest coins. He called his disciples to him. "Truly," he said, "this poor widow has given more than all the rest who are giving to the treasury, for they have put in out of their superfluous wealth, and she has given out of her poverty; yes, given even all the living that she had."

As the days of this week went by, it became more and more evident to Jesus that the men who had power in Jerusalem had set their faces hard as flint against him. They would not receive his gospel of the love of God. They were determined to consider it as only blasphemy that he should be thought of as Messiah. Increasingly the teachings of Jesus took on a more solemn note. Looking ahead, he knew that the sort of destruction which more than once had fallen on Jerusalem would fall on it again. There should be times of terror from which not many would escape. The exact meaning of some of his words, as these have come through the remembrance of his hearers and have been recorded in the Gospels, is not easy to understand. As we read what he said, we cannot clearly tell when he is referring to actual wars and desolations which he foresaw as coming in Palestine, or when he is using instead great spiritual symbols for the awful judgments of God which should come upon an indifferent nation. But two things are unmistakable. Jesus saw that his world stood at its hour of crisis. Issues of life and death were at hand for every man's destiny. He himself might have to die; and if he did die, then the whole nation's chance for present salvation would have to go down into the dust. That was one truth. And the other of which his soul was sure was this: that whatever happened, the power of God which he felt within himself would triumph. "In those days, after that tribulation, the sun shall be darkened, and the moon shall not give her light. And the stars shall be falling from the heavens, and the powers that are in heaven shall be shaken. And then shall they see the Son of man coming in the clouds with great power and glory."

The great word for those who desired to follow him was "Be ready!" The first certainty was that they should suffer. Let them trust God, keep their courage, and face whatever should happen, unafraid. "Watch and pray," he said, "for you know not when the time is." It should be with them, he said, as it is with men whose master has gone into a far country and left them, meanwhile, in charge of his house, giving to each one his own work and duty, and commanding the porter at the door to watch. "Watch therefore," he said, "for you cannot know when the lord of the house will come, whether at evening, or at midnight, or when the cock begins to crow, or in the morning. Let him not come suddenly and find you sleeping. And what I say to you I say to all, Watch."

This same recurring note of watchfulness clangs like a bell through two other parables which he told. "The kingdom of heaven," he said, "is like ten maidens, taking their lanterns and going out to meet the bridegroom. Five of them were foolish, and five were wise. The foolish ones, when they took their lanterns, took no oil with them. But the wise took extra oil with theirs. But as the bridegroom was long in coming, they all grew sleepy, and presently they slept. At midnight there was a cry, 'Look, the bridegroom comes; go out to meet him.' Then all those maidens rose and trimmed their lanterns, and the foolish said to the wise, 'Give us some of your oil, for our lanterns are going out.' But the others answered: 'No, for there may not be enough for us and for you. Go to someone who sells oil, and buy for yourselves.' But while they hurried off to buy, the bridegroom came, and those who were ready went in with him to the marriage feast, and the door was shut. Presently came also the other maidens, saying, 'O sir, O sir, open the door for us.' But he answered, 'I tell you solemnly, I do not know you.'"

The other picture which Jesus drew of the suddenness with which men might be called to account was this: There was once a man who, because he was going abroad, summoned his servants and gave to them large sums of money to administer for him while he was gone. Then at last he returned and called his servants to see what they had done with that which he had entrusted to them. Two of them had so managed what had been put into their hands that they had doubled the value of it. But the third came with shifty excuses why he had done nothing. He had been afraid he might lose everything. He thought his master was a hard man and would punish him if there were any loss. So he had wrapped up his money and buried it; and here it was. He brought back to his master exactly what belonged to him, no more and no less. But those who had used their opportunities greatly were rewarded, and the one who had done nothing with his trust was "cast into outer darkness"; for only those who have been faithful in their first chance can be trusted with a second.

Once, in the earlier days, someone had asked Jesus whether there were only a few who should be saved. What sort of persons, that is to say, should be able to stand before the face of God? As was so often true, Jesus did not answer such a question by bare words of definition. With the swift artistry of his thought, he painted the answer so that the mind's eye could see it, and like a painting full of symbolism it looks out upon us from the pages of the first Gospel.

"When the Son of man shall come in his glory, and all the holy angels with him, then shall he sit upon the throne of his glory. And before him shall be gathered all nations: and he shall separate them one from another, as a shepherd divideth his sheep from the goats. And he shall set the sheep on his right hand, but the goats on the left.

"Then shall the King say unto them on his right hand, 'Come, ye blessed of my Father, inherit the kingdom prepared for you from the foundation of the world. For I was an hungered, and ye gave me meat: I was thirsty, and ye gave me drink: I was a stranger, and ye took me in: Naked, and ye clothed me: I was sick, and ye visited me: I was in prison, and ye came unto me.'

"Then shall the righteous answer him, saying, 'Lord, when saw we thee an hungered, and fed thee? or thirsty, and gave thee drink? When saw we thee a stranger, and took thee in? or naked, and clothed thee? Or when saw we thee sick, or in prison, and came unto thee?' And the King shall answer and say unto them, 'Verily I say unto you, Inasmuch as ye have done it unto one of the least of these my brethren, ye have done it unto me.'

"Then shall he say also unto them on the left hand, 'Depart from me, ye cursed, into everlasting fire, prepared for the devil and his angels: For I was an hungered, and ye gave me no meat: I was thirsty, and ye gave me no drink: I was a stranger, and ye took me not in: naked, and ye clothed me not: sick, and in prison, and ye visited me not.'

"Then shall they also answer him, saying, 'Lord, when saw we thee an hungered, or athirst, or a stranger, or naked, or sick, or in prison, and did not minister unto thee?' Then shall he answer them, saying, 'Inasmuch as ye did it not to one of the least of these, ye did it not to me.' And these shall go away into everlasting punishment: but the righteous into life eternal."

CHAPTER XLIV

IN WHICH APPEARS THE DARK FIGURE OF JUDAS TAKING A BRIBE TO
BETRAY HIS MASTER, AND IN WHICH JESUS EATS THE PASSOVER SUP-
PER WITH HIS DISCIPLES; THEN GOES OUT INTO GETHSEMANE TO PRAY,
AND IS SEIZED THERE BY THE TEMPLE GUARD, AND CARRIED AWAY
FOR TRIAL IN THE COURT OF CAIAPHAS, AND TAKEN THE NEXT DAY
BEFORE PILATE IN THE ROMAN'S JUDGMENT HALL.

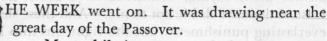

THE WEEK went on. It was drawing near the great day of the Passover.

Meanwhile it was not only from the circle of his avowed foes that danger threatened Jesus. There was disaffection even in the little group who had been nearest him. One of the twelve was Judas Iscariot. If he had ever loved Jesus well, his love had cooled. As to what the reasons were, we can only guess. If Judas Iscariot means Judas of Kerioth, then Judas was a native of a Judæan town. Thus he was the only one of the twelve who came from the proud province in which Jerusalem itself was situated. Judæans were sometimes apt to look upon the men of Galilee as an inferior class. Yet Judas had seen the Galilæans among the twelve take places of prominence which had not been given him. It was James and John and Peter who were nearest Jesus in his great experiences; these three, but not Judas. Judas may have been jealous of the others, and this jealousy may have embittered his feeling toward Jesus also.

Or it may be that Judas was never able to master some sort of an ambition similar to that which for a time possessed James and John. They had believed that Jesus would be the sort of Messiah who would build an earthly kingdom, and that they would be sharers in it. Judas may have thought that too; not only thought it, but passionately insisted that it must be so. When the days went on, and there was no sign that Jesus would establish this sort of kingdom, Judas was offended. It may have seemed to him that he had been led to follow Jesus under false pretenses. He was disappointed and disillusioned. If Jesus had failed him, why—he asked himself—should he go on being faithful to Jesus?

Then came his opportunity. The chief priests in Jerusalem wanted exceedingly to learn two things. They wanted a proof that Jesus had positively claimed to be the Messiah, so that they might accuse him of blasphemy. One of his disciples could give that proof. Furthermore, they wanted to know from someone who would intimately know of Jesus' movements where and when they might be able to seize him without danger that the crowd should know of it, and so perhaps defend him. They could learn that also only from one of Jesus' friends. Some rumor of what they wanted may have come to Judas. This, then, was his chance, and he would take it—this chance to separate himself from the cause of Jesus, which, so far as what he wanted was concerned, already seemed a failure—his chance to win honor and reward from those who were powerful in Jerusalem.

So Judas went secretly to the Sanhedrin, which was the ruling council of the Jewish Church. He was willing to tell them what Jesus had said. He was willing to show them how they could get Jesus into their power. Did they want to know that? They did. And what would they give for the knowledge? Thirty silver pieces they would give, and they weighed them out in his presence.

From that time on, Judas watched his opportunity to betray his Master.

The evening of the Passover came. Jesus sent two of his disciples to a certain house in Jerusalem, the house, it would seem, of someone he already knew; and there they would find, he said, a large upper room furnished and ready. In that they were to prepare the Passover meal. When the evening fell, he came with the rest of the twelve, and they sat down to eat the Passover meal of unleavened bread and the lamb which, according to the ancient traditions, had been eaten by the Israelites on that night long centuries before when they had set out under the leadership of Moses from the slavery in Egypt.

In the Gospel of John, and there only, there is an account of what happened when Jesus and the disciples first came into the upper room. In Eastern countries a mark of welcome for guests was that their sandals should be removed, and their feet, dusty from the road, be bathed. To bathe the feet of guests was the function of a servant; but there was no servant here. No one of the twelve wanted to take the servant's place. No one wanted to seem less important than the others.

Then Jesus arose. He took a towel and girded it about him, put water into a basin, and began to wash the disciples' feet and to wipe them with the towel. From one to another he went. Peter, always the quick-spoken one, protested, and the others sat silent and ashamed. But he washed the feet of Peter and of the others also; and this he did, says the Gospel, "knowing that he came from God, and went to God." When he had finished, he said: "Do you know what I have done to you? You call me Master and Lord, and you well say so, for so I am. If I then have washed your feet, you also ought to wash one another's feet; for I have given you an example that you should do as I have done to you."

They began to eat the Passover. Presently Jesus took bread and broke it; and as he gave it to them, he said, "This is my body which is broken for you; do this in remembrance of me." Then he took the cup of wine; and he said, "This cup is the new covenant in my blood, which is to be poured out for you."

They did not understand him very well; only they felt the shadow of some dark thing impending. Then Jesus said, "One of you who eat with me now shall betray me."

Distressed, they began each one to ask him, "Is it I?"

He answered: "It is one of the twelve that eats with me from this dish. The Son of man shall go even as it is written of him: but woe to the man through whom he is betrayed! It were better for that man if he had never been born."

Then Judas said, "Is it I?" Jesus answered, "It is as you have said."

THE WELL OF SYCHAR

MARY MAGDALENE AT THE SEPULCHER

Judas arose and went out. And it was night.

For a while longer Jesus sat in the upper room with the eleven. In the Gospel of John, from the fourteenth to the seventeenth chapters, there echoes the memory of what he said and of how he prayed. Then at length, when they had sung a hymn together, they went out into the Garden of Gethsemane, at the foot of the Mount of Olives.

Back of them glimmered the lights of Jerusalem. In the garden it was dark, and very quiet in the shadows beneath the olive trees.

Jesus bade the main group of the disciples sit together at a certain place and wait for him. With Peter and James and John he went deeper among the trees. These three men, who had been with him at most of the great moments of his ministry, he drew round him again in this his darkest hour. In them there was a comradeship of understanding which he wanted now. "My heart is sad," he said, "even to the point of death. Stay here and watch."

Leaving them there, he went forward and fell on the ground, and the awe-struck disciples could hear him pray. Like one in agony he was wrestling with what confronted him. For a long time he had foreseen the enmity which was closing round him and the possibility of his death. But now he faced the imminent fact of it, the fact not only of physical torture and of death, but of the scattering of his disciples and the seeming defeat of the gospel he had proclaimed. He prayed that the bitter hour might pass away.

"Abba, Father," the disciples heard him say, "all things are possible to thee; take this cup away. Nevertheless, not what I will, but what thou wilt." Then in the silence his figure still was kneeling, waiting for his answer from on high.

Presently he arose and came back to the three who were nearest him. They were all asleep. He looked down at Peter, and he said to him: "And you are sleeping! Could you not watch with me a single hour? Watch and pray, lest you fall into temptation. The spirit is willing, but the flesh is weak."

A second time he went away among the trees, and prayed,

"O my Father; if this cannot pass away unless I drink it, thy will be done!"

When he came back again, they were asleep once more, for their eyes were heavy. He must keep his vigil all alone.

Again he prayed; and for the third time he returned. There were sounds now coming nearer through the night, and he knew what they meant. He stood and looked at the disciples. "So you would sleep and take your rest," he said. Then he called them: "Enough of sleeping; the hour is come; look, the Son of man is betrayed into the hands of sinners. Up, let us be going; see how he who is to betray me is at hand!"

While he spoke there was a trampling of feet and a confusion of voices. The guard which had been furnished by the priests of the Temple were coming into Gethsemane. At their head was Judas.

Judas came up to Jesus, and kissed him. This was the sign by which in the darkness he was to identify Jesus, so that the soldiers of the priests could seize him. Peter, awakened from sleep, had snatched a sword, and he struck at those who were closing in on Jesus, and wounded one of the high priest's men. But Jesus said: "Have you come out to arrest me like a robber, with swords and clubs? When I went among you day by day in the Temple, you did not touch me; but this is your hour, and the dark power has its way."

His captors led Jesus away to where the Sanhedrin, the ruling council of the Jewish Church, had been hastily assembled. They met in the house of Caiaphas, the high priest. A strong man was Caiaphas, and ruthless when he had a purpose to pursue. He had been appointed high priest by Valerius Gratus, procurator of Judæa; and, though high priests before him had held their positions for an average of hardly more than a year each, Caiaphas had been high priest for eighteen years. He regarded Jesus as a disturber who endangered his authority, and he had made up his mind already to bring him to death.

Before the Sanhedrin various witnesses were brought to testify against Jesus. Some of them, perhaps with confused impressions of what they had heard him say about his own death and rising again, declared that they had heard him say that he would destroy the Temple which had been made with hands, and that in three days he would raise up another temple not made with hands. But their testimony was contradictory and unconvincing. The case for Jesus' condemnation was not moving forward well.

Then stood up Caiaphas. "Why do you answer nothing?" he said. "What is this that these men are witnessing against you?" But Jesus held his peace, and only looked at Caiaphas without a word. Again the priest demanded, "Are you the Messiah, the Son of the Blessed?"

Then Jesus spoke. "I am," he said: "and you shall see the Son of man sitting at the right hand of power, and coming in the clouds of heaven."

It was the answer that Caiaphas had wanted above all. Here was ground enough for condemnation. "Blasphemy!" he cried. "There is no need of any more witnesses." He turned to the council. "You have heard his blasphemy," he said. "What do you think?" Vehemently they all condemned him to death. Some of those who stood near him began to strike him, to spit upon him, and, blindfolding him, to taunt him, saying, "Prophesy who is it that strikes you!"

In the courtyard of Caiaphas, meanwhile, outside the room or balcony where Jesus was arraigned, was Peter. All the disciples had fled from the garden when Jesus was taken. But Peter had had the courage at least at a distance to follow him. Now he was crouching in the shadows beyond the rim of the light cast by a fire which was burning in the courtyard. A maidservant of the high priest came and stared at him. "You were with the Nazarene, with this Jesus," she said.

But Peter denied it. "I do not know what you are saying," he protested.

But the woman was not to be put off. She said to some of the others who were standing about, "This fellow is one of them."

Again Peter denied it. The others joined in. They said to

Peter: "You certainly are one of them; you are a Galilæan; your speech shows it."

But Peter broke out into curses and oaths. "I do not even know this man!" he said.

Somewhere off in the distance a cock crew. The sound of it shocked Peter into remembrance—remembrance of words which Jesus had spoken that night in the upper room: "Before the cock crow twice, you shall three times deny me." Peter went out from the courtyard of the high priest, bitterly weeping.

The day came, and the whole Sanhedrin had now a formal consultation. They bound Jesus and made ready to take him before the Roman procurator, Pontius Pilate, that Pilate might order him to be crucified. They themselves had power of judgment in cases affecting their own people; but they had been deprived by the Romans of the authority to carry any death penalty into effect. To the palace of the governor, therefore, by the tower of Antonia, they went, carrying Jesus, and with Caiaphas at their head. Caiaphas knew Pilate. He had not been high priest these many years and studied Roman officials, and especially this one, for nothing. He was familiar with Pilate's record and with his character. He knew that Pilate could bluster and then back down. He knew that already, on more than one occasion, accusations had been made against Pilate to the emperor, and that Pilate would not want to have serious protest lodged against him again. When the priests and those who were with them had brought Jesus into the courtyard of the governor, they sent word in to him that they wished an audience.

Pilate came out on the balcony above the court. "What accusation do you bring against this man?" he asked.

The chief priests knew that their real accusation would have little standing in a Roman court. They wanted Pilate to deliver him up without too much questioning. "If he were not a criminal," they answered, "we would not have brought him to you."

Pilate let those words pass with contemptuous silence. He ordered Jesus to be brought into his judgment hall alone. With curiosity, and doubtless with a strange sort of bewilderment, he looked at this man who had stirred such passions in Jerusalem.

"So you are a king," he said. "Are you a king?"

"Do you say this of yourself? Or did others tell you so?" Jesus answered.

Scornfully Pilate replied: "Am I a Jew? Your own nation and the chief priests have delivered you to me. What have you done?"

"My kingdom is not of this world," said Jesus. "If my kingdom were of this world, then would my followers fight, that I should not be delivered up; but my kingdom is not from hence."

"Are you a king, then?" Pilate persisted.

And Jesus answered: "You say that I am a king. To this end was I born, and for this cause came I into the world, that I should bear witness to the truth."

The Roman looked at him incredulously. What bandying of words was this? A kingdom of the truth! "What is truth?" he said.

Pilate led Jesus with him then out upon the balcony. "I find no fault in him at all," he said.

But instantly the crowd in his courtyard broke out into angry protest. "He stirs up the people," they cried, "teaching through all Judæa, from Galilee, where he began, and now even here in Jerusalem."

From Galilee! That gave Pilate a quick suggestion. Herod, the tetrarch of Galilee, happened to be in Jerusalem. Jesus belonged in his jurisdiction. Let Herod have charge, then, of this troublesome matter. So he sent Jesus to Herod.

But Herod would have none of it. He was curious to see if Jesus would work some miracle. When Jesus would not even answer his questions, he was bored, and sent him back to Pilate.

Pilate by another means tried to avoid his dilemma either of condemning Jesus without reason or else of rousing the hatred of the priests and the mob by letting him go. He remembered that there was a custom that at the time of the Passover the Romans should pardon some notable offender as a favor to the Jews. He reminded them of this. Even if Jesus were guilty of something, he could be forgiven now. He would release Jesus and let him go. But the crowd in his court cried out their angry repudiation. There was a notorious highwayman named Barabbas, whom the people admired because at least he had defied the power of Rome; and Barabbas was in prison. They demanded that Barabbas should be released. But what, then, should he do with Jesus, Pilate asked; and the mob shouted, "Crucify him, crucify him!"

Pilate had one more expedient. He handed Jesus over to his soldiers to be scourged; and then he brought Jesus back, bleeding from the scourging, upon the balcony where the crowd could see him. He thought they might be placated by this. But they were only the more fierce. "Crucify him, crucify him!" they cried again.

"But shall I crucify your king?" said Pilate.

"We have no king but Cæsar," they shouted; and then, "If you let this man go, you are not Cæsar's friend. Anyone who makes himself king, speaks against Cæsar."

They had struck Pilate at his point of vital weakness. He did not dare to be accused to Rome of having dealt gently with one who might be called a revolutionist. Sullenly, with an empty gesture first of washing his hands as though disavowing responsibility, Pilate handed Jesus over to the will of the priests, and to the hands of his soldiers to be crucified.

CHAPTER XLV

THE CRUCIFIXION OF JESUS ON CALVARY BETWEEN THE CROSSES OF
TWO THIEVES, AND THE WORDS WHICH HE SPOKE BEFORE HE CRIED,
"IT IS FINISHED!"

HE SOLDIERS led Jesus away to a court called
the prætorium, and summoned the rest of their
company. They took a purple cloak and put
it about him, and wove a crown out of thorn-
bush twigs and put this on his head.   Then
they pretended to salute him.   "Hail, King of
the Jews!" they said; and while they struck him and spat upon
him, they went down on their knees and made as though they
worshiped him.   Then they took the cloak off, and put his own
garments on him, and led him out to crucifixion.

In the crowd which quickly gathered and followed on the
way were the priests and others who had clamored already for
his death.   There may have been also some of the Galilæans
who had known and admired him; but if they were there, they
were overawed by the Roman guard and by the hostile Jerusalem crowd.   Through the streets of Jerusalem the procession
went, with the heavy beams of the cross laid on Jesus' shoulders.
On the way a certain man named Simon of Cyrene, happening
to come in from the country, was called upon to help Jesus bear
his cross.   Along the way many of the women of Jerusalem,
watching the tragic procession passing by, began to wail and
lament.   Jesus said to them, "Daughters of Jerusalem, do not
weep for me, but weep for yourselves, and for your children."

Outside the walls of the city they went to a low hill called
Golgotha, because its shape was that of a skull.   The soldiers
fastened the cross-beam to the upright of the cross, and nailed
the hands of Jesus to it with iron nails, then dragged the cross
upright and let the foot of it drop into the hole which had been

dug as its socket in the hill. On the right and left of Jesus two others were crucified, men who had been condemned for robbery.

To Jesus and the others the soldiers offered the usual drink, which was supposed to stupefy the senses and to numb the pain, wine mingled with myrrh; but Jesus would not take it.

At the foot of the cross the soldiers sat down to gamble for clothes which they had taken from Jesus. He hung above them, his hands and feet fastened by the nails. His lips moved in prayer. "Father," he said, "forgive them, for they know not what they do."

Meanwhile the crowd jostled round the circle which the soldiers kept clear near the crosses. Over the head of Jesus they had put a rude placard on which was inscribed, "The King of the Jews." Among the crowd this roused both anger and mockery. "Ah," they shouted, "you who would destroy the Temple and build it in three days, save yourself then, and come down from the cross!" And the priests said: "So this is the one who saved others! Well, he cannot save himself. Let this Christ, the King of Israel, come down now from the cross, so that we may see and believe."

Of the two thieves who were crucified beside him, one reviled him. "So you are the Messiah," he said. "Then save yourself and us." But the other thief replied: "Have you no fear of God, seeing you are in the same condemnation? And we have been condemned justly; for we are only receiving the due reward of what we have done; but this man"—and he lifted his eyes to Jesus—"this man has done nothing amiss." Then he said to Jesus, "Remember me when you come into your kingdom!" And Jesus answered, "I tell you certainly that to-day you shall be with me in paradise."

As the time went on toward noon, the day grew dark; and about three o'clock in the afternoon Jesus cried with a loud voice, "Eloi, Eloi, lama sabachthani?" Some of the people thought he was calling upon Elijah to come and take him down; but what he was doing was to quote the Hebrew of the psalm that began, "My God, my God, why hast thou forsaken me?"

Then there was silence for a time. At length he said, "It is finished!" And again, "Father, into thy hands I commend my spirit." And when he had said this, he breathed out his last breath, and his body hung still upon the cross.

Whether his disciples were near at hand, we do not know. The Gospels tell how some of the women who had loved him were there, and the Gospel of John says that his mother was near the foot of the cross, and that Jesus gave her into the keeping of John. Also the Roman centurion, who had been in charge of the crucifixion, was moved as he had watched Jesus and listened to him there. "Truly," he said when it was over, "this man was the Son of God."

Evening came, and a man named Joseph of Arimathæa— who seems to have been one who loved Jesus, but had perhaps not before this time dared to say that he was a disciple—went to Pilate and asked that the body of Jesus might be given to him. And so, with Pilate's consent, he took the body of Jesus down from the cross, and wrapping it in a linen cloth, he laid it in a tomb which had been hewn out of a rock, and rolled a stone before the door. And Mary Magdalene and another Mary were there when Joseph laid the body thus to rest.

CHAPTER XLVI

F THE record of the life of Jesus had concluded with the crucifixion, that would have been the end of Christianity. The disciples thought it was the end, the end of everything. Notwithstanding all that Jesus had said to prepare them for his death, they had not really believed that it could happen. When the swift events of the last week came to their climax in the crucifixion, when Jesus had actually been condemned and put to death, and they saw his body hanging on the cross, it seemed to them that in his dying all their hopes had gone down to darkness and defeat.

But the crucifixion was not the end; it was only the beginning. After the crucifixion came the resurrection, and Jesus who had died was alive again; and because they were sure of that, the disciples themselves began to live with such a joy and strength as they had never had before.

The Gospel accounts of the resurrection are in some ways not easy to understand. They leave us with questions here and there as to what it was exactly that happened, and as to how it happened. We shall think of those questions presently; but the first and important thing is to listen to what the Gospels say, and to see again through their various scenes the shining figure of Jesus alive again and making faith and life for his disciples start anew.

Through the day following the crucifixion the disciples were somewhere in Jerusalem. Perhaps they crept together in hiding for fear lest the men who had crucified their Master should also hunt them down. It may be that they began to remember those words which Jesus had spoken when he was in Galilee, the words in which he foretold his death and said that he would rise again. Wistfully they recalled these now. A faint hope was burning in their hearts, but they did not really believe. Jesus was dead. That was the only thing they seemed certainly to know.

Then came the first day of the week. Early on that morning some of the women who had loved him started out from Jerusalem for the tomb in the little garden where Joseph of Arimathæa had laid the body when he took it down from the cross. They were Mary Magdalene, another Mary, and Salome. They had brought fragrant spices, that they might lay these in the tomb.

It was early. Over the rim of the world the sun was rising, and the long, low light streamed along their way. As they went along the silent road, they were asking one another what they should do when they reached the tomb. A great stone had been rolled across the door of it. How should they ever roll away that stone?

They came to the garden. To their amazement, the stone was rolled away; and at the doorway of the tomb they saw a figure that looked like a young man, clothed in a white robe. When he saw the look upon their faces, he said: "Do not be amazed. You are seeking Jesus of Nazareth, who was crucified. He is risen, he is not here. See, here is the place where they laid him. Go now, tell his disciples, and tell Peter. He will go ahead of you into Galilee; and there you shall see him, as he promised."

Awed and silent and frightened at first, they drew back from the tomb. Then the thought of what it all might mean began to burst upon them. With trembling joy they ran to where the other disciples were, and cried out to them the words that they had heard—"He is risen!"

At first these others could not believe; but Peter sprang up to go to the garden to see for himself, and John went with him. Eagerly they ran, and the younger John ran faster than Peter and came first to the open tomb. He stopped there, not venturing to go in; but Peter, coming after him, entered, and the two of them found the tomb empty, as the women had said.

Mary Magdalene had come back now to the garden. There in mingled hope and fear, she was weeping; and as she wept, she saw a vision of two angels.

"Why do you weep?" she heard them say.

She answered, "Because they have taken away my Lord, and I do not know where they have laid him." When she had said this, she turned around, and there before her was a figure standing. It was Jesus, but she did not know that it was he.

"Why do you weep?" he said. "Whom do you seek?"

She thought that it was the gardener. "Sir," she said, "if you have borne him hence, tell me where you have laid him, and I will take him away."

Then Jesus spoke one word. "Mary," he said; and all her heart leaped to recognition.

"Master!" she cried, and stretched out her hands toward him.

But Jesus bade her not to try to touch him. She was to go to the disciples and to tell them that he was ascending presently to God.

That evening two of the disciples were going out from Jerusalem to a village called Emmaus. They talked together of all the things which had been happening. They had heard the news which the women and Peter had brought back from the garden, but they were not convinced.

Along the darkened road they went, deep in conversation; and as they talked a figure drew near them, and came and walked at their side. It was Jesus; but they did not know him. "What are these things which you are saying to each other?" he asked.

They stopped, and their faces showed how sad they were. One of them, whose name was Cleopas, answered, "Are you only a visitor in Jerusalem, and so do not know the things which have happened there in these days?"

"What things?" he asked.

"All the things concerning Jesus of Nazareth," they said. "He was a prophet mighty in word and deed in the sight of God and all the people; but the chief priests and our rulers handed him over to be condemned to death, and they crucified him— when we had hoped that it should be he who would redeem our people, Israel. Yet that is not all. This is the third day since those things happened, and some women of our company amazed us after they had gone out early to the tomb. They did not find his body there, and they came back saying that they had seen a vision of angels, who said that he was alive. Yes, and some of the others of those who were with us went to the tomb and found it to be as the women said; but him they did not see."

Then Jesus, the Jesus whom they did not know, began to speak. He asked them why they were so slow of heart to believe what all the prophets had made them hope for. Did they not know that it was necessary that Christ should suffer? Had they no understanding of all that was written in the old Scriptures as to the way in which he should come?

They drew near to the village for which they were bound, and Jesus showed that he would go farther. But they begged him to come in and stay with them. "The day is far spent," they said.

So Jesus went in to tarry there. Then as they sat down together at the table, he took bread and blessed it and broke it and handed it to them. Instantly their eyes were opened. Perhaps it was the look of his face as he gave thanks, perhaps the gesture of his hands. Whatever it may have been which made them see, they knew that this was Jesus; but even as they recognized him, he was gone.

Then they said to each other, "Were not our hearts burning within us as he talked with us on the road, and as he interpreted the Scriptures to us?" And, springing up, they went back to Jerusalem, and found the eleven disciples—for Judas now had gone—and others of the little company who had loved Jesus. They were telling how the Lord had risen and appeared to Peter. But Cleopas and his companion recited all that had happened on the road to Emmaus, and how that Jesus had been known in the breaking of the bread.

Then, while they were gathered together in the room, Jesus himself appeared. At first they were terrified; but he spoke to them and told them to be at peace. Then he showed them his hands and his feet, in which were the wounds made by the nails. And on another day, so the Gospel of John recounts, he came again when Thomas, who had been absent before, was there, and bade him touch these wounds in his hands and feet, so that he might be sure that it was Jesus.

In the Gospel of John there is another and beautiful story of the appearance of Jesus, not in Jerusalem, but this time in Galilee. The disciples had gone back to the old home and to the land they loved and to their fishing-boats on the familiar lake. Simon Peter said, "I am going fishing," and the others said, "We will come with you." That night they fished, but took nothing; and as the day was breaking, there stood Jesus on the shore. But the disciples did not know that it was he.

"Boys," he said, "have you anything to eat?"

And they answered, "No."

"Drop the net on the right side of the boat, and you will find fish," he said. John looked up and said to Peter, "It is the Lord!"

When Peter heard that, he snatched up his fisherman's coat and leaped into the sea, and the other disciples came rowing after him, dragging the net of fishes. When they reached the land, they found a fire of coals there, and fish laid on it, and bread. And Jesus said, "Bring some of the fish you have caught." So Simon Peter brought the net full of fishes, and Jesus said, "Come and have breakfast." No one of the disciples dared to ask, "Who are you?" for they knew it was the Lord. So Jesus came and took the bread and fish and gave it to them.

When they had finished breakfast, Jesus said to Simon Peter, "Simon, son of Jonas, do you love me more than these?"

He answered, "Yes, Lord, you know I love you."

He said to him, "Feed my lambs."

A second time he asked him, "Do you love me?"

Peter answered, "Yes, Lord, you know I love you."

Jesus said to him, "Tend my sheep."

A third time he asked, "Simon, son of Jonas, do you love me?"

It grieved Peter to have Jesus ask him three times if he loved him. He said, "Lord, you know everything; you know I love you!"

Jesus said, "Feed my sheep." Then he went on to tell Peter how that, when he, Peter, was young, he went where he would and did everything he pleased, but, when he grew old, he should be bound by others and made to go in ways that he had not chosen; and so he signified to Peter how he too some day should go to prison and to death for his Master's sake.

But Peter, as he turned, saw John, and he said to Jesus, "Lord, what shall this man do?"

Jesus answered: "If I should will that he tarry till I come again, what has that to do with you? You follow me."

Such, then, are the accounts of the appearances of the risen Jesus. As we have already said, they do not all fit easily together, and out of them there rise questions which we can never fully answer. What was it that happened on Easter morning? Where was the body of Jesus? In what sort of form did he appear? One account tells how Jesus came among the disciples when they were gathered behind doors which were shut and locked, which only a spiritual body, and not a body of flesh and blood, could be thought to do; but the account of the appearance on the Lake of Galilee, as written in the Gospel of John, tells of Jesus as eating a meal of bread and fish with his disciples. It may well be that some of the details of the resurrection stories belong to tradition rather than to the first and simpler facts. Any account of a great experience is bound to be colored in different ways as it is handed on from those who first knew it to those who hear of it from them.

But none the less through the various descriptions of the risen Jesus one great fact comes clear: the disciples who had thought that Jesus was dead knew now that he was alive; his spirit was in their midst, and their spirits caught fire from that conviction. They were so sure that he was living that they did not stop to trim all their recollections into agreement; and neither did the writers of the Gospels. They put down the memories of how this one or how that one had known or heard that the Lord appeared. That he had appeared and that he was alive, they had no need to question. The changed and joyous lives of those to whom he had come back were proof enough of that. They had been afraid, and now they were not afraid. They had been hopeless, but now they had more than hope; they had a certainty which made them into heroes. A while ago they had been as Peter was in the courtyard of Caiaphas, not daring to admit that they were Jesus' followers. Now they went out to proclaim what they knew of him in the face of all the world.

So it was that, on looking back, they could think of Jesus as one who had said, "All authority has been given to me in heaven and in earth." They were going out now to preach him everywhere. They would tell the good news of how he had lived and died, and of how his spirit would live in the hearts of all who loved him. They were ready to meet anything and everything in the power of his promise: "I am with you always, even unto the end of the world."

CHAPTER XLVII

THE BEGINNING OF THE CHRISTIAN CHURCH, WITH THE CHOICE OF
A NEW APOSTLE TO TAKE THE PLACE OF JUDAS, AND WITH PETER'S
SERMON ON THE DAY OF PENTECOST; AND THE HEALING OF THE
LAME MAN AT THE TEMPLE BY PETER AND JOHN, AND THE BOLDNESS
OF THESE TWO DISCIPLES WHEN THEY WERE SEIZED AND TRIED.

FTER A TIME the disciples ceased to have
their experiences of Jesus as a figure seen and
heard. As an invisible Presence which seemed
always to be moving with help and encouragement at their side, he was no less a power than
he had been before; but there were no more
appearances such as those recounted in the concluding chapters
of the Gospels. Jesus was with God, and God was his Father
and their Father, and would never fail them. This was what
they felt sure of after men said that Jesus had gone, and this was
what mattered. Of course the question would be asked, *How*
had he gone; and the early church answered it with a tradition
which was framed in the ideas which all men then had of the
sort of world they lived in. There above the earth was the
sky, and in the sky was heaven. It was to heaven, therefore, that
he had gone. So the tradition grew and was handed down that
a company of disciples outside of Jerusalem saw him ascending
from the earth toward the sky until a cloud received him out of
their sight.

Meanwhile a new chapter of life and work was opening for
the disciples. They had a commission from Jesus that they
should be his witnesses. They must begin in Jerusalem itself.

The first thing they did was to fill up again the number of
the twelve. Judas, who had betrayed his Master, was dead.
But twelve was to them a sacred number. It was the number
which Jesus originally had chosen. It was the number of the

twelve tribes of Israel. So all the little company of those who had loved and followed Jesus met together in Jerusalem, and they chose another to take the place of Judas. His name was Matthias.

With his election there begins the formation of the early church in Jerusalem. The history of the beginnings of the church is written in the opening chapters of the Acts of the Apostles. To understand these rightly it must be remembered that they were compiled later on in the first century from materials which had been handed down from the first generation to the next. By that time there was a tendency to glorify the early church and to represent it as pure in discipline, utterly devoted in spirit, and marked by many miracles of special heavenly favor. But as we learn presently from the letters of Paul, which make up so large a part of the New Testament, the members of the early church were very human men and women, with their faults and difficulties which the spirit of Jesus only little by little began to change. When we come to the story of the life of Paul, we shall be reading history which is in large measure contemporary with its facts. But when we read the story of the first days in Jerusalem, we must remember that we are reading what men in the next generation liked to think that the church was at the beginning. They had good reason to reverence it, because it had dared to receive and to preach the gospel of Jesus when this was very dangerous; and so it is not strange that the tradition represented this first church as one in which great virtues flourished and in which sin met immediate and dramatic judgment. Here and there its incidents are wrapped in the magnifying mist of time; but, nevertheless, the outlines which matter most are clear—namely, that here was a group of men and women made courageous by their faith in the living Christ, who created a fellowship which was to extend across the world.

After the election of Matthias, there came the feast of Pentecost, one of the great festivals of the Jewish year. The disciples were still members of the Jewish Church, for they still believed that the whole Jewish people might yet accept

Jesus as the Messiah. They observed the holy days as they had always done, and worshiped according to the ancient ways.

At the time of Pentecost many pilgrims were in Jerusalem. The disciples were meeting together somewhere, perhaps in the same upper room where Jesus had held the supper of the Passover. As they met and as they prayed, they were filled with a new Spirit. There seemed to come a sound from heaven as of a rushing, mighty wind, and cloven tongues as of fire.

Then to a throng of people who had come together in the streets Peter began to preach. All sorts of men were there, not only the people of Jerusalem and of Judæa, but those who had come from many different provinces—Parthians, and Medes, and Elamites, men from Mesopotamia, Egypt, Arabia, and Rome. The rush and power of Peter's utterance held them all spellbound. Every man seemed to hear in his own tongue the message which Peter was conveying. He preached to them of the prophecies of the Old Testament and of the promise of the day when God would pour out his Spirit upon all flesh: "And your sons and your daughters shall prophesy, and your young men shall see visions, and your old men shall dream dreams." He told them of Jesus, how he had lived, how he had been crucified, and how he was risen, and how this crucified Master had been made by God the Saviour of all.

Many were stirred, and wanted to know what they should do. Peter told them they should repent of their sins and be baptized. So they were baptized—three thousand of them, says the book of Acts—and "they continued steadfastly in the apostles' doctrine and fellowship, and in breaking of bread, and in prayers." Moreover, they decided to hold all their possessions in common, selling what each one owned, and dividing among the whole fellowship according to the needs of everyone. It was said too of them afterward that they used all to go with one accord every day to worship in the Temple, and that in the houses of different ones of them in Jerusalem they met to break bread together "with gladness and with singleness of heart," and that, as they went on their way praising God, they found favor with all the people.

But, as a matter of fact, there were many by whom this little group of the followers of Jesus was regarded with the opposite of favor. The priests and other rulers had no mind to see the followers of one whom they had crucified making converts in Jerusalem.

One day Peter and John went up to the Temple at the hour of prayer, and they saw there a man who was carried each day to the gate of the Temple which was called "The Beautiful Gate," where he sat and begged of those who went by. When he saw Peter and John, he asked them to give him alms. Peter, turning his eyes upon the beggar, as he and John stood there together, said, "Look at us," and the beggar looked up expectantly, thinking that Peter was about to give him money; but Peter said: "I have no silver nor gold; but what I do have, that I give you. In the name of Jesus Christ of Nazareth, rise up and walk."

He took the beggar by his right hand and lifted him up; and immediately the man's feet and ankle bones had new strength. He leaped up and walked, and went with them into the Temple, rejoicing and praising God.

The people who saw this were filled with wonder, and, gathering round Peter and John in that part of the Temple which was called "Solomon's Porch," they listened while Peter preached again as he had preached at Pentecost. But meanwhile the authorities of the Temple had heard of what was going on. They broke in upon the gathering, indignant that Peter should be preaching the name of Jesus there in the very Temple. They arrested Peter and John and put them into prison till the next day.

Then in the morning, when Caiaphas the high priest, and Annas his father-in-law, and others of the chief priests, were assembled, they brought Peter and John before them, and they demanded by what power and in what name they had done this. Again it was Peter who made answer; and he told them that it was through the power which had come through Jesus that the lame man had been made to walk. The priests conferred. They said that Peter and John were unlearned and ignorant men.   How did they dare to be so bold?   Then they remembered Jesus, and they took note that these men had been with him.

But there standing by was the man who had been healed. It was hard to say anything against that healing.   They put Peter and John and the beggar out of the room, and took counsel together.   What should they do next?   They could not deny what had happened; but, nevertheless, something must be done to stop this activity in the name of Jesus.   So they called Peter and John in again, and commanded them that they should not preach in Jesus' name at all.   But Peter and John answered: "You can judge for yourselves whether it seems to you right in the sight of God to pay more heed to you than to God.   As for us, we cannot help but tell what we have seen and heard."   So the council of the priests, having threatened Peter and John further, let them go, since they saw no way in which they could punish them.

Back then to the little company of Christians in Jerusalem Peter and John went.   They lifted up their voices in a hymn of praise to God, and they prayed together, and the Spirit came upon them all with power.

CHAPTER XLVIII

MORE STORIES OF THE EARLY CHURCH IN JERUSALEM AND OF HOW
IT SPREAD FROM THENCE, INCLUDING THE STORY OF ANANIAS AND
SAPPHIRA, THE MARTYRDOM OF STEPHEN, THE PREACHING OF PHILIP,
THE CONVERSION OF SAUL, AND PETER'S VISION AND HIS BAPTISM
OF CORNELIUS, THE CENTURION.

T WAS remembered of the early church in
Jerusalem that its members had tried to prac-
tice a sharing of all their goods. It was said
that "Neither was there any among them that
lacked: for as many as were possessors of land
or houses sold them, and brought the prices
of the things that were sold, and laid them down at the apostles'
feet; and distribution was made unto every man according as
he had need."

It was later found that this experiment had not worked so
well as the church had hoped, and it was not continued. But
there were many who looked back upon it as the way of the
church in its earliest and happiest years. In that time, they
said, the church was so nearly perfect that those who were false
to its ideal fell into immediate judgment. They recalled the
tradition of what had happened to a man named Ananias and
Sapphira, his wife.

Ananias had sold some of his possessions, and pretended
that he was bringing the whole price of them as a gift to the
church; but what he did was to keep back part and bring the
other part to the apostles as though it were the whole. Then
said Peter: "Ananias, why has Satan filled your heart, so that
you lie to the Holy Spirit and keep back part of the price of the
land? While you had it, was it not your own? And after it
had been sold, did you not have it in your power to do what
you chose? Why have you planned this thing? You have not
lied to men, but to God."

When Ananias heard this, he fell down dead, and there was fear among all who heard of what had happened. Some young men came and wrapped his body, and took it out and buried it.

About three hours after that, in came his wife, not knowing what had happened. Peter said, "Tell me whether you sold the land for such and such a price," and she said "Yes." Then said Peter: "How is it that you have agreed together to tempt the Spirit of the Lord? Look, the footsteps of those who have buried your husband are there at the door, and those same men shall carry you out also."

Down fell Sapphira at Peter's feet, and she died also, and the same young men who had buried her husband came to bury her.

Thus Peter had grown to be thought of as a man of such authority that at his rebuke people's hearts stopped beating. Moreover, it was said that many signs and wonders were wrought among people by Peter and the other apostles, and that the sick people, brought on beds and couches into the streets, were placed where even the shadow of Peter might fall upon them, and that then they were healed.

It was told of Peter also that once he went down to a town called Lydda, and found there a man named Æneas, who had been sick with palsy for eight years. "Æneas," said Peter, "Jesus Christ makes you well. Up, and make your bed." And immediately this palsied man got up, to the astonishment of all who knew him in the town.

But more too was told of Peter. It was said that in Joppa there was a woman named Tabitha, who was also called Dorcas, beloved by all in the city for her charities and good deeds. But she fell sick and died, and all the poor women of Joppa were there, weeping, and showing the garments which Dorcas had made for them. Then some of the disciples in Joppa, hearing that Peter was in Lydda, sent two messengers, begging him to come as quickly as he could. He came, and, entering the room where Dorcas lay, he put outside all who were there, and kneeled down and prayed. Turning then toward her, he said,

"Tabitha, arise." And she opened her eyes; and when she saw Peter, she sat up. He gave her his hand, and lifted her up; and when he had called her friends in again, he gave her to them alive.

Also there was a story of what happened when he and others of the apostles were arrested by the high priest and others of the ruling council and thrust into the common prison. That night an angel of God opened the prison doors and let them out, and said, "Go, stand and speak in the Temple to the people all the words of this life." So early the next morning into the Temple they went; and when those who had ordered them to be put in prison sent to have the prisoners brought before them, they received a message saying the prison was found locked, and the prison keepers standing on guard at the doors, but that, as for the inside of the prison, nobody was there.

At that same moment, there came a man who said, "Look, the men whom you put in prison are standing in the Temple, teaching the people." At this the Temple commander, with the other officers, went and brought them, though without violence, for they were afraid of the people, and they led the apostles in before the court. Then said the high priest: "Did we not strictly order you not to teach in this name? And here you have filled Jerusalem with your doctrine, and intend to bring this man's blood on us."

But Peter and the other apostles answered, "We ought to obey God rather than men." And again Peter spoke boldly about Jesus, and of how he and the others must be Jesus' witnesses. When the authorities heard that, they were so angry that they began to talk together of how they could put Peter and the others to death.

But in their council there stood up a Pharisee, named Gamaliel, a teacher of the law, who was held in high reputation among the people. He had the prisoners put out of the room for a time; and then he said to the council: "You men of Israel, take heed what you intend to do concerning these men. For in earlier days there arose a man named Theudas, who boasted to be somebody. A number of men, about four hundred, joined themselves to him; but Theudas was slain, and all who rallied to him were scattered, and their movement came to nothing. After him, there appeared Judas, a Galilæan, in the days of the taxing, and he drew many people after him; but he perished also, and all who followed him were dispersed. So now I tell you, keep clear of these men, and let them alone; for if this idea or this work be of men, it will come to nothing; but if it be of God, you cannot overthrow it. Beware, lest you should be found fighting against God."

As Gamaliel spoke, the rest agreed. So when they had brought the apostles in again, and had had them flogged, and ordered them not to speak in the name of Jesus any more, they let them go. But of the apostles it was remembered that, leaving the presence of the council, they went on their way "rejoicing that they were counted worthy to suffer shame for his name. And daily in the Temple, and in every house, they ceased not to teach and preach Jesus Christ."

By this time the church in Jerusalem had begun to have need of more people appointed to manage its affairs. There arose a complaint among those who were not Hebrews because, they said, their widows were not being given their share in the daily distribution of food. So the twelve called together all the disciples, and said: "It is not wise that we should leave off preaching God's word and serve tables. So, brethren, look about among yourselves, and find seven men of reputation for honesty, who are full of the Holy Spirit, and have good sense, and we shall appoint them to have charge of this business. But we will give ourselves continually to prayer, and to the ministry of preaching."

The whole group listened to this with approval, and they chose seven men—Stephen, Philip, Prochorus, Nicanor, Timon, Parmenas, and Nicolas. These they brought to the disciples, who prayed, and laid their hands upon them, to appoint them to their new work.

But Stephen did more than the work to which he had been set apart. He was a man of great faith and power; and when he found himself in a debate with some members of one of the Jewish synagogues, he spoke with such understanding and spirit that they were not able to answer him. In their anger, they had him arrested and brought before the ruling council. There Stephen made his defense. He traced the history of the people of Israel from the beginning. He showed how often they had refused to listen to the word of God, and he ended by denouncing the priests and other rulers there before him as having been the murderers of Jesus. When they heard him say this, they were so furious that they gritted their teeth. But Stephen, lifted out of himself, gazed up with his whole face lighted as by a vision, and he cried, "Behold, I see the heavens opened, and the Son of man standing at the right hand of God!"

Then those who heard him gave an angry shout, and stopped their ears, and rushed upon him. They hurried him outside the city, to stone him to death. Flinging off their garments, they put them at the feet of a young man whose name was Saul. And as they were stoning Stephen, Stephen called upon God, and he prayed, "Lord Jesus, receive my spirit." Then he kneeled down and cried again with a loud voice, "Lord, do not lay this sin to their charge." And when he had said that, he died.

Now this same Saul who had stood there and approved the killing of Stephen was a leader in making havoc of the church. After Stephen's death, a great persecution broke out in Jerusalem, and many of the disciples were driven here and there through Judæa and Samaria. But Saul went from house to house, hunting out men and women who were followers of Jesus, and dragging them off to prison. Nevertheless, those who had scattered from Jerusalem were still preaching everywhere in Jesus' name.

Among these was Philip, who preached in the city of Samaria with such effect that there was great joy in that city, and many were baptized. When the apostles who were still in Jerusalem heard this, they sent Peter and John to Samaria; and they, when they had come to the city and to the gathering of new disciples there, prayed for them, that they might receive the

Holy Spirit; and when they laid their hands upon them, this gift of the Spirit came.

Meanwhile, there was a man there named Simon, who had pretended to be a great magician. When he saw the change that came to the people of Samaria, he offered money to Peter, in order that he might be taught the secret of giving people such joy and courage as he had seen these disciples gain. But Peter spurned his money, and rebuked him, and bade him repent of his wickedness, and pray God that the thought he had had might be forgiven; and the frightened Simon asked for Peter's prayers on his behalf.

After that, Peter and John went back to Jerusalem, preaching the gospel in various villages of the Samaritans on the way. Meanwhile, Philip set out on a journey toward Gaza on the Mediterranean coast; and as he went, he met upon the road a man who was an officer at the court of Candace, Queen of Ethiopia, returning from Jerusalem, where he had been to worship. In his chariot he was reading from the writings of the prophet Isaiah, and Philip asked him, "Do you understand what you are reading?" "How can I," he answered, "unless some man should guide me?" And he asked Philip to come up into the chariot with him. The words which he was reading were these: "He was led as a sheep to the slaughter; and like a lamb dumb before his shearer, so opened he not his mouth. In his humiliation his judgment was taken away: and who shall declare his generation? for his life is taken from the earth."

"I pray you," said the Ethiopian, "tell me of whom the prophet was speaking this. Was it of himself, or of some other man?"

Then Philip began with this writing of Isaiah, and told of Jesus, and of how the prophecy had come true in him. By this time, the chariot had come to a place where there was water, and the Ethiopian said: "Look, there is water here. What should prevent me from being baptized?"

Philip said: "If you believe with all your heart, you may;" and he answered, "I believe that Jesus Christ is the Son of God." And he stopped his chariot, and he and Philip went down to the water, and Philip baptized him there. After that, Philip departed, and the man of Ethiopia went on his way rejoicing.

But while these things were happening, the persecution of the followers of Jesus still was spreading. Saul had secured letters from the high priest to the authorities of the synagogue in a city as far away as Damascus, which gave him the right, if he could find any men and women who were of Jesus' way, to bring them bound to Jerusalem. But as he journeyed northward, and had now come near Damascus, suddenly there blazed round about him a light as from heaven. Falling down to the earth, he heard a voice saying, "Saul, Saul, why persecutest thou me?"

"Who art thou, Lord?" he asked.

And the answer came: "I am Jesus whom thou persecutest. Stand up, and go into the city, and it shall be told thee what thou must do."

Those who traveled in Saul's company were standing speechless, hearing a voice, but seeing no man. Then Saul arose; but when he lifted his eyes, he could not see, and men led him by the hand and brought him to Damascus, where for three days he was blind, and neither ate nor drank.

Now, in Damascus there was a disciple named Ananias, and in a vision he heard his own name spoken; and he said, "Behold, Lord, I am here." Then a message came to him: "Up, and go into the street which is called Straight, and ask at the house of Judas for one called Saul, of Tarsus, for he is there, praying; and in a vision he has seen a man called Ananias coming and putting his hand upon him, and praying that he might receive his sight."

"Lord," said Ananias, "I have heard from many people of this man and of all the evil he has done to the saints of Jerusalem. And here he has authority from the chief priests to put in chains all who call upon thy name."

But to Ananias came the voice again: "Go upon your way. He is my chosen instrument to bear my name before the Gentiles, and kings and the people of Israel.   For I will show him what great things he must suffer for my name's sake."

Out went Ananias, then, and came to the house where Saul was; and putting his hands on him, he said, "Brother Saul, the Lord, even Jesus who appeared to you on the way as you were coming hither, has sent me, in order that you may recover your sight, and that you may be filled with the Holy Spirit."

Then it was as though scales fell from Saul's eyes.   His sight came back.   He stood up, and was baptized, and presently, when he had taken food, he was strengthened.

For a time Saul remained among the disciples in Damascus, but not for long.   Apparently after the great shock and crisis of his conversion he needed to go away into solitude and silence to reorder his thoughts and shape the decisions to which now he would be committed.   Consequently, he went away into Arabia; and there in the deserts, perhaps in that rocky wilderness of Sinai where the mighty memories of Moses brooded, he pondered the change which he must make from defense of the law, for which he had long been a zealot, to the preaching of the new gospel of the love of Christ which was shaping in his heart.

Two or three years went by, and then he returned to Damascus.   There he began to preach Christ in the synagogues, that he is the Son of God.   Those that heard him were amazed, and they said: "Is not this the same man who destroyed in Jerusalem those who called on the name of Jesus?   Did he not formerly come here for this purpose, to arrest all whom he might find, and bring them in chains to the chief priests?"   But Saul increased in power, and he confounded the Jews in Damascus with his proof that in Jesus the Messiah had come.   Before many days had passed, the Jews began to plot among themselves to kill him, but Saul learned of this.   He learned too that day and night they had set a watch at the gates of the city, in order to kill him if he tried to escape; but the disciples there let him down over the wall at night, and so he made his way back to Jerusalem, entering the city again for the first time since that day, three years before, when he had set out for Damascus to arrest and imprison the Christians there.

In Jerusalem he tried to join the disciples; but they were all afraid of him. They could not believe that he was a disciple. But there was one man among them, great-hearted and generous, named Barnabas; and he took Saul and brought him to the apostles, and told them how Saul had seen Christ on the road, how Christ had spoken to him, and how Saul had preached boldly at Damascus in the name of Jesus. So from that time on, Saul went in and out among the followers of Jesus in Jerusalem and boldly preached in his name until here also threats were made against him, and there was danger that he would be killed. So when the other disciples in Jerusalem knew this, they took Saul to Cæsarea, and sent him away to Tarsus, which was his home.

At Tarsus and in the region round it, Saul remained for about ten years. In that time the churches in Judæa did not see his face; but as he wrote afterward to the Galatians, they heard this of him, "That he which persecuted us in times past now preaches the faith which once he destroyed." These years in and near Tarsus were not so exciting as the years which followed were to prove; but in them Saul must have been developing the depth and certainty of the message which in the next decade he was to proclaim across the world.

Presently Saul should become the greatest figure in the fellowship of the disciples; but in the earliest recollections it was still Peter who stood foremost, and there is told of him, as having happened about this time, something that showed a new way in which the church was growing. In the city of Cæsarea there was a Roman centurion named Cornelius, commander of the Roman soldiers there in the so-called Italian regiment. He was a religious man, who worshiped God with all his family, and he gave much alms to the people, and was a man of prayer. One day, about three o'clock in the afternoon, he had a vision of an angel of God coming to him and calling him by name. While he wondered what the vision meant, he heard the voice of the angel telling him that his prayers and his gifts to the poor had gone up like a memorial of him to God, and that now he was to send men to Joppa to call for one named Simon, whose surname was Peter, who was lodging with another Simon, a tanner, in a house by the seaside, and that Simon Peter should tell him what he ought to do.

When his vision of the angel passed from before him, Cornelius called two of his household servants, and a devout soldier from among those who waited on him; and when he had told them what had happened, he sent them to Joppa.

The next day, as they went on their journey, and drew near to Joppa, Peter had gone up upon the housetop about noon to pray. He grew hungry, and wished that he had something to eat; but while the meal was being made ready in the house, he fell into a trance. He saw heaven opened, and what seemed to be a great sheet tied up at the four corners let down toward the earth. In this were all sorts of four-footed beasts and reptiles and wild birds. There came a voice, "Rise, Peter; kill, and eat." But he heard his own voice answering, "Not so, Lord; for I have never eaten anything common or unclean." Then a second time the voice spoke, "That which God has cleansed, you shall not call common." Three times this happened. Then the great sheet was drawn up into the skies.

When Peter awoke from his trance and wondered what this vision which he had seen could mean, the men who had been sent from Cornelius to inquire for Simon's house had arrived and were standing at the gate. They called and asked whether Simon, surnamed Peter, was lodging there. Then Peter went down to the gate, and he said: "I am the man for whom you are seeking. What is the errand on which you have come?" They told him how Cornelius the centurion had been told by an angel to send for him and to hear what Peter might say. So Peter brought the men into the house and gave them lodging; and on the next day he started off with them, and some other disciples from Joppa kept him company.

When they reached Cæsarea, Cornelius was waiting for them, and he had called together his kinspeople and near friends. He greeted Peter eagerly, and fell down on his knees before him. But Peter lifted him up. "Stand up," he said.

"I am only a man myself." Then going into the house, he found all those whom Cornelius had brought together, and he said: "You know how it is against the law for a man who is a Jew to keep company with one of another nation and to come into his house; but God has shown me that I must not call any man common or unclean; so I came to you without objection as soon as I was sent for. I ask you, therefore, what your intention is in sending thus for me."

So Cornelius told Peter of his vision, and when Peter heard of that, he said, "Truly I see that God is no respecter of persons; but in every nation the man who fears God and does good is acceptable in his sight." Then he went on to tell Cornelius and his friends of Jesus; and when they rejoiced to hear the gospel, Peter asked that water should be brought, that those who desired it might be baptized

After that, when Peter came back to Jerusalem, and news of what he had done in Cæsarea had gone ahead, there were those among the stricter disciples who were offended. In their view, no one had a right to belong to the fellowship of Jesus except those who were Jews by birth or by circumcision. They came to him protesting, and they said, "You went in to the house of uncircumcised men, and you ate with them."

But Peter told the whole story from the beginning to the end, the story of his vision on the housetop at Joppa, of the coming of the messengers from Cornelius, of his going to Cornelius' house, and of the way in which those who were there responded when he preached of Jesus; and he said: "I remembered then the word of the Lord, how that he said, 'John indeed baptized with water, but you shall be baptized with the Holy Spirit.' If God then gave to these Gentiles the same gift which he did to us, who already have believed on the Lord Jesus Christ, what was I, that I should stand in the way of God?" So when they heard this, the disciples in Jerusalem who had objected could say no more, but admitted that God must have set before the Gentiles also an open door to repentance and to life.

THE MESSENGERS TO PETER

SAINT PAUL AT JERUSALEM

CHAPTER XLIX

IN WHICH THE GREAT ADVENTURE OF CHRISTIAN MISSIONS BEGINS
WITH THE SENDING OUT OF PAUL AND BARNABAS FROM ANTIOCH;
AND THE PERILS THROUGH WHICH THEY WENT IN THE CITIES OF ASIA
MINOR, AND THE REPORT THEY BROUGHT BACK TO THE APOSTLES
AT JERUSALEM.

FTER THE persecution of Stephen, some of
the disciples who had scattered from Jeru-
salem had gone, as we have already seen, to
Samaria. Others had gone still farther. They
had reached the great city of Antioch in the
north, and had begun to preach there, at first
to the Jewish people only; but afterward they brought their
message to the Greek population also, and many became be-
lievers in the gospel of Jesus. News of this was brought to Jerusalem, and the apostles there sent Barnabas to Antioch. When
he came and had seen how the grace of God was working, he was
glad, and he encouraged all the new disciples to be loyal to the
Lord with their whole heart. For Barnabas was a good man,
and full of faith and of the Holy Spirit; and many people were
added to the fellowship.

Then Barnabas remembered Saul. Saul could help in this
new work at Antioch. So off to Tarsus he went to look for
Saul, found him, and brought him to Antioch. For a year they
worked together, and taught many people, and it was there in
Antioch that the disciples were first called Christians. In those
days it was prophesied that a great famine was coming through
the world, which did occur in the time of Claudius Cæsar. So
all the disciples in Antioch, each one according to his ability,
determined that they would send help to those who lived in
Judæa, and they brought their gifts and put them into the
hands of Barnabas and Saul, that they might carry these to
Jerusalem.

To Jerusalem Barnabas and Saul went; but when they got there, they found that something even worse than famine was afoot. A new persecution had broken out. James, the brother of John, had been killed. Peter was imprisoned. But Peter escaped from the prison—and when he was free, he came to the house of Mary, the mother of John Mark, where many of the disciples were gathered together, praying. He knocked upon the door, and a maid named Rhoda came within to listen to see who this might be who was knocking. When she recognized Peter's voice, she was so overcome with joy that she did not open the door but ran in and told the others how it was Peter standing there. They thought she had gone mad, but she steadily declared that it was so. "It is his spirit," they said. But Peter kept on knocking; and when they opened the door and saw him standing there, they were astonished; and as he told them how he had escaped, they believed that it was an angel who had set him free.

It was, as we have already said, to the house of the mother of John Mark that Peter came. The young John Mark himself was a cousin of Barnabas; and when Barnabas and Saul went back from Jerusalem to Antioch, they took John Mark with them. They had not been there very long before the Spirit moved the church in Antioch to appoint Barnabas and Saul for a special work. They were to be sent out as missionaries to carry the gospel of Christ to other lands. So they, feeling that they were sent by the Holy Spirit, went down to the seacoast and took ship for Cyprus, taking John Mark; and in the city of Salamis they preached the word of God in the synagogue of the Jews. After various adventures there, they sailed for the mainland of Asia Minor, and landed at Perga, in the province of Pamphylia. But there John Mark, dismayed by dangers which he believed might lie ahead, left them and went home.

Barnabas and Saul (who from this time on is called Paul) went northward along the rough and hazardous ways to the important city of Antioch (not the Antioch in Syria which they had left, but Antioch in the interior of Asia Minor). Here, as in so many other cities of the Roman Empire, there was a colony of Jewish people who had a synagogue, and into the synagogue Paul and Barnabas went on the seventh day. After the reading of the law and the prophets, the leaders of the synagogue sent a message to them, saying that, if they had any word of exhortation for the people, they were invited to speak. So Paul stood up, and began, "Men of Israel, and you that fear God, give me hearing." Then he went on to trace the history of the people of Israel from the time when they had been brought out from captivity in Egypt down to the days of David the king. And then he said that, from among the descendants of David, God had raised up a Saviour in Jesus. He told the congregation how Jesus had been crucified, and how he had risen again and appeared to his disciples in Jerusalem and in Galilee, and that now, in the name of Jesus, he had come to preach the good tidings of the forgiveness of sins.

When he had finished, there was a difference of opinion among the congregation. Some of those of Jewish blood were interested, and some were hostile. But the Gentile people wanted to hear Paul again, and they urged that he should preach to them on the Sabbath following.

So the next week a great crowd from the whole city were gathered together to hear this new preaching of the word of God; and when the Jews saw the multitude, they were annoyed, and began to contradict what Paul was saying. Then Paul and Barnabas made a bold decision. They said to the Jews: "It was necessary that the word of God should first have been preached to you; but now that you have rejected it, and have passed judgment on yourselves as being unworthy of eternal life, we turn to the Gentiles. For so it is that God commanded us when he said, 'I have set thee to be a light to the Gentiles, that thou shouldest be for salvation to the ends of the earth.'" When the Gentiles heard that, they were glad, and many of them believed Paul's gospel, and all through the surrounding region ran the report of what he preached. But the Jewish group, always easily angered by anything which seemed to take away their particular religious privilege, stirred up many of the leading people in Antioch, and roused such threats of violence against Paul and Barnabas that they were driven out of the city. So they shook the dust of Antioch off their feet, and went on to another city, Iconium.

In Iconium they entered, as they had done in Antioch, into the Jewish synagogue on the Sabbath, and this time their preaching drew many converts both from among the Jews and the Gentiles. But here again the Jewish group stirred up the townspeople, and poisoned their minds against Paul and Barnabas, so that, although they stayed for a considerable time in Iconium, the feeling of the city was more and more divided about them. At length there was a riot, and a mob began to move toward Paul and Barnabas, to seize them violently and to stone them. But they, learning of it, escaped to the country near the cities of Lystra and of Derbe, and in these cities they continued to preach their gospel.

In Lystra there was a man who had been lame from his birth and had never walked. He listened so intently when Paul preached that Paul began to look at him, and he saw that this man had faith sufficient to be healed. So with a ringing voice Paul cried, "Stand up on your feet." And the lame man leaped up and walked. When the crowd saw that, they began to say excitedly that here were gods come down in the likeness of men. Barnabas, they said, must be Jupiter, and Paul, who was the chief speaker, must be Mercury.

Presently came the priest from the temple of Jupiter, which was near the gates of the city, bringing oxen with garlands around their necks to the gates, in order to offer a sacrifice. When Paul and Barnabas heard of this, they rent their clothes and sprang in among the crowd of people, crying out: "Men, what do you mean by doing such things as these? We also are men of the same natures as your own, and we are preaching to you that you should turn from these empty superstitions to the living God, who made heaven, and earth, and the sea, and all that they contain." But even so, they had difficulty in preventing the people from offering a sacrifice to them.

But the feeling of the crowd was to have a dangerous change. To Lystra came some Jews from Antioch and Iconium, who won over the crowd, so that they took Paul and stoned him, and left him lying outside the city, thinking that he was dead. But as his friends stood round him, he stirred, and then got up upon his feet, and came in to the city, and the next day he left with Barnabas to go to Derbe. There also he preached, and taught large numbers of people.

It seemed to him and Barnabas that the time had come to go back to Antioch in Syria, from which they had started out. They could have gone on a way which would not have led them through the cities where they had been threatened and assaulted; but what they did was to turn back on this same dangerous road which they had traveled before. To Lystra, to Iconium, and to Antioch in Asia Minor, they went again, strengthening the spirits of those who had become disciples, and encouraging them to continue in the faith, and to be loyal to the kingdom of God, even if it should mean for them much suffering. Moreover, they ordained elders for the new churches in these towns, and with prayer and fasting they entrusted them to the Lord on whom they had learned to believe. And passing through the province of Pisidia, they came back to Pamphylia, and when they had preached again in Perga they took ship at the seaport of Attalia, and sailed homeward to Antioch, where they had first been commended to the grace of God for the work which now they had fulfilled. There in Antioch, when they arrived, they gathered the whole church together, and told them the story of what God had done with them, and how he had opened the door of faith to the Gentiles also.

For a considerable time they remained in Antioch with the disciples there, and there was peace in the church until some men who had come from Judæa began to talk to the people in Antioch and to tell them that they could not be saved unless they first were circumcised—as all strict Jews believed to be required by the law which had come down from the time of Moses. Paul and Barnabas had sharp debates with them about this matter, and at length it was determined that Paul and Barnabas and some of the others should go to Jerusalem and consult the apostles and others of the leaders in the church there about this question. So they started southward, passing on their way through the various towns where there were Christian congregations, and telling them the story of how the Gentiles were being converted, which news was listened to with great joy.

At Jerusalem they were welcomed by the church in general and by the apostles, and they recited all the things that God had done through them. But some of the Christians who formerly had been of the party of the Pharisees declared that all who were to come into the Christian fellowship must be circumcised according to the ancient law. When, therefore, there had been much discussion in the council, Peter stood up and reminded them of his own experience, and of how he had been led to preach to Gentiles and to baptize Cornelius. "And God," he said, "who knows the hearts, was their witness that he gave them the Holy Spirit as truly as he has given him to us; and he put no difference between us and them, but purified their hearts by faith. Now, then, why should you tempt God, and put a yoke upon the neck of these disciples, which neither our fathers nor we ourselves were able to bear? It is by the grace of the Lord Jesus Christ that we must be saved, and so must they."

There was silence in the council when Peter finished speaking, and then they all listened, as Barnabas and Paul recited the signs and wonders which God had wrought among the Gentiles by them.

Still no one ventured to give a verdict until James arose. He began by referring to what Peter had said, and with Peter he agreed. He advised, then, that the Gentiles should not be required to keep the Jewish law except that they should keep away from any worship of idols and from evil living, from the flesh of animals which had been strangled, and from the taste of blood. These regulations he considered should be enough.

So the church at Jerusalem assented to this decision, and they chose two men, Judas Barsabas and Silas, to go to Antioch with Paul and Barnabas (whom they spoke of as "men who have hazarded their lives for the name of the Lord Jesus Christ") and to carry to the church in Antioch a letter, telling them the opinion of the apostles and the Jerusalem church that the Christians need be under no other special rules beyond those which they had named. So when the delegation had come to Antioch, and had read the letter to the church there, the Christians of Antioch rejoiced and were much encouraged. For a while Judas and Silas remained in Antioch, preaching, and heartening the disciples.

The controversy, however, was not fully over. There were Jewish Christians who still held stubbornly to the old ideas, and believed that no man had a right to come into the Christian Church unless he was ready to obey all the Jewish law. It seems that even Peter himself wavered in this matter. Perhaps it was about this time that he made the visit to Antioch of which Paul afterward wrote in one of his letters, the Epistle to the Galatians. In that letter Paul referred to the Council in Jerusalem, and then he went on to say: "But when Peter had come to Antioch, I opposed him face to face, for he was to blame. At first he ate with the Gentiles; but when some men came up from James in Jerusalem, he drew back and separated himself, because he was afraid of those who belonged to the circumcision party. And other Jews acted disloyally along with him to such an extent that even Barnabas was carried away with their disloyalty. Now, when I saw that they were not behaving honestly according to the truth of the gospel, I said to Peter before them all, 'If you who are a Jew live in the way of the Gentiles, and not according to the Jewish rules, why do you compel the Gentiles to live as the Jews do?'"

Then in this letter of his, Paul went on to show how the new life of the Christians did not come through the old law, but through the grace which was given in Jesus Christ. And he swept on to these great and unforgetable words: "I am dead to the law, that I might live unto God. I am crucified with Christ. Nevertheless I live; yet not I, but Christ lives in me. The life which I now live in the body I live by the faith of the Son of God, who loved me, and gave himself for me."

CHAPTER L

PAUL SETS OUT ON A NEW MISSIONARY JOURNEY, WHILE BARNABAS
TAKES JOHN MARK AND GOES ANOTHER WAY; PAUL CROSSES THE
ÆGEAN SEA INTO MACEDONIA, IS IMPRISONED AND RELEASED AT
PHILIPPI, PREACHES IN THESSALONICA, IN ATHENS AND IN CORINTH,
AND COMES BACK AGAIN AT LENGTH TO CÆSAREA AND TO ANTIOCH.

OR A WHILE longer Paul and Barnabas con-
tinued in Antioch, teaching and preaching the
word of the Lord. Then one day Paul said to
Barnabas, "Let us go again and visit the
brethren in all the cities where we preached
before, and see how they are faring."

Barnabas was ready to go. He wanted to take John Mark
with them. But Paul did not think well of this. He had no
intention of having again the man who had left them in Pamphylia and would not go on with them in the work. So the
disagreement between them was so sharp that they separated,
and Barnabas, taking Mark, sailed to Cyprus; and Paul chose as
his companion Silas, one of the two men who had come up
from Jerusalem, and they went through Syria overland into
Asia Minor, to encourage the churches which he and Barnabas
had established there.

When Paul and Silas came to Derbe and Lystra, they found
a young disciple named Timothy, son of a Jewish mother and a
Greek father, and one well spoken of by all the Christians at
Lystra and also at Iconium. Paul wanted Timothy to go with
Silas and himself as their companion; and in order not to inflame
the prejudices of the Jews in those regions, he caused Timothy
to be circumcised. Passing on through the towns of the region,
he delivered to the little Christian groups the message from the
council in Jerusalem; and the churches, strengthened in their
faith, were increasing in numbers daily.

Through the provinces of Phrygia and Galatia they went

until they came to Troas, on the western coast of Asia Minor. There in the night Paul had a vision of a man standing on the shore of Macedonia across the intervening sea, praying him to come over into Macedonia and help them.

At this point in the history which is written in the book of Acts it begins to be said, not that "they," but that "we" did so and so. From this point on, Luke himself, who was the writer of all, or a considerable part of the Acts, has joined Paul as his companion. He was a Greek, and in Paul's own words he was also "the beloved physician." So the group of at least four, as it would seem, Paul, Silas, Timothy, and Luke, set sail from Troas, and came presently to Philippi, the chief city in north-eastern Macedonia, and a Roman colony. For some days they remained there, and then on the Sabbath day they went out to the banks of the river, where there was held a service of prayer. They sat down and began to talk to a group of women who came together there. Among them was a woman named Lydia, a dealer in purple dyes, and one who reverenced God. Her heart was touched as she listened to the things which Paul spoke; and after she and all her family were baptized, she begged Paul and his companions to come and stay at her house.

Then on another day, as they were going out to the place of prayer, they met a certain young girl who went into trances and told fortunes, and who brought in much money to those who controlled her. She followed Paul, and cried, "These men are the servants of the most high God, which show us the way of salvation." Day after day she did this, until Paul, pitying her, turned and said to the spirit in her, "I command you in the name of Jesus Christ to come out of her." That moment she was changed. And when her masters saw that their hope of profit was gone, they seized Paul and Silas and dragged them into the market place before the magistrates. "These men, who are Jews," they said, "are exceedingly disturbing to our city. They are teaching customs which it is against the law for us to receive or observe, for we are Romans." So a crowd began to gather against them, and the magistrate commanded that they should be stripped and beaten; and when they had been beaten with many lashes, they were thrown into prison, with a charge to the jailer to keep them securely. So he, having received that order, put them into the deepest part of the prison, and locked their feet in the stocks.

At midnight Paul and Silas were praying and singing praises to God, so that the other prisoners heard them. Suddenly there was a heavy earthquake, so that the foundations of the prison were shaken, and all the doors were wrenched open, and every man's chains were loosed. The prison-keeper, waking out of his sleep, and seeing the prison doors open, snatched his sword, and was about to kill himself, supposing that the prisoners had escaped. But Paul shouted aloud, "Do not harm yourself; we are all here."

Then the keeper called for a light, and sprang in trembling, and fell down before Paul and Silas. He led them out, and he said: "Sirs, what must I do to be saved?" "Believe on the Lord Jesus Christ," the answer came, "and you shall be saved, with all your family." Then they explained the gospel to him, and also to all who were in his house; so that, there in the night, he took them and washed their wounds where they had been beaten, and he and all his family were at once baptized. Then in his own house he set food before them, and he rejoiced because he and all his family believed in God.

When the next morning came, the magistrates sent officers, saying, "Let those men go." So the prison-keeper came and told Paul: "The magistrates have sent to let you go. You can leave, then, and go in peace." But Paul said: "They have beaten us publicly, when we had not been condemned. we who are Roman citizens, and they have thrown us into prison; and now shall they get rid of us secretly? Certainly not. Let them come themselves and escort us out." So the officers took this message back to the magistrates; and they were afraid when they heard that Paul and his companions were Roman citizens, and they came and apologized, and brought them out, and asked them to leave the city. Then from the prison they went to Lydia's house; and when they had seen the disciples and encouraged them, they went away.

Through Amphipolis and Apollonia they came to Thessalonica, where there was a synagogue. Paul, according to his custom, went in, and for three Sabbath days he reasoned with them out of the Scriptures, making plain that it was necessary that Christ should have suffered, and should have risen again from the dead, and that Jesus whom he preached was indeed the Messiah. Some of them believed and joined Paul and Silas; and among the Greeks and among prominent women of Thessalonica many more. But ringleaders stirred up the lower elements of the population and set the city in an uproar. They assaulted the house of a man named Jason, where Paul and Silas were supposed to be; and when they did not find them, they caught Jason and certain other disciples, and dragged them off to the authorities of the city, shouting, "These men who have turned the world upside down and now have come here, this Jason has welcomed; and all of them are defying the decrees of Cæsar, and saying that there is another king, one Jesus." Both the people of the city generally and the authorities were disturbed when they heard this, so they put Jason and others with him under bonds to keep the peace. Immediately, then, the disciples sent Paul and Silas away by night to Berea.

There again they went into the synagogue of the Jews, who were, as it happened, of a finer sort than those in Thessalonica. They listened to the message of Paul and Silas with open-mindedness, and they read diligently in the Scriptures to see whether the things they said were so. Many of them believed, as did also a group of prominent Greeks, both men and women. But when the Jews of Thessalonica heard the news that Paul was preaching at Berea, they came thither and stirred up the people, so that again Paul had to be sent away quickly by the disciples as though he were going to sea; but Silas and Timothy remained in Berea. Those who escorted Paul brought him to Athens, and then went home, having a message from him to Silas and Timothy to come to him as quickly as they could.

Now, while Paul was waiting for them in Athens, his spirit was stirred within him at the sight of the idols which filled the city. He debated, not only in the synagogue with the Jews and with other devout persons, but in the market place also every day with those who gathered there. Certain philosophers of the Epicureans and of the Stoics encountered him. "What is this that he is babbling about?" they inquired. And others remarked, "He seems to be setting forth strange gods"—because he preached of Jesus and the resurrection. Then they took him to the Areopagus, and they said: "Let us hear what this new teaching which you have been speaking about may be. These ideas you are bringing sound strange to our ears. We should like to know what they mean." (For all the Athenians, and the visitors in Athens, spent their time in nothing else but telling or hearing the latest novelty.)

Then Paul, standing at the center of Mars' Hill, said: "Men of Athens, I see signs everywhere that you are very religious. For as I passed by and saw your objects of worship, I found an altar with this inscription, 'To the Unknown God.' This God, therefore, whom you worship in ignorance, him I proclaim to you. The God who made the world and all things in it, since he is Lord of heaven and earth, does not dwell in temples made with hands, neither is he served by human hands, as though he needed anything, since it is he who gave men life and breath and all things else; and he has made of one blood all nations of men who dwell on the face of this earth, and has fixed their destinies and the boundaries which they are to inhabit. And his purpose is that they should seek the Lord, and that they might feel after him and find him, since he is not far from any one of us. For in him we live, and move, and have our being. Yes, as certain of your own poets have said, 'We also are his creation.' Since then we are of the nature of God, we ought not to think that God's likeness can be put into gold, or silver, or stone, which is carved by art and man's device. The times of ignorance God overlooked; but now he commands men everywhere to repent, for he has appointed a day in which he will judge the world justly by that One whom he has appointed, and of this he has given proof to all by raising him from the dead."

When they heard of the resurrection of the dead, some

mocked, and others said, "We will listen to you about this another time." So Paul said no more. Dionysius the Areopagite, a woman named Damaris, and a few others, were drawn to him and believed his message; but these were all.

Some time afterwards, Paul left Athens and came to Corinth, and there he found a Jew named Aquila, who had been born in Pontus, but had lately come from Italy with his wife Priscilla, because the Emperor Claudius had compelled all Jews to leave Rome. Aquila and Priscilla were tent-makers; and as Paul was skilled in this same craft, he went to live and to work with them. On the Sabbaths he spoke in the synagogues and persuaded both Jews and Greeks. When Silas and Timothy arrived from Macedonia, Paul was intent with his whole soul upon his preaching, and upon his effort to convince the Jews that Jesus was Messiah. It was thus to the people of his own race and blood that Paul preached first; but when they set themselves against him, and spoke abusively, he said at last: "Your blood must be upon your own heads; I am clean of it. From henceforth I will go to the Gentiles." So he left the synagogue, and entered into the house of a devout man named Justus, who lived close by. Crispus also, the president of the synagogue, together with all his family, had been converted by Paul's preaching; and many of the Corinthians, hearing this, believed and were baptized.

The message with which Paul's heart was on fire then has passed like an undying torch across the years. We know what he said, and the very words in which he said it. When he had left Corinth, he wrote letters back to the church which he had founded there, and two of his letters, the first and second Epistles to the Corinthians, are part of the New Testament. He describes what he felt when he came to Corinth, and what it was he wanted to do. Even on the printed page, the words flame with the passion of his soul. "Brethren," he wrote, "when I came to you, I did not come with elaborate words of wisdom. I determined not to know anything among you but Jesus Christ, and him crucified. My words and my preaching were not with plausible words of the wisdom of men, but in demonstration of the Spirit, and in wisdom and power; so that your faith should not be based on men's wisdom, but on God's power."

And again he wrote: "For the preaching of the cross is foolishness to those who are perishing, but to us who are saved it is the power of God. It is written, 'I will destroy the wisdom of the wise, and will bring the cleverness of the prudent to nothing.'

"Where are the wise? Where are the scribes? Where are the disputers of this world? Has not God made the wisdom of this world foolishness? For when the world with all its wisdom could not know God, it was God's will by the foolishness of preaching to save those who believe. For the Jews want a sign, and the Greeks want wisdom. But we preach Christ crucified, who is to the Jews a stumbling-block and to the Gentiles sheer folly. But to those who are called, both Jews and Gentiles, he is Christ the power of God and the wisdom of God. For the foolishness of God is wiser than men; and the weakness of God is stronger than men."

They may not have seemed a very promising lot, these Corinthians to whom Paul preached. Corinth was a seaport; and like every seaport, where the ships bring men from the ends of the earth, there was plenty of weakness and vice. The first disciples were obscure men and women who would have had a hard time being good in such a place as Corinth; and, good or bad, they would have seemed to the city too unimportant for it to matter, one way or the other, what they were. But Paul summoned these men and women to a new greatness in the sight of God. "You see your calling, brethren," he wrote, "how that not many wise men according to the flesh, not many mighty ones, and not many noble ones are called. God has chosen the foolish things of the world to put the wise ones to confusion; and God has chosen the weak things of the world to confound those that are mighty. The base things of the world, and the things which are despised has God chosen; yes, he has chosen the things which are not, to bring to nothing things which are; so that no flesh should glory in his presence. . . .

But, rather, as it is written, 'He that glories, let him glory in the Lord.' "

They had many problems, these Corinthians. They were involved in many temptations, and some of them fell into very ugly sins. Paul writes of those in his letters, about irreverence in worship, about impurity and lust, about the confusion of mixed marriages, and the enticements of the pagan world round them. But to these Corinthians, nevertheless, he gave the utmost treasures of his mind and heart. It was to them he wrote his immortal words about the resurrection, which end like a burst of music with his, "Thanks be to God which giveth us the victory through our Lord Jesus Christ!"

And it was to these Corinthians that he wrote his hymn to Christian love which begins, "Though I should speak with the tongues of men and of angels, and have not love, I am become as sounding brass, or a tinkling cymbal. And though I have the gift of prophecy, and understand all mysteries, and all knowledge; and though I have all faith, so that I could remove mountains, and have not love, I am nothing. And though I bestow all my goods to feed the poor, and though I give my body to be burned, and have not love, it profiteth me nothing." And then it sweeps on to this great climax: "And now abideth faith, hope, love, these three; but the greatest of these is love."

These were no light words for Paul to utter. They had been wrought out of the trials and triumphs of his own spirit. In turbulent Corinth he was met often, not with love, but with vindictive opposition. Nevertheless, he held on his way. Once in the night he had a vision, and in the vision he heard the voice of God. "Be not afraid," it said, "speak, and be not silenced, for I am with thee. No man shall set on thee to hurt thee. I have many people in this city." So in Corinth, for a year and six months, Paul continued, teaching the word of God.

Later, when Gallio was proconsul of Achaia, the whole Jewish population made an uprising against Paul and brought him before the bar of judgment. "This fellow is persuading men to worship God contrary to the law," they cried. And as Paul was about to answer, Gallio, interrupting, said to the Jews,

"If this were a question of crime or violence, it would be reasonable that I should bear with you Jews; but if it is a question
of words and names and of your law, see to the matter yourselves; for I will be judge of no such questions." And he drove
them out from his tribunal. Whereupon the Greeks took
Sosthenes, the president of the synagogue, and beat him in the
judgment hall, and Gallio took no notice of them.

For a considerable time longer Paul tarried in Corinth,
and then, taking leave of the brethren, he sailed for Syria, taking
with him Prisciila and Aquila; and reaching Ephesus, he left
these two there; but he himself went into the synagogue, and
reasoned with the Jews. When they urged him to stay a longer
time, he would not consent; but bidding farewell to them, he
said, "I will return to you again, if it is God's will." And so he
sailed from Ephesus. Landing at Cæsarea, and greeting the
church there, he went on once more to Antioch.

CHAPTER LI

PAUL'S THIRD MISSIONARY JOURNEY, HIS LONG MINISTRY IN EPHESUS,
AND THE RIOT WHICH BROKE OUT AGAINST HIS PREACHING THERE;
HIS FURTHER ADVENTURINGS IN MACEDONIA AND HIS RETURN TO
JERUSALEM, WHERE HE SPEAKS TO THE PEOPLE AND IS ASSAILED BY
THE MOB, IS RESCUED BY ROMAN SOLDIERS AND TAKEN DOWN TO
CAESAREA, WHERE HE PLEADS HIS CASE BEFORE FELIX THE GOVERNOR.

AUL'S SECOND long journey as a missionary
of the gospel was finished, but his work was
not completed. After he had spent some time
in Antioch, he set out again and went through
the region of Galatia and Phrygia, encouraging all the disciples there. When he had
traveled across all the width of Asia Minor, he came again to
Ephesus.

There in Ephesus was a Jew named Apollos, born in Alexandria, an eloquent man, and mighty in the Scriptures. Being
of an eager spirit, he preached and taught earnestly the things
he knew, though all he knew of baptism was the baptism of
John. With boldness he was preaching in the synagogue, where
Aquila and Priscilla heard him. So they took him home, and
explained the Christian way more perfectly. Then when he
felt moved to go across into Achaia, the brethren wrote urging
the disciples there to welcome him; and when he had come,
he brought much help to those who by God's grace had believed,
for he carried great conviction, even among the Jews, as he
publicly showed from the Scriptures that Jesus was Messiah.

It was after Apollos had left Ephesus and gone to Corinth
that into Ephesus and to the disciples there came Paul. He
asked them, "Have you received the Holy Spirit since you
believed?"

They answered, "We have not even heard whether there
is such a thing as the Holy Spirit."

527

"How, then, were you baptized?" he asked.

And they answered, "Into John's baptism."

Then Paul said, "John truly baptized with the baptism of repentance, telling people that they should believe in Him who should follow him, that is, on Jesus the Christ."

When they heard this, they were baptized in the name of the Lord Jesus; and after Paul laid his hands on them, the Holy Spirit came upon them, and they burst into ecstatic speech, and prophesied.

Into the synagogue, then, Paul went, and for some three months he boldly preached, persuasively reasoning about the kingdom of God. But when many of them were hard and unbelieving, and spread malicious reports of the way of Christ among the crowd, Paul withdrew; and separating the disciples from the rest, he went with them to the school of one Tyrannus, where every day he carried on his argument. For two years this continued, so that widely among the people of this part of Asia, both of Jews and Greeks, the word of the Lord Jesus was made known.

Paul had caught the attention of Ephesus now. Men felt his power, and constantly greater beliefs grew up as to what he did, and what he was able to do. They said that if they even touched their handkerchiefs to his body, the handkerchiefs had virtue in them, and could be used to cure diseases and to drive out evil spirits. There was a group of charlatans who thought they might imitate Paul with profit. They would go to demented people, and call over them the name of the Lord Jesus. "We adjure you by the Jesus whom Paul is preaching," they said. By this second-hand method they thought that they could get Paul's results. But one man upon whom they tried this device cried out, "Jesus I know, and Paul I know; but who are you?" Then he sprang upon the group of frauds with such wild violence that they fled, naked and wounded. After which there was much fear among the people in Ephesus who had been practicing various magical arts. They took their books and burned them.

Thus far the work of Paul was greatly effective; but trouble was to arise from a new quarter. In the city of Ephesus there was a great and magnificent temple to the goddess Diana. Crowds of pilgrims came to the city to worship in the temple before the image of the goddess. Silversmiths in Ephesus made little images like the great one, which the worshipers bought and carried home. It was a profitable business; but now this business was in danger. Paul's preaching was drawing people away from the worship of Diana. Not so many images were being bought. Among the silversmiths was a man named Demetrius, who called together one day all the workmen of his trade. "Men," he said, "you know that by this craft we get our living; but you can see that, not only in Ephesus, but almost throughout Asia, this Paul has persuaded many people and turned them away. He has said that there are no such gods as these we make with our hands. The result is that, not only is our craft in danger of being ruined, but the temple of the great goddess Diana will be despised and her magnificence destroyed, —Diana whom all Asia and the world worships."

When they heard this, their anger rose, and they shouted, "Great is Diana of the Ephesians!" until the whole city was thrown into confusion. Then the mob, led by Demetrius, caught Gaius and Aristarchus, men of Macedonia who were Paul's traveling companions, and rushed with them into the theater. Into the theater Paul also started to go; but the disciples prevented him; and some of the chief men of Asia who were his friends sent him a message, begging him not to take the risk of entering there.

Meanwhile the crowd was crying, some one thing and some another, and in the confusion the larger number did not know what it was they had come together for. A man named Alexander, a Jew, was pushed forward; but when he gestured for silence, and was about to speak, they drowned his voice with shouts, and for two hours went on shouting, "Great is Diana of the Ephesians!" The town clerk tried to bring them to quiet and to order. Everybody knew, he said, that all the Ephesians were worshipers of Diana. No one could question that. They ought to keep calm and do nothing reckless. If Demetrius and the other silversmiths had any case that would stand in law, let them bring it before the proper authorities. "We are in danger," he said, "of being called to account for this day's uproar, and there is no way by which we can give a reason for this rioting." He dismissed the assembly then; and when the city was quiet, Paul called the disciples round him and embraced them, and departed to go to Macedonia.

Into Macedonia then he went, through various adventures and the danger once of assassination, down to Achaia, back to Macedonia, and across the sea once more to Troas. On Sunday, when the disciples gathered for the breaking of bread, Paul, who was to leave on the next morning, began to preach. Until midnight he went on; and in the upper room where his listeners were gathered, there were many lamps. In the hot room at midnight, even Paul's preaching could be too much, and a young man named Eutychus fell fast asleep; and as Paul preached on and on, he slipped down from his seat and fell out of the third-story window, and was picked up for dead. Paul went down, and threw himself upon him and embraced him, and he told the others not to be frightened or distressed. Eutychus was not dangerously hurt.

When they were reassured about Eutychus they went upstairs again and had the Lord's Supper together. Through the rest of the night Paul went on talking to the disciples, until the day broke and he set out upon his way. Luke and Timothy and Silas had sailed to Assos, and at Assos Paul met them; and in the ship they went together to Chios and Samothrace, and presently to Miletus, a seaport not far from Ephesus. Paul had gone past Ephesus because he did not want to delay in Asia, but was hastening, if possible, to be in Jerusalem for the feast of Pentecost.

When, however, Paul arrived at Miletus, he sent thence a message to the church in Ephesus, asking the elders to come to him. So when they had gathered round him, he said: "You know the way in which I have been with you in all seasons since the day I came into Asia, serving the Lord with humbleness of mind, with many tears and trials which came to me through the plots of the Jews. You know that I have kept back nothing that was helpful to you, but have showed you and taught you openly from house to house, preaching both to the Jews and also to the Greeks repentance toward God and faith in our Lord Jesus Christ. And now you see I go a prisoner of the Spirit to Jerusalem, not knowing what things may happen to me there. Only I know that the Holy Spirit in every city testifies to me that bonds and afflictions are awaiting me. But none of these things move me, nor do I count my life dear to myself, if only I may finish my course with joy and fulfill the ministry which I received from the Lord Jesus, to proclaim the gospel of the grace of God.

"And now I know that all of you among whom I have gone preaching the kingdom of God shall never again see my face. I call you to witness that I am pure from the blood of all men, that I have not flinched from declaring to you the whole purpose of God. Take heed, then, to yourselves, and to the whole flock over which the Holy Spirit has made you guardians, that you may feed the Church of God, which he has purchased with his own blood. I know this, that after my going deadly wolves will enter in among you, and not spare the flock. Moreover, from your own midst men shall arise, speaking perverse things, to draw disciples after themselves. Watch, then, and remember that for three years I did not cease to warn each one of you night and day with tears.

"And now, my brethren, I commend you to God, and to the word of his grace, which is able to build you up and to give you an inheritance among all those who are being made into saints. I have not coveted any man's silver or gold or apparel. Yes, you yourselves know that these hands of mine have provided for my necessities and for those of my companions. I showed you how that, working thus, you ought to support the weak, and to remember the words of the Lord Jesus, as he said, 'It is more blessed to give than to receive.'"

When he had spoken thus, he knelt down and prayed with them, and they all wept, and fell upon Paul's neck, and kissed him, sorrowing most of all because he said that they should see his face no more. And they went with him to his ship.

So from Miletus Paul and his companions put out to sea, and past the islands of Rhodes and Cyprus they went until they landed at Tyre, where the ship was to discharge her cargo. Finding there a group of Christians, they tarried with them seven days, and these disciples begged Paul not to go to Jerusalem. But he went on his way, nevertheless, after the congregation at Tyre had escorted him out of the city and kneeled down on the shore and prayed. Farther down the coast he stopped at Ptolemais, and the next day went on to the larger port of Cæsarea, where he and those who were with him went to the house of the evangelist Philip.

While they were there, there came down from Judæa a man named Agabus, who was a prophet. He took Paul's girdle, and bound his own hands and feet, in order that in this dramatic fashion he should show the message which he said he had received from the Holy Spirit. Thus, he said, would the Jews at Jerusalem bind the man who owned that girdle, and deliver him into the hands of the Gentiles.

When they heard that, all Paul's companions and all the disciples of Cæsarea begged him not to go to Jerusalem. But Paul answered, "What do you mean by weeping and breaking my heart? I am ready, not only to be bound, but also to die at Jerusalem for the name of the Lord Jesus." So when they saw that he would not be dissuaded, the others ceased their efforts, and they said, "The will of the Lord be done."

Then Paul and his company set out for Jerusalem; and arriving there, they were received with affection by the church. On the next day Paul called upon James and the other elders who were with him. He gave them a report of what had happened in his ministry among the Gentile peoples.

They listened with approval mingled with caution. They reminded him that there were thousands of Jews who had become Christians, and they were all zealots for the law. They said that these Jewish Christians had heard that Paul was teaching the Jews in other countries to forsake the Jewish customs. So they urged him to correct this impression. They told him that there were four men who had vows which they must discharge in the Temple. Let Paul go with these men and take part with them in the Temple ritual which, as good Jews, they were about to observe. Paul was willing to do this. Champion of the liberty of Christianity among the Gentiles though he was, he was ready to show his sympathy also with those Jewish Christians whose consciences held to the old ways. So he went up to the Temple with the men of whom James had told him; but when he had arrived there, certain Jews from Asia saw him and recognized him, and they stirred up an angry crowd to seize him. "Men of Israel," they shouted, "this is the man who talks everywhere against our people, and against the law, and against this Temple. And here he has brought Greeks into the Temple, and defiled this holy place."

As a matter of fact, no Greek was there; but the men of Asia had seen Trophimus, an Ephesian, with Paul in Jerusalem, and they chose to think now that it was he whom Paul had brought with him into the sanctuary. So the city was in a tumult, and a crowd rushed together and took Paul and dragged him out of the Temple, and the doors were shut behind him.

As they were about to kill him, it was reported to the commander of the Roman garrison that all Jerusalem was in an uproar. He immediately took soldiers and ran down into the crowd, who, when they saw the Romans, stopped beating Paul. So the commander came up and seized Paul, and ordered him to be bound with chains. He demanded also who he was, and what he had done. He could not get a clear answer from the clamorous crowd, for some shouted one thing, and some another. So he ordered Paul to be carried into the barracks. When he reached the stairs, the violence of the mob had become so great that Paul had to be carried by the soldiers, and the whole mass of the people followed, shouting, "Away with him!"

As Paul was being taken into the barracks, he said to the commander, "May I speak to you?" And he answered in surprise, "Can you speak Greek? I thought you were that Egyptian who a while ago made an uproar and led four thousand murderers out into the desert." But Paul said, "I am a Jew of Tarsus, a city in Cilicia. I am a citizen of no mean city. I appeal to you to let me speak to the people." So when the commander had given him permission, Paul stood on the stairs; and beckoning to the crowd, who suddenly fell silent, he began to speak to them in Hebrew.

"Men," he said, "my brothers, and fathers, hear now my defense which I make before you." When they heard that he was speaking in Hebrew, the silence grew still more deep, and Paul went on to describe his life, his birth in Tarsus, his studies in Jerusalem as a pupil of Gamaliel, his persecution of the Christians, his conversion on the road to Damascus, and his commission to preach the gospel of Christ. They listened to him until he told them that he had heard the voice of Jesus say, "Go; I will send you far away to the Gentiles."

When they heard that, they burst into an angry shout: "Away with such a fellow from the earth! He is not fit to live." They yelled, and tore off their clothes, and flung dust into the air.

Then the commander ordered Paul to be brought into the barracks and to have him examined under the lash, so that he might find out what was the reason why the crowd was shouting so against him. As the soldiers were tying Paul, he said to the centurion who was standing by, "Are you allowed to scourge a man who is a Roman and has not been condemned?" Hearing that, the centurion went and told the commander, "Be careful what you do, for this man is a Roman."

Startled by this report about his prisoner, down came the commander then and said to Paul, "Tell me, are you a Roman?" He answered, "Yes." Then said the commander, "I obtained this citizenship with a great deal of money." "And I," said Paul, "was born a citizen." With that, the men who had been ordered to examine him moved off, and the commander himself was afraid, now that he knew Paul was a Roman citizen, and that he had put him in chains.

Next day, because he was still anxious to find out what the

real facts were concerning which the Jews were accusing Paul, he freed Paul from his fetters; and having ordered the chief priests and all their council to appear, he brought Paul down, and placed him in their midst. Then Paul, looking earnestly upon the council, said, "Men and brethren, I have lived in all good conscience before God to this day." The high priest Ananias ordered some that stood by him to strike him on the mouth. "God shall smite you, you whited wall," said Paul; "do you sit there to judge me by the law, and then order me to be struck contrary to the law?" Those that stood near him said, "Do you revile God's high priest?" "I did not know," said Paul, "that he was the high priest; for it is written, 'Thou shalt not speak evil of the ruler of thy people.'"

Again Paul looked at the council. His swift discernment saw that part of them were Pharisees, and part of them Sadducees. "Brothers," he said, "I am a Pharisee, the son of a Pharisee, and it is of the hope of the resurrection of the dead that I am called in question." When he had said that, the Pharisees and Sadducees immediately broke into disagreement, for the Sadducees denied that there is any resurrection, or angels, or spirits; and the Pharisees affirmed them all. There arose a great clamor, and the scribes, who belonged to the party of the Pharisees, stood up and contended: "We find no fault in this man. What if an angel or spirit has spoken to him? Let us not fight against God." Then there ensued a violent division, and the commander, fearful lest Paul might be torn in pieces, ordered the soldiers to go down and take him by force from among them, and to bring him into the castle.

That night Paul saw the Lord standing by him, and he heard him say: "Be of good cheer, Paul, for as you have testified of me in Jerusalem, so you shall bear witness also in Rome."

But the next day a crowd of the Jews formed a conspiracy, and bound themselves by an oath that they would not eat nor drink until they had killed Paul. To the chief priests and elders they came, and told them of their oath. They had a plan too as to how they might get Paul into their hands. Let the council send a message to the commander of the garrison, asking him to bring Paul down next day on the plea of examining him more thoroughly. "Before he ever gets here," they said, "we shall kill him."

But by chance Paul's nephew, the son of his sister, heard of their plot; and gaining entrance into the barracks, he told Paul. So Paul sent for one of the centurions, and said to him, "Take this young man before the commander, for he has something to tell him." The centurion took him, therefore, and he told the commander what he had learned of the conspirators who meant to lay an ambush for Paul. "There are more than forty of them," he said, "and now they are ready, looking for a promise from you." Whereupon, the commander let him go, having instructed him to say nothing to any man else of what he knew.

He called then two centurions. "Get ready two hundred soldiers to go to Cæsarea, with seventy horsemen, and two hundred spearmen. They are to be ready to start at nine o'clock to-night. Have horses ready also, so that Paul may be mounted and brought safe to the governor, Felix." Also he wrote a letter that read thus: "Claudius Lysias to his Excellency the Governor Felix, greetings: This man was taken by the Jews, and would have been killed by them, but I came with a detachment, and rescued him, having heard that he was a Roman. And when I wanted to learn the reason why they had accused him, I brought him to their council. I saw then that he was accused of questions in their law, but that there was nothing laid to his charge to deserve death or imprisonment. Then when it was reported to me that the Jews had laid an ambush for the man, I sent him immediately to you; and I gave orders to his accusers also to say before you what they had against him. Farewell."

Then the soldiers, following their orders, took Paul and brought him by night to Antipatris. The next day, the infantry left the horsemen to go with him, and they returned to the barracks. The horsemen, when they reached Cæsarea, delivered Claudius Lysias' letter to the governor, and brought Paul also into his presence. When the governor had read the letter, he asked of what province Paul was; and when he learned that he was of Cilicia, he said, "I will hear you when your accusers have also come." And he ordered him to be kept meanwhile in Herod's judgment hall.

Five days later Ananias the high priest, together with some of the others, came down to Cæsarea, and with them a certain orator, Tertullus, who denounced Paul to the governor. "We have found him," he said, "a pestilent fellow, a leader of sedition among the Jews in all the world, and a ringleader of the sect of the Nazarenes." He went on to tell how they were about to dispose of him when Lysias, the commander of the garrison, had snatched him out of their hands. Felix, he hoped, would deal with Paul in a different manner. To which the priests and the others voiced their complete assent.

With a gesture toward Paul, the governor gave him leave to reply. He began to speak, and Felix listened to him until Paul began to speak of the resurrection. To the Roman it did not seem that either the accusation or the defense had much to do with any law that he was concerned with. He stopped the hearing. "When Lysias the commander comes down, I will find out the truth about the matter," he said. So he ordered the centurion to take charge of Paul, to let him have liberty, and to permit his friends to see him.

Now Felix's wife Drusilla was a Jewess, and some days later he sent for Paul, and listened to him as he spoke of faith in Christ. And as Paul reasoned of righteousness, and of self-control, and of the judgment to come, Felix trembled, and he said: "Go away for the present. When I have a convenient season, I will call you." At the same time he had a hope that Paul would give him a bribe, and so he might set him free; and with this in mind, he sent for him the oftener, and conversed with him.

But after two years, Portius Festus came to take Felix's place; and Felix, willing to show the Jews a favor, left Paul bound.

CHAPTER LII

HEN THE new governor, Festus, had come into the province, he tarried in Cæsarea only three days, and then went up to Jerusalem. There the high priest and other Jewish leaders lodged a complaint against Paul, and urged Festus to send for him and have him brought to Jerusalem, their secret purpose being to lay an ambush on the road and kill him; but Festus answered that Paul should be kept at Cæsarea, and that he himself would shortly return there. Those who wanted to accuse Paul could come down with him when he went.

Some ten days he stayed in Jerusalem, and then returned to Cæsarea; and taking his seat next day in the hall of judgment, he ordered Paul to be brought in. When Paul had entered, the Jews who had come down from Jerusalem crowded about and made many vehement complaints against him, which, however, they could not prove; and meanwhile Paul's answer was that neither against the Jewish law, nor against the Temple, nor against the emperor, had he given any ground of offense. Festus, however, willing to ingratiate himself with the Jews, answered Paul, and said, "Are you willing to go up to Jerusalem and be tried there before me concerning these charges?"

Then said Paul: "I stand at the judgment seat of Cæsar, where I ought to be judged. To the Jews I have done no wrong, as you well know. If I am a criminal, or have done anything which could deserve death, I do not flinch from dying; but if

538

there is no proof in these charges which they bring against me, then no man can hand me over to their vengeance. I appeal to Cæsar."

That appeal Festus did not dare treat lightly; and when he had conferred with his council, he said: "So you have appealed to Cæsar? To Cæsar, then, you shall go."

Several days went by, and Herod Agrippa, the king, and Bernice, his wife, arrived in Cæsarea to salute Festus. When they had been there now for a long stay, it occurred to Festus to tell Agrippa about Paul. "There is a certain man," he said, "left here in custody by Felix, about whom, when I was in Jerusalem, the chief priests and the Jewish elders brought me information, and wanted to have him condemned. I answered them that it is not the Roman way to hand over any man to be put to death before the accused is confronted by his accusers face to face and is allowed to make his own answer as to the crime which is charged against him. So when they had come here to Cæsarea, promptly the next day I sat at the tribunal and ordered him to be brought out. When his accusers stood up, they did not bring accusations of any such matters as I had supposed, but they had certain questions against him which had to do with their own superstitions and with one Jesus, who was dead but whom Paul claimed to be alive. Now, because I was puzzled about such quibbling as this, I asked him whether he would go to Jerusalem and be tried with reference to these matters there; but he entered an appeal that his case should be reserved for hearing before the emperor. So I ordered him to be kept until I could send him to Cæsar."

Said Agrippa to Festus, "I should like to hear the man myself."

"You shall hear him then," said Festus, "to-morrow."

Then on the next day, when Agrippa and Bernice had come with great pomp into the hall where the hearing was to be conducted, together with the army commanders and the leading men of the city, at Festus' order Paul was brought in. Then said Festus:

"King Agrippa, and all you who to-day are here present

with us, you see this man in regard to whom the whole multitude of the Jews, both here and at Jerusalem, have beset me, clamoring that he ought not to be left alive. But when I found that he had done nothing which deserved death, and that he of his own accord had appealed to the emperor, I determined to send him to Rome. Yet I have nothing definite to write about him to the sovereign; and so I have brought him here before you, and especially before yourself, King Agrippa, that, after this examination is conducted, I might have something to write, for it seems to me unreasonable to send a prisoner to Rome and not at the same time indicate the crime with which he is charged."

Agrippa then said to Paul, "You are permitted to speak for yourself."

So Paul began:

"I count myself happy, King Agrippa, in that I shall make answer for myself before you to-day concerning all the things of which I am accused of the Jews, especially because I know you to be expert in all Jewish customs and questions. I pray you, therefore, to hear me patiently.

"My way of life since I was a youth among my own people at Jerusalem, all the Jews know. Yes, those who have known me from the beginning, if they would speak, must testify that, according to the strictest sect of our religion, I lived a Pharisee. And now I stand and am tried for the hope of the promise which God made to our fathers, which promise our twelve tribes, earnestly serving God night and day, hope to achieve. It is for this hope's sake, King Agrippa, that I am accused by the Jews.

"Why should it be a thing incredible to you that God should raise the dead? I, indeed, believed once that I ought to do many things contrary to the name of Jesus of Nazareth, and so I did in Jerusalem. Many of the saints I shut up in prison, having been armed with authority from the chief priests; and when they were put to death, I voted for their execution. In every synagogue, and often, I punished them. I forced them to blaspheme; and in my rage against them I persecuted them even to foreign cities.

"Then as I went to Damascus, with authority and permission from the chief priests, at midday, O king, I saw on that road a light from heaven, brighter than the brightness of the sun, flaming round about me and those who journeyed with me. And when we had all fallen to the ground, I heard a voice speaking in the Hebrew tongue, which said: 'Saul, Saul, why persecutest thou me? It is hard for thee to kick against the pricks.' I said, 'Who art thou, Lord?' and he said: 'I am Jesus whom thou persecutest. But rise, and stand upon thy feet, for I have appeared unto thee for this purpose, to make thee a minister and a witness both of these things which thou hast seen and of those things in which I shall appear to thee, delivering thee from the people, and from the Gentiles, unto whom I now send thee, to open their eyes, and to turn them from darkness to light, and from the power of Satan to God, that they may receive forgiveness of sins, and an inheritance among those who are redeemed by faith in me.' So, King Agrippa, I was not disobedient to the heavenly vision; but I showed first to men in Damascus, and in Jerusalem, and through all the boundaries of Judæa, and then to the Gentiles, that they should repent and turn to God, and do works fit for repentance.

"It was for these causes that the Jews caught me in the Temple and were about to kill me. But by God's help I have gone forward to this day, bearing witness both to small and great, and saying nothing else than that which the prophets and Moses said should come to pass; that Christ should suffer, that he should be the first to rise from the dead, and that he should show light to the people and to the Gentiles."

When Paul had spoken thus far in his defense, Festus interrupted loudly: "Paul, you are beside yourself. Your great learning is making you mad."

But Paul answered: "Most noble Festus, I am not mad. I am uttering the solemn words of truth. For the king has knowledge of these things, and therefore before him I speak freely. I am convinced that none of these matters are obscure to him, for all this was not done in a corner."

He turned toward Agrippa. "King Agrippa," he said, "do

you believe the prophets?" And as Agrippa hesitated, he went on, "I know you believe."

"With a little more of this," said Agrippa, "you might persuade me to be a Christian."

If he spoke with cynicism, Paul answered him in flaming earnestness. "I would to God that, not only you, but also all the others that hear me this day were both almost and altogether such as I am, save only for these fetters."

At that the king stood up, and the governor also, and Bernice, and those who had been seated with them. They withdrew to confer among themselves. "This man has not done anything that deserves either death or imprisonment," they said; and Agrippa summed up the matter thus: "If he had not appealed to the emperor, this man might have been set at liberty."

To Italy, therefore, it was determined that Paul must go. So Festus handed him, and certain other prisoners, over to the charge of a centurion named Julius, of the imperial regiment; and Paul, with Luke and perhaps other companions also, went on board ship; and after touching at Sidon, and sailing south of Cyprus, where the ship encountered head winds, they came to Myra, a port of Lycia. There Paul and his companions were transferred to another ship, from Alexandria, which was bound for Italy. Making slow progress, the vessel reached Cnidus with difficulty, sailed under the lee of Crete, and barely managing to pass it, came at length to a place called Fair Havens, not far from Lasea. By this time it had grown late in the season, and sailing was dangerous. So Paul warned those upon the vessel. "Men," he said, "I foresee that this voyage will end with great hurt and damage, not only to the cargo and the ship, but also to our lives."

But the centurion believed the captain of the ship, and the owner, more than the words of Paul. They considered that the harbor was not sheltered enough for the ship to winter there, and so the majority voted to put to sea, if by any possibility they could reach Phenice in Crete, and winter there in its harbor, which opens to the southwest and the northwest. When the south wind blew softly, they thought they could seize their chance; and loosing their moorings, they sailed close along the shore of Crete.

But not long afterward there sprang up a furious head wind, called Euroclydon, and so the ship was caught and could not keep her head up into the storm, and they let her drift before it. Running under the lee of the isle of Clauda, they had heavy work to undergird the ship with ropes; then, fearful lest they should be driven into quicksands, they lowered the sail and let the ship drive. That day and night the ship was violently tossed about in the storm, and the next day the crew flung the cargo overboard. On the day afterward they threw over the ship's gear; and, when day after day neither sun nor stars appeared, and the hurricane still raged, all hope that they should be saved seemed gone.

But when they had been for a long time without food, Paul stood up in the midst of the ship's company, and he said: "Men, you ought to have listened to me, and not have loosed from Crete, and so have got into all this danger. But now I bid you be reassured; for though the ship may be lost, there shall be no loss of the life of any single man among you. For last night there stood by me an angel of God, whose I am, and whom I serve; and the angel said, 'Have no fear, Paul; you are to be brought before Cæsar, and God has given you all those who sail with you.' And so I say, Be cheerful, for I believe God, and that it will happen exactly as it was told me. However," he said, "we are going to be cast upon some island."

This premonition of Paul's was coming true. When the fourteenth night had come, as they were being driven up and down in Adria, about midnight the sailors thought that they were drawing near land. They took soundings, and found the water twenty fathoms deep; and a little farther on, they sounded again, and found the water fifteen fathoms. Then fearing lest they should be driven on rocks, they threw out four anchors from the stern of the ship, and they wished for day.

A group of the sailors let down the small boat under pretense of putting out anchors from the bow; but what they meant was to try to get away to safety. Then said Paul to the centurion and to the soldiers, "Unless those men stay on the ship, you cannot be saved." So the soldiers cut the ropes of the small boat, and let her fall off.

As the day was dawning, Paul urged on them all to have something to eat. "This is now the fourteenth day," he said, "that you have had little or nothing to eat. I beg you now to take food. Your health requires it. This will keep you in condition, and not so much as a hair from the head of any one of you shall be lost." When he had said this, he took bread, and offered thanks to God before them all; and when he had broken it, he began to eat; and they all began to be cheerful, and they also took some food—there being in the ship two hundred and seventy-six souls. When they had eaten enough, they lightened the ship again by throwing out into the sea the wheat with which she was laden.

When day broke, they did not recognize the land; but they descried a sort of creek with a beach, and they thought they might run the ship ashore there. Cutting away the anchors, and leaving them in the sea, and untying the rudders, and hoisting the mainsail to the wind, they pointed the ship inshore. Coming to a reef, where the waves beat two ways, they ran the ship aground. The bow of the boat stuck fast, so that it could not be got off; but the stern began to be smashed to pieces by the pounding of the waves. The impulse of the soldiers was to kill the prisoners, lest any of them should swim ashore and escape. But the centurion held them back because he wished to save Paul. He gave orders that all who could swim should dive into the sea first and go ashore, and that the rest should save themselves as best they could on boards and broken pieces of the ship. And so it resulted that the whole company escaped safely to the land.

Natives of the region, drawn to the shore by the sight of the wrecked ship, gave them friendly help. They built a fire, and brought all the rescued men close round it, for not only were they dripping from the sea but rain had begun to fall, and it was cold. As they clustered there, Paul gathered up some wood to put it on the fire; and as he did so, a viper wriggled out of the wood and fastened on his hand. When the natives saw this poisonous snake coiled round his hand, they said, "Evidently, this man is a murderer who has escaped the sea, but has not escaped justice." When Paul shook the snake off into the fire, they watched him, supposing that he would begin to swell and presently fall down dead with the poison; but after they had stared at him a long time, and saw no harm had come to him, they changed their minds, and began to say that he must be a god.

Not far away on the island—for it was the Island of Malta upon which the ship had been wrecked, and on which Paul and the rest of the ship's company had landed—there lived a leading citizen named Publius. He received Paul and his companions; and for three days they lodged at his house. The father of Publius was ill; but Paul went into his room, and prayed, and laid his hands upon him, and the man was healed. And other sick folk of the island were brought to Paul, begging for his healing touch.

Three months went by, and at length the centurion and his soldiers were able to embark again with Paul on a ship from Alexandria which had been wintering at Malta, a ship which had Castor and Pollux as its figure-head. To Syracuse and Rhegium, then to Puteoli the vessel shaped her course, and from Puteoli, where Paul found a little company of Christians, he went forward on his way to Rome. Out from Rome to meet him came some of those who in the imperial city already belonged to the Christian brotherhood. They met Paul at a place called the "Three Taverns" on the Appian Way; and when Paul saw them, he thanked God and took courage.

Arrived at Rome, the centurion delivered his prisoners to the local authority; but Paul was allowed to live by himself with a soldier as his guard. After three days, he called together the leading Jews of Rome. He told them how he had been arrested in Jerusalem, and how he had appealed to the emperor; and how it was thus that he had come to Rome. He said that he was bringing no accusation against his own people. Rather, it was for the sake of the hope of Israel that he had been ready to be put in chains.

At first they seemed ready to listen to him. They said they had had no messages from Judæa concerning him, and no other reports unfavorable to Paul had come to them. They were ready to listen to what he had to say; but they told him that, as for the Christian sect in general, they believed that it was being condemned everywhere. They fixed a day when a larger number would come to his lodgings; and on that day, beginning in the morning and lasting till night, he told them what he believed about the kingdom of God and about Jesus, as he had been foreshadowed both by Moses and the prophets. Some of them were convinced, and others were not; and when there was a disagreement among them, they turned to go away. Then Paul added his final message. He quoted the words of the prophet Isaiah concerning those who should hear and not understand, and, seeing, should not perceive, because their hearts were callous and their ears were dull. They must know then, he said, that now God's salvation should be sent to the Gentiles, and that the Gentiles would hear.

So when the people of his own blood had left him, as had happened more than once before, Paul still proclaimed his gospel to all others who would listen. Two years he remained in his lodging at Rome, welcoming all who came to visit him; and he preached of the Lord Jesus Christ openly and undisturbed.

With this record we come to the end of the book of "The Acts of the Apostles." It would appear that Luke perhaps had meant to write a further history of the final years of Paul, but, for one reason or another, he did not do so. From the letters, however, which Paul wrote, and which are included now in the New Testament, and from the traditions of the early church, it is possible to know in general the story of what followed.

Evidently, the charges against Paul were considered by the emperor or his advisers to be so unconvincing that no action was taken upon them, and Paul was left to live in Rome with no restriction on his freedom except that a soldier was assigned as his guard to make sure that, when he was wanted, he could be produced. During this time Paul not only taught in Rome, but he wrote letters to Christian individuals and to congregations in other parts of the Roman world. He wrote a lovely letter to Philemon concerning Onesimus, a runaway slave. He wrote a letter to the church at Philippi, and in it is a mirror of his own mind when he says to the Philippians, "This one thing I do, forgetting those things which are behind, and stretching forward to the things which are before, I press on toward the goal unto the prize of the high calling of God in Christ Jesus." And then he said again: "Finally, brethren, whatsoever things are true, whatsoever things are honorable, whatsoever things are just, whatsoever things are pure, whatsoever things are lovely, whatsoever things are of good report; if there be any virtue, and if there be any praise, think on these things."

After some two years the case against Paul was so far dismissed that he was allowed to leave Rome entirely. Where he went is not certain. In his letter which he wrote to the Christians in Rome, which is printed in the New Testament as "The Epistle of Paul to the Romans," he speaks of his desire to go into Spain; but there is no certainty that he did go there. He did, doubtless, go again to the East, to Ephesus probably, and to other cities in Asia. Somewhere, and for some cause, he was arrested again; and this time, when he was taken to Rome, the result was different. He was held in close imprisonment; and at last, when Nero was emperor, he was put to death. He who had stood by when Stephen had become the first martyr for the name of Christ, now laid down his own life for the sake of the same Lord. The long record of persecutions, which he summed up in his second letter to the Corinthians, had come to its climax, and his record was complete. He had been "as sorrowful, yet always rejoicing; as poor, yet making many rich; as having nothing, and yet possessing all things." And in the great words of the second letter to Timothy, he could say, "I have fought the good fight, I have finished the course, I have kept the faith."

He had become of those who are "as unknown, and yet well known; as dying, and behold, we live."

In the New Testament there are letters which bear the names of James, of Peter, and of John. All of them reveal the faith and courage of the little groups of Christians who in the first century were maintaining their faith against a hostile world. They carried it like a torch which all the winds of danger and of death could not extinguish, and they passed its flame on to little communities here and there in the Roman world, and in turn the Christian faith was passed on to other countries and to undiscovered continents. In the later years of the first century, when persecution sometimes was fierce, the Christians did not always dare to write their communications to one another in forms which their enemies could use against them, and so sometimes they expressed these in veiled forms and symbols which only those who belonged to the brotherhood would understand. Such a writing is the book of "The Revelation," with which book the New Testament comes to its conclusion. In magnificent imagery it lifts up before the eyes of the faithful its visions and its promise of Christ triumphant, the "Alpha and Omega, the beginning and the ending, which is, and which was, and which is to come."

In the final vision of the Holy City to be builded four-square upon the earth, where "the nations of them which are saved shall walk in the light of it; and the kings of the earth do bring their glory and honor into it," there is proclaimed the truth that the life of our world can be redeemed only when the spirit of Christ dwells in its midst.

"Even so, come, Lord Jesus," the seer of the Revelation prays.

And then, as a prayer and a promise, come the last words which are included in the Bible, "The grace of our Lord Jesus Christ be with you all, Amen!"

SOME SUGGESTED READING

From among the almost numberless books about the Bible the following are a few of those which may most directly help the general reader who wants to know more about the reasons for the sort of interpretation of the Book which this STORY OF THE BIBLE has presented.

The Abingdon Bible Commentary. The Abingdon Press, New York.

How to Know the Bible. George Hodges. The Bobbs-Merrill Company, Indianapolis.

The Modern Use of the Bible. Harry Emerson Fosdick. The Macmillan Company, New York.

An Outline of the Literary History of the Bible. Margaret B. Crook. The Abingdon Press, New York.

Archæology and the Bible. George A. Barton. American Sunday School Union.

The Background of the Bible. Henry Kendall Booth. Charles Scribner's Sons, New York.

Historical Geography of the Holy Land. George Adam Smith. Harper & Brothers, New York.

Narratives of the Beginnings of Hebrew History. Charles Foster Kent. Charles Scribner's Sons, New York.

The Book of the Twelve Prophets. George Adam Smith. Harper & Brothers, New York.

The Old Testament Speaks. Carl Sumner Knopf. Thomas Nelson & Sons, New York. (Which includes a comprehensive bibliography on the Old Testament.)

The Literature of the Old Testament in Its Historical Develop-ment.[1] Julius A. Bewer. Columbia University Press, New York.

---

[1] A book to which in the course of writing this STORY OF THE BIBLE I have been particularly indebted.—W. R. B.

The Growth of the Gospels. Frederick C. Grant. The Abingdon Press, New York.

New Testament Times in Palestine. Shailer Mathews. The Macmillan Company, New York.

The World of Jesus. Henry Kendall Booth. Charles Scribner's Sons, New York.

Portrait of a Carpenter. Winifred Kirkland. Charles Scribner's Sons, New York.

The Master; A Life of Jesus Christ. Walter Russell Bowie. Charles Scribner's Sons, New York.

The Literature of the New Testament. Ernest F. Scott. Columbia University Press, New York. (Which includes a comprehensive bibliography on the New Testament.)

The Mysticism of Paul the Apostle. Albert Schweitzer. Henry Holt and Company, New York.

INDEX

A

AARON, older brother of Moses, 87; goes with Moses to court of Pharaoh, 91-95; holds up hands of Moses, 103; speaks to Israelites for Moses, is made priest, 104; makes golden calf, 107, 108; is disaffected and begs forgiveness, 111; dies, 119

Abednego, 377-381

Abel, 31, 32

Abiathar, 202, 230, 241, 242, 245

Abigail, 206-208

Abijam, 259

Abimelech, 146-148

Abiram, 111

Abishag, 244

Abishai, 229, 231, 235, 237, 238

Abner, 209, 216-218

Abraham comes from the East to Canaan with Sarah and Lot, 40-45; offers up Isaac, 46-48; seeks bride for Isaac, 49-53; his death and burial, 53

Absalom, 224-233

Achan, 127, 128

Adam, 28-33

Adonijah, 241-244

Adonizedec, 130

Æneas, 501

Agag, 186-188

Ahab, 261-277

Ahasuerus (Xerxes), 365-371

Ahaz, 300, 305, 306

Ahaziah, king of Israel, 269, 270

Ahaziah, king of Judah, 285-287

Ahijah, 251, 253, 257

Ahimaaz, 232, 233

Ahimelech, 201, 202

Ahinoam, 208

Ahithophel, 229, 231

Ai, 127, 128

Alexander the Great, 375

Amalekites, 103, 186-188

Amasa, 235, 237, 238

Amos, 292-297

Amram, 87

An angel visits Mary, 398; angel Gabriel appears to Zacharias, 399

Ananias, a disciple of Damascus, 507

Ananias, husband of Sapphira, 500, 501

Anathoth, 325

Andrew, called by Jesus, 417; one of the twelve apostles, 432

Antioch in Asia Minor, 512-515

Antioch in Syria, 511, 515, 517

Antipater, 389

Apollos, 527

Apostles, names of, 431, 432

Aquila, 523, 526

Ararat, Mount, 36

Araunah, and the threshing floor, 239

Ark, built by Noah, 35-37; Ark of the Covenant, 109, 110; taken around walls of Jericho, 126; taken by Philistines, 173; carried to house of Abinadab in Kirjath-jearim, 174, 175; taken to Jerusalem, 220, 228

Artaxerxes, 341

Asa, 259

Ascension, 495

Ashtoreth, 250

Assyria, 300, 306, 307-311, 320

Athens, 521-523

Augustus Cæsar, 394-401

B

BAAL, 142, 264-266, 289

Babel, Tower of, 38, 39

Babylon, 237, 320, 334, 340

Balaam, 116-119

Balak, 116-119

Baptism, 505, 519, 528

Barabbas, 484

Barak, 137, 138

Barnabas, 507, 511

Bartholomew, one of the twelve apostles, 432

Baruch, 329

Barzillai, 236, 244

Bathsheba, 221, 241-244

Beatitudes, 424

Beersheba, 59

Belief in Jesus as Son of God, 505

Belshazzar, 383, 384

Benaiah, 241, 242, 245, 246

Benhadad, 272-274, 283, 285

Benjamin, 66, 74-84